Cities of the
Heartland

Midwestern History and Culture

General Editors
James H. Madison and Thomas J. Schlereth

CITIES OF THE HEARTLAND

The Rise and Fall of the Industrial Midwest

Jon C. Teaford

INDIANA UNIVERSITY PRESS
Bloomington and Indianapolis

First Paperback Edition 1994

The following illustrations appear courtesy of the Chicago Historical
Society: #4, ICHi-05632; #5; #9, ICHi-00484; #11, ICHi-06577;
#15, CRC-136H; #16, ICHi-03545; #17, DN-59357; #18; #19, photo by Richard
Nickel, ICHi-21070; #20, ICHi-18895; #22, ICHi-22216.

The paper used in this publication meets the minimum requirements of American
National Standard for Information Sciences—Permanence of Paper for Printed
Library Materials, ANSI Z39.48-1984.

 ™

Manufactured in the United States of America

Library of Congress Cataloging-in-Publication Data

Teaford, Jon C.
    Cities of the heartland : the rise and fall of the industrial
Midwest / Jon C. Teaford.
        p.   cm. — (Midwestern history and culture)
    Includes bibliographical references and index.
    ISBN 0-253-35786-1 (cloth : alk. paper)
        1. Cities and towns—Middle West—History.   2. Middle West—
Industries—History.   3. Urbanization—Middle West—History.
I. Title.   II. Series.
HT123.5.A14T43   1993
307.76′0978—dc20   92-19931
    ISBN 0-253-20914-5 (pbk.)

    2 3 4 5 6 99 98 97 96 95 94

Contents

The Urban Heartland

From Cleveland to Milwaukee and Cincinnati to Saint Louis stretch the cities of the heartland. Through much of the nineteenth century they were the wunderkinds of the American family of cities, infant prodigies that astonished travelers from throughout the world with their remarkable precosity. By the beginning of the twentieth century they had grown to maturity and stood tall among the nation's urban centers. Four of them ranked among the ten largest cities in America, and six were on the list of the top twenty. The leader of this midwestern band was broad-shouldered Chicago, the nation's second largest metropolis and a city famed for its strutting self-confidence and feisty bravado. By the second half of the twentieth century, however, Chicago and the other midwestern metropolises had grown old, and their graying business districts and sagging industries became the focus of news stories and travelers' tales. The term *rust belt* entered the American vocabulary, and Youngstown, Detroit, and Peoria offered a visible definition of this new concept. By the close of the twentieth century, the cities of America's Midwest appeared to have passed through the entire urban life cycle.

This book offers a biography of that life. It examines the cities in the area of the Old Northwest Territory as well as adjacent Saint Louis, a metropolis that straddles the border of Missouri and Illinois and whose development was intrinsically tied to its rivalries with Cincinnati and Chicago. It considers the economic rise of these communities and their yearnings for cultural success. In other words, the following pages recount the midwestern city's desire to prove itself not only an industrial dynamo but also an intellectual giant. Moreover, this book perceives the heartland centers not as monoliths but as mosaics. They became home to people of diverse ethnic backgrounds and of every social and economic status. Rich and poor, black and white, German and Pole, all sought their fortunes in these hubs. Chicago, Cleveland, and Detroit were each a pluralist's paradise, rife with ethnic and economic conflict but noisy with cries for accommodation and compromise.

Unlike some recent histories, this work does not define an urban region simply as a market area tied together by a network of mutual trade links. Instead, it conceives of the Old Northwest as a region whose cities possessed certain social, political, economic, cultural, and ethnic characteristics that distinguished them as a class apart from the other metropolises in the nation.[1] Trade was not the only link that led Chicagoans, Detroiters, and Toledoans to conceive of themselves as residents of a common region. A variety of factors defined the heartland cities and made them somewhat distinguishable from American metropolises to the east, south, and west.

For example, the states of Ohio, Indiana, Illinois, Michigan, and Wisconsin shared not only common political roots within the Northwest Territory but also certain unifying bonds that determined their economic development and urban growth. The Ohio River on the south and the Great Lakes on the north tied these states together, and along these common waterways and their tributaries the chief cities developed. These water routes to the East and South were the umbilical cords that fed the nascent urban settlements stretching from Ohio to Wisconsin. Since the chief cities of all of these states first appeared on the map before the dawn of the railroad era, the Ohio-Mississippi river system and the Great Lakes were all-important access routes.

Geography also influenced the rise of midwestern cities as prominent rail centers. The prevailing flat terrain of the region was conducive to railroad construction, and the cities' inland location made them greedy for rail links to the seacoast. Consequently, by the late nineteenth century, Chicago, Saint Louis, and Toledo were to claim top rank among the nation's rail hubs. More than the cities of the East or South, the midwestern metropolises were railroad towns tied to each other and the rest of the world by a dense network of iron roads.

The natural resources of the region further encouraged a distinctive pattern of development for these cities. With expansive coal fields stretching across the three southern states of Ohio, Indiana, and Illinois and rich iron ore deposits along Lake Superior, primary metals and the fabrication of metal products were to become the industrial mainstay of one city after another. The rich soil of the area also contributed to the dominance of midwestern cities in the processing of livestock and grain throughout the nineteenth century. And the proximity of millions of agrarian consumers meant that fabrication of farm implements, the construction of wagons, and the business of rural-oriented mail-order houses would thrive in the cities of the heartland.

Benefiting from these rich natural resources and the dense railroad network, the cities of the Old Northwest would develop into manufacturing giants, smokestack metropolises dependent to a large degree on heavy industry. This distinguished them from the cities of the trans-Mississippi Midwest. In the late nineteenth and early twentieth centuries the nation's industrial belt reached as far west as Saint Louis and Rockford; beyond that western limit cities remained primarily hubs for wholesaling and shipping. Kansas City, Omaha, Minneapolis, and Des Moines were the sites of many mills and factories, but they were not Detroits, Milwaukees, or Garys. Geographers and business leaders alike grouped the cities from Saint Louis eastward under the rubric of "Industrial Midwest," correctly perceiving them as an element apart from the less industrialized area to the west.

Moreover, the tide of German migration that swept over the industrial Midwest in the nineteenth century ensured a common ethnic base that distinguished heartland hubs from the Irish metropolises of the East and the native-born population of the South. New Englanders founded certain midwestern cities, whereas Pennsylvanians and Virginians were more prevalent in other of these interior centers. But by the Civil War a common Germanic population overlaid these differences, ensuring similar cultural, political, and social patterns in Milwaukee, Saint Louis, and Cincinnati.

Geography, resources, and ethnicity did not dictate a monotonous uniformity throughout the region. The river cities differed from the lake metropolises, and Milwaukee was not a carbon copy of Indianapolis. But neither was Chicago a smaller version of New York nor Cleveland a western clone of Boston. The cities of the heartland enjoyed a distinctive heritage, and their history was not a replay of the life and times of the eastern centers.

One characteristic that persistently influenced the development of midwestern cities was a common heartland consciousness, a realization that for better or worse they were in the interior of the continent, removed from either coast and one giant step from access to the world beyond the seas. During the earliest period of white settlement prior to the Civil War, this heartland consciousness was seen in the persistent desire to gain an outlet to trade centers east of the Appalachians. Cities developed along routes of commerce to the Gulf of Mexico or the Atlantic seaboard, and promoters of each future metropolis boasted of its water links to the outside world. The litmus test of urban success was the number of steamboats annually bound for New Orleans or the number of schooners sailing each year for Buffalo. Midwestern cities were chiefly doors to the East and South; their growth and prosperity was directly related to their success as connecting points between the midwestern agricultural hinterland and the southern and eastern markets.

During the first half of the nineteenth century, midwestern cities were also deemed cultural ports where cargoes of those valued commodities known as civilization and refinement regularly disembarked. At Cincinnati, Saint Louis, Cleveland, and Detroit the culture of the outside world penetrated into the interior, offering hope that the heartland might some day become truly as civilized as New York City or Philadelphia. Just as they boasted of commercial access to the East and South, proud residents of midwestern urban centers never stopped drawing attention to evidence of literary life, fine hotels, or genteel society in their cities. Underlying both the commercial and cultural promotion of the heartland cities was this consciousness that urban success meant breaking down the barriers to the outside world. The future great city of the heartland supposedly would be that metropolis which could overcome the isolation of the midcontinent.

During the late nineteenth and early twentieth centuries, the heartland consciousness assumed a more positive tone. In the minds of an increasing number of Midwesterners, location in the interior of the continent no longer connoted isolation but rather centrality. Urban boosters bragged that Chicago, Saint Louis, Detroit, and Indianapolis were central to the nation's resources and markets. The chief emphasis was no longer on links with the world east of the Appalachians. Instead, chambers of commerce advertised the cities' proximity to coal fields, iron ore, and agricultural wealth. They claimed that the belt running from Cleveland to Milwaukee was the heart of industrial and commercial America and in closer contact to the bulk of American consumer dollars than any other region. Economically, the heartland was not on the frontier; it was in fact at the heart of wealth and business.

Culturally and politically, the interior no longer seemed such a backwater but instead a hub. In the eyes of Midwesterners, the region was the nation's most typically American area with all the positive attributes that implied in an age of nationalism. It was the valley of democracy and the land of Lincoln, supposedly the very embodiment of the political virtue of the nation. It was the principal breeding ground of progressive reform, the locale where American democracy was purifying itself and attempting to reach ever higher levels of perfection. Moreover, such Midwesterners as Frank Lloyd Wright and the other architects of the Prairie School were creating a new American style. The midwestern landscape itself was the inspiration for this new architecture that promised liberation from European conventions. Others of the Chicago school of architecture were constructing the first skyscrapers, inventing a new building form that was to revolutionize central business districts throughout the world. And a Chicago literary school was now writing of the hog butcher of the world and seeking creative stimulus from the Midwest's greatest metropolis.

Yet a lingering sense of cultural inferiority persisted. London, Paris, and New York continued to set the standards for Western civilization, and no matter how loudly boosters might praise the brawny vitality and the brash freshness of Chicago, most still regarded it as a city with too many rough edges, a city at the heart of the nation's economy but remaining on the cultural frontier. For too many urban Midwesterners "interior" still implied "inferior."

During the 1920s and 1930s the industrial Midwest remained at the heart of the nation's economy, solidifying its claim as the workshop of North America. Millions of automobiles rolled from heartland assembly lines, each one a symbol of the manufacturing might of the Midwest. Yet the nation's new boomtowns were to the south and west in sunny Florida and golden California. Already there was an emerging sense that the Midwest's metropolises were peaking, and any astute observer could see the first signs of the decentralization of America's wealth, a decentralization that would shift cash from the pockets of Ohioans and Hoosiers to the wallets of Westerners and Southerners. Moreover, Detroit, Cleveland, and even Chicago retained their status as cultural colonies of the East, way stations in the east-west transmission of fashion and culture.

This heartland sense of being "out of it" and one step removed from the action grew stronger in the second half of the twentieth century. As the industrial belt corroded into the rust belt, it seemed increasingly clear that the center of economic vitality had moved west of the Rockies and south of the Ohio River. Journalists and shortsighted observers might identify periodic booms and busts, but the long-term trend was less erratic. It was a gradual slide from a position of economic supremacy, that slide beginning prior to World War II and persisting throughout the remainder of the century. Midwestern cities no longer were economic miracles as in bygone days. Whereas in 1915 Detroit and Akron were famed boomtowns, in 1975 they were grim jokes, symbols of precipitous economic decline. In the decades before the Civil War, the heartland cities had shared a consciousness of the interior as frontier; by 1900 they shared a sense of the interior as central to American life; at the close of the 1970s they all feared an emerging vision of the interior as void. The nation was bicoastal, with New York and Los Angeles setting the styles and dominating the media. In the minds of many Americans, that long flat expanse between the coastal capitals was culturally as dull as its monotonous terrain. Meanwhile, the nation's southern rim was attracting both people and dollars. Indianapolis might still claim to be the crossroads of America, but most urban leaders recognized that an increasing amount of the traffic on Hoosier roads was headed south. Midwestern cities were on the defensive, and their economic and political leaders would employ every tactic, offer every lure, and unleash every power at their command to keep a corporate headquarters, revive an aging steel plant, or halt the slow death of downtown retailing. Corporate wanderlust was the nightmare of every mayor and chamber of commerce, because few midwestern chieftains had any confidence that business was willing to wander in their direction.

Throughout the past two centuries, then, an interior mentality was a common characteristic of the cities of the heartland. They sensed that they were cut off from the world, and this attitude influenced their economic, social, and cultural development. In the antebellum period it was seen in the obsession with gaining access to the East and replicating the civilization of the Atlantic seaboard. At the beginning of the twentieth century it was evident in the prevailing belief that the Midwest was the heart and soul of America and in the proud boast that Chicago was the most American of cities. Yet the persistent sense of cultural isolation and the concurrent tendency toward cultural imitation was just another symptom of this heartland consciousness. And in the late twentieth century, when the rim of the nation prospered seemingly at the expense of the hub, this interior mentality was likewise a factor in the public policies of cities.

During these decades of ascent and decline, of boom and bust, of brash confidence and nagging doubt, the midwestern metropolises each tried to cope with the economic, social, political, and cultural woes confronting them. They shared many problems common to cities throughout the industrializing world of the nineteenth and early twentieth centuries. And they faced the dilemmas endemic to urban areas throughout the postindustrial world of the late twentieth century. They were not creatures totally apart from New York, Baltimore, London, or Glasgow.

But their story is a special one. A common mentality and consciousness link the cities of the industrial Midwest, underlying an identifiable urban culture peculiar to the region. Just as the cities of the American South reflect the unique characteristics of their region, so the metropolises of the heartland are a product of a region that has traditionally claimed to be the American norm but is in fact a distinguishable fragment of the national whole. There is, then, merit in examining the midwestern city as a distinctive phenomenon. It is a legitimate subspecies of urban life.

Cities of the Heartland

1.

Creating the Urban Network

In 1848 the Ohio town-site speculator and journalist Jesup W. Scott predicted in the pages of a national magazine that commerce and manufacturing were "destined to build up in [the Midwest's] fertile valley, the greatest cities of the world."[1] This was not the first time Scott made this claim. As early as the 1830s he envisioned a spectacular urban future for the Midwest. But he was unsure which locale was to be the future great city of the world. In 1841 he ventured the prediction: "Within one hundred years . . . , Cincinnati will be the greatest city in America; and by the year of our Lord two thousand, the greatest city in the world."[2] The following year he told an appreciative audience in Maumee, Ohio, their community was destined for first rank among interior cities and would house at least a million inhabitants within a century.[3] In 1843, however, he told the readers of a national publication that Chicago was also on the list of leading contenders for top urban honors. "On the whole," he observed, "we deem Chicago alone, of all the lake towns, entitled to dispute future pre-eminence with Maumee," and he argued that the emerging Windy City might at least "sustain the second place among the great towns of the North American valley."[4] By the 1850s Scott was identifying Toledo and Chicago as the two chief rivals for coming greatness. As late as the 1860s he was publicizing the superior advantages of Toledo over Chicago and arguing that the Ohio city, where he had extensive real estate holdings, was destined eventually to overtake its western competitor.[5]

Scott was not the only optimist investing in midwestern town sites. Others also believed that the virgin forests and prairies would give way to urban greatness within a century. But for these boosters just as for Scott, the big question was where the good fortune of urban growth would strike. Which sites would prosper and become metropolises to rival those of the Atlantic seaboard and Europe? Which towns would emerge as secondary commercial cities? Which would remain small county seats? And which would disappear altogether, victims of the battle for survival of the fittest? These were the great questions that dominated the thinking of urban promoters throughout the Midwest in the first two-thirds of the nineteenth century.

During these formative decades town-site development proved a serious gamble with poor odds for the investor. In the 1840s the Cincinnati writer James Hall already recognized this fact of economic life. "Town making," he wrote, "has not generally proved profitable. Of the vast number of towns which have been founded, but a small minority have prospered, nor do we think that . . . the founders of these have been greatly enriched." Even a site "at the junction of two noble rivers," with "plats beautifully executed" and "immense sums of money . . . supposed to have been collected abroad," had ended up "the residence only of frogs and mosquitoes, while hundreds of towns and cities ha[d] grown up within the same period without effort."[6] In the mind of a longtime western resident such as Hall, who perhaps had suffered a few too many losses in speculation, town-site investment was as risky as a toss of dice. Too often the dice seemed loaded against the investor.

Midwestern urban development, however, was not a lottery, with Chicago, Cincinnati, and Detroit succeeding simply because they chanced to have the lucky number. Despite Hall's doubts, there were factors that improved the odds for certain town sites. Most notably, before 1850 a site on a navigable body of water was essential for any community with commercial aspirations. Whether in the form of a river, lake, or canal, water was the cheapest mode of transportation and the only viable means of access to outside markets. As Jesup Scott himself recognized, Easterners would reject his prognostications with the query: "How can Cincinnati, situated nearly a thousand miles from the sea, almost in the very centre of the continent, rival our great seaports . . .?"[7] It could only do so if Ohioans, Hoosiers, and their neighbors could create yet another seacoast along the Ohio River. Or along the Mississippi or the Great Lakes. If frontier residents took advantage of these navigable highways, then merchants could earn a profit from the surplus produce of the interior, and commercial cities could flourish. Moreover, networks of canals would further enhance the commercial possibilities of interior settlements, enabling them to reach north of the Ohio and south of the Great Lakes to capture the trade of previously landlocked areas. Water was, then, the one ingredient that seemed necessary to urban development in the early Midwest. Town-site speculation remained a gamble, but to invest in a community not on a navigable waterway was like betting on a horse with broken legs. Without water transportation a town did not have the means to win.

Some towns did develop as government centers with inland sites dictated by political considerations. Moreover, after 1850 the railroad offered a new mode of transportation to the East, improving the odds for towns remote from navigable streams. But during the first two-thirds of the nineteenth century, the Mississippi and Ohio rivers and the Great Lakes remained the Tigris and Euphrates of midwestern urban civilization. These bodies of water carried the commerce which built great cities. These transportation routes determined the urban map of the heartland.

River Cities

The first white American settlements in the Midwest were strung along the Ohio River. The southern borders of Ohio and Indiana and the Ohio and Mississippi river banks of Illinois attracted the earliest settlers, and only

TABLE 1

Largest Cities in the Midwest, 1840 and 1850

1840		1850	
City	*Population*	*City*	*Population*
Cincinnati	46,338	Cincinnati	115,436
Saint Louis	16,469	Saint Louis	77,860
Detroit	9,102	Chicago	29,963
Cleveland	6,071	Detroit	21,019
Dayton	6,067	Milwaukee	20,061
Columbus	6,048	Columbus	17,882
Zanesville, Ohio	4,768	Cleveland	17,034
Chicago	4,470	Dayton	10,977
Steubenville, Ohio	4,247	New Albany, Ind.	9,895
New Albany, Ind.	4,226	Indianapolis	8,091
Chillicothe, Ohio	3,977	Madison, Ind.	8,012
Madison, Ind.	3,798	Zanesville, Ohio	7,929

Sources: Department of State, *Compendium of the Enumeration of the Inhabitants and Statistics of the United States* (Washington: Thomas Allen, 1841); J. D. B. DeBow, *Statistical View of the United States* (Washington: A. O. P. Nicholson, 1854).

gradually did population move northward to the Great Lakes. It was, then, the Ohio and Mississippi rivers that nurtured the preeminent heartland cities of the first half of the nineteenth century. As seen in Table 1, in both 1840 and 1850 the population of the Ohio River metropolis of Cincinnati far exceeded that of any other midwestern community. Saint Louis, the chief port on the upper Mississippi River, ranked second, with almost twice the population of the largest lake city in 1840 and with more than two and a half times the inhabitants of the lake metropolis of Chicago in 1850. At midcentury the largest city in Indiana was not in the interior or on Lake Michigan. Instead, it was the Ohio River port of New Albany. In 1840 all of the Midwest's twelve largest cities were ports on navigable rivers, canals, or lakes, and in 1850 only tenth-ranked Indianapolis did not enjoy water access to the outside world. But it was the Ohio River that sired the preeminent urban center of Cincinnati, the renowned Queen City of the West.

In the 1830s and 1840s virtually everyone acknowledged the urban preeminence of Cincinnati in the Old Northwest, though boosters in Saint Louis may have viewed that preeminence as temporary. Outsiders regarded the Queen City as the true capital of the northern heartland, and few travelers exploring the newly settled region west of the Appalachians failed to visit the Ohio metropolis. What impressed many of these visitors, however, was not simply the size of Cincinnati but the rapidity of its growth. According to one traveler touring the city in 1840, "We . . . were quite astonished—not because we had never seen larger and finer cities, but that this should have

arisen in what was so lately a wilderness."⁸ Its Horatio Alger story of rapid
ascent from wilderness backwater to urban dynamo was a visual testimony
to the potential greatness of the Old Northwest and a source of hope for
urban boosters elsewhere. If Cincinnati could achieve such a wonderful
transformation virtually overnight, so might Toledo or Peoria or every other
settlement struggling for a place on the map.

During the 1830s and 1840s Cincinnati was not only an inspiration to town-
site developers from Cleveland to Saint Louis, it was also the cultural hub
of the region. Just as its merchants distributed the commercial goods of the
outside world throughout the Old Northwest, so its educated elite viewed
the city as the fount of learning, letters, and the arts, the purveyor of culture
to the backwoods. Through those years when it reigned unchallenged as
Queen City of the West, it proudly offered cultural as well as commercial
access to the eastern seaboard and Europe. As western monarch, its domain
included not only the world of barter but that of books.

During its first decade Cincinnati offered few signs of this future regal
bearing. Founded in 1788, during the 1790s it was the capital of the Northwest Territory and the site of one of the region's chief military posts. Yet
by 1800 it could claim only 750 residents, and as late as 1805 it contained
only 173 houses, fifty-three of them log structures and a mere seven built of
brick. Moreover, in 1800 Chillicothe became the capital of the Ohio Territory, depriving Cincinnati of its political distinction. Henceforth commerce
was to be the engine of growth in the nascent Queen City.

Throughout the first decade of the nineteenth century flatboats and keel-
boats carried the city's cargoes down the Ohio, but by 1815 Cincinnati residents were looking forward to the advantages bestowed by the newly
invented steamboat. Writing in that year, Daniel Drake of Cincinnati observed: "No country on earth, equally fertile with this, can be more benefited by such boats." According to Drake, the steamboat would result in "the
reduction of the voyage from New-Orleans to Cincinnati from a hundred, to
thirty days, . . . or to the annihilation of two-thirds of the distance."⁹ This
was good news for a settlement whose future depended on overcoming the
isolation of the interior valley. With steam propulsion, markets would draw
nearer and the Cincinnati region could move from a largely subsistence
economy to a life of trading and commerce.

By 1816 Cincinnatians were constructing their first steamboat, and two
years later they launched five of these vessels. A euphoria prevailed in the
emerging Ohio city as immigrants from the East flooded its streets, and the
population soared from approximately four thousand in 1813 to almost ten
thousand in 1819. In 1819 alone Cincinnatians constructed some three hundred new structures, but despite this building boom housing space was tight
and in some cases a half dozen families were forced to share a house of six
to eight rooms. Property values rose rapidly, and community leaders were
eager to speculate in town lots. A British visitor marveled at the economic

boom and observed: "Such an active scene I never expected to see amongst the back woods of America."[10]

This boom, however, was built on credit, and when in 1819 the Bank of the United States began to demand redemption of notes, a bust ensued. The boom-bust cycle was a common phenomenon in the Old Northwest during the first half of the nineteenth century. America's interior valley had more land than hard cash, and speculation often exceeded production. The result was a series of waves of prosperity succeeded by setbacks, which in turn were followed by years of recrimination when all confessed their earlier folly. The panic of 1819 struck Cincinnati with particular ferocity. In June 1820 one visitor noted: "The town does not now present anything like the stir that animated it about a year and a half ago. Building is in a great measure suspended, and the city which was lately over crowded with people, has now a considerable number of empty houses."[11] Not only were once-wealthy land speculators ruined, so were the many artisans engaged in the formerly booming building trades. According to one Cincinnati resident, "One of our boss carpenters bought a wood-saw and buck and went about sawing wood. Our leading bricklayer procured a small patch of ground . . . and raised watermelons, which he sold himself in the market."[12] Moreover, the downturn added fuel to the arguments of eastern detractors who still regarded Cincinnati and the Northwest as an isolated wilderness. A sad but loyal Cincinnatian admitted: "The high expectations we had formed for our city, and which seemed so cruelly nipped in the bud, gave point and zest to the sneers and sarcasms with which we were assailed."[13]

Cincinnati's embarrassment, though, was only temporary. By the mid-1820s, the Queen City was truly becoming monarch of northwestern commerce. In 1826 the city's boatyards launched seventeen steamboats, and within a single week in February 1827 twenty-one steamboats arrived at and departed from the Ohio port. Ten years later a Cincinnatian appropriately raised the inventor of the steamboat to demigod status when he wrote: "The name of Fulton should be cherished here with that of Washington[;] . . . if the one broke the chains that bound us to a foreign country, the other has extended the channels of intercourse, and multiplied the ties which bind us."[14]

Enhancing Cincinnati's fortunes was the opening of the Miami Canal to Dayton in 1828. In 1831 one recent New England migrant described the quantity of produce passing through the Miami Canal as "beyond conception." "Boats arrive from the interior daily," he recorded, "loaded down with thousands of barrels of flour, pork, whiskey, hams, lard, corn, and every kind of produce."[15] Not until 1845 was the Miami Canal completed all the way to Toledo, thus linking Cincinnati to Lake Erie. But as this waterway gradually extended northward, it offered cheap transport for the rich harvests of western Ohio. In 1845 the opening of the Whitewater Canal from Richmond, Indiana, to Cincinnati also ensured lower freight rates for goods funneling into the Queen City from the eastern half of the Hoosier state. Both these canals encouraged the development of commercial agriculture in interior counties and represented further victories over the isolation that plagued the early heartland.

Trade figures testified to Cincinnati's commercial expansion. During the depression year 1819, the value of imports to Cincinnati was only $500,000. By 1826 this figure had risen to $2.5 million, and in 1829 it reached $3.8 million. Prosperity in the early 1830s yielded to business doldrums in the late 1830s and early 1840s followed by renewed growth during the second half of the 1840s. From 1852 to 1853 Cincinnati's imports amounted to $51.2 million. Moreover, steamboat arrivals at the Queen City that year topped four thousand and supplementing this were almost six thousand flatboat arrivals.[16] By midcentury Cincinnati boosters were claiming that their city was "the greatest provision market in the world." In the words of one commentator, "ENTERPRISE is written on its forehead."[17]

Even more remarkable was the progress of Cincinnati's manufacturers. Meat packing was the premier industry, and consequently the city soon won the unlovely sobriquet of "Porkopolis." By the mid-1840s Cincinnati packed an average of 247,000 hogs annually, or approximately one-quarter of all hogs processed in the region of the Midwest and Kentucky. Second-ranked Louisville packed only about one-fourth as many.[18] In 1834 the visiting poet Charles Fenno Hoffman described the "immense slaughter-houses" as "the most remarkable . . . of all the establishments of Cincinnati." According to this observer, "The minute division of labour and the fearful celerity of execution in these swinish workshops would equally delight a pasha and a political economist." As a result of this brutal efficiency: "The fated porker, that was but one minute before grunting in the full enjoyment of bristling hoghood, now cadaverous and 'chap fallen,' hangs a stark and naked effigy among his immolated brethren."[19] The environmental impact of this gory business, however, added no laurels to the Queen City's crown. In 1847 a critic wrote of "the effluvia . . . from a hundred slaughter-houses in different parts of the city, which sen[t] forth rivers of blood."[20] A few years later a commentator recorded that he had seen Cincinnati's Deer Creek "running with blood, from the hogs killed upon it." He added more poetically, "The stream is crimsoned till it mingles with the Ohio."[21]

Less colorful but also significant was the array of other manufacturing establishments in the Queen City. As early as 1826 there were five steam engine works employing 126 workers, three steamboat yards with two hundred employees, twenty-nine boot and shoe shops with 257 workers, and thirty-five clothing manufacturers employing 599 men and women. Virtually every other type of industry was represented as well, though the author of a directory for that year noted regretfully: "There is no Umbrella Factory in this city."[22] During the ensuing twenty-five years Cincinnati further consolidated its supremacy as the manufacturing capital of the Midwest. Whereas its population increased 150 percent between 1840 and 1850, the value of its manufactured goods soared 200 percent, with the number of industrial workers rising from 10,608 to 33,098.[23] In 1850 the New York editor Horace Greeley commented: "Cincinnati is destined to become the focus and mart for the grandest circle of manufacturing thrift on this continent."[24] A year later a leading local booster referred to manufacturing as "the great source of the prosperity of Cincinnati, and the great element of its progress."[25] And in 1855 a local business figure reported: "The great and substantial elements of manufactures are progressing with almost incredible speed."[26]

At midcentury manufacture of iron goods exceeded all other industries in number of employees and was second only to food processing in value of product. Just as rivers of blood flowed from the packing houses, billows of smoke issued from the city's many foundries. In 1847 an observer wrote of Cincinnati as "nearly enveloped in black smoke" and commented on "that dingy, sooty appearance, which characterize[d] all the buildings."[27] Seven years later another described a typical Cincinnati iron factory as a "dingy volcanic establishment, pouring forth flame and smoke."[28] For many Cincinnati residents, however, the blood and smoke of manufacturing spelled dollars and were symbols of the Queen City's much-vaunted industrial success.

Yet not all Cincinnatians shared in this commercial and industrial good fortune. Especially unfortunate were the often friendless newcomers who exhausted their resources on the trip west and reached the Queen City penniless. In the 1820s one commentator reported on the "great number of emigrants" who "were but too often wretchedly furnished with money" and of families who "were crowded in a single, and often in a small and uncomfortable apartment." According to this observer, "many suffered, died, and were buried by charity."[29] By the middle of the century the problem of poverty seemed even more apparent. In the early 1850s a local newspaper reporter wrote of a "small, dirty, dilapidated" tenement room containing "confused heaps of filthy rags for beds, and a meagre supply of old and broken furniture."[30] Writing of the seeming hopelessness of the Queen City's poor, an editorial commented: "They feel they are doomed to the wretched squalor of their present state of misery and neglect, and . . . writhe out their woeful day of reckless indifference, like a den of pent-up serpents, amongst themselves."[31] Meanwhile, a Methodist cleric added to this grim catalog of woe when he told of a mother who said "she had kept herself and four children on dry bread for a whole week, and only thirty-seven and a half cents worth of it at that." He found the woman's children "in the back part of an Irish whiskey shop, a little girl six years of age, nestled down with a pig and two dogs trying to keep warm."[32]

Queen City residents responded to such accounts with a long list of charities. As early as 1818 John Kidd bequeathed $1,000 per year, forever, for the "education of poor children and youth of Cincinnati."[33] Three years later the Ohio legislature incorporated Cincinnati's Commercial Hospital and Lunatic Asylum "for the common benefit of the poor" and those transient "diseased boatmen" who plied the Ohio River.[34] In addition, by 1841 the city claimed three orphan asylums, a "House of Employment for Female Poor," and a Charitable Intelligence Office, which served "as a means of collecting information respecting the poor," and provided "in various modes relief for their wants."[35] Moreover, Cincinnati's benevolent citizens did not ignore employed but depraved persons at the bottom of the social ladder. In the words of an early city directory, the Cincinnati Boatmen's Bethel Society sought "to afford means of grace and moral improvement to boatmen and those residing in the river vicinity."[36] These and other benevolent organizations that followed in the 1840s and 1850s not only testified to the generosity of Cincinnati residents but also to the economic inequities of the city. Had more urban dwellers shared in the bounty of the rich heartland, the list of charities would have been shorter.

Disproportionately represented among the poorer residents of Cincinnati were African Americans. The states of the Old Northwest were free, and thus in the minds of many blacks the Queen City of that region symbolized an escape from slavery. Yet the Ohio River did not mark the northern boundary of racial prejudice. In 1815 a leading white Cincinnatian described the city's blacks as "a thoughtless and good humored community, garrulous and profligate; generally disinclined to laborious occupations, and prone to the performance of light and menial drudgery."[37] Such a disparaging attitude prevailed among the white elite throughout the first half of the nineteenth century and ensured that blacks would have more difficulty than others in climbing the social ladder. By 1850 more than 80 percent of the black work force were unskilled laborers, employed as servants, stewards on steamboats, and roustabouts on the docks. Though African Americans were found in every ward of the city, at midcentury 75 percent of them lived in the least desirable districts of the central waterfront and East End with Bucktown, Little Bucktown, and Little Africa especially identified in the public's mind as black domains.

Prevailing racial prejudice also led to periodic outbreaks of violence between blacks and whites. In 1829 "some two or three hundred of the lowest *canaille*" launched a raid on black homes, and a racial clash ensued.[38] According to a contemporary account, during one weekend in September 1841 a race riot left the city "almost entirely at the mercy of a lawless mob, ranging in number from 200 to 1500." The white mob attacked black residents who in turn fired repeatedly upon their assailants. The whites then obtained "an iron six pounder from near the river, loaded with boiler punchings, etc.," and "the cannon was discharged several times." Eventually "strong patrols of military and citizens . . . prevented any further outbreak."[39]

Blacks were a minor element in Cincinnati's population compared to the large and growing German contingent. By 1850 the Queen City could claim immigrants from dozens of countries, including such diverse locales as China, Turkey, Guatemala, and Denmark. But in Cincinnati as in all the cities of the Old Northwest, Germans predominated by the time of the Civil

War. In 1860 the Irish constituted the largest foreign-born group in twenty-two of the twenty-five northeastern cities of over twenty thousand population; Germans ranked first in only three. Likewise, the Irish prevailed in nine of the eleven cities with more than twenty thousand residents in the South and West. But in all seven of the midwestern cities in this population category, Germany held first place.[40] The Queen City and her sister heartland hubs were German territory, and throughout the remainder of the century the urban Midwest would bear a strong Teutonic stamp distinguishing it from other regions of the nation.

During the 1830s Cincinnati experienced the first great influx of Germans. Whereas in 1830 persons of German birth accounted for only 5 percent of Cincinnati's population, by 1840 the German share was up to 23 percent and in 1850 the figure was 27 percent. At midcentury almost one-half of the population was foreign born, and almost as many Queen City residents listed Germany as their place of birth as listed Ohio. By the 1840s these Teutonic newcomers already claimed the area north of the Miami Canal as their own, winning for this neighborhood the nickname Over-the-Rhine. As early as 1826 Cincinnati Germans established a weekly newspaper, and by 1850 the city could boast of four German-language papers. Other signs of German influence also were increasingly evident. In 1851 twenty-one breweries were in operation, quenching the thirst of many newcomers. German singing societies appeared, and in 1849 the three largest of these choral groups invited melodic compatriots from Louisville and Madison, Indiana, to share their talents in a *Saengerfest,* a three-day festival of singing and camaraderie.[41]

This influx of newcomers from the eastern states and abroad resulted in a distinctive urban demography in the Old Northwest. Cincinnati and the other nascent hubs of the region were disproportionately male, with a large young adult population, but with fewer children than the surrounding rural areas. In 1840 all the major northeastern Atlantic seaboard cities, with the exception of Boston, had more women than men, whereas in the six largest cities of the Old Northwest the pattern was just the opposite. In 1850 Boston fell in line with the eastern norm, yet each of the midwestern cities retained a male majority. A Cincinnati directory for 1841 identified two causes for the preponderance of males over females in heartland cities: "First, many persons among the males, emigrating, precede their families for the purpose of testing the advantages of the measure at the least expense; and, in the second place, numbers of young and unmarried men, from the eastward, are continually arriving here in search of employment."[42] Thus young men were in the vanguard of urban settlement in the Old Northwest, creating a community with a disproportionate share of footloose, lively males and less than its share of stable families and mature patriarchs.

Transient young men, however, have traditionally been the most crime-prone element of the population, and consequently Cincinnati's demographics did not bode well for public order and tranquillity. Though promotional literature boasted of the city's sober, industrious citizenry, less prejudiced sources deplored the violence and immorality blighting the river port. In 1839 a young Cincinnati medical student wrote to a friend in Boston: "If you desire to live in a population where no confidence exists—where drunkenness, licentiousness and crime prevail—come to the west, and locate somewhere on its great thoroughfares." According to this witness, "Here you will find a floating population . . . without position, names or homes . . . getting their living by gambling, robbery, and thieving, and polluting what otherwise might be a virtuous and respectable community."[43] Writing in 1832, a young law clerk in Cincinnati told an eastern friend: "At this moment we are infested by a gang of desperadoes, as fearless as they are wicked. Three steamboats, one saw-mill, one iron establishment and the two magnificent Hotels of the city have been destroyed by incendiaries within the four past weeks."[44] Moreover, racial animosity was not the only cause of rioting. For example, in 1842 an unruly mob of an estimated two thousand people violently protested the failure of local banks. In the words of one observer, "The Mob tore down the Bank of Cinc., Miami Ex. Co., Exchange Bank of Cinc. and Savings Bank of Louisville—in all 4 Institutions. They entered the offices and scattered the books[,] papers and blank notes to the winds."[45]

During the 1820s, 1830s, and 1840s, Cincinnati was, then, a young, somewhat raucous city, an economic boomtown admired for its commercial and industrial development, but also a place of limited promise for thousands of poor residents and for African Americans living just one step above slavery. Like all emerging heartland hubs it was obsessed by the need to develop transportation links that could carry the region's agricultural bounty to the outside world. And like the other interior cities it was assuming a Germanic flavor that would distinguish the Midwest for many decades. It was, however, different from the other communities in the Old Northwest, for as late as 1850 it stood unrivaled in its success. In the minds of its boosters and of many other Americans, it was truly a queenly city, a city that had risen to the top of the urban heap and that momentarily reigned supreme.

Moreover, it was eager to claim all the cultural and social trappings worthy of a queen. Just as Cincinnati was the preeminent example of economic success in the interior, it also sought to establish itself as living proof that civilization and refinement could flourish in the former wilderness. Located deep in the heart of the continent, Cincinnati and the other midwestern cities were far removed from the traditional centers of European culture. Deeply aware of their relative isolation, midwestern urban dwellers felt compelled to advertise loudly their amenities and cultural attainments. Owing to the widely read criticisms of Frances Trollope, Cincinnati was especially defensive about its claims to civilization. This English woman lived in the Queen City from 1828 to 1830 and then profited from her sojourn on the urban frontier by writing a disparaging account entitled *Domestic Manners of the Americans*. According to Trollope, the queen of the West was actually a common, money-grubbing wench. Writing of Cincinnati, the acerbic Briton observed, "Every bee in the hive is actively employed in search of that honey . . . vulgarly called money; neither art, science, learning, nor pleasure can seduce them from its pursuit." "All animal wants are supplied profusely at Cincinnati," Trollope admitted, "but . . . the total and universal want of manners . . . is so remarkable, that I was constantly endeavouring to account for it."[46] If Cincinnati was to prove that Queen City was a more appropriate nickname than Porkopolis, it had to demonstrate the falsehood of Trollope's charges.

By midcentury Cincinnati could boast of a number of proud symbols of its civilization. Expressing the sentiments of many of his fellow citizens, a devoted Queen City promoter pronounced the local Catholic cathedral "the finest building in the west, and the most imposing, in appearance, of any of the cathedrals in the United States." Yet he betrayed the bookkeeper's mentality so abhorrent to Frances Trollope when he noted that the ceiling stuccowork, though "equal in beauty to that of any cathedral in the world," was executed "for a price less than one-half of what it would have cost in Europe."[47] In the secular realm, Cincinnati's Burnet House was oft-cited proof of the city's success in overcoming the interior wilderness. Opened in 1850, local boosters regarded this structure as "undoubtedly the most spacious, and probably the best, hotel in its interior and domestic arrangements, of any in the world."[48] Moreover, a national periodical seconded this assessment when it praised the 342-room, domed hostelry as "one of the most stupendous and magnificent establishments suited for the reception of the traveling public now in existence in either of the two great continents of the world."[49] Meanwhile, the Cincinnati Observatory offered concrete evidence of the Queen City's dedication to science. Funded through contributions from hundreds of Cincinnatians including professionals and artisans alike, the observatory stood atop Mount Adams and housed a "magnificent telescope, one of the largest and most perfect in the world."[50] At the time of its opening in 1845, a New Orleans newspaper proclaimed, "Well done, the Queen City!"[51]

In an era when even Atlantic seaboard cities suffered from muddy thoroughfares, roaming livestock, and at best haphazard sewerage, Cincinnati's municipal services also seemed commensurate to those of the supposedly more civilized East. As early as 1816 the Cincinnati town council granted a private company the privilege of supplying piped water to the community. In 1839 the city purchased the waterworks, and by 1851 it had laid more than forty-five miles of pipe.[52] Meanwhile, in 1841 the city council awarded its first gas franchise; ten years later five hundred gas street lamps lighted the thoroughfares.[53] The Queen City's most notable municipal achievement, however, was the creation of the world's first professional fire department. Until 1853 companies of volunteers had fought the city's blazes, but during the late 1840s and early 1850s there were mounting complaints about the low character, incompetence, and violence of the volunteers. The *Cincinnati Commercial* editorialized: "The fire department . . . has degenerated from a body of high-minded, noble, daring, and energetic men, into a mere horde of brawlers and rioters, . . . clustering in crowds around the various engine houses, annoying the neighbors, and insulting every female who may chance to pass, with gross and insulting language."[54] Responding to the criticism, a local mechanic built a steam-powered fire engine that could pump more water with less labor than the traditional hand pumpers. Cincinnati's city council purchased the new machinery, thereby eliminating the need for hundreds of volunteers. In place of the maligned brigades, it created a smaller paid force which became a model for cities throughout America and Europe.

Fire engines, gas lights, water mains, observatories, lavish hotels, and cathedrals all spelled civilization. But Cincinnati's claim to refinement went beyond these amenities. During the 1830s and 1840s the Queen City was also attempting to extend its domain over the arts and literature. To overcome the sense of cultural inferiority and isolation so prevalent in the heartland, the leading city of the Old Northwest would have to produce poetry and sculpture as well as pork and steam engines. Literary clubs, highbrow reviews, and artistic salons would offer final proof that Cincinnati was part of the civilized world and not simply an overgrown backwater outpost.

A long list of literary journals carried the Queen City's banner into the battle for cultural glory. One common denominator of these publications was the desire to prove to the world that the interior valley was civilized and did nurture literary talent. In 1827 the editor of *The Western Monthly Review* expressed a typical sentiment: "We have seen . . . with what a curl of the lip, and crook of the nose an Atlantic reviewer contemplates the idea of a work written west of the Alleghany mountains. What, say they, a back woods man write!"[55] A quarter century later the editors of *The Genius of the West* were still engaged in the same crusade, fuming over a speaker who had proclaimed, "The West has no literature." The editors replied: "The West HAS a literature—a literature of her own—fresh, bold, vigorous, and beautiful—not refined into stupidity—not degenerated into obscenity—but looming up like her own mountains—fertile as her rich soil—attractive as her blooming prairies."[56]

Yet the high mortality rate among Cincinnati's short-lived literary periodicals seemed to reinforce eastern skepticism rather than allay it. Soon after founding the *Cincinnati Literary Gazette* in 1824, the publisher realized that "it could not be maintained in a city of 10,000 inhabitants, all so busily engaged in their various pursuits that a man of leisure was unknown among them."[57] In 1837 the editor of the faltering *Western Monthly Magazine* unsuccessfully pleaded to readers to save his journal and thereby disprove eastern writers who argued that "the West was not yet ripe for a literature of her own." Though he claimed that many heartland residents were unwilling "to see the Great West subservient to the East for its literature," his journal was doomed.[58] Four years later the editor of the expiring *Western Messenger* expressed equal frustration: "Our people, perhaps, have as yet no literature because they have nothing to say. They are busy living, doing, growing."[59] Moreover, Midwesterners' own doubts about the literary talent of their region may have undermined these journals. Commenting on the "wonderful mortality" of heartland publications, in 1844 the editor of the *Western Literary Journal and Monthly Review* admitted: "I have at times thought that [Midwesterners] were more attracted by the beauty and glitter of works . . . from the East, than by the substantial merits of those that have been written and published among themselves."[60]

Thus by midcentury the dedicated efforts of Cincinnati's literary lights had proved largely unavailing. In 1855 a venerable Cincinnatian commented on the repeated and masochistic attempts to establish literature in the Queen City. "No warnings of experience," he wrote, "can restrain the desire of multitudes to take the place of those lame ducks that annually waddle forth from the wrecks of their fortunes to warn others that success is the exception and ruin the rule."[61] Though Queen City residents tried again and again, they could never establish themselves as the true literary rival of Boston. This cultural failure remained a theme in midwestern history. During the first half of the nineteenth century and for many decades afterward, heartland residents were burdened with an awareness that their hubs suffered a severe cultural trade deficit, importing brilliance from the East but offering few intellectual exports in return. Those Cincinnatians, like Harriet Beecher Stowe and the poets Alice and Phoebe Cary, who did acquire some literary recognition usually achieved their greatest success only after resettling in the East. In 1850 Cincinnati was still better known for pork than for poetry.

At midcentury, however, Cincinnati could boast of its success as a major book publishing center, earning it the appellation "literary emporium of the West." As early as 1831 Queen City presses were producing books at the rate of 350,000 a year. Ten years later, estimates of production ranged from one to two million volumes annually. By 1850 the Midwest metropolis ranked fourth in the nation in output of books, behind only New York, Philadelphia, and Boston. School books were the chief merchandise of Cincinnati publishers with the famous McGuffey Reader outselling all others.[62] But this primer failed to bolster the literary pretensions of the Queen City. Cincinnati led the nation in the rudiments of learning; New York and Boston were monarchs of high culture.

In the fine arts Cincinnati could also claim some achievements, though again it failed to dispel nagging doubts of cultural inferiority. Much of the Queen City's success in the realms of painting and sculpture was owing to the patronage of Nicholas Longworth. After amassing a fortune in real estate, Longworth retired to a life as the city's leading cultural benefactor. His most applauded protégé was the sculptor Hiram Powers who began his career making wax figures for the chamber of horrors in a local "museum." His talent attracted Longworth's attention, and the wealthy Cincinnatian financed a trip to Italy for the budding sculptor. Powers never returned to the Queen City, but his ensuing success in Europe and the East made him a hero in his hometown and a model for other young Cincinnatians dreaming of fame and fortune. Describing the impact of the Powers legend on the Queen City, Longworth wrote: "I scarcely meet a vagrant boy in the streets, who has not a piece of clay in his hands, moulding it into the human face divine."[63] In 1848 a local critic referred to Powers as "the Canova of the West," and three years later a Queen City booster described this favorite son "as the sculptor of the age, if not of all ages past and to come."[64]

Longworth was also to finance the travels and training of a number of painters. According to one of the patron's admirers, "There was never a young artist of talent who appeared in Cincinnati, and was poor and needed help, that Mr. Longworth, if asked, did not willingly assist him."[65] Other Queen City citizens rallied around the cause of art as well. In 1847 a number of city residents launched the Western Art Union, which maintained a gallery and distributed works of art to its members by means of a lottery. This organization sought "to render the city a school for art, a mart for the elegant productions of the pencil, the burin, and the chisel—a center for the concentration of the patronage of the arts of our country."[66] With almost five thousand members by 1850, the Art Union seemed to demonstrate that Cincinnati was as refined as any of the exalted eastern centers.

In 1851, however, the Western Art Union disbanded after deep rifts split the group. Moreover, its failure was not the only indication that Cincinnati's vaunted culture was merely a thin gilt veneer veiling a continuing sense of inferiority. Cincinnati may have been the home of many noted artists at the beginning of their careers, but most departed for Europe or the East as soon as funds were available. In fact, Longworth's patronage consisted primarily of paying the travel expenses of those who wanted to get out of town and establish themselves in the true art centers of the world. Longworth sponsored an artistic diaspora not the creation of an artistic hub. Even as subject matter, the interior valley seemed unworthy compared to the Italian campagna or the Hudson River. In an 1848 review of the Western Art Union exhibition, a Cincinnati critic complained: "Is the majestic forest which stretches to the West . . . devoid of interest? . . . Hath the empire West of the Alleghanies . . . . nothing worthy of the pencil in her history?"[67] Cincinnati was the incubator for many nascent artists, but it was an inspiration for neither brush nor chisel.

The Queen City may not yet have rivaled Paris or London, but it was unquestionably the cultural and commercial giant of the Ohio River Valley and the Old Northwest. It was not the only river city, however, with pretensions of future greatness. To the west other emerging trade centers sought to parlay steamboat traffic into regal status of the type enjoyed by Cincinnati. For example, the two rivals for urban supremacy in Indiana were the river ports of New Albany and Madison. Madison remained slightly behind in population, but its boosters perceived a nobler future. As early as 1833 an observer reported that "within the months of March and April last, an amount not less than $120,000 in merchandise, was imported in this town, which was chiefly sold to country merchants at wholesale, on terms as fair as could be had at Cincinnati or Louisville."[68] By the 1840s Madison ranked third in pork packing in the region comprising the Midwest and Kentucky, though it processed less than one-fourth the number of hogs as renowned Porkopolis.[69] In wholesaling and packing Madison may have been making its mark in the Hoosier state, but it posed no serious threat to the supremacy of the Queen City.

Meanwhile, New Albany was futilely attempting to defeat neighboring Louisville. Though Indiana's largest city, New Albany remained in the shadow of the Kentucky metropolis across the Ohio River. Expressing the prevailing sentiment of the Hoosier community, in 1836 a New Albany newspaper bitterly referred to Louisville's shadow as an "Anaconda embrace, devouring everything it can feed upon."[70] The Indiana metropolis did, however, excel at steamboat building, and by the mid-1850s of all the cities west of the Alleghenies only Pittsburgh surpassed New Albany in the number of craft constructed.[71]

The only real threat to the Queen City's supremacy was Saint Louis, the monarch of the upper Mississippi. In the 1830s and 1840s it was the second largest city of the northern interior and its rate of growth boded ill for Cincinnati. Between 1840 and 1850 alone, its population increased 373 percent as compared with a 149 percent rise for the Queen City. At midcentury there seemed no limit to the expansion of Saint Louis.

Founded in 1764 by the French, during the next half century Saint Louis developed slowly as a fur trading center. Its location, however, destined it for a greater fate. Seated on a limestone shelf safely above the waters of the Mississippi, Saint Louis was only twenty miles below the mouth of the Missouri River and forty miles south of the outlet of the Illinois River. In other words, it was near the union of three great navigable waterways, and produce from the Upper Mississippi River valley and the interior of Missouri and Illinois naturally flowed to its docks. In 1833 a student of the West observed that owing to this fortuitous location, "It must necessarily become a large town."[72] According to a British visitor in the mid-1840s, "It occupies . . . the central point, from which the great natural highways of the Union diverge in different directions . . . [and] it is destined soon to become the greatest internal entrepôt of trade in the country."[73]

This glorious destiny was not far distant, for in terms of trade Saint Louis already was striding ahead of other interior cities. In 1846 the pages of one business journal reported: "In her commerce, St. Louis presents a spectacle which, we believe, is not equalled by any other interior port in the world."[74] The following year local boosters claimed that it had "grown to be the greatest steamboat port, next to New Orleans, in the world," though one Cincinnatian quickly labeled this a "fallacy."[75] By 1850, however, the hard data seemed to be on the side of the Missouri metropolis. In that year Saint Louis was able to boast that the steamboat tonnage enrolled at its port amounted to almost twenty-five thousand tons as compared with less than seventeen thousand tons at the supposedly reigning city of Cincinnati.[76] Eyewitness testimony confirmed these statistical findings. In 1852 an Ohioan well acquainted with Cincinnati reported from Saint Louis: "The wharf . . . is in a constant tumult, and as you look upon the closely wedged masses of human beings, horses, mules and ox teams, you wonder how they all can move." Traveling along the waterfront, this observer marveled: "There were not far from three miles of steamboats, in solid phalanx, bordering the city, their dark chimneys looking like a blighted forest of mighty oaks."[77]

Like the Queen City, Saint Louis had overcome the commercial isolation of the heartland and brought the continent's interior into economic contact with the world. But nature's gift to Saint Louis was even greater than that bestowed on Cincinnati. In an age of preeminent water transportation, the river network radiating from Saint Louis was the dream of any inland town. Saint Louis certainly seemed to enjoy the mandate of heaven, the divine imprimatur for success.

As yet, however, Saint Louis ranked well behind Cincinnati in manufacturing. In 1854 the Missouri metropolis's most ardent promoter admitted: "St. Louis, as a manufacturing city, is yet in its minority—I may say, its infancy." Until recently "almost all kinds of goods and manufactured wares were brought [to Saint Louis] from other cities chiefly from those on the Ohio." Much to the disgust of this booster, Saint Louis still had no glass factories or paper mills. Moreover, he decried "the immense sums of money annually paid by St. Louis to the boat builders and furnishers and mechanics of the Ohio."[78] In the early 1850s, Saint Louis was perhaps the greatest port but not the preeminent workshop. The Queen City retained that honor.

Cincinnati also far outshone Saint Louis in the realm of culture and refinement. Even its most fervent supporters did not proclaim Saint Louis the Athens of the West or the new Boston. Attempts to establish western literature and western art centered on Cincinnati and not on the Missouri hub. Though it possessed some up-to-date hostelries as well as a fine cathedral embellished by supposedly original works of great European painters, Saint Louis remained relatively rough and unhewn. Moreover, some found the Saint Louis populace distressingly intemperate and uncouth. According to a newly arrived Ohio woman, "If the daily reports of the police may be accredited, there are a vast number that are prompted by the *spirits within them*, . . . to do many unseemly things." Lamenting her move to the unreformed and unrefined Missouri city, this disenchanted soul cried, "Ohio, how I love Ohio!"[79]

Thousands of German immigrants, however, were flooding into the Missouri city, and prospects for future industrial growth were definitely glowing. The population and manufacturing gap between Cincinnati and Saint Louis seemed to be narrowing, and possibly even the Queen City's cultural status might prove vulnerable. Certainly Saint Louis boosters were not discouraged. In their mind, it was simply a matter of time before the westward march of civilization would ensure their city first place in the interior valley, if not in the nation.

Yet both the Queen City and Saint Louis faced unexpected competition from a string of new cities to the north. If future urbanization focused on the Great Lakes rather than the rivers, then perhaps Cleveland, Detroit, or Chicago might exceed the glory of both southern metropolises. By 1850 the race for urban supremacy had more than two contestants. The field remained open.

Cities of the Lake Region

Though the Ohio and Mississippi rivers assumed an early preeminence as water highways linking the Midwest to the outside world, to the north the Great Lakes were to offer a second route to the East and Europe. Like the rivers, the lakes provided the access that could transform the Old Northwest from an isolated interior wilderness into an economic Eden, enriching the pockets of millions of enterprising settlers. And like the rivers, the lakes nurtured a group of cities that acted as conduits funneling eastern money, migrants, and culture into the heartland. Cincinnati and Saint Louis commanded the chief commercial portals of the Midwest, but the Great Lakes offered a convenient and tempting back door to the interior that had a potential for ushering in much business and many newcomers.

Until the late 1820s, however, this back door generally remained closed, with relatively few traders passing through it. Only with the opening of the Erie Canal in 1825 did the commercial potential of the Great Lakes begin to be realized. Linking the Hudson River at Albany with Lake Erie at Buffalo, the Erie Canal offered a continuous water highway to the East that was far shorter than the circuitous route down the Mississippi River to New Orleans and then around Florida to the Atlantic seaboard. In other words, by the late 1820s the Ohio shore of Lake Erie was much closer to eastern markets than were river communities like Cincinnati or New Albany. Moreover, the construction of midwestern canals linking the Great Lakes with the Ohio and Mississippi valleys further enhanced the competitive advantage of the lakeshore communities. In 1833 the state of Ohio completed the Ohio Canal from Portsmouth on the Ohio River to Cleveland on Lake Erie, and henceforth an increasing amount of produce would head north to the lakes rather than south to the river. At the same time Ohio was constructing a second canal from Cincinnati to Toledo, whereas Indiana was also building a water route from the Ohio River to Lake Erie, and Illinois was digging a waterway to connect the Illinois River and Lake Michigan. Together the lakes and canals would shift the focus of settlement northward and nurture trading centers that would eventually unseat the Queen City from her throne.

Chief among the emerging lake ports were Cleveland, Detroit, Chicago, and Milwaukee. Though both Detroit and Cleveland had existed since the eighteenth century, development in all four of these cities only took off in the 1830s in the wake of the opening of the Erie Canal. All were actually products of the speculative boom of that decade, and thus compared with Cincinnati each was a latecomer to the race for urban supremacy in the Midwest. By 1850 they ranked third, fourth, fifth, and seventh in population among the region's cities, and each had established itself as the trading center of an expanding northern hinterland. Yet the largest, Chicago, remained only one quarter the size of Cincinnati.

The impact of canal construction was especially evident in the development of Cleveland and Chicago. Founded in 1796, Cleveland remained a sleepy outpost for the next three decades. As late as 1825, it claimed only five hundred residents, and contemporaries described it as "a pretty place nested upon a high bluff and composed of some fifty houses" with "its clear atmosphere as yet unpolluted by smoke."[80] That same year, however, work began on the Ohio Canal with Cleveland as its northern terminus. Canal traffic between Cleveland and Akron commenced in 1827, and six years later the waterway stretched to the Ohio River. Meanwhile, Cleveland's population soared from 1,100 in 1831 to 3,323 in January 1834 to 5,080 in August 1835. Commenting on the resulting housing shortage, a Cleveland newspaper complained, "There is not even a room to be rented and families have been compelled to take shelter in barns."[81] The number of ships arriving at the Cleveland port rose from 775 in 1830 to 2,761 in 1844, and throughout the 1840s Cleveland was the chief grain forwarding center on the Great Lakes.[82] Not until 1855 would Chicago deprive it of that distinction. By 1845 Cleveland boosters were justifiably promoting their city as the "Queen City of the Lakes," and according to one local enthusiast, "Already Cleveland wields a potent wand over the watery empire ranging away from its shores."[83]

Whereas completion of a canal spurred Cleveland's growth, the simple prospect of a waterway was the ignitor of Chicago's boom. Only ten miles of low prairie separated the foot of Lake Michigan from the Des Plaines River which in turn ran into the Illinois River, a tributary of the Mississippi. As early as 1673 the French explorer Joliet recommended construction of a canal at this point, for nowhere would it be easier to join the waters of the Great Lakes and the Mississippi River. Thus during the early 1830s Illinois began implementing plans for a state-constructed waterway along the Des Plaines–Chicago route, and state canal commissioners laid out the original town site of the future Windy City. At the beginning of 1832 there were still only twelve houses on the site, but as the state proceeded with plans for the canal, investors turned their attention to the nascent town. Any community at the northern terminus of a waterway linking the nation's two great inland water routes seemed to be certain of a grand destiny, and nobody wanted to be left out of the boom that ensued.

During the mid-1830s land prices soared. A town lot that brought $66 in October 1833 was sold for $800 on November 30, 1833.[84] In 1836 a Chicago newspaper bragged about a piece of local property that had "risen in value at the rate of *one hundred per cent per* DAY, on the original cost ever since [1830]."[85] A British traveler recorded that Chicago's "streets were crowded with land speculators, hurrying from one sale to another" and observed that "it seemed as if some prevalent mania infected the whole people." "A young lawyer of my acquaintance," she reported, "had realized five hundred dollars per day the five preceding days, by merely making out titles to land."[86] Meanwhile, the number of buildings rose from twelve at the beginning of 1832 to 450 in 1837, and the population likewise skyrocketed. In 1834 a New York visitor observed that "four fifths of the population [had] come in since last spring," and he was already predicting that the infant settlement would become the "New Orleans of the North."[87] By 1837 another traveler was proclaiming Chicago and its transformation from wilderness to city as "the greatest wonder" of the Northwest. According to this awestruck observer, "the wand of the magician, or the spell of a talisman, n'er effected changes like these; nay, even Aladdin's lamp, in all its glory, never performed greater wonders."[88]

Between 1837 and 1843, however, the bottom fell out of the land market as boom turned to bust. These years of economic depression slowed the growth of every emerging midwestern town, but its catastrophic impact on the former capital of speculation was especially severe. In 1839 a local business leader wrote that "one fourth of 1836 prices [could] hardly be obtained for much business property," and two years later he reported sadly: "Property has depreciated monstrously. It often happens that property which sold for hundreds, even thousands, is not now worth even ten dollars."[89] Another Chicagoan observed melodramatically that "the land resounded with the groans of ruined men and the sobs of defrauded women, who had entrusted their all to greedy speculators."[90] The city directory of 1844 referred to the late 1830s as Chicago's "season of mourning and desolation."[91] In 1841 the bankrupt state of Illinois suspended construction of the canal, leveling one more blow at the once-booming community. But work resumed in 1843, and five years later celebrations marked the opening of the much vaunted waterway. Finally Chicago stood astride the water route between the two great highways of commerce.

By 1850 Chicago was the largest lake city, but it had not yet smoothed some of the rough edges associated with frontier existence. It was still known for its muddy thoroughfares and jerry-built structures as well as its crude boosterism. In fact, a Swedish visitor claimed: "Chicago is one of the most miserable and ugly cities which I have yet seen in America, and is very little deserving of its name, 'Queen City of the Lake.'" "Sitting there on the shore of the lake in wretched dishabille," this observer reported, "she resembles rather a huckstress than a queen."[92]

Such cutting remarks must have won applause from Detroit and Milwaukee, for at midcentury they were still not ready to award the urban crown to their upstart Illinois competitor. Founded by the French in 1701 as a military and fur trading post, Detroit continued to serve this limited function for the next 125 years, only gradually attracting American settlers during the early nineteenth century. As late as 1827 probably as many as half the population bore French surnames. Spurred by the boom of the 1830s, however, Detroit's population rose from 1,517 in 1828 to almost 5,000 in 1834, and by the latter date French settlers constituted less than a sixth of the inhabitants.[93] In 1831 a local observer wrote that "demand for stores and dwelling houses" was "unprecedented." "We have not been prepared to meet the exigencies arising from so rapid an increase of our numbers," he complained, "and almost every building that can be made to answer for a shelter is occupied and filled."[94] Moreover, as in Chicago land speculation preoccupied the growing city, and residents of Michigan proved no more immune to the mania than the citizenry of Illinois. In 1835 the *Detroit Journal* reported: "Buying and selling is the order of the day. Our city is filled with speculators who are all on tip-toe."[95]

The economic debacle of the late 1830s and early 1840s struck Detroit just as it did Chicago, but by the second half of the 1840s the Michigan city had resumed its rapid growth. At midcentury Detroit was clearly the unchallenged metropolis of Michigan and some local boosters were anticipating an even broader domain for their ascendant hometown. After reviewing Detroit's manifold advantages, in 1849 an eager promoter predicted that his city might well become "the great workshop as well as central mart for the lake country."[96]

Meanwhile, Milwaukee was also claiming to be the "Queen City of the Lakes."[97] Settlement of the future Wisconsin metropolis began in 1834 and by 1836 a Green Bay newspaper was reporting, "Land speculators are circumambulating it and Milwauky is all the rage."[98] That same year a correspondent boasted that in five years Milwaukee's population would surpass Chicago's, because nature had "given it a marked superiority in every particular essential to the growth of a great city."[99] Though it could claim only seventeen hundred inhabitants in 1840, during the following decade the Wisconsin city caught up to Detroit, in part owing to a marked influx of German immigrants. By 1850 Milwaukee's population was 64 percent foreign born, and 57 percent of these immigrants were from Germany.[100] Thus Milwaukee was already establishing itself as the preeminent German city in an increasingly Germanic Midwest.

Before Cleveland, Chicago, Detroit, and Milwaukee emerged as the chief lake cities, however, they had to defeat an array of competing towns that dreamed of an equally grandiose future. At the mouth of each creek entering the Great Lakes, speculators laid out a town and promoters boasted of an exemplary natural harbor capable of sheltering a fleet. Scores of paper towns and wilderness trading posts vied for top position. In the battle for commercial supremacy that raged during the 1830s and 1840s the urban "big four" of the Great Lakes had to vanquish these hopefuls, either by exposing the falsehood of their claims or by ensuring that lawmakers did not authorize canals or harbor improvements that benefited these rivals. Only the fittest would survive the competition for urban supremacy, and consequently, at midcentury the shores of Lake Erie and Lake Michigan were strewn with the remnants of defeated ports that had been forced to bow before the triumphant quartet of Cleveland, Chicago, Detroit, and Milwaukee.

For example, the Ohio cities of Sandusky and Toledo momentarily posed a threat to Cleveland and Detroit. Located on a large protected bay, Sandusky was, according to one local booster, "the most eligible point in the whole Northwest for a great commercial city" and a leading contender for the northern terminus of the Ohio Canal.[101] Instead, in what Sandusky residents viewed as the "most stupendous fraud perpetrated," Ohio's legislators named Cleveland as the outlet for the waterway. Years later business leaders in the angry city were still complaining of "the partiality and blindness of early state legislation" which "retarded the wise designs of nature, by building up rivals."[102]

Situated at the mouth of the Maumee River and the northern outlet of the Wabash and Erie and Miami and Erie canals, Toledo enjoyed advantages that Sandusky lacked. Prognosticators of urban greatness frequently placed it at the head of the list of future metropolises, above both Cleveland and Detroit. Yet Toledo's promise far outpaced its performance, and with only thirty-eight hundred residents in 1850 it was running considerably behind its competitors. Local newspapers lamented that Cincinnati at the southern terminus of the Miami and Erie Canal was stealing trade from the lake port.[103] Moreover, the commerce that passed through Toledo seemed to generate little local employment. In 1850 the *Toledo Blade* admitted: "The fact that but few men are necessary to do an immense commercial business, is perhaps more strikingly illustrated in the history of our city than in any other port in the Union."[104] With less than a quarter the population of Cleveland and one-fifth the inhabitants of Detroit, Toledo was already permanently overshadowed. An early lead gave its rivals economic supremacy.

Meanwhile, to the west Hoosier promoters hoped to produce their own version of Chicago at the town site of Michigan City. Surveyors claimed that the site offered the best anchorage along the short Indiana coast of Lake Michigan, though sand frequently blocked the harbor, preventing ships from unloading at the shore line. Perhaps more advantageous was Michigan City's designation as the northern terminus of the Michigan Road, a state-constructed highway running from the Ohio River to the Great Lakes. During the speculative boom of the mid-1830s, the combined attractions of port and road lured perhaps as many as three thousand residents to Michigan City, and the dollars of scores of investors poured into the community. A young settler from Connecticut wrote his parents that those who invested "in land early in the spring" would "double and treble [their investment] in the course of six months."[105] Yet federal appropriations for harbor improvements proved inadequate, and the economic bust of the late 1830s deprived the Hoosier port of possibly as much as one-third of its population. At the close of 1837 a local storekeeper summed up the prevailing opinion when he wrote: "This place is not what we anticipated for business—and besides that, not a pleasant place to live in."[106] Chicago surged far ahead of its Hoosier competitor, and by midcentury Michigan City had an unenviable reputation as the graveyard of Great Lakes shipping. Visiting its hazardous harbor, one observer recorded: "Standing upon the pier, as far as the eye can reach, you can see wrecks on either beach."[107]

Chicago and Milwaukee also faced initial competition from hopeful rivals on the western shore of Lake Michigan. Both Racine and Kenosha, then known as Southport, were laid out in the 1830s, each at the mouth of a minor river leading into the lake. Like Milwaukee and Chicago, these settlements needed federal appropriations for harbor improvements if they were to surpass their competitors, and consequently the goal was to obtain funds for one's own port while denying money to one's rivals. In 1839 a Racine resident expressed a common sentiment when he wrote: "Everything depends upon our getting an appropriation for a Harbor next winter." "If we fail and Milwaukee and Southport succeed," he observed, "the value of the property will at once sink one half from its present value."[108] When in 1840 a federal government survey favored appropriations for Racine over Southport, a resident of the latter town lamented: "It is a Dark period for Southport, our only hope [is] that Racine doesn't get a harbor."[109] In all of the cities, federal aid fell short. But with superior, though flawed, natural anchorages, Milwaukee and Chicago pulled well ahead of Racine and Kenosha. At midcentury, Racine had only five thousand residents and Kenosha an unimpressive thirty-five hundred.

Thus by 1850 Cleveland, Detroit, Chicago, and Milwaukee had risen above the pack and dashed the hopes of former rivals. In an age when water access to the East was all-important, the superior harbors and canal connections of these cities made them winners in the urban race. The harbors of Racine, Kenosha, and Michigan City proved inferior, and Sandusky remained without a canal link. As a consequence, none would ever enter the front ranks of midwestern cities.

In the interior of the northern half of the Midwest, however, some.towns developed during the 1830s and 1840s that laid the manufacturing foundations of the region. Located at the falls of rivers and the locks of canals, these communities became milltowns, owing as much to an abundance of water power as to a strategic position on highways of commerce. Though they would never threaten the quartet of lake metropolises let alone the Queen City of Cincinnati, they would develop into prominent manufacturing centers in a region that would later become the nation's industrial heartland. In the first half of the nineteenth century, trade was still the chief building block of midwestern cities. But in some nascent communities the impact of available sources of industrial power was already evident.

For example, the canal town of Akron benefited from waterborne trade, but it enjoyed the added advantage of profitable mill sites. When in 1825 an Ohio newspaper announced the laying out of Akron, it reported that "power for manufacturing purposes" would be "obtained from water supplied by the canal."[110] Six years later Dr. Eliakim Crosby began construction of a mill race that carried the waters of the Little Cuyahoga River down a one-hundred-foot fall to the Ohio Canal, thereby further enhancing the community's power resources. In the late 1830s Crosby and some partners then embarked on the building of another canal intended to convey the falling waters of the Cuyahoga River to a point just north of Akron. Though this last scheme was never completed, it stirred high hopes, with the *Ohio Gazetteer* predicting that Akron would possess "a water power unsurpassed in the known world."[111] In the pages of the *New York Tribune* Horace Greeley compared Akron of the future with the greatest eastern milling centers, prophesizing that Crosby's site would become the "Lowell of the West."[112]

Hoosiers also believed that rushing millstreams offered one key to urban growth. South Bend lay in the path of the Michigan Road, but available waterpower distinguished the community from less favored town sites along this trade route. In 1843 promoters of the South Bend Manufacturing Company began construction of a dam across the Saint Joseph River with mill races on either side. Along these races developed the town's first industries, precursors of the many factories that would transform the infant settlement into a workshop. In 1850 the *Indiana Gazetteer* claimed that South Bend's "fine situation, excellent water power and the enterprise of its citizens" ensured that it would be "among the largest towns in northern Indiana."[113]

At the same time, waterpower was aiding Grand Rapids, Michigan, and Rockford, Illinois, to become something other than country crossroads. Seated astride the rapids of the Grand River, the appropriately named Michigan settlement seemed especially blessed with mill sites. In 1837 a local newspaper extolled the virtues of the community, among which were an "immense hydraulic power." Comparing the future city with upstate New York's greatest milling center, the newspaper argued that Grand Rapids was destined to become "the Rochester of Michigan."[114] Harnessing the waters of the Rock River likewise seemed to promise greatness for Rockford. In 1844 the Rockford Hydraulic Company began construction of the necessary dam and races, and shortly three sawmills, a grist mill, a woolen factory, and a foundry and machine shop opened for business.[115] By the 1870s local observers were claiming that the development of the Rock River's water power was responsible for having made their community the "leading inland manufacturing city of the Northwest."[116]

During the 1830s and 1840s, then, certain towns were emerging from the mass of contenders and establishing themselves as prospective manufacturing hubs. These were fluid decades with urban fortunes rising and falling; there was no sure formula for success. Yet waterpower seemed a basic ingredient to the elixir that brought life to some settlements. Just as a good harbor and a canal link were invaluable in boosting the prospects of port cities like Chicago and Cleveland, so a dam and some mill races certainly were vital to the Akrons and Rockfords.

Yet during the 1830s and 1840s not only were rival towns battling to see which came out on top, so were sections of emerging cities. Just as fierce as the competition between Racine and Kenosha or Sandusky and Cleveland was the clash between the east side and the west side, the north end and the south. Whether a prospective canal or road was located east of the river or west was a question worth thousands of dollars to land speculators who were gambling that their town lots would garner the highest prices. Similarly, the location of a bridge or a courthouse could determine the site of the business district and the flow of commerce and population with significant rewards for lucky property holders. Thus to the individual investor the issue was not just whether Milwaukee or Detroit triumphed; the ultimate question was which section of Milwaukee or Detroit would hit the real estate jackpot.

This type of rivalry was evident, for example, in Cleveland. Ohio City lay on the west bank of the Cuyahoga River and Cleveland on the east. The Ohio Canal passed through the east side, thereby boosting Cleveland, but Ohio City residents refused to concede defeat to their east bank rivals. In 1837, however, a developer built a bridge across the Cuyahoga that threatened to divert traffic from Ohio City businesses to the merchants of the east side. Faced with another strike against them, west siders took action, initiating a "bridge war." The Ohio City council declared the bridge a public nuisance, and the town marshal applied an ample charge of blasting powder to the span in an attempt to destroy it. The sturdy structure survived, but now east siders rose to the challenge. According to a contemporary observer, one fiery east side speaker threatened: "Before we will cowardly submit to this great injustice, we will give them war! War to the knife, and the knife to the hilt!"[117] East siders drew a cannon up to their end of the bridge and readied themselves for attack. When an army of west siders appeared, led by the pastor of the Ohio City Presbyterian church, the two forces exchanged a volley of stones and bullets without incurring any fatalities. Yet the bridge remained, and the east side would become the focus of commerce in Cleveland.[118] Hard feelings persisted, but in 1854 Cleveland annexed Ohio City, and the east and west sides gradually assumed a stance of peaceful coexistence.

Clevelanders, however, were not the only belligerents in the struggle over bridges. Milwaukee also fought a bridge war, and again the issue was whether the east side or west side would attain commercial supremacy. The east and west sides had competed bitterly since the founding of the community, trading charges as to the unhealthiness and inadequacies of their rival's territory. In the words of one resident of the period: "Every man, and especially every woman, on the east side declar[ed] that on the west side the ague went forth bodily at night, and that the pestilence stalked at noon-day, while they on the west side threw back the taunt."[119] Yet bridges became the crux of controversy. The east bank of the Milwaukee River needed bridges to connect it to its agricultural hinterland, but west siders regarded such spans as obstructions to navigation benefiting only their rivals. The issue came to a head in 1845 when west siders removed the western end of the Chestnut Street bridge, causing the eastern end to collapse into the river. Moreover, west siders destroyed the western approach to the Oneida Street bridge rendering it impassable. Again as in Cleveland, "guns were fired and flaming speeches made," but eventually the two sides negotiated a ceasefire.[120] The central business district developed along both banks of the river, happily enriching east and west.

Citizens of Akron and Rockford were engaged in similar battles. Through much of the 1830s North Akron and South Akron fought to determine which was the true Akron. Churches had to locate on the neutral ground between the two sections to avoid alienating parishioners. Because the Baptist meeting house faced south, a schism almost split the congregation.[121] In Rockford the rivalry was between the east bank of the Rock River and the west bank. Each side of town was surveyed separately, and neither section would adjust its street pattern to harmonize with the other. Consequently, to this day the bridges across the Rock River must angle awkwardly to link the thoroughfares. Controversy over the location of the county courthouse divided the two sides in the early 1840s. Each section offered to pay for construction of the county buildings if the county commissioners chose a site on its side of town. Eventually the commissioners turned down the east side proposal, so the west side won the honor of building the public structures without the expenditure of one cent by the county.[122]

West Rockford was the seat of county government; Cleveland's business district was developing on the east side of the Cuyahoga River; Chicago, Milwaukee, Detroit, and Cleveland were the dominant lake ports. By 1850 the various parts of the lake region's emerging urban hierarchy were falling into place. Certain communities and sections of town were dropping out of the race for top honors and the list of possible winners was narrowing. But the contest was not over. Chicago led, yet Detroit and Milwaukee were not too far behind. The east and west banks of the Milwaukee River were still neck and neck for the prize of commercial supremacy in the Wisconsin metropolis. Moreover, the question remained whether any of the northern contenders could overcome the head start that the river metropolises of Cincinnati and Saint Louis enjoyed.

Capital Cities

Though navigable rivers and lakes were the chief avenues of urbanization in the Midwest, some cities developed not because of their water links to the outside world but because of their role as centers of state government. In the case of these communities, transportation to the South and East counted for less than accessibility to the various corners of the states they governed. And in each of the heartland states lawmakers equated ease of access with a central location. Thus to win capital-city status, a city had to be in the heart of the state. This automatically precluded a site on the Great

Lakes or Mississippi or Ohio rivers because these waterways formed the boundaries of each of the states of the Old Northwest.

The demand for a centrally located capital away from the great water highways ensured that in four of the five states of the Old Northwest the centers of commerce and government would not coincide. Cincinnati, Cleveland, Detroit, Milwaukee, and Chicago were preeminent in trade and manufacturing. All of them perched at the edge of their states, however, and consequently they lost governmental honors to Columbus, Lansing, Madison, and Springfield. Of the capital cities only Indianapolis became both the political and the commercial hub of its state, and it did not achieve that distinction until the dawning of the railroad era. Elsewhere, the command center of the private sector was destined to operate far from public sector headquarters. Government remained in exile in the interior, removed from the business and culture of the greatest urban centers.

The easternmost state of Ohio first faced the task of selecting a capital city, and in many ways its experience was typical. On entering the union in 1803, Ohio's capital was Chillicothe, located equidistant from the state's eastern and western borders. Yet it was far south of the state's center and thus deemed unacceptable as a permanent seat of government. Consequently, in 1810 the general assembly selected a five-member commission to recommend a new capital site, which the lawmakers specified should "not be more than forty miles from what may be deemed the common center of the state."[123] The commissioners chose a location twelve miles north of present-day downtown Columbus. Ohio's legislators, however, failed to act on the recommendation, probably because the owners of the recommended tract had little to offer the state in exchange for selection of their land as a capital site. Basic to the establishment of state institutions throughout the Old Northwest was the assumption that the owners or residents of the selected site would contribute generously to the realization of state plans. Governmental honors were generally bought rather than freely bestowed, and if townsite promoters wanted their tract to become the capital of Ohio, they would have to offer the state a good deal.[124]

In 1812 an enterprising syndicate made Ohio's legislators such an offer. These promoters proposed to lay out a capital city on the high east bank of the Scioto River, fifty miles north of Chillicothe and within the forty-mile radius of the state's geographic center. They would give Ohio a ten-acre plot as a site for the state house and auxiliary offices and provide without charge an equal-sized tract for the penitentiary. Moreover, this syndicate promised to pay $50,000 toward the construction of the new state buildings. In other words, the developers would shoulder the expense of laying out the town, grant the state land for its public institutions, and pay 60 percent of the state's building costs. Despite these favorable terms, some legislators seem to have been reluctant to fix forever the seat of government, so the promoters offered an amendment that guaranteed capital status for their town site only until 1840. Ohio's lawmakers agreed, and thus was born the capital city of Columbus.[125]

In Ohio as in other heartland states, however, some localities retained hope of winning the capital title for many years after the question was seemingly settled. When the state's guarantee to Columbus promoters expired in 1840, boosters of rival towns throughout central Ohio began agitating for relocation of the capital. "The question of the location of the seat of government has become an open one," a group of legislators argued, "and Columbus . . . is entitled to the same consideration, as to her claims to the permanent capitol of the state, as any other town within our border, and no more."[126] Meanwhile, opponents of removal claimed that selection of a new capital would violate the contract between the Columbus town-site promoters of 1812 and the state of Ohio. The promoters had fulfilled their part of the bargain; consequently the state was honor-bound to keep the seat of government in Columbus. The majority report of a legislative committee concluded that abandonment of Columbus would constitute "such a forfeiture of the faith of the State as would certainly not be justified by any code of morals."[127] Eventually in 1843 the Ohio Senate voted to reopen the search for a permanent seat of government, but fortunately for Columbus the House rejected the resolution. Finally in 1851 the new Ohio constitution specifically identified Columbus as capital, giving added authority to the city's position as political hub of the state.

In Indiana an emphasis on central location also characterized the process of capital selection. But Hoosier legislators did not make any deals with private town-site developers. Instead, Indiana's capital was a product of public enterprise. It was built on state-owned land, a state-employed surveyor laid it out, and the state treasury collected the proceeds from the sale of town lots.

In 1816 at the time of Indiana's admission to the union, the state capital was Corydon, just fifteen miles north of the Ohio River. As in the case of Ohio, however, the white population was gradually extending northward, and a centrally located seat of government seemed necessary. Moreover, when Indiana was admitted, Congress authorized the donation of four square miles of public land for the site of a state capital. Hoosier lawmakers could select whatever site they wished, and Congress would donate the chosen tract. Consequently, in 1820 the state legislature appointed a commission to find the best location for a seat of government, and this body predictably chose a plot directly in the middle of the state on the banks of the White River, a stream that the commissioners erroneously believed would be navigable and thus would provide water access for legislators traveling to the new capital. The state legislature confirmed the selection, christened the new community Indianapolis, and appointed another group of commissioners to lay out the site. These commissioners, in turn, hired a Scottish surveyor who had aided in laying out Washington, D.C. He drafted a plan deemed appropriate for a capital city, with broad streets and diagonal avenues radiating from a central circle, which was intended to be the site of the governor's house. Then the state auctioned off the town lots, depositing the receipts in the Public Building Fund, which financed the construction of the state house and other public offices. From selection to sale, then, Indianapolis was a state creation molded by the public sector.[128]

Though one relied on private developers and the other did the job itself, both Ohio and Indiana built their capitals from scratch. In contrast, Illinois chose an existing centrally located town to be its political hub, elevating a humble county seat to capital status. Like Ohio and Indiana, Illinois had selected a town far south of its center to serve as capital during the state's early years. Yet as in the other states the imperative of a central location soon forced reconsideration of the seat of government. In 1833 the legislature authorized a statewide referendum to determine which of six nominated places should be the capital. The nominees were Alton, Jacksonville, Peoria, Springfield, the existing capital of Vandalia, and an uninhabited site known simply as the Geographical Center of the state. In the election Alton won the most votes, though Vandalia and Springfield followed closely behind.[129]

A third-place finish, however, did not discourage Springfield boosters. Founded in 1821, Springfield was the seat of Sangamon County and boasted of fourteen hundred residents by 1835. Moreover, in the Sangamon County delegation were some of the most politically adroit legislators in the state, including the young Abraham Lincoln. These Sangamon lawmakers championed their county seat, and in 1837 they logrolled a bill through the legislature making Springfield the capital. The Sangamon delegation agreed to support bills financing canal and railroad construction vital to other towns if the representatives of these localities backed Springfield as the seat of government. To sweeten the deal, Springfield residents also pledged $50,000 for the construction of state buildings in the new capital.[130]

Rival towns feared and bewailed Springfield's good fortune. An Alton newspaper cried: "ALTON is doomed to utter extinction. Tremble, now O, JACKSONVILLE! and be thou mightily afraid, O, PEORIA! . . . destruction will come upon you like a whirl-wind, and your names be forever blotted from the face of the earth."[131] Vandalia critics described the new capital as set in "a large wet prairie or field, full of bogs and springs" and labeled it "Swampfield."[132] But on hearing the news of the Sangamon delegation's victory, jubilant Springfield residents built a huge bonfire and rejoiced. One observer summed up the feelings in the new capital when he wrote: "The owner of real estate sees his property rapidly enhancing in value; the merchant anticipates a large accession to our population, and a correspondent additional sale for his goods; . . . indeed every class of our citizens look to the future with confidence that we trust, will not be disappointed."[133]

An examination of the capital selection process in Wisconsin in 1836 and in Michigan in 1847 reveals many of the same themes evident in Ohio, Indiana, and Illinois. A central location was of prime significance, and the winning sites of Madison and Lansing both were near the heart of the most populated sections of their states. Because of the absence of dense settlement in the frigid northern reaches of either state, however, the seats of government were far south of the geographic center. The Michigan legislator who introduced the bill to name Lansing capital emphasized its ideal location by also introducing a map on which "a bright red wafer was placed at the point called Lansing and from this point to each lake town was drawn a broad black line." According to this lawmaker, "These lines were so large as to be seen across the hall of the House, and thus ocular demonstration was presented that Lansing was an extremely central point."[134] Moreover, an adept use of political influence reminiscent of the Sangamon delegation's manuevers was a factor in the northern states. The developer of the Madison town site was James Duane Doty, a leading Wisconsin politician who wielded his clout to win capital status for his investment. Enhancing his political influence were more tangible assets. According to legend, Doty freely distributed Madison corner lots to undecided legislators, thereby buying votes for his side.[135]

In both Michigan and Wisconsin as elsewhere, competition for the title of capital was brisk. Arrayed against the Lansing site was the incumbent capital of Detroit as well as such other contenders as Marshall, Jackson, and Ann Arbor. A property holder in Lansing offered free land for a state house and volunteered "to erect on an adjoining lot, suitable buildings for the temporary use of the legislature . . . without charge, till permanent buildings [were] erected."[136] Other localities made similarly tempting offers in order to block the Lansing initiative, and some lawmakers ridiculed the Lansing site as a "howling wilderness." "What, shall we take the capital from a large and beautiful city," asked foes of the future seat of government, "and stick it down in the woods and mud on the banks of Grand river, amid choking miasma . . ., where the howl of wolves . . . and groans of bull frogs resound to the hammer of the woodpecker and solitary note of the nightingale?"[137] Lansing's victory did not quiet the scoffers. In fact, the story soon spread that legislators voted for the Lansing site only because they thought it was "a good joke to locate the capital in the woods."[138] Joke or not, Lansing remained the seat of government.

Contending for the Wisconsin prize were a multitude of sites, including such real settlements as Fond du Lac, Milwaukee, and Racine as well as such largely mythical creations as the City of Four Lakes and Wisconsinapolis. As late as 1870 Milwaukee boosters seriously tried to lure the state government from Madison. Yet the natural beauty of Madison's site proved a strong argument in favor of that community. Positioned on an isthmus between two lakes, the Madison site early won a number of admirers. In 1834 two years before the selection of Madison as capital, one observer said of the area's lakes: "They are the most beautiful bodies of water I ever saw."[139] Doty himself felt that the natural beauty of the site made it especially appropriate for a seat of government. The Madison lakes did not provide avenues of transportation to the community nor did they generate appreciable water power. They were attractive rather than functional. But Madison was created as a capital city not as a commercial hub, and thus aesthetic value took precedence over economic worth. Whereas in Milwaukee water was for floating cargoes and moving turbines, in Madison it was for visual pleasure.

In none of the states of the Old Northwest were commercial considerations of prime importance in selecting the seat of government. Consequently, before 1850 none of the capitals matched the growth of the chief river and lake ports, and none ranked first in population in its state. Located on a branch of the Ohio Canal, only Columbus enjoyed the benefits of a navigable waterway, and with eighteen thousand inhabitants the Ohio capital remained more than twice as populous as the next largest capital city, Indianapolis. By 1850 Springfield had fifty-one hundred residents as compared with nearly thirty thousand in Chicago, Madison could boast of less than seventeen hundred persons in contrast with Milwaukee's twenty-one thousand, and recently founded Lansing had only a little more than one thousand inhabitants. Designation as state capital clearly did not advance a community to the head of the urban pack.

In fact, the capital cities had a reputation for dullness and lethargy relieved only by a few months of activity each year when the legislature was in session. In 1820 one bored New Englander serving as secretary to Ohio's governor reported of Columbus: "This is a scene of dullness to which my eye has been hitherto unaccustomed and to which my disposition has always been a stranger."[140] Thirteen years later another New Englander wrote of the social life during the legislative sessions in "this little village in the Western wilderness," noting, "Wine parties are frequent [and] . . . there be two billiard tables, two Roulette tables, and at the chief Hotel a room open to the game of Faro." Yet upon his return to Cincinnati, he wrote a friend: "Thank God I at last am in *the* city."[141] Throughout the first half century of its existence, Columbus was a graveyard for manufacturing enterprises, none of them surviving for very long. In 1843 even a local booster had to admit: "Of mills and manufactories, further than the common branches of mechanism, we have nothing to boast."[142]

Other capital cities likewise seemed to show little promise of a great urban future. Accounts of Indianapolis referred to it as "a dull country village," and an early history claimed that before the late 1840s "it had been a mere country town, which owed all its importance to the possession of the Capital." "Its business was purely local," this chronicler reported; "it produced little, and it distributed little that it did not produce."[143] With its ample supply of mud and roaming pigs Springfield also suffered criticism. Springfield resident Abraham Lincoln often told the story of a speaker seeking permission from the Illinois Secretary of State to deliver lectures at the state house on "the second coming of [the] Lord." "It's no use," replied the Secretary of State; "it is my private opinion that if the Lord has been in Springfield *once,* he will not come the *second time.*"[144] While the Illinois legislature was meeting, parties, balls, and banquets filled the social calendar, but the cultural delights and commercial bustle of a Cincinnati were absent. More primitive was the city of Madison where, according to one early resident, loose hogs slept in the cellar of the state house and "not infrequently their music was less enchanting than Aeolian harps, or grand old organ tones."[145]

The growth and development of these struggling little seats of government depended in part on their success in attracting other state institutions besides just the legislature. Penitentiaries, schools for the blind and deaf, insane asylums, universities, and state fairs all meant jobs and money, and nascent midwestern towns vied for these government plums. The capital cities captured many of the institutions, but boosters elsewhere did not necessarily defer to these seats of government. Instead, at times the competition could be stiff.

Columbus was most successful in acquiring state facilities. A state penitentiary opened in the capital just one year after the city's founding, a "deaf and dumb asylum" followed in 1829, an institution for the blind began instruction in 1837, and that same year the cornerstone was laid for a "lunatic asylum." In 1850 Ohio's first state fair was held in Cincinnati, though Columbus hosted the event the following year. Seeking to make a clean sweep of the state institutions, Columbus residents urged fixing the fair permanently in the capital city. But for once Columbus suffered a setback. The editor of the *Ohio Cultivator* opposed a fixed site, arguing, "The object of . . . the State Fairs is to benefit *the State at large*—not one particular portion." By moving the site each year more Ohioans would be able to exhibit and attend, thereby receiving "the stimulus to improvement which such Fairs afford[ed]." Moreover, the *Cultivator* reported that during the 1851 fair many "found great difficulty in procuring lodgings, or . . . they were charged exorbitantly for hotel accommodations, etc., while at Columbus."[146] At the 1852 meeting of the State Board of Agriculture some board members complained that "several hundred dollars were yet due on the subscription of the city of Columbus, towards the expenses of the Fair of 1851," and a resolution to locate the fair permanently at Columbus "lost by a decided majority."[147] For the next twenty years the fair rotated among ten cities in the state, and not until the 1870s could Columbus finally claim to be the permanent home of this event.

Indianapolis also obtained the state schools for the blind and deaf and the mental hospital, while the state fair was held in various cities until the late 1860s. The penitentiary, however, was in the Ohio River settlement of Jeffersonville, and Bloomington was the site of the state university. Legislators showed some reluctance to concentrate all institutions in the capital city, and the act of 1844 creating the school for the deaf provided that nothing in it should be "construed to make any permanent location of the asylum for the deaf and dumb at Indianapolis."[148] Yet the trustees of this asylum lobbied for a location in Indianapolis, claiming that the institution "should be located at such place as to be under the immediate supervision of the Legislature."

Moreover, Indianapolis's central location played a role in the trustees' decision. Since the institution was intended "for the benefit of persons scattered all over the State," the trustees believed it needed to "be located as conveniently as . . . possible to all." In addition, Indianapolis, though a dull country town, was not quite as dull as most Hoosier settlements, and thus it could prove enlightening to those deprived of hearing. The trustees explained: "The inmates of the Deaf and Dumb Asylum, being dependent upon their eyes for all that they know, should be placed in situations where as great a variety of objects as possible might be brought within the limits of their observation."[149] Indianapolis supposedly offered a greater variety of objects than rival towns.

Elsewhere the arguments for the capital city seem to have been less persuasive, for Springfield, Madison, and Lansing did not prove so successful. Madison won the odd combination of the state university and mental hospital, whereas the schools for the blind and deaf went to Janesville and Delavan, respectively, and the state fair eventually was fixed in Milwaukee. Wisconsin's capital vied for the state prison, and its advocates cited the community's "proverbial salubrity and beauty of location" as somehow conducive to the punishment and reformation of evildoers. But a generous booster of the village of Waupun offered to donate twenty acres as a prison site, and the state readily opted for the Waupun tract.[150] Michigan's institutions were scattered throughout the state with Ann Arbor winning the university, Jackson the prison, Kalamazoo the "asylum for the insane," and Flint the school for the deaf and blind. The state did not, however, freely bestow such institutions. Kalamazoo's citizens donated a ten-acre site plus $1,500, and the more generous people of the Flint area gave twenty acres as well as $3,000.[151] According to a local history, "there was great rejoicing in Jackson" over passage of the act establishing the prison. Yet Jackson bought its happy victory at the cost of sixty acres of land.[152]

Jacksonville, Illinois, however, was most aggressive in acquiring state institutions. In 1837 it lost out to Springfield in the battle for the seat of government, but it soon compensated for this defeat by establishing itself as the institutional capital of Illinois. In 1839 Jacksonville's legislators secured the Deaf and Dumb Asylum, and local citizens raised almost $1,000 to purchase a seven-acre tract for the new school. Local legislators faced a tougher battle in obtaining the state mental hospital. To stir support for this institution, in 1846 Jacksonville boosters persuaded the well-known reformer Dorothea Dix to come to Illinois and prepare a shocking exposé on the mistreatment of the insane. Dix aroused the consciences of the state's lawmakers, but she also betrayed her Jacksonville sponsors by supporting a bill that named Peoria as the site of the hospital. Both Peoria and Chicago sought the institution, and Jacksonville legislators spared little rhetoric in exposing the shortcomings of these rival towns and in presenting the virtues of their own community. They succeeded, acquiring a second institution for ambitious Jacksonville. Seeking to win the triple crown of institutional combat, in 1848

Jacksonville citizens founded a school for the blind supported solely by tuition fees and local donations. With the school already in operation, the next year Jacksonville legislators succeeded in making it a state institution.[153] Though Springfield had secured the vaunted title of capital, Jacksonville proved that a community could rise from the ashes of political defeat and capture most of the secondary rewards that a state had to offer.

By 1850, then, the states of the Old Northwest had selected their capitals and placed their institutions in communities eager for any boost to their fortunes. In some states, such as Ohio and Wisconsin, private entrepreneurs had laid out the capital, whereas in Indiana the state had taken the initiative and in Illinois the legislature had transformed an existing city into the seat of government. Everywhere the title of capital had been much sought after. Springfield had defeated Alton, Vandalia, Jacksonville, and Peoria, and Lansing had vanquished Detroit, Marshall, Jackson, and Ann Arbor. Moreover, those communities seeking the state's rewards generally had outbid rivals, presenting a package of cash and land that the legislature could not afford to ignore.

Yet a state house and insane asylum had not proven as effective engines of urbanization as a safe haven on the Great Lakes or an advantageous location on the Ohio or Mississippi rivers. Jacksonville may have scored well in the contest for institutions, and Springfield may have won the honor of serving as capital. But by 1850 Chicago had already far outpaced them in population and wealth. The governmental centers formed at best the second string of the emerging urban network. Commerce was king, and commercial hubs were to win the first lap of the race for urban glory in the heartland.

The Advent of the Railroad

During the 1850s and 1860s the rapid proliferation of rail lines across the Midwest introduced a new element in the evolution of the region's young cities. No longer was water the all-important means for overcoming the isolation of the heartland. Rails now linked East and West and changed the odds in the game for urban supremacy. By 1870 a hierarchy of cities had clearly emerged, with the largest metropolises assuming an unchallenged prominence that they would retain throughout future decades. And one of the factors that determined which cities joined the list of winners and which were among the losers was the number of railroad lines linking the community with the outside world.

In fact, in no area of the nation did railroads assume such a prominence during the mid-nineteenth century as in the Old Northwest. With a long-standing demand for transportation lines to the East and a flat terrain that made railroad construction relatively easy, the Old Northwest developed the most extensive network of railways in the nation. Between 1850 and 1860,

Cities of the Heartland

TABLE 2

Largest Cities in the Midwest, 1860 and 1870

1860		1870	
City	Population	City	Population
Cincinnati	161,044	Saint Louis	310,864
Saint Louis	160,773	Chicago	298,977
Chicago	109,260	Cincinnati	216,239
Detroit	45,619	Cleveland	92,829
Milwaukee	45,246	Detroit	79,577
Cleveland	43,417	Milwaukee	71,440
Dayton	20,081	Indianapolis	48,244
Indianapolis	18,611	Toledo	31,584
Columbus	18,554	Columbus	31,274
Peoria	14,045	Dayton	30,473
Mill Creek, Ohio*	13,844	Quincy, Ill.	24,052
Toledo	13,768	Peoria	22,849

Sources: Department of Interior, United States Censuses of 1860 and 1870 (Washington: Government Printing Office, 1864 and 1872).
*A suburban area adjoining Cincinnati and not actually a municipality.

the railroad mileage in the Old Northwest soared from 1,276 to 9,715, and in the latter year Ohio and Illinois ranked first and second respectively among the states in the length of their rail lines. Chicago was to emerge as the nation's leading rail center, whereas East Saint Louis, Illinois, and Toledo were also to rank near the top in railroad traffic. Locomotives were able to overcome the Appalachians' commercial blockade of the heartland and disarm the region's chief enemy, distance from world markets. Recognizing this, the Midwest readily embraced its liberator and became the rail hub of the continent.

With scores of iron roads stretching westward, midwestern cities grew rapidly, though some benefited more than others. As seen in Table 2, the lake cities, and especially Chicago, continued to surge ahead, rivaling the older river ports. The chief rail lines linking the Midwest to New York City skirted Lake Erie and passed through northern Indiana to Chicago, thus giving northern centers the fastest and cheapest access to the nation's metropolis. Cincinnati and Saint Louis retained their advantage in trading with the South. But the Civil War momentarily halted this trade, and by the late 1860s access to the devastated and impoverished former Confederacy certainly was not worth as much as a connection to the wealthy Northeast. The rivers that had nurtured both Cincinnati and Saint Louis flowed in the wrong direction; a direct rail line to New York was a much more potent stimulant for an urban economy than a water route to New Orleans.

Cincinnati's drop from first place among midwestern cities was indicative of the urban shift northward. Some observers claimed that the Queen City was too ready to rest on past laurels and was lacking in initiative, but throughout the 1850s and 1860s Cincinnati entrepreneurs sought desperately to attract rail links and fretted about any perceived slippage in their community's position. As early as 1850 a local leader warned of excessive faith in the river as a commercial mother lode, claiming: "Cincinnati has no . . . monopoly of natural advantages [and] may gain far more than she can lose by the Locomotive; which . . . now raises and depresses towns and cities, at its pleasure."[154] Likewise, that same year a Cincinnati newspaper admonished its readers that the city could not bask "in the glory of pork and poetry, in the grandeur of past achievement, in the deceptive dream of a future greatness that is to come without watchfulness or toil."[155] Expressing the fears of many Queen City residents, one contemporary observed that the lake shore railroads had left Cincinnati "high and dry on the banks of the beautiful Ohio . . . out of the way of the stream of humanity."[156]

Responding to such dire warnings, Queen City leaders sponsored a long list of rail projects, the most ambitious being the Ohio and Mississippi Railroad which would complete a rail link from Baltimore to Saint Louis via Cincinnati. In 1850 the Cincinnati city council agreed to loan $600,000 for construction of this rail line, and in a referendum the electorate overwhelmingly endorsed the loan. Meanwhile, enthusiastic Queen City business leaders personally subscribed to $80,000 of the railroad's stock in a single hour. Construction proceeded slowly, however, and by 1855 the mismanaged railroad was approaching bankruptcy. Coming to the rescue, the Cincinnati city council purchased from the company a tract of wharf property for an inflated price of $500,000. Finally the heavily subsidized line opened to traffic in 1857 amid lavish celebrations. Emphasizing its central location in the nation as opposed to the northern lake shore railroads, the celebrants labeled the Ohio and Mississippi Railroad the "American Central Line" or the "Great National Route." According to local boosters, the Baltimore-Cincinnati-Saint Louis line was the commercial axis of the nation, and of course, the Queen City was at the center.[157]

Yet Cincinnati boosters were wrong. Baltimore was not the great eastern hub; New York City was. Thus the eastern terminus of the nation's commercial axis had to be New York City, and the line west from that metropolis passed through Cleveland, Toledo, and Chicago, far to the north of Cincinnati. Cincinnati was increasingly high and dry and, in the words of a contemporary, "not a fossil or in danger of having a signally fossiliferous tendency, but out of line."[158] In other words, the Queen City retained a good deal of life, but it was becoming farther removed from the heart of the midwestern economy. In 1860 it ranked an impressive third among the nation's cities in value of manufactures, surpassed only by New York and Philadelphia. During the following decade, however, it even lost its distinction as America's leading pork packer. The center of hog production was shifting westward to the rich farmlands of Illinois and Iowa, distant from the packing plants of

Cincinnati. Whereas from 1857 through 1860 Cincinnati accounted for 18 percent of all hogs packed in the region of the Midwest plus Kentucky, the Queen City's share for 1861 through 1864 dropped to 14 percent. Meanwhile, Chicago's proportion of the packing business rose from 7 percent to 25 percent.[159] At the close of the Civil War, Porkopolis no longer deserved its nickname.

According to the population figures for 1860 and 1870, Saint Louis was Cincinnati's successor for top honors in the midwestern urban network. It placed only slightly behind Cincinnati in 1860, and the census bureau ranked it first ten years later. Yet its position was not secure, and despite much boasting about its ideal location at the confluence of great waterways, most Saint Louis leaders realized that their city had to become a rail hub. In 1854 one local booster wrote of "artificial means of communication" which were "already being built" and whose tendency was "to turn some of the business from St. Louis into other channels, to other places." Supporting these new rail lines were urban rivals, most notably Chicago, who looked "with envious eyes upon St. Louis" and whose efforts would be "combined to cripple, or at least deplete her." "St. Louis, . . . if she will maintain her position must have Railroads," this booster concluded, "and these artificial arms, instead of detracting from, will be found absolutely to increase, and in a great ratio, her present steamboat interests."[160]

This was the standard wisdom of the Missouri metropolis, and it produced a flurry of rail projects intended to reinforce the city's God-given destiny as America's commercial hub. Saint Louis vigorously supported the Ohio and Mississippi Railroad with a large majority of the electorate approving a proposal authorizing the city government to loan $500,000 to the rail line. But the most ambitious of the city's rail schemes was the Pacific Railroad. Dedicated to ensuring that Saint Louis stood squarely astride the long-sought passage to the Orient, in 1849 local leaders initiated plans for a railroad linking the Missouri metropolis to San Francisco Bay. In the words of a memorial to Congress prepared by a Saint Louis promoter, the railroad would bring "Europe and Asia into contact through the heart of our North American continent" and become "the greatest common carrier of the world." It would supposedly make the United States "the half-way house upon the highway of nations," but what thrilled the Missouri backers was that Saint Louis would lie at the junction of this world highway with the greatest inland water route, the Mississippi River.[161] If completed, the Pacific Railroad seemed to ensure Saint Louis's magnificent destiny. The commerce of the world would gravitate toward its wharves and depots, and the once isolated heartland metropolis would enjoy artificial links to the great eastern and western oceans as well as the natural waterway running north and south.

To realize this project, the city government again contributed $500,000, whereas the state of Missouri provided $2 million and the federal government authorized a generous land grant to subsidize construction. Construction costs, however, exceeded estimates, and laying of the track proceeded at a slow pace. Moreover, in 1855 a railroad bridge collapsed under a trainload of Saint Louis dignitaries traveling to Jefferson City to celebrate the opening of the rail line to that community. Twenty-nine persons were killed, and the incident added one more black mark to the reputation of the line. Then in the early 1860s guerilla warfare by Confederate sympathizers further retarded progress on the road, and not until 1865 did it reach Kansas City. After more than fifteen years of effort and millions of dollars of public and private investment, the Pacific Railroad had only arrived at the western border of Missouri not the western shores of the United States.[162]

In fact, by the late 1860s the rival city of Chicago was fast approaching Saint Louis in population, and the Missouri metropolis seemed out of breath from its efforts to keep ahead. Though it was on the "American Central Line," it was farther from New York City than was Chicago, and the Mississippi River was a serious barrier to eastbound traffic. With no bridge yet spanning the waterway at Saint Louis, all rail freight going to and from the east had to be ferried across the Mississippi, an expensive process that encouraged manufacturers to locate in the newly founded community of East Saint Louis, Illinois, rather than on the Missouri side of the river. Unable to honestly win the race with Chicago, in 1870 Saint Louis chose to cheat. That year census takers in Saint Louis withheld their figures until Chicago's returns were reported; then the Saint Louis enumerators announced a fallacious population count for their hometown that topped Chicago by twelve thousand. Officially Saint Louis was monarch of the Midwest, but it held that title only through fraud.[163]

In contrast, by 1870 Chicago was a city that did not need to cheat. Railroads were radiating in all directions from the Illinois metropolis, ensuring its ultimate victory over Cincinnati and Saint Louis. Located at the southern tip of Lake Michigan, Chicago did not suffer the inconvenience of a water barrier hampering its rail access to the east. Moreover, due west of Chicago lay the richest farmland in the world. Thus as rail lines stretched westward the unrivaled cornucopia of Iowa was to become a province within the Windy City's expanding commercial empire. Far removed from the conflict of the Civil War, Chicago enjoyed another advantage over its rivals to the south. Confederate raiders did not threaten the Windy City's hinterland as they did Missouri or the Kentucky region across the Ohio River from Cincinnati. During the 1860s grain and hogs from northern Illinois and Iowa proceeded without interruption to Chicago and eventually into the stomachs of the Union Army.

In 1848 the first locomotive chugged out of Chicago and unleashed an era of rail development that transformed the city. By 1852 an enthusiastic citizen was boasting of over two hundred miles of rail lines completed within Illinois "and free access, at all times, to every city on the sea-board, from Portland to Savannah!" According to this booster, Chicago was inevitably destined to become "the great store-house of the East and the West,—the Central Exchange of the Nation."[164] Five years later this destiny seemed closer to realization, for eleven trunk lines converged on the city and 120 trains arrived and departed daily.[165] As Chicago's rail lines reached the Mississippi they diverted traffic from Iowa, Minnesota, western Wisconsin and western Illinois that had formerly sailed downstream to Saint Louis. By the late 1850s Chicago had definitely shorn the great river port of its northern markets.

Moreover, all this was accomplished without the city government of Chicago committing one dollar to rail development. Whereas the public authorities in Cincinnati and Saint Louis borrowed and begged to finance rail construction, good fortune simply dropped into Chicago's lap with eastern investors largely footing the bill for transportation lines. Diversion of the bounty of the Midwest northward to Chicago ultimately would aid New York City, the Windy City's natural eastern outlet. Consequently, New York capitalists, as well as their Boston counterparts, preferred the lake cities to the river ports and readily invested in Chicago's railroads. In addition, New Yorkers had much more capital than Baltimore residents. Thus private money flowed much more freely for the northern route than for the much-vaunted central line of Baltimore-Cincinnati-Saint Louis. "What built Chicago?" asked one resident. "Let us answer, a junction of Eastern means and Western opportunity. . . . Greatness was forced upon Chicago as a golden subjugation."[166]

By the 1860s Chicago was reveling in its golden subjugation and already claiming to have vanquished all rivals. Chicagoan John Wright wrote an entire book on the success of his hometown relative to all competitors and especially noted: "The nonsense that centrality on the rivers insures large superiority to St. Louis, is a bubble which has long wanted pricking."[167] A guide to the city published in 1868 unequivocally described Chicago as "the largest and most important city in the Northwest, and, in its rapid growth, the most remarkable in the Union."[168] Meanwhile, Windy City residents fondly recounted the advice of an Englishman to a compatriot visiting America: "See two things in the United States, if nothing else,—Niagara and Chicago."[169] The falls and the city were the two wonders of the continent, and most Chicagoans probably doubted that the roaring cataract was really worthy to be classed with their hometown. Granted, Chicago was still a parvenu; Cincinnatians would have sneered at the idea of finding "culture" in the Illinois metropolis. But Chicago was first in pork, and many Windy City residents were confident that poetry would surely follow.

Perhaps no city felt the dramatic impact of the railroad as much as Indianapolis. Landlocked in the heart of Indiana far from any navigable body of water, Indianapolis remained a small town until the late 1840s, lagging behind the Hoosier river ports of New Albany and Madison. In 1847 the completion of the Madison and Indianapolis Railroad linked the Indiana capital to the Ohio River, almost immediately transforming the community. According to a contemporary chronicler, before 1847 Indianapolis "had been shut out from the world . . . by an almost impassable expanse of mud" and "a death-like quiet pervaded the place."[170] By 1857, however, eight trunk lines converged on the city with the population quadrupling in the ten years since the first locomotive roared into town. Local boosters proudly referred to it as "the Railroad City of the West," and the Board of Trade proclaimed: "Indianapolis is 'the place where the ways meet,' and is more a centre of transit by Railroads than any other inland town in the world."[171] Likewise, a local politician described the Hoosier capital as "the hub of the wheel, with the railroad spokes pointing to the circle, including the whole field of Western production, consumption and demand."[172] After a quarter of a century being in the middle of nowhere, Indianapolis had become a regional crossroads.

Propelled by its newfound success as a rail center, Indianapolis moved upward among the ranks of midwestern cities. From tenth place in 1850, it progressed to eighth position in 1860 and then to seventh in 1870. Moreover, by the latter year it had clearly established itself as the preeminent metropolis of Indiana, with second-place Evansville less than half its size. The Madison and Indianapolis Railroad was the first and last rail line constructed to Madison; all later railroads bypassed the has-been port. New Albany became even more of a subsidiary of adjacent Louisville than it had been before, and its glory as a builder of steamboats waned as river traffic diminished in significance. By 1870 the railroads had made Indianapolis the commercial as well as the political capital of Indiana, and this was an honor it would retain.

After a half century of contention Indianapolis was the first city of Indiana, Chicago was, or was soon to be, the first city of the Midwest, and Cincinnati, Saint Louis, Milwaukee, Detroit, and Cleveland were recognized as significant centers surpassed only by the Windy City. In other words, by 1870 the urban pattern of the Midwest had crystallized, with cities fixed in a position of prominence or a status of subordination. Throughout future decades urban centers would continue to jockey for a better position, and some would run ahead of others. Quincy, Illinois, would falter and Akron spurt forward. But by the close of the Civil War it was generally clear which were to be the big cities and which the small. The Zanesvilles and New Albanys had dropped from the list of leading midwestern towns, and the once-absent Milwaukees and Toledos had taken their place. The main bout in the urban battle for survival and success was over.

Moreover, by 1870 Midwesterners had finally won the great struggle to overcome the commercial isolation of the heartland. Throughout the formative era of midwestern urban development the vital issue was access to the outside world. Communities with such access would grow; towns without links to the East or South would die. Prior to 1850 navigable waterways were, then, the key to urban success. Yet ultimately the railroad proved to be the answer to the midwestern dilemma. It overcame the Appalachian barrier and offered an economically feasible means of exchanging goods with the Atlantic seaboard. Even during the early decades of the railroad era, access to the East determined urban fortunes. Thus the lake cities led by Chicago flourished because of their superior connection with New York City. But by 1870 America's great interior valley was no longer the "remote West," far removed from the nation's markets. Iron rails bound East and Midwest, joining Chicago to New York and drawing the heartland cities toward economic maturity.

1. Rows of steamboats at the landing in Cincinnati during the early 1850s were a sign of the Queen City's commercial prominence. Ohio Historical Society.

2. This broadside testified to Cincinnati's manufacturing development in the 1830s. Ohio Historical Society.

3. Hog-butchering establishments such as this one earned Cincinnati its early title of Porkopolis. Ohio Historical Society.

4. Chicago in 1830 was simply a military stockade and trading post. Chicago Historical Society.

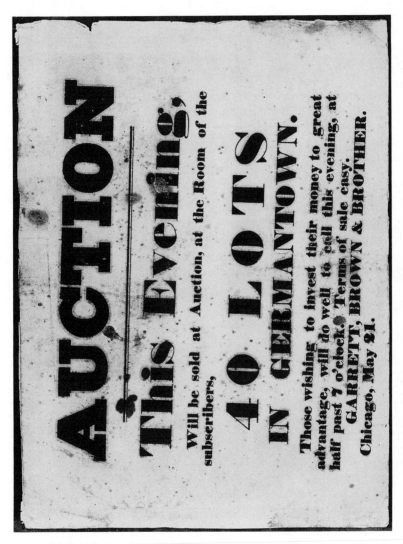

5. This Chicago broadside from 1836 advertises the chief pursuit of most midwestern cities of the 1830s: land speculation. Chicago Historical Society.

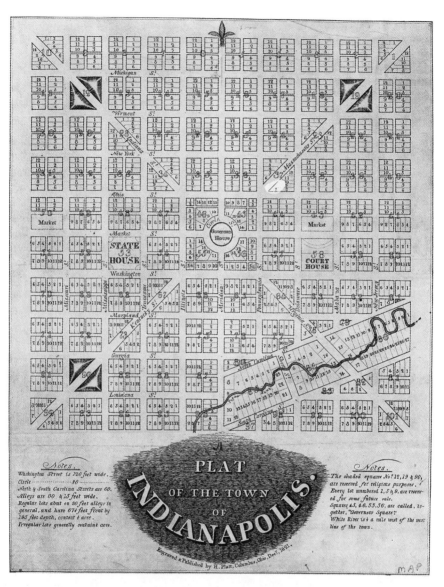

6. With its radiating boulevards and broad avenues, the original plan for
Indianapolis seemed appropriate to a capital city. Indiana State Library.

WASHINGTON STREET—1825.
View Looking West from Pennsylvania Street.

7. An artist's rendition of how the principal street in the frontier capital of Indianapolis might well have looked in 1825. Indiana State Library.

2.

The Emerging Center of Urban America

In 1874 a Chicago periodical wrote of its hometown as "the concentrated essence of Americanism" and published a poem that proclaimed: "The East is asleep or is dead; . . . Her genius is gone to the West—Her genius, her empire, her prestige."[1] With these words the Chicago journal summarized the emerging belief of most Midwesterners. No longer was the land west of the Appalachians at the edge of the nation and remote from the markets and ideas of the civilized world; no longer was it a wilderness to be conquered and tamed by transplanted European culture. By the 1870s and 1880s, it seemed truly the heart and essence of the nation, not only central to the national existence but the source of the nation's vitality. According to midwestern urban boosters of the late nineteenth century, the nation's rail lines radiated from Chicago and Saint Louis, the agricultural produce of the Mississippi Valley was unsurpassed, and the mineral and timber resources of the heartland offered the raw materials for boundless industry. The Midwest possessed the prerequisites for great cities as no other region, and in the rich interior valley supposedly lay the future of urban America. In the 1870s and 1880s Chicago was not an outpost of American enterprise and civilization; it was America.

Bolstering the faith of these midwestern boosters were the soaring population figures reported in each successive census. Thousands of new migrants from the East and abroad were swelling the population of heartland cities, pushing Chicago, Cleveland, and Detroit forward in the ranks of the nation's metropolises. As seen in Table 3, by 1890 Chicago was home to more than one million people and Saint Louis was approaching the half-million mark. Whereas in 1860 no midwestern city ranked among the nation's five largest and only three were among the top fifteen, thirty years later both Chicago and Saint Louis held a place among the five leading metropolises, and a total of five heartland cities were among the fifteen most populous. In 1860 Chicago was only one-eighth the size of New York City; by 1890 it was two-thirds as populous as the nation's greatest metropolis. Clearly the gap was closing between the interior hubs and those on the Atlantic seaboard, lending support to the belief that the Midwest would soon become the nation's preeminent urban region.

The flood of newcomers to heartland cities not only boosted the census

TABLE 3

Population and Rank of the Largest Midwestern Cities, 1890

City	Population	Rank among the Nation's Cities
Chicago	1,099,850	2
Saint Louis	451,770	5
Cincinnati	296,908	9
Cleveland	261,353	10
Detroit	205,876	15
Milwaukee	204,468	16
Indianapolis	105,436	27
Columbus	88,150	30
Toledo	81,434	33
Dayton	61,220	45
Grand Rapids	60,278	47
Evansville	50,756	56

Source: Census Office, *Compendium of the Eleventh Census: 1890* (Washington: Government Printing Office, 1892), 1: 434.

rankings of their new hometowns but provided the labor for thousands of factories arising throughout the region. These laborers were to form a working class that grew increasingly restive during the last decades of the nineteenth century. Strife thus tarnished the reputations of Chicago, Milwaukee, and Cleveland, causing heartland capitalists to have momentary doubts about the magnificent destiny of the region. Yet from 1870 throughout the early 1890s wealth and population continued to gravitate westward, and it was the optimistic hope of most urban Midwesterners that the bulk of the nation's people and their money would settle once and for all in the fertile plain between the Appalachians and the Rockies.

Manufacturing and Marketing

Underlying the population growth of heartland cities was a firm foundation of economic expansion, and especially expansion in manufacturing. Before the Civil War all of the nascent midwestern cities, with the exception of Cincinnati, were primarily trade centers specializing in the export of raw materials from the heartland and the import of merchandise from the East. Their prosperity depended on advantageous transportation ties with the East and South, for they were chiefly transfer points where grain and pigs departed and textiles, coffee, and iron goods arrived. Only in Ohio's Queen

City was manufacturing for the western market a mainstay of the local economy.

After the Civil War, however, Midwesterners witnessed the gradual transformation of their cities into manufacturing hubs rivaling those of the East. In 1860 Cincinnati's Hamilton County was the only county in the Midwest to rank among the nation's top ten counties in value of manufactures. Saint Louis County held the twelfth place in the nation, and Chicago's Cook County lagged behind in twenty-second position. Six of Massachusetts's fourteen counties ranked ahead of the Windy City. By 1890, though, Chicago had a firm hold on second place, Saint Louis had moved into fifth position while Cincinnati clung to seventh place. In 1860 only two of the nation's top twenty manufacturing counties were in the Midwest; by 1890 the Old Northwest plus Saint Louis accounted for seven of the twenty cities with the greatest value of manufactures.[2]

Rising output also meant an increased number of manufacturing jobs and a population increasingly dependent on factory employment. The population of Chicago rose tenfold between 1860 and 1890, yet the number of Chicagoans employed in manufacturing soared at least thirty-fold. Likewise, in Cleveland, Detroit, and Milwaukee the size of the industrial work force grew at double the pace of the increase in population.[3] Though the midwestern cities were still major trade centers with steamboats lining the river levees and schooners crowding the lake ports, the proportion of factory hands in the labor force was growing and overshadowing the long-standing army of stevedores, porters, and haulers.

Spurring this industrial boom was the region's advantageous position with regard to resources, transportation, and markets. The days of isolation were over, and in the 1870s and 1880s midwestern cities could boast of rail lines as well as water routes offering enviable access to rich mineral deposits, bountiful agricultural produce, and millions of consumers in the rural hinterland. In the late nineteenth century midwestern urban boosters no longer emphasized access to the East or Europe but boasted of their hometowns' access to the markets and raw materials of the wealthy Midwest. The Midwest was becoming the nation's economic heart and proud cities crowed about their good fortunes as hubs of America's most favored region.

Especially significant was access to the raw materials of manufacturing. Coal literally fueled the industrial revolution of the nineteenth century, and Ohio, Indiana, and Illinois all had virtually inexhaustible deposits of this vital commodity. Moreover, Ohio could draw on the limitless deposits in nearby West Virginia, eastern Kentucky, and western Pennsylvania. If coal was the fuel of the age, iron was the essential metal, and here again the Midwest was blessed. The upper peninsula of Michigan was the chief source of iron ore in the late nineteenth century, and the lake ports of Detroit, Cleveland, Chicago, and Milwaukee all enjoyed inexpensive water access to this mining region. Moreover, Missouri's much-vaunted Iron Mountain, a solid mass of ferrous ore, was only seventy-five miles by rail from Saint Louis, and Wisconsin's Iron Ridge was fifty miles northwest of Milwaukee.

Wisconsin and Michigan also could claim the chief timberlands of the era, producing millions of board feet of lumber. And together the midwestern states formed the nation's granary with an abundance of corn and wheat as well as millions of corn-consuming hogs. Beyond the Mississippi, more recently settled states were challenging the agricultural supremacy of the Old Northwest. But even the rich lands of Iowa were actually an economic dependency of Chicago, invariably sending their produce along the many railroads terminating in the Windy City. In the late nineteenth century the Midwest was, then, the nation's chief source of lumber, iron ore, grain, and livestock, and a leading supplier of coal. Sitting amid these natural riches, midwestern cities seemed inevitably destined to manufacturing glory.

These facts were well known to the region's urban boosters, and one city after another proclaimed its sure-fire destiny as an industrial giant. In 1886 a Milwaukee publication observed that the Wisconsin metropolis had "at her doors a country rich with many kinds of raw material which come from forest, from mines, and from farms."[4] The following year a boosterish account of Detroit's industries emphasized "the wealth of Michigan in iron, copper and other metals, her unexcelled forests, and her vast supplies of other raw materials for manufacture, and the proximity of ample supplies of fuel of every kind to Detroit."[5] According to a similar advertisement of Cincinnati's industrial success, "The great natural resources that lie almost within our grasp, are among the prominent advantages of the city in the lines of industry."[6] Likewise, in 1878 Cincinnati's Board of Trade boasted of the city's "proximity to boundless fields of coal and iron, and other minerals; to forests of timber yet measurably unbroken; . . . and to the immense granaries of our country."[7]

Adding to the Midwest's good fortune was its unequaled transportation network that facilitated the distribution of goods to their markets. Many manufacturers moved to Chicago because it offered the cheapest, fastest rail transportation to a multitude of locations in the nation's interior. Not only was it "situated on the only great east and west water-way in North America," but according to one writer in 1887, it also was "at the centre of a web of steel whose radii reach[ed] the ocean in three directions, and to the northward touch[ed] the limit of civilized life."[8] Smaller cities also bragged of their advantages as transportation hubs when selling themselves to prospective manufacturers. An Indianapolis publication claimed: "The city is the nucleus of a railroad system which had few equals and no superiors."[9] According to Columbus boosters, Ohio was "the middle State of the Union" and Columbus was "the 'Hub' of Ohio," and in the words of the local board of trade, "the great railway center of the state."[10]

Not only did cities like Chicago, Indianapolis, and Columbus sit amidst enviable natural resources and boast of unsurpassed transportation links, they also enjoyed access to a mass of relatively wealthy consumers. Though midwestern farmers often protested their hard times, they unquestionably enjoyed the highest standard of living of any of the world's tillers of the soil. Whereas sharecroppers in the American South had little disposable income for urban manufactures and subsistence farmers throughout the world lived on the edge of starvation, the millions of midwestern agrarians were ready customers for the latest farm implements and household goods. Midwestern city dwellers themselves had a standard of living superior to that of their European counterparts. Moreover, with the development of the Great Plains and Rocky Mountain states there was enormous demand for lumber and iron goods, and the Midwest was the closest supplier of these commodities.

With raw materials, excellent transportation facilities, and a ready market for its output, the midwestern city, then, had the chief prerequisites for manufacturing success. During the antebellum period New England may have taken an early lead in the industrial revolution, but now it was the Midwest's turn to flex its manufacturing muscles. In the 1870s and 1880s rising smokestacks marked the advent of the region's industrial era.

Especially notable was the expansion of the iron and steel industry. Midwestern cities could obtain the prerequisite coal and iron ore cheaply, and the rapid westward expansion of railroads meant there was a demand for the product. Thousands of miles of iron rails and iron-wheeled railroad cars were needed for the new lines, not only in the Old Northwest but also in the states west of the Mississippi. Moreover, steam was the chief source of industrial power west of the Appalachians, and thus factories required an ever increasing output of iron boilers. And every new farm homestead and city residence needed an iron stove for heating and cooking.

Consequently, midwestern fabricators of iron and steel products proliferated in the post–Civil War era. By 1890 foundry and machine shop products ranked first in value added among the industries of Cleveland and Detroit, held second place in Milwaukee, and were third in Chicago and Cincinnati. These five midwestern cities alone accounted for approximately 30 percent of the nation's foundry and machine shop output.[11]

Cleveland's fortunes were especially tied to metal working concerns. In the 1850s that city's entrepreneurs had pioneered iron ore shipments from Michigan's Upper Pensinsula, and Cleveland vessels continued to dominate this trade. With ample coal supplies to the south in Ohio and Pennsylvania, as early as 1868 the local board of trade boasted: "[Cleveland's] many natural advantages . . . bid fair to render her, at no distant day, the great Iron Mart of the West."[12] Fifteen years later there were 136 establishments in Cleveland "devoted to the manufacture of iron and steel, and their products," and together these firms employed over seventeen thousand hands. In the late 1880s the enormous Cleveland Rolling Mills alone claimed over four thousand employees.[13]

Owing in part to the enterprise of Captain E. B. Ward, Detroit and Milwaukee rivaled Cleveland in the fabrication of iron and steel products. A

Great Lakes ship captain engaged in the iron ore trade, Ward established an iron works in Wyandotte, twelve miles outside of Detroit, and here in 1864 he introduced to the United States the Bessemer process for producing steel. Seeking to expand his holdings, in 1867 Ward organized the Milwaukee Iron Company and began construction of a giant mill in Bay View, a village abutting the southern boundary of Milwaukee.[14] According to a Milwaukee periodical, by 1873 the sprawling Bay View works was "the second in importance in the United States" and possessed "fifteen smoke-stacks, adding to the vast sulphurous cloud, day and night hanging over the place."[15]

More significant than Ward's mills were the numerous factories in both Detroit and Milwaukee which fabricated products from iron and steel. In 1887 a Detroit observer boasted of the local stove factories which had proved so successful that the Michigan city's stove output was "larger than that of any other in the United States." Similarly, with an abundance of both iron and lumber, "in the production of freight cars Detroit exceed[ed] in out-put any other city on [the] continent."[16] One Detroit enthusiast claimed that between 1865 and 1883 the Michigan Car Company produced over forty-eight thousand cars and if placed end to end they would stretch "two hundred and eighty-four miles, or across the State of Michigan and beyond Chicago."[17] As early as 1873 the Milwaukee machine shops of E. P. Allis and Company covered six acres and visitors to the works were "struck with astonishment at the bewildering maze of revolving machinery" which produced a "deafening" noise.[18] The following year a Milwaukee publication proclaimed that Allis-manufactured grist and sawmills were "grinding and sawing all over the Northwest, and away in Utah and Montana." According to this account, "The Mikado of Japan, having tried the quality of their flouring mills a year ago, has just ordered from this enterprising house a first-class gang saw-mill."[19]

Other midwestern cities were likewise sending iron and steel manufactures throughout the continent and the world. By the late 1880s Chicago ranked second in the nation as an iron and steel center, and it produced 15 percent of the nation's farm machinery.[20] Smaller centers such as Youngstown, Ohio, were also building an industrial base on the iron and steel industry. By 1875 twenty-one blast furnaces operated in the Youngstown area as well as nine rolling mills employing almost twenty-five hundred workers.[21] Pittsburgh remained the nation's iron and steel capital, but this branch of industry was moving westward and adding to the wealth of cities throughout the heartland.

Meanwhile, the Midwest was also acquiring a growing share of the nation's woodworking industries. For example, furniture manufacturing offered employment to thousands of urban Midwesterners and was becoming the economic mainstay of communities like Grand Rapids, Michigan, and Rockford, Illinois. Both Grand Rapids and Rockford enjoyed ready access to the vast timber resources of the upper Midwest, and they parlayed this asset into a multi-million-dollar industry. Though cabinetmakers had served the local market before the Civil War, not until the 1870s did Grand Rapids begin to

establish its reputation as the furniture capital of America. A display of
Grand Rapids furniture at the Centennial Exposition of 1876 attracted national attention to the city; especially impressive was a three-piece bedroom
suite embellished with niches containing statuettes of such figures as George
Washington and Christopher Columbus and surmounted by eagles with out-
stretched wings.[22] By 1891 one Grand Rapids furniture manufacturer boasted
of his city's far-flung sales, remarking that "the Royal Hawaiian Hotel in
Honolulu bought twenty carloads of furniture from Grand Rapids firms . . .
and Emperor Hirohito of Japan used a hand-carved office suite from Grand
Rapids."[23] During these same years the arrival of thousands of Swedish
immigrants with woodworking skills encouraged the growth of furniture
manufacturing in Rockford. Never as famous as their Grand Rapids rivals,
Rockford's furniture factories dominated the economy of the Illinois city
and by the beginning of the twentieth century employed almost one-fourth
of the local work force.[24]

The name Grand Rapids became synonymous with furniture, but by the
1890s the nation's largest maker of home furnishings was actually Chicago.
As early as 1886 one author reported: "In parlor furniture especially, Chicago leads the world, the annual sales of upholstered goods and frames
equaling those of New York, Boston and Cincinnati combined."[25] By 1895
the value of Chicago's furniture output exceeded that of New York City by
$4 million and was twice that of third-place Grand Rapids.[26] Like Grand
Rapids and Rockford, Chicago benefited from its proximity to the necessary
raw materials, and in 1878 a correspondent for *American Cabinet Maker*
said of the Chicago furniture manufacturer: "He has the advantage . . . of
vast forests of lumber almost at the very door of his workshop, so cheap
has transportation by the network of railroads become, as well as superior
navigation facilities."[27] Moreover, Chicago became a mecca for skilled woodworkers from Germany and Scandinavia who lent their expertise to the
production of chairs, desks, beds, and cabinets.

The forest resources of the Midwest not only fostered the manufacture of
furniture but also provided the foundation for a flourishing wagon and carriage industry. Whereas Chicago led the nation in sofas and chairs, Cincinnati was queen of carriage manufacturing, drawing on the hardwood forests
of southern Ohio and Indiana as well as eastern Kentucky. By 1891 the value
of the output of its carriage and wagon works was more than twice that of
second-place New York City, and in 1894 a local commentator boasted that
Queen City's production exceeded "both in quantity and value that of any
four cities in this country."[28] Other midwestern centers were making their
names in this industry as well. Columbus believed it ranked first in the nation
in the manufacture of high-class carriages. The Columbus Buggy Company,
which claimed to be "by far the largest carriage factory in the world," turned
out a new buggy every eight minutes.[29] At the same time the Studebaker
brothers were making South Bend, Indiana, famous as a center of wagon
manufacturing, and in Flint, Michigan, William C. Durant founded a carriage

factory that together with the community's other cart and wagon works earned Flint the proud nickname "The Vehicle City."[30] Midwestern farmers provided a ready market for wagons and buggies, and cities like Columbus, South Bend, and Flint were taking advantage of the demand.

Not only did the mines and forests of the Midwest provide raw materials for an industrial boom, so did the region's bountiful farms with their livestock and rich harvests of grain. Even before the Civil War, Cincinnati was renowned for its meat-packing plants, but by the 1870s and 1880s other cities had gained fame in this field. In fact, the name Chicago was to become as closely associated with hog butchering as Grand Rapids was with furniture. In 1865 Chicago entrepreneurs constructed the Union Stock Yards which by the 1870s included 146 acres of yards and pens capable of holding 25,000 head of cattle, 100,000 hogs, and 22,000 sheep.[31] Enormous packing houses opened at the yards, solidifying Chicago's position as the largest slaughtering center in the world. "They say every Englishman goes to the Chicago stockyards," observed Rudyard Kipling in 1889.[32] And this seemed hardly an exaggeration, for every traveler's account of the Windy City during the late nineteenth century included an obligatory description of the lethal efficiency with which Chicagoans daily doomed thousands of cattle and swine. One "handbook for the traveler" noted that "the object of greatest interest to strangers" was "unquestionably, the slaughtering" where a visiting British editor "saw for some time hogs having their throats cut at the rate of eight every minute, or nearly 500 an hour."[33] Another guidebook of the city clearly summed up the view of many visitors when it boasted: "Whoever comes to Chicago and fails to visit the Great Union Stock Yards, loses an opportunity to be found in no other city on the habitable globe."[34]

Other midwestern cities tried to emulate the success of Chicago's stockyards. In 1871 construction began on the Saint Louis National Stock Yards located on four hundred acres in East Saint Louis, Illinois, and that same year Cincinnatians organized the Union Railroad Stock Yard Company with the city's chief packing houses building plants adjacent to the new yards. Milwaukee, Indianapolis, and Peoria also sought a major share of the slaughtering business through the laying out of modern stockyards.[35] Yet Chicago stood head and shoulders over all the rest. From 1895 to 1896 it accounted for over one-third of all hogs packed west of the Appalachians, processing more than six times as many pigs as Saint Louis and ten times as many as Cincinnati.[36]

The by-products of slaughtering were also fostering midwestern industry. For example, in Cincinnati, soap manufacturers made use of the animal fats from the packing houses and one of these, Procter and Gamble, was to become world famous. As early as 1883 Procter and Gamble employed five hundred workers and produced 20,000 bars of soap daily as well as 100,000 candles. Already mastering the techniques of advertising, the soap manufacturer was winning customers nationwide by proclaiming Ivory Soap "99$\frac{44}{100}$% pure."[37]

At the same time Milwaukee residents were profiting from the tanning of animal hides. The tanning business thrived in Milwaukee not only because of plentiful hides from nearby packing houses but also because of the city's proximity to the chief sources of hemlock bark in Wisconsin and Michigan. The eastern states had already exhausted their supply of this bark which was a vital ingredient in the tanning process. Consequently, tanneries gravitated westward, and by 1886 Milwaukee boasted of fifteen tanning establishments employing one thousand people.[38]

Beer, however, was the commodity that would make Milwaukee famous. With their abundant grain supplies and their equally abundant population of German immigrants trained in brewing and thirsty for beer, all the midwestern cities were well suited to the production of malt liquors. Yet it was Milwaukee and Saint Louis that took the lead in this industry, and by 1890 brewing ranked first among the manufacturing industries in both cities. In 1895 the nation's largest brewer was Pabst of Milwaukee, followed in second place by Anheuser-Busch of Saint Louis and Schlitz of Milwaukee in third position.[39] Milwaukee supposedly benefited from the destruction of Chicago's breweries in the Great Fire of 1871. Without a local source of beer, desperate Chicagoans turned to Milwaukee brew and they found it to their liking.[40] As early as 1873 the Milwaukee Chamber of Commerce bragged: "At every railroad station throughout Wisconsin, Illinois, Iowa, Minnesota, and Michigan, the familiar words: 'Milwaukee Lager Beer,' embellished with a representation of a mug of the foaming fluid, meets the eye of the traveler."[41] Yet Saint Louis was a worthy competitor, and in 1892 one periodical describe the Anheuser-Busch works as occupying "some forty city blocks" and employing "an army of men."[42]

Midwestern granaries not only supplied the brewing industry but also provided raw materials for the production of distilled liquors. Sitting in the heart of the corn belt with a plentiful water supply and nearby coal fields, Peoria became the preeminent distilling center of the late nineteenth century. With such a huge output, Peoria became the largest source of the federal government's whiskey tax revenues. In 1893 a local publication claimed that Peoria exceeded "by fifty per cent any revenue district in the United States in the amount of revenue tax it pa[id], to the government." In fact the Peoria district contributed as much as the combined total for the Chicago and Cincinnati districts. According to this account, the city's fourteen distilleries had a capacity to produce 185,000 gallons of alcohol each day.[43]

In the fields of malt and distilled liquors, tanning, meat packing, wagons, furniture, and iron and steel goods, midwestern cities ranked either first in the nation or among the largest producers. No longer isolated outposts in the nation's economic boondocks, cities like Cleveland, Detroit, and Chicago were realizing the full potential of the region's natural resources, transportation network, and consumer market. Only in the area of textile manufacturing did eastern supremacy virtually preclude midwestern competition. Though Chicago, Milwaukee, and Cincinnati boasted of thriving manufacturers of men's clothing, the cotton and wool cloth for this apparel came from the East. Metal and wood industries and processing of livestock and grain formed the backbone of midwestern manufacturing. Cloth largely remained an import.

Manufacturing growth, however, was not the only evidence of the Midwest's new economic maturity. During the late nineteenth century midwestern advances in marketing and merchandising were also attracting national attention. Department stores like Chicago's Marshall Field's were capturing a larger share of the consumer dollar and offering shoppers in the interior all the latest fashions from the East and Europe. Moreover, the Gimbel family opened its first department store in Milwaukee, founding a retailing chain that would spread eastward to Philadelphia and New York City.[44] In every major midwestern city, giant emporiums were developing that would soon rival the best stores in the nation.

During the late nineteenth century the Midwest would also develop a new mode of marketing, the mail-order catalog. This was Chicago's great contribution to American shopping, and the Illinois metropolis would remain preeminent in the mail-order field. Mail-order shopping arose from the peculiar circumstances of the rural Midwest. Midwestern farmers and small-town residents were relatively affluent and well educated but remote from big-city stores. Elsewhere in the world the remote rural dweller had little income to spend on the clothing, watches, and hardware offered in catalogs and if illiterate, as was often the case, could not read advertising copy or fill out order forms. But the combination of isolation, affluence, and education in the rural Midwest provided the prerequisites for mail-order merchandising. Moreover, Chicago's unparalleled rail network, offering cheap transportation to all points of the compass, made the Windy City a natural hub for the distribution of merchandise to the rural Midwest. The heartland had an eager body of mail-order customers and the transportation lines necessary to make the system work.

Aaron Montgomery Ward first realized the possibilities of mail-order marketing. Others had conducted a mail-order business in specialized fields, with seed companies distributing seed catalogs and agricultural machinery firms sending out illustrated listings of their farm implements. Ward's contribution was the general catalog offering a broader range of merchandise than any rural store stocked or any specialized catalog sold. In 1872 the enterprising Chicagoan mailed his first catalog, and later that year Ward secured appointment as purchasing agent for the Illinois Grange. The Grange was a powerful farmer's organization dedicated to bettering the economic lot of midwestern agrarians. It sought to do this through government regulation of railroad rates but also through lower prices for goods purchased by farm families. By buying in bulk directly from the factory and eliminating the wholesaler, mail-order businesses seemed to provide the means for achieving these lower prices. Ward convinced Grange leaders that this was the case, and with the official imprimatur of the powerful farm organization, Ward's business flourished. To boost his business Ward spoke at Grange meetings and advertised his firm as the "Original Grange Supply House." By 1883 the Ward catalog listed over ten thousand items and had expanded to 240 pages.[45]

Elsewhere in the nation established department stores sent out mail-order catalogs but none met with a success that matched Ward's. Chicago, however, was to nurture one competitor which would later overshadow Montgomery Ward. In 1886 Richard Sears, a railroad station agent in North Redwood, Minnesota, persuaded fellow station agents along the rail line to help him sell a shipment of watches he had purchased. The original consignment sold so quickly that Sears ordered additional time pieces. Within a year he quit his job, started a mail-order business specializing in watches, and moved to Chicago, lured by that city's superior transportation facilities and central location. Needing a watch repairman, he hired Alvah Roebuck who became Sears's partner. Thus was born Sears, Roebuck Company. Gradually Sears added new items to his listings and by the mid-1890s was offering a general merchandise catalog.[46] Together with Montgomery Ward, Sears would make Chicago the unchallenged mail-order capital of the world.

Thus by the 1890s Chicago's central location and unequaled accessibility had transformed it into a manufacturing and marketing center second in the nation only to New York City. Whereas in the first half of the nineteenth century the interior was equated with isolation, in the late nineteenth century the heartland had become the nation's hub and its cities had benefited accordingly. Chicago was at the crossroads of America's railroads, within a day's travel of millions of consumers and abundant agricultural and mineral riches. Together with its sister cities in the Midwest, it appeared to be at the emerging center of urban America.

The Workers

The factories, wholesalers, retail stores, and rail lines of America's heartland depended on the labor of millions of workers who flooded into midwestern cities during the late nineteenth century. Many came from abroad, continuing the flow of European immigration evident in the 1830s, 1840s, and 1850s. For example, in 1880, 65 percent of Chicago's manufacturing employees were born outside the United States.[47] And in Cleveland, Detroit, and Milwaukee the proportion was much the same. Coal, iron ore, lumber, grain, and hogs were the raw materials fueling the Midwest's industrial boom, but it was workers from Europe that turned these commodities into profits for midwestern manufacturers.

Midwestern cities were, then, far from homogeneous. Instead, they displayed a cosmopolitan character that impressed all visitors but troubled many residents. By 1890 Milwaukee had a smaller proportion of native white residents of native parentage than any other American city of over 100,000 population. Chicago had the third smallest proportion of native born of native parentage, and Detroit ranked fourth. Less than 13 percent of Milwaukee's residents were whites born in the United States of American-born parents, and only about 21 percent of Chicago's and Detroit's inhabitants were in this category. Of the seven heartland cities having over 100,000 residents, only Indianapolis could claim a majority of inhabitants who were native of native parentage. Moreover, more than one-third of the population of Chicago, Detroit, Milwaukee, and Cleveland were foreign born as were approximately one-fourth of the inhabitants of Saint Louis and Cincinnati.[48] In 1883 one observer reported: "No one who visits Milwaukee can fail to be struck with the semi-foreign appearance of the city."[49] The same could be said of urban areas throughout the heartland.

As during the antebellum period, German immigrants were most prevalent and formed the backbone of the work force. In 1890 in each of the ten most populous heartland cities, the largest number of foreign born came from Germany, and in seven of the ten cities Germans constituted a majority of those born abroad. They represented, in fact, more than two-thirds of the foreign population in Cincinnati, Milwaukee, and Dayton.[50] In no region of the country was there such a heavy concentration of Germans. Consequently, in 1890 as in 1860 midwestern cities had a distinctively Teutonic flavor, and to some observers a city like Milwaukee seemed more German than American.

Germans were especially well represented in the industrial work force, providing much of the skilled labor necessary to midwestern manufacturing. In 1880 the German born made up only 15 percent of Chicago's population but represented 26 percent of its industrial work force. In some trades they were especially prevalent. By 1890, 48 percent of Chicago's bakers were German-born males as well as 40 percent of the city's cabinetmakers, 34 percent of the butchers, and 33 percent of the boot and shoe makers.[51] Likewise, in Cincinnati in 1890 17 percent of the city's total population was born in Germany, but 64 percent of the cabinetmakers and 63 percent of the bakers were German born as were half the workers in the leather processing and tailoring industries.[52] Regional origins influenced which positions German immigrants occupied. Census data from 1880 for a German neighborhood on the northwest side of Chicago revealed that only 15 percent of the immigrants from the rural provinces of northeastern Germany were skilled workers as opposed to almost two-thirds of those from more industrial regions like Saxony and Silesia.[53] Newcomers from the farms of Europe performed the unskilled tasks, whereas those trained in European workshops could secure more lucrative jobs as skilled woodworkers or tailors.

Though disproportionately represented in the industrial labor force, Germans were not found solely at the factory workbench. A number opened their own businesses and became leading manufacturers. For example, brewers were usually German and names like Pabst or Busch testified to the success of some Teutonic businessmen. But Germans also operated thousands of small workshops, and by 1890, 27 percent of all Cincinnatians classified by the census as "manufacturers" were German born. Less impressive were the figures for the professions. Though natives of Germany constituted one-sixth of Cincinnati's inhabitants, they accounted for only 12 percent of the physicians and 7 percent of the lawyers.[54]

Germans were, however, making their mark on midwestern urban politics, rising to the highest positions in city government. During ten of the sixteen years from 1869 to 1885, German-born men served as mayor of Toledo, and in 1875 a native of Hannover, Germany, became mayor of Columbus. Saint Louis's first German-born executive, Henry Overstolz, occupied the mayor's seat from 1876 to 1881; in 1879 Cincinnati chose its first mayor of German birth, Charles Jacob; and in 1884 Milwaukee voters elected an immigrant from Berlin to their city's highest public post.[55] Cincinnati's Jacob was representative of upwardly mobile Germans in the midwestern city. Born in Bavaria, he learned the butchering trade from his father in Germany before emigrating to Cincinnati at the age of sixteen. In the Queen City he established a pork packing concern and helped found the German Banking Company as well as joining various German fraternal organizations. After service on the city council, he attained the mayor's office, demonstrating to his compatriots the opportunities available to foreign-born strivers in the Queen City.[56]

In 1890 in eight of the ten largest midwestern cities the Irish were the second most numerous foreign-born group, and in Detroit and Milwaukee they ranked third. Yet unlike in the East, they were considerably overshadowed by the mass of Germans. In the two leading New England cities of Boston and Providence, the Irish born outnumbered the German born seven to one and twelve to one respectively. But in each of the ten largest midwestern urban centers there were at least twice as many German born as Irish born, and in Cincinnati, Detroit, Milwaukee, Toledo, and Dayton the natives of Germany outnumbered the Irish by better than four to one.[57] Irish immigrants, however, continued to provide much of the unskilled labor, and in 1890 in Chicago a greater percentage of the Irish born were unskilled workers than were the German or Scandinavian born. Irish workers were most successful in gaining access to public employment, especially in the police department. In 1900 the Irish born and those of Irish parentage constituted 14 percent of Chicago's male work force but accounted for 43 percent of the watchmen, policemen, and firemen.[58]

This success in winning municipal jobs was in part owing to the political clout of the Irish. By 1885 those of Irish birth or parentage held fourteen of the eighteen positions on Chicago's Democratic City Central Committee, and five years later with one-sixth of the city's population they occupied over one-third of the city council seats.[59] Yet Chicago, Saint Louis, and Detroit were not Boston or Providence, and Irish politicians had to exercise greater ingenuity in the Midwest to win at the polls. Irish political success in midwestern cities could not rely on ethnic appeal alone. Memories of the Emerald Isle simply did not stir the souls of that many voters.

By the 1870s and 1880s Irish strength in the work force and political arena were further being diluted by the growing number of Scandinavians finding jobs in the heartland cities. In 1890 almost seventy-two thousand natives of Norway, Sweden, and Denmark lived in Chicago, and together they actually outnumbered the Windy City's Irish born. Moreover, Chicago could claim the largest Scandinavian settlement in America, with more than double the Nordic population of second-place Minneapolis. In fact, by the turn of the century one out of every ten Swedish-Americans lived in the Illinois metropolis, and it ranked as the second largest Swedish city in the world, surpassed only by Stockholm.[60]

Coming from heavily forested Norway and Sweden, it was natural that many Scandinavian males were attracted to the furniture and miscellaneous woodworking industries or practiced the carpenter's trade. In 1880 Scandinavians accounted for 20 percent of Chicago's skilled furniture workers, and by 1900 this figure had risen to 30 percent.[61] With their seafaring heritage, many Norwegians served as crew members on the lake vessels operating out of Chicago's harbor. As early as 1870 one Norwegian estimated that 65 percent of all the seamen on Lake Michigan sailing vessels were first or second generation Norwegian-Americans. In 1874 a proud Nordic shipowner boasted: "If all ships on the Chicago River hoisted flag according to the nationality of their crew the Norwegian would be more numerous than that of any other."[62] Young Scandinavian women most often found employment as domestics, and Chicago matrons seemed to have prized a Swedish maid above an Irish one.[63]

Many Scandinavian newcomers found employment in factories owned by compatriots who had arrived earlier and successfully established themselves. In fact, in some cases Scandinavian-American factory owners paid for the transatlantic passage of eager workers. These immigrants often came to the Windy City without any knowledge of English, but to ensure that they arrived at their correct destination they wore signs around their necks bearing the address of the factory. Factories thus became homogeneous ethnic oases in the heart of the polyglot city. For example, the Norwegian Andrew Johnson founded the Johnson Chair Company which by the close of the century employed five hundred workers, almost all of them Norwegian. Though Johnson proved a paternalistic overseer of his fellow countrymen, he did not necessarily pursue a benevolent paternalism. Many of Chicago's Norwegians referred to the Johnson Chair Company as *"fattighuset,"* "the poor house," because of the low wages paid, and Johnson reportedly stood at the factory gate and tore up the union cards of employees who dared to join labor organizations.[64]

Among the smaller midwestern cities the most notable concentration of Scandinavians was in Rockford. By 1890 more than half of the foreign born in Rockford's Winnebago County were natives of Sweden, and the Swedish born accounted for approximately one-fourth of the city's total population. Again many of these Swedes were attracted to the furniture industry. In

Rockford a number of the furniture factories were, in fact, cooperatively owned by the Swedish employees. For example, in 1876 a group of Swedish cabinetmakers who were tired of periodic wage cuts organized the Union Furniture Company on a cooperative basis. According to one of the founders, "Our whole capital was only $12,000, and most of that was paid in by deducting small amounts every month from the payroll of the workers."[65]

Though Rockford and Chicago could claim large Scandinavian communities, in many of the other midwestern cities Slavic newcomers far outnumbered Nordic immigrants. By 1890 Poles constituted the second largest foreign-born group in Milwaukee and were in third position in Toledo, whereas Czechs (then known as Bohemians) held fourth place in Cleveland. The Slavic migration had not yet peaked, but already midwestern cities were attracting a disproportionate number of these newcomers. Chicago alone had twice as many residents of Czech or Polish birth as lived in all of the twenty largest cities of the eastern states. As in the antebellum period, Central Europeans clustered in the central regions of North America whereas newcomers from the periphery of Europe were more common along the east coast of the United States. Thus Chicago, Detroit, and Cleveland were German, Czech, and Polish territory whereas New England, New York City, and Philadelphia were to hold a special attraction for the Irish from Europe's Celtic fringe and Italians from the continent's southern rim. Though many Italians would eventually penetrate into America's heartland, the Midwest could never rival the East in the number of Southern Europeans. In 1890 four times as many Italian-born persons lived in New York City as lived in the ten largest midwestern cities combined.[66]

The Midwest drew Slavic immigrants, in part, because of the concentration of metal-working industries in cities like Cleveland, Detroit, Chicago, and Milwaukee. Employers deemed Slavs especially well suited for the heavy labor of the foundry, blast furnace, and machine shop. Thus a disproportionate number of Detroit's Poles found employment with the American Car and Foundry Company in the years before the advent of the automobile industry.[67] Similarly, the huge Cleveland Rolling Mills was a magnet, drawing Slavic workers to the Ohio metropolis.[68] Factory managers may have been impressed by Polish brawn, but ethnic stereotypes as well as lack of training and education kept most Poles from obtaining skilled positions or jobs as foreman. In Milwaukee the Pabst Brewing Company mostly hired Germans, employing Poles, generally young females, to perform only the least skilled operations in the bottling department.[69] Czechs were more likely than Poles to obtain skilled jobs, but usually Slavic newcomers remained at the bottom of the industrial hierarchy.

Not all Slavic immigrants, however, were condemned to a lifetime of hard labor in the iron and steel mills. Especially among the Czechs, who arrived earlier in the Midwest than the Poles, there was some movement upward into the ranks of the employer. According to a report of the Illinois Bureau of Labor Statistics in 1892, the operators of sweatshops in Chicago were "all of foreign birth or parentage, principally of foreign birth," and "Bohemians" owned more of these establishments than any other group, operating 232 with almost twenty-seven hundred employees. Scandinavians followed in second place with 154 shops and also twenty-seven hundred workers. These shops did much of the sewing for the clothing industry and were notorious for exploiting poorly-paid workers, most of whom were of the same nationality as the boss of the shop. The bureau report found that the employer tended "to recruit his employees from those who [could] speak no other language but his," and consequently, "The race [i.e., ethnic] characteristics of shops are very marked." Many of the earlier Czech and Scandinavian migrants were, then, building their prosperity on the cheap labor of their compatriots. Though generally deploring the sweatshop system, the state investigators did remark admiringly of the enterprising Bohemian and Scandinavian bosses: "They are thrifty people who aspire to own and improve real estate."[70]

One of the largest but most ignored elements of the midwestern labor force was the native-born American worker. Though visitors and residents alike frequently commented on the Germanic flavor of Milwaukee and the multitude of tongues heard on the streets of Chicago, they often overlooked the fact that thousands of native-born Americans from the rural Midwest were also migrating to cities and staffing the factories and offices. This American migration was especially important in Indianapolis and Columbus where in 1890 the foreign born accounted for only 14 percent of the population. Between 1860 and 1890 each of these cities had increased in population approximately fivefold, growing just as rapidly as Detroit, Milwaukee, and Cleveland. But the newcomers to these burgeoning metropolises were more often native-born Americans from the farms of Indiana and Ohio than Slavs or Scandinavians. The lake cities may have been assuming a "foreign" cast, but the state capitals remained bastions of the American born. Hoosier or Buckeye natives were operating the lathes and forges of these urban centers.

Likewise, an ethnic gap was developing between the river metropolises of Cincinnati and Saint Louis and their counterparts on the Great Lakes. Though both the Queen City and the Missouri metropolis included a substantial foreign-born population, they were not attracting as many immigrants as in the past. Slavic newcomers especially gravitated to the lakes and eschewed the river cities. In 1890 Cincinnati had thirty-five thousand more residents than Cleveland, but Cleveland's Slavic-born population was thirteeen times greater than that of the Queen City. In other words, the river cities as well as Indianapolis and Columbus were growing more American in their ethnic composition as the older German immigrants died and the new Slavic migrants bypassed them in favor of Cleveland, Detroit, and Chicago. Whereas in the mid-nineteenth century, midwestern cities shared a common Germanic flavor, by the end of the century there were increasing differences in the ethnic composition of the heartland hubs. The river cities remained aging German centers, the capital cities of Columbus and Indianapolis were heavily native born, but the lake ports retained a German base to which was added an increasing number of Slavic newcomers and Scandinavians.

One ethnic group that was not notably increasing its share of the midwestern urban population was the African Americans. Though the black population of Cleveland almost quadrupled between 1860 and 1890, its proportion of the whole slipped from 1.9 percent to 1.2 percent. Likewise, the black share of Detroit's population fell from 3.1 percent in 1860 to 1.7 percent in 1890, in Chicago the percentage of blacks only inched upward from 0.9 to 1.3, and in Cincinnati the figure rose from 2.3 percent to 3.9 percent.[71] Moreover, few of these African Americans became part of the expanding industrial work force. Factory jobs were for whites; blacks remained servants, waiters, janitors, laundresses, or dockworkers. Only in the river city of Evansville, Indiana, was there a dramatic increase in the percentage of blacks in the population. Located adjacent to the slave state of Kentucky, after the Civil War, Evansville experienced a sharp rise in its African-American population, blacks increasing from 0.8 percent of the population in 1860 to 10.9 percent in 1890.[72] But again the black newcomers earned their income largely from domestic service or menial labor on the river wharves.

In contrast to the relatively unchanging role of blacks was the marked change in the position of women in the work force. Just as Slavs and Scandinavians filled the labor needs of the rapidly expanding cities so did thousands of women who secured jobs in factories and offices. During the single decade of the 1880s the proportion of women sixteen years of age and older who were earning a wage or salary in the five states of the Old Northwest rose from 10.6 percent to 14.6 percent. Whereas in 1880 fewer than 350,000 women in these states were employed outside their homes, ten years later over 600,000 had jobs.[73] In 1890 a report of Ohio's state labor bureau commented on "the alarming presence of so many females in the gainful occupations" and noted that the number was "increasing with a rapidity that [was] bewildering."[74] "Employers of labor are continually preparing for the entry of women into new branches of industry," announced the Michigan Bureau of Labor just two years later.[75] In 1894 the comparable agency in Indiana argued that "the almost ubiquitous presence of women in the field of labor" justified its lengthy study of women wage-earners in Indianapolis. In fact, the Hoosier bureau concluded that the working woman was "no longer the unfortunate exception, but a self-reliant, free and independent person, demanding and receiving increasing respect both for herself and for her industrial abilities."[76]

Working women were especially common in the cities, and by 1890 approximately 20 to 25 percent of all midwestern urban females over ten years of age engaged in gainful occupations. In the heartland metropolises, however, women were less likely to work than in eastern urban areas. For the twelve midwestern cities with over fifty thousand population, the median proportion of women gainfully employed was 21 percent as compared to a median of 25 percent for the twenty-eight eastern cities in this population category. This difference was largely owing to the concentration of apparel and textile firms in the eastern states. These establishments most frequently employed women, and in some New England textile centers more than 40 percent of the females were employed.[77] With its focus on metals, woodworking, butchering, and brewing, midwestern industry drew more heavily on male labor. Yet the data indicated that in Chicago as in New York the expanding work force was attracting an increasing number from the female population.

Work was not necessarily a liberating experience for the women of midwestern cities. Wages were lower than those of men, and employers often hired females because they believed women were pliant and readily exploited. One manufacturer told an Ohio labor investigator: "I prefer women to men because they are more tractable, more easily managed, will do harder work and more of it without complaining and will work overtime whenever our interests require it." According to this employer, "Why, a decent girl will work till she drops rather than risk losing her place."[78] Ohio labor investigators were also "frequently brought face to face with the fact that women and men working in the same factory received a difference of from 25 to 50 per cent in wages."[79] In 1889 a female watchmaker from Canton, Ohio, complained: "If a girl's expenses are the same as a man's, . . . why not pay her the same wages as a man gets, when she can do the work just as well."[80] Such arguments proved fruitless, however, and female factory workers remained in the most poorly paid positions, performing unskilled labor that required manual dexterity or a delicate touch. Female fingers were thus deemed best suited for such tasks as needlework, dipping chocolates, and book binding.

Women, migrants from midwestern farms, and newcomers from Bohemia, Sweden, and Germany together formed the motley labor pool necessary for rapid industrial growth in the late nineteenth-century Midwest. With factories rising and business expanding, cities like Chicago, Cleveland, and Detroit needed all the workers they could get, and this included recruits from distant lands as well as women lured from their traditional sphere in the home. The new demands of manufacturing were, then, transforming the midwestern work force and creating a massive industrial army unlike anything that existed in the first half of the century.

This new army, however, was not a docile force, responding mechanically to every management order or dictate. Instead, as the industrial force expanded, tensions between management and labor likewise increased. The female watchmaker from Canton was not the only worker discontented with her lot. Midwestern workers were willing to organize strikes, participate in violent confrontations with the authorities, and generally shake the foundation of the region's economic base. Though boosters proclaimed Chicago, Milwaukee, and Indianapolis as the new industrial dynamos of the world with glorious destinies, the working class too often seemed ready to smash these dynamos and shatter the capitalists' dreams of the future. In the late

nineteenth century, the midwestern city not only appeared to be the emerging center of American industry; too often it also seemed to be the volatile
vortex of industrial discontent.

Contributing to the labor radicalism of the Midwest was the heavy concentration of radical Germans and Bohemians in the population. Whereas Irish
immigrants joined the police force and remained fiercely loyal to the Roman
Catholic church, the Central Europeans were more likely to be rebels against
church, state, and property. Many of the Germans were refugees from the
autocratic repression that followed the revolutionary struggles of 1848, and
many of the Czechs were foes of the Habsburg regime ruling their homeland
and bore a hatred for the Habsburg's allies in the Catholic church hierarchy.
The homeland of Karl Marx and Friedrich Engels, Germany was the European hotbed of socialism, and many German immigrants carried their con-
tempt for the capitalist status quo to the New World. German names filled
the rosters of socialist political organizations in America, and German-language newspapers were often dedicated to toppling the industrialist and the
banker. As the most German section of the nation, the Midwest was naturally
the center of anti-capitalist unrest, and nowhere did the threat of the foreign
anarchist seem more imminent.

Midwestern factories also tended to be larger than eastern establishments,
and thus midwestern workers perhaps more strongly perceived the imper-
sonal exploitation often associated with the modern factory system. The
difference in size was in part owing to the Midwest's focus on metalworking,
machinery, and meat packing, industries characterized by large-scale plants,
as opposed to clothing which was produced in smaller units. Yet even when
establishments in the same industry were compared, the midwestern units
tended to be larger. For example, there were sixty-seven employees per
foundry and machine shop in the five midwestern cities of Chicago, Cleveland, Cincinnati, Detroit, and Milwaukee. By comparison, there were only
forty-one workers per foundry and machine shop in the five largest eastern
cities of Baltimore, Boston, Brooklyn, New York, and Philadelphia.[81] With
giant rolling mills, sprawling farm implement factories, and expansive railroad car works, the Midwest faced special labor problems. Disciplining and
cajoling the industrial masses and keeping a lid on unrest was not to prove
an easy task.

Statistics on strikes indicate that midwestern industrialists were relatively
unsuccessful in capping discontent. According to the federal commissioner
of labor, New York City led the nation in number of work stoppages during
the period 1881 through 1900. But when labor unrest was measured by the
cash amount employers lost owing to strikes, Chicago led New York by a
two-to-one margin. Since New York was considerably more populous than
Chicago, the difference in per capita cost of strikes was even greater. Chicago and Saint Louis ranked first and second in the nation in per capita loss
to employers from strikes, the Windy City's per capita figure being four

times that of New York and the figure for the Missouri metropolis was twice that of the nation's largest city.[82] The other midwestern centers were more in line with eastern averages, but in the region's largest metropolis the typical work stoppage was on a larger scale than in the East and was considerably more costly. Chicago's labor tumult was draining the employer's pocket to an extent unequaled among the leading cities of the nation.

Dissatisfaction over wage levels and the length of the working day ignited many of these costly strikes. In an 1892 survey conducted by the Indiana Department of Statistics, an Indianapolis laborer in the iron and steel industry complained: "A man don't get wages enough to enable him to pay for provisions and clothing." "A man can not dress as a citizen of the United States ought to, nor can he have enough to eat," agreed an Indianapolis moulder.[83] In 1885 a carpenter from Columbus, Ohio, expressed much the same sentiment when he proclaimed: "The producers demand a fair share of the wealth which they create."[84] Disgusted by a working day that averaged ten hours or longer, an Evansville worker claimed that "it would be right to call nine hours a day's work." According to this Hoosier laborer, "That would give a man a chance to rest so that he would have an appetite and feel like eating his supper."[85] Likewise, in 1889 a Youngstown iron worker complained to Ohio's labor commissioner that his hours were "too much for any man to stand in a rolling mill, as the labor [was] excessive, and hot."[86]

But some Midwesterners believed that an eight- or nine-hour day and a dollar more per week was not the answer to the workers' ills. For an emerging body of socialists, the existing capitalist system was at fault and it needed to be destroyed. In 1877 a Cincinnati socialist editor claimed: "The present mode of owning wealth is productive of gigantic evils." "Capital under its present shape is a 'gorgon' that is swallowing the earnings of the great mass," concluded this radical.[87] Three years later Detroit's *Labor Review* began its war on capitalism, announcing to its readers that it intended to tear "the mask from off" the false economic system and display it "in such a light as to make even those . . . blind see the folly of hugging to their bosoms this thing so hideous and so cruel."[88] Another socialist journal published in Detroit summed up the attitude of the radical Midwesterner when it argued that only socialism struck "at the very root of the labor troubles."[89]

Such rhetoric especially unnerved midwestern business leaders and industrialists. Shorter working hours and higher wages were negotiable demands that might be considered if the existing level of profits permitted. But the existence of socialists and sundry radicals opposed to the economic system as a whole was a threat to the very foundations of urban capitalism in the Midwest. And as the rhetoric became hotter and the mobs more unruly, the repression became more violent. State militias marched against angry workers, socialist editors retaliated with demands for the destruction of capitalism, and friends of capitalism responded with warnings about alien anarchists and bomb-throwing Bohemians. Thus during the 1870s, 1880s, and early 1890s midwestern cities experienced not simply rumblings of discontent but pitched battles in the streets as management and labor and capitalism and socialism fought for the upper hand.

For example, in 1877 a wave of labor violence swept midwestern cities, shocking residents unaccustomed to such bitter economic confrontations. In July of that year eastern railroads suffering from the prevailing economic depression slashed the pay of their workers by 10 percent. The employees retaliated with a violent strike that halted freight traffic and led to armed conflict between the militia and workers in Baltimore and Pittsburgh. The strike quickly swept westward producing a week of tense confrontation in Saint Louis, Chicago, and other midwestern centers.

Leading the strike activity in the Missouri city was the Workingmen's Party, a socialist organization with strong German and Bohemian contingents. At a public meeting of the Saint Louis strikers, one fiery socialist speaker noted ominously: "There was a time in the history of France when the poor found themselves oppressed to such an extent that forebearance ceased to be a virtue, and hundreds of heads tumbled into the basket." "That time may have arrived with us," cried this incendiary.[90] Strikers marched through the Saint Louis streets with a brass band playing the French revolutionary anthem, the *Marseillaise*. Those workers still at their jobs were pressured to lay down their tools and join the strike, and according to a local newspaper, mobs roamed the city shouting "the savage cry of 'Come out! You sons of bitches,' . . . to the workmen in the various shops."[91] Meanwhile, the British consul in Saint Louis reported to his government that "the city was practically in the hands of a mob[;] . . . nightly mass meetings were held in the most public places, where thousands of the most ignorant and depraved in the community were made riotous by the incendiary speeches of their orators."[92] At the close of the week an armed force organized by business leaders quelled without bloodshed what seemed an incipient revolution, but in a post mortem a Saint Louis newspaper warned that the strikers would have been "destructive and pitiless enough if they could have had their way."[93]

Chicago also experienced unrest and an outpouring of socialistic rhetoric. Mobs threatened railroad property and either convinced or forced thousands of factory workers to walk out of their shops. A local anti-labor newspaper printed the melodramatic headline: "TERROR'S REIGN. The Streets of Chicago Given Over to Howling Mobs of Thieves and Cut-Throats."[94] Especially volatile was a west-side Bohemian district which a *Chicago Tribune* reporter called "a hotbed of communism." With "dresses . . . tucked up around the waists" and "brawny sunburnt arms brandish[ing] clubs," women in this neighborhood attacked a door and sash factory in a clash which one newspaper reported as an "outbreak of Bohemian Amazons."[95] Police suppressed the revolt, but at the close of the week at least thirteen people had lost their lives in the Chicago conflict.

Lesser protests erupted in Detroit, Cleveland, and a number of smaller midwestern centers. A newspaper in normally tranquil Fort Wayne, Indiana, reported at the close of the railroad strike: "Fort Wayne has been resting on a powder magazine during the past twelve days and only a spark was needed to produce an explosion which would wipe out all that makes this city what it is."[96] Editors throughout the heartland would have agreed whole-heartedly with this assessment. Not everywhere was the situation so volatile nor the class divisions so pronounced, but reports from the largest cities frightened many middle-class heartlanders. In 1877 the battle between em-ployer and employee had flared, illuminating the class conflict which was accompanying the industrialization of the midwestern city.

Moreover, in the following decade radicals endeavored to heighten class consciousness throughout the Midwest and convince workers of the errors of capitalism. From 1880 the Socialist Labor Party was headquartered in Detroit, a natural choice since the party executive committee acknowledged that the Detroit chapter was "always sound" and characterized by "the great-est harmony, and active agitation."[97] The next year Chicago radicals founded a "Revolutionary Socialist Party" which specifically rejected the electoral process as a means of righting capitalist wrongs. Faith in the ballot box was, according to the Chicago radicals, the "great American superstition."[98]

Then in 1883 these same leftist firebrands were among the founders of the International Working People's Association (IWPA), an anarchist organiza-tion which opposed the authority of church, state, and capitalist overlord. Chicago supplied the largest delegation to the organization's initial meeting and became the home of the IWPA's Bureau of Information, the central office charged with aiding local chapters. In the words of one historian, Chicago "became the Mecca of the anarchist movement, to which adherents from all over the country looked for advice and support."[99] The IWPA won its chief support among the Germans and Bohemians, and of the fourteen newspapers published by the association between 1883 and 1886, nine were in the German language, two in Czech, and only two in English.[100] With its large German and Czech population, as well as its history of labor strife, Chicago seemed naturally destined for radical preeminence.

In 1886 Chicago radicals were to make national headlines and earn notori-ety that only confirmed the Windy City's reputation for upheaval and unrest. Labor leaders throughout the nation urged a general strike in support of the eight-hour day, the work stoppage to begin on May 1, 1886. During the first half of May an estimated 350,000 workers nationwide did join in the eight-hour protests, but 110,000 of these were in Chicago alone.[101] Workers struck at plants throughout the city and gathered in the streets to hear speeches that bolstered their courage. Then on May 3 fighting broke out between police and protesters at the McCormick Reaper Works, leaving one dead and several injured. Angered by the bloodshed, anarchist editor August Spies published twenty-five hundred circulars calling for revenge against "the fac-tory-lords." "Annihilation to the beasts in human form who call themselves rulers," Spies appealed, "uncompromising annihilation to them!"[102] The following day labor radicals announced a mass meeting at the Haymarket. Meanwhile, the newspapers carried headlines that screamed "Riot Reigns" and referred to workers "Wrought up to a Frenzy by Anarchistic Harangues."[103]

When police arrived at the Haymarket meeting that evening, someone tossed a bomb at them, killing or wounding several officers. A battle ensued between the police and armed workers which left many more dead or wounded. In retaliation the authorities rounded up anarchist leaders, even though there was no evidence that they had thrown the bomb or conspired to do so. The anarchists were convicted, sentenced to death, and in 1887 four of them, including Spies, died on the gallows. Moreover, to protect the city against further radical uprisings, Chicago citizens successfully petitioned the federal government to establish an army base, Fort Sheridan, only an hour's ride north of the city. In the words of one Chicagoan, "In 1886 red anarchy threatened Chicago with [a] form of barbarism, and Fort Sheridan was erected to protect civilization and maintain peace."[104]

During May 1886, fifteen thousand workers also struck in Milwaukee. In the most violent clash of the Milwaukee conflict, the state militia fired on strikers "armed with sticks, knives, pistols, and stones" who were attempting to assault the Bay View Rolling Mills. Five people died in the battle. Again the authorities placed the blame on labor radicals, most notably on the Central Labor Union led by German socialist Paul Grottkau.[105]

Throughout the Midwest many claimed that such foreign agitators were the chief source of trouble. Wisconsin's Commissioner of Labor Statistics concluded that the Central Labor Union "was composed mostly of foreign-born people, many of them new-comers and not citizens of the United States." These aliens had "brought the May riots upon Milwaukee, always before so peaceable, so thrifty, so contented."[106] Similarly, a Chicago manufacturer claimed: "This trouble in our works was caused entirely by a few aliens, who had been in this country only from three months to a year." According to a fellow Windy City manufacturer, "There is a large . . . atheistic German element who still cherish the anarchist desire to divide with those who have more than they."[107] A Chicago German denied this association between Germans and radicalism, claiming: "The oft-repeated assertion that anarchy in the United States is a curse for which the Germans are particularly responsible, is entirely erroneous."[108] Yet most Americans believed otherwise. Anarchism and communism were social diseases transmitted by Central Europeans, and midwestern cities with their disproportionate share of Central Europeans appeared particularly infected by these radical plagues.

Further reinforcing Chicago's reputation as a center of radicalism and discontent was the Pullman strike of 1894. When employees of the giant Pullman railroad car company struck, railway workers supported them by refusing to service Pullman-manufactured cars. Rail service into and out of Chicago was halted, a mob of ten thousand laborers destroyed hundreds of thousands of dollars of railroad property, and troops from Fort Sheridan invaded the city to restore order. Again Chicago newspapers heightened the tension by printing such incendiary headlines as: "THIRSTY FOR BLOOD—Frenzied Mob, Still Bent on Death and Destruction."[109] Again Chicago became the American symbol for violence and rebellion. According to the commissioners appointed to settle the strike, the "vast metropolis" was "the center of an activity and growth unprecedented in history, and combining all that this implie[d]." It also included "many of a certain class of objectionable foreigners." Giant, rapidly growing with only shallow roots, and a hotbed of foreign agitation, Chicago thus seemed the most volatile location in the country. In the opinion of the commissioners, "No more dangerous place for . . . a strike could be chosen."[110]

By the mid-1890s, then, the midwestern cities had a large and diverse working-class population drawn from all parts of Europe and North America, but disproportionately from Central Europe. It was not, however, a docile mass; instead the Midwest's largest metropolis had acquired an unenviable reputation for disorder, and data demonstrated that Chicago employers were suffering unparalleled losses owing to the city's strikes. The Midwest was not the calm center of American life but a cauldron of class conflict. Unrest and upheaval had accompanied the industrialization of the midwestern city, and the battle between labor and management remained far from resolved.

Yet throughout the Old Northwest investment in factories continued to soar and the army of workers swelled. Conflict did not seriously stem the flow of cash into mills and foundries, for urban Midwesterners believed that their economic star was still rising. The apex of manufacturing fortunes remained in the future, and strikes and violence did not yet seem to dim the industrial prospects of the region's cities.

3.

Skyscrapers, Symphonies, and Ballparks

The Changing Physical and Cultural Complexion of the City

Chicago's Auditorium Building rose seventeen stories and contained offices, a hotel, and the largest theater in the world. At the theater's opening in 1889 the President and Vice President of the United States were both present, as were the governors of several states. Renowned opera star Adelina Patti sang "Home Sweet Home" to the cheering attendants, and an orchestra and five-hundred-voice chorus performed the specially-commissioned "Auditorium Festival Ode." The gala ceremony was a well-deserved tribute to the Auditorium, which symbolized magnificently the physical and cultural changes sweeping midwestern cities. Throughout the Midwest, cities were rising toward the sky in an attempt to meet the demands of commerce. At the same time they were dressing themselves in the accoutrements of culture in a continuing effort to prove that they had finally come of age. A towering office block housing a symphony hall, the Auditorium Building was proof of the progress of heartland cities and just one more sign in the mind of Midwesterners that the center of urban America was moving westward to the Mississippi Valley and the shores of the Great Lakes.

By the 1870s and 1880s the signs of physical change and advancing urban culture were everywhere. Not only did new office blocks line downtown streets, but the city limits extended miles farther from the center, with thousands of homes arising along streets unknown twenty years earlier. No longer dots of habitation in a vast sea of farmland, the largest cities were beginning to sprawl across the countryside and throw out satellite settlements at commuter stations along the railroads. Museums joined symphony halls as landmarks of the new maturity. But baseball stadiums offered further evidence that the midwestern hubs were truly urban and could compete with New York, Philadelphia, and Boston on the playing fields as well as in the census columns.

In his address at the opening of the Auditorium, Illinois's governor expressed the spirit of the region when he claimed that the new theater stood "as proof that the diamond of Chicago's civilization ha[d] not been lost in the dust of the warehouse, nor trampled beneath the mire of the slaughter pen." "This Auditorium," the governor intoned, "proves that culture and art are here keeping pace with a material development not surpassed by any in the world."[1] In the mind of the governor and his fellow Midwesterners, the region was in the forefront of material development and making rapid strides toward cultural refinement. He did not need to rely simply on population figures and manufacturing statistics to support this contention. He could look to the Auditorium itself as proof positive of the changing cultural and physical complexion of the region's cities.

Upward and Outward: The Physical Growth of the Urban Heartland

With the rapid increase in population and the advent of large-scale industrialization, midwestern cities expanded both upward and outward. By the close of the century tall buildings rose in the central business districts and rows of new frame houses stretched along monotonous miles of straight streets. In fact, this upward and outward movement distinguished the midwestern city from the largest eastern hubs. The skyscraper was a midwestern invention, and Chicago was the vertical city par excellence during the 1880s and 1890s. But at the same time home ownership and the single-family dwelling were also more characteristic of the midwestern city than of eastern centers, and consequently Chicago, Detroit, and Cleveland sprawled outward with new housing subdivisions engulfing acres of corn fields and prairies. Moreover, the emerging pattern of stretching skyward in the urban core and spreading horizontally on the fringes would persist in future decades.

Underlying this concentration of commerce at the center and dispersion of housing at the edges was the development of mass transit during the late nineteenth century. In 1859 horse-drawn street railways operated for the first time in both Chicago and Saint Louis, and that same year Milwaukee and Cleveland authorized construction of such lines. Over the next few decades an expanding network of streetcar tracks reached out from the center of each major midwestern metropolis, freeing urban dwellers from their traditional reliance on their feet as the chief means of transportation. With the advent of horsecars some city dwellers could now live farther from the urban core, and the introduction of cable lines accelerated the centrifugal flow of population. The cable system was not dependent on the horse; instead the cars were linked to a moving underground cable which pulled them along the street's surface. In 1882 Chicago opened its first cable line, offering speedier service than the four-mile-per-hour pace of the lumbering horsecars. In 1885 Saint Louis likewise introduced cable cars, and during the late 1880s Cleveland experimented with this newfangled mode of transportation.[2]

Yet the electrification of streetcar lines in the late 1880s and early 1890s was the most significant development in late nineteenth-century mass transit. Electric streetcars traveled faster and farther than the old horsecars and proved more reliable and cheaper to operate than cable cars. By the last decade of the century every community from Youngstown to Peoria worthy of the name *city* could boast of an electric transit system. Like the horsecars, the electric trolleys spurred an outward migration of population, but also like the horsecars they encouraged the concentration of retailing and business in the city center. In each of the Midwest's major hubs streetcar lines converged on the core. At the Public Square in Cleveland, the intersection of Broad and High streets in Columbus, Fountain Square in Cincinnati, and Monument Circle in Indianapolis the chief lines crossed, drawing people from every section of the city and making these central locations ideal for offices and stores which sought to attract as many patrons and shoppers as possible. Thus at the same time streetcar development exercised a centrifugal influence on residential construction, it exerted a centripetal pull on commerce. In the compact cities of the past, business and housing stood side by side, and the urban core included the residences of the wealthy as well as stores, saloons, and warehouses. By the 1880s and 1890s midwestern cities were increasingly segregated according to function, with business claiming its share of urban space and housing occupying a separate turf.

As the urban core became the focus of commerce, demand for downtown property soared. Business growth in the rapidly expanding midwestern hubs further accelerated this demand. Chicago, Cleveland, and Detroit were now big cities with an increasing number of stores, hotels, banks, and administrative and professional offices. All of these businesses preferred to locate in the center where they could enjoy optimal access to clients and customers and maximum opportunity for face-to-face dealing with fellow entrepreneurs. Thus expanding business and a centripetal transit network together produced a bonanza for downtown property holders. In Chicago the average value for a quarter acre of land in the central business district rose from $130,000 in 1880 to $900,000 in 1890 and $1,000,000 in 1891.[3] With more bidders vying for the finite ground space at the city center, prices inevitably skyrocketed.

As demand mounted and land values rose, real estate developers recognized the necessity of building upward. Only from giant multistory structures could they realize sufficient rental income to profit from their investment in the costly land. As early as 1875 New York City boasted of several office buildings rising nine or ten stories, but it was the midwestern metropolis of Chicago that was to steal the architectural laurels from Gotham and give birth to the first wave of skyscrapers. Besides increased demand and rising property values, two additional factors helped Chicago assume the lead in the construction of tall buildings. First, the Great Fire of 1871 which had destroyed one-third of Chicago ignited a rebuilding boom that drew many of the most promising young architects to the Windy City. These men had the imagination, ingenuity, and engineering skill to break building traditions and soar skyward. Second, Chicago had a reputation as a miracle city where any investor might profit, and everything was possible and even probable. Thus money was available for the untried and the audacious. The Illinois metropolis had evolved in a single generation from an Indian trading post to a metropolis and then had risen like a phoenix from the flames of 1871 and quickly reestablished itself. With such a past, it seemed a good bet that Chicago might reach heaven itself.

During the early 1880s nine- and ten-story buildings had begun appearing on the Chicago skyline. Traditional brick or stone walls, however, bore the weight of these buildings, and with such construction techniques additional height was only possible by creating ever thicker walls at the base of the structure. Thus the masonry load-bearing wall was ill-suited for tall structures. In 1885 Chicago architect William LeBaron Jenney liberated builders from the masonry support wall when he constructed the first office building with structural steel beams. The building's interior steel cage carried the weight of the structure, and the masonry walls had no support function, serving only as a screen separating the indoors from the outdoors. Using this construction method, builders could add floor after floor, and since the walls provided no support, more space could be devoted to windows.

During the next decade, Jenney's innovation nurtured scores of so-called skyscrapers with ten to twenty stories and broad expanses of windows offering light and air to office workers. "Tear down that old rat trap and erect a sixteen-story building" became the standard cry of downtown developers, and by the early 1890s steel-beam construction became so closely associated with the Windy City that it was referred to as "Chicago construction."[4] In 1890 the firm of Burnham and Root designed the twenty-one story Masonic Temple, then labeled the "tallest building in the world." The *Chicago Tribune* described this office high rise as "a building of such magnificent height that . . . the Tower of Babel itself would have looked like a pigmy structure beside it."[5] Two years later the architectural partnership of Adler and Sullivan completed the Schiller Building, creating a slender seventeen-story tower that expressed the new verticality of the city.[6] And in 1893 Holabird and Roche's seventeen-story Old Colony Building opened for tenants, followed the next year by the same architects' sixteen-story Marquette Building. Using steel frame construction, Holabird and Roche provided ample window space in both structures. In 1894 an observer commented of the Old Colony: "One thing that strikes both the layman and the student of this kind of architecture . . . is the exceptional amount of lighting surface in this building."[7]

Another striking feature of these buildings was their utilitarian design. Though some structures suffered from fussy exterior ornamentation, most were unusually stark for the Victorian era and pretentious only in their size. At the turn of the century a distinguished eastern architecture critic observed: "The 'business block,' strictly utilitarian in purpose and solidity of construction, is the true and typical embodiment . . . of the Chicago idea."[8] Similarly, in 1891 one local author concluded of Chicago office building architecture: "The requirements of commerce and the business principles of real estate owners called this style into life. Light, space, air, and strength were demanded by such requirements and principles as the first objects and exterior ornamentation as the second.[9] The Chicago office building was an unabashedly commercial structure, and Windy City architects never forgot this basic fact. Their job was to create attractive but functional vertical boxes containing a maximum of rentable space.

Visitors to Chicago marveled at these giant commercial hives with their thousands of busy office workers. Like the stockyards, the downtown office towers were concrete monuments to the city's phenomenal pursuit of the dollar. "I stopped at Chicago," wrote a correspondent of the *American Architect,* "and gazed in wonder at its 'cliff dwellings' which, say what you will in regard to lack of design, flatness, etc., are among the unique things of the world."[10] In 1894 a booster of the city likewise wrote: "The fame of Chicago has spread to the uttermost ends of the earth and her name is associated with many great modern achievements, but with none more inseparably than the huge office buildings, the 'sky-scrapers' that rise like some strange growth from the level of the city."[11] And Baedeker's 1893 "Handbook for Travellers" to the United States reported that Chicago had "become identified with the erection of enormously tall office-buildings." "The architectural beauty of these is often questionable," the guidebook admitted, "but no one can fail to admire the wonderful skill of their architectural engineering."[12]

Though Chicago was the site of the most significant of the early skyscrapers, Windy City architects were extending the Chicago style and construction techniques to other midwestern cities as well. In Saint Louis, Adler and Sullivan's Wainwright Building was completed in 1892. With a facade of tall brick piers alternating with recessed window panels, the Wainwright Building conveyed a soaring quality appropriate to the new metal-cage office structures, and latter-day critics were to proclaim it a landmark in the evolution of skyscraper architecture. A year later Adler and Sullivan also completed the taller but less noteworthy Union Trust Building just two blocks from the Wainwright.[13] Meanwhile, Chicago's Daniel H. Burnham and Company, the successor firm to Burnham and Root, designed the Cuyahoga Building, the first structure in Cleveland with a complete steel frame.[14] Detroit was not far behind, for in 1896 the fourteen-story Majestic Building opened. Another creation of the Burnham firm, the Majestic was Detroit's tallest building and proof that the Michigan metropolis was catching the soaring Chicago spirit in architecture.[15]

Thus throughout the Midwest, and the rest of the nation as well, Chicago was determining the course of commercial building. As the birthplace of the skyscraper, the Midwest's greatest metropolis was clearly an emerging center of architecture that haughty Easterners could no longer ignore. Some contemporaries viewed the Chicago-style giants as tasteless reminders of the Windy City's preference for Mammon over the muses of Art. But Chicago was making its mark on American business districts, and downtowns across the nation would never be the same again.

Chicago may have been famed for its tall buildings, yet throughout most of the city the horizontal prevailed over the vertical. Across the level prairies spread thousands of one- or two-story structures housing a million Chicagoans. Moreover, the long lines of frame and brick cottages were proliferating at a breakneck pace as builders tried to keep up with the city's population growth. In the Illinois metropolis and in other heartland centers mass transit allowed workers to move farther from the core, and real estate developers were profiting from this mobility. At the edge of every city was a motley array of subdivisions advertising ideal sites for new homes and the promise of a better life.

Such subdivisions were inordinately commonplace in the Midwest, because the single-family, owner-occupied dwelling was more characteristic of the heartland cities than of most of their counterparts elsewhere in the nation. Especially marked was the contrast with northeastern cities where multi-family structures and rent paying were the norm. This was evident in the figures for the 1890 census. When the sixteen cities of over 50,000 population in New England, eastern New York, and northern New Jersey were ranked according to number of persons per dwelling, the median community had 7.9 occupants for each residence. By comparison, for the twelve cities of this population category in the Old Northwest plus Saint Louis the median was only 5.6. New York City had 18.5 persons per dwelling, whereas the highest figure for any midwestern city was less than half this number. Fourteen of the sixteen northeastern cities had at least seven persons per dwelling; only three of the twelve midwestern cities recorded a density of this magnitude. Likewise, among the sixteen northeastern cities the median percentage of families owning their home was only 22 percent. For the twelve heartland cities the median was 36 percent. In only one of the northeastern cities did more than 30 percent of the families own their dwellings; in nine of the twelve midwestern cities more than 30 percent did so.[16]

Compared to the nation as a whole the Midwest also stood out as a region of homeowners. Of the fifty-eight American cities having over 50,000 inhabitants in 1890, Toledo ranked first in percentage of home ownership, recording an impressive 46 percent, and Grand Rapids occupied second place with almost 45 percent. Milwaukee, Detroit, and Dayton were not far behind, with more than four out of every ten families owning their dwellings. New York City, however, ranked last with only six percent, and the southern cities with their many impoverished black residents ranged between 18 and 23 percent.[17]

The Midwest was not, then, a region characterized by large tenement houses of the type found in New York City. Instead, the typical midwestern urban center boasted of being a city of homes where one could raise a family free from the worst aspects of urban life found in overcrowded Manhattan.

In 1884 a Detroit booster proudly noted of his hometown: "Few, if any, cities have so large an area in proportion to population, or furnish so much dwelling room to their inhabitants."[18] Six years later the distinguished Chicago architect John W. Root likewise noted that in cities west of the Appalachians, "residences much more frequently occup[ied] considerable space, being entirely detached from other houses and surrounded by their own trees and lawns." There was "a notable absence, compared with cities in the East, of houses built in blocks" giving midwestern dwellings "a general suburban aspect."[19] This was a claim any good Cleveland resident or loyal Milwaukeean might well have seconded, for their cities offered an alternative to the triple-decker rental housing of Boston and Providence or the multi-family flats of Jersey City and Newark.

The two exceptions to the midwestern pattern were the river cities of Cincinnati and Saint Louis. Both had more persons per dwelling and fewer homeowners than the typical midwestern city, and their housing patterns more closely approximated those of the East. This was especially true of Cincinnati, a city known for its congested working-class tenements. One notorious example was a five-story tenement called Big Missouri, which housed approximately three hundred tenants in ninety-five rooms. Ill-ventilated and unsanitary with only one outdoor hydrant providing water for the three hundred residents, Big Missouri was, in the words of a Cincinnati health officer, "an outrage against decency and humanity."[20] In 1888 the annual report of the United States Commissioner of Labor observed of the Queen City: "The streets are dirty and closely built up with ill-constructed houses, holding from two to six families. Many poorer parts of Cincinnati are wretched as the worst European cities."[21]

This, however, was not the midwestern norm. Though the poor and working class of Cleveland or Detroit often lived in shabby, unsanitary cottages, fewer of these families shared a dwelling than did their counterparts in Cincinnati or the East, and they were more likely to own their humble abodes. With only 1.09 families per dwelling in 1890, Indianapolis was a community where the single-family structure prevailed among all social classes. "The suburbs of the city contain a great number of cottages of from two to six rooms each," reported an investigator of labor conditions in the Hoosier capital, "and these are the usual homes of the working people." Moreover, according to this source, "Many of these homes are owned by those who occupy them."[22] Repeating what he called "an undisputed belief," a Milwaukee author of the 1880s said of his hometown: "No other city of its size in the world contains so many workingmen who own their own homes." "Go into the wards where the laboring classes reside," he told his readers, "and it is surprising to see the numbers of little houses, comfortable and cleanly, which bear the marks of ownership."[23]

Yet some of these were not actually single-family dwellings. Many of Milwaukee's Polish immigrants built new foundations under their frame cottages and created basement apartments which they rented to relatives or other newcomers from their homeland. And both Germans and Poles often constructed two houses on the same lot, one facing the street and the other a "rear house" on the back alley. Again this provided rental income for the immigrant property owner who usually lived in the front house, but it also increased the population density of poorer neighborhoods.[24] The rear house was increasingly common in Chicago as well, depriving families of yard space and forcing children to play in the city's notoriously muddy streets.[25] Yet in the late nineteenth century, Chicago's immigrant districts remained primarily a collection of one- or two-story buildings, and in neither Milwaukee nor the Windy City did working-class neighborhoods bear a resemblance to Manhattan's teeming Lower East Side.

As midwestern cities grew outward some of the new subdivisions were specifically for working-class purchasers. A German building and loan society subdivided and sold much of Chicago's Humboldt Park development, and in 1880, 62 percent of the district's heads of household were manual workers.[26] Four years later a Chicago real estate journal offered a rosy description of the neighborhood as "a most charming spot" with "fresh air, plenty of room, and a rapidly growing population of industrious workers."[27] Often such developments arose near outlying factories to provide needed housing for the workers. For example, in 1890 a Toledo real estate broker advertised Cycledale, a "New and Handsome Addition surrounding the Bicycle Factory."[28] In the 1880s an account of South Chicago noted its burgeoning manufacturing establishments but observed that there was "great need of cottage residences." With the expected influx of workers to the area there would be "a splendid opportunity for investment" in "dwellings of the simpler class," for the workers "would hail new cottages with joy."[29]

Better publicized and more highly lauded, however, were the new homes of the wealthy that arose in former crop lands and country pastures. In every city fashionable avenues lined with pretentious mansions were reaching out from the city center. In Milwaukee there was Prospect Avenue, in Indianapolis, North Meridian Street, and in Columbus, East Broad Street. One of the most famous was Cleveland's Euclid Avenue, for according to a guidebook from the 1870s, "No avenue in the world can present to the delighted visitor such a continuous succession of charming residences and such uniformly beautiful grounds for so great a distance."[30] In Saint Louis the wealthy preferred private streets to avenues. Marked off by intimidating gates, these streets were owned and maintained by their residents and were protected by numerous deed restrictions. During the late nineteenth century, Saint Louis's wealthiest citizens wished to escape the hubbub and economic heterogeneity of the core, and thus they created private streets along the western fringe of the city to serve as residential havens.[31]

Humboldt Park, Cycledale, the eastern reaches of Euclid Avenue, and the private streets of Saint Louis all exemplified the residential expansion of the midwestern city. Some subdivisions were for the rich and others for the working class, but in every major heartland city builders were extending the frontier of urban settlement. To keep up with this outward flow, midwestern municipalities were forced to redraw their boundaries and annex ever larger tracts. The late nineteenth century was, in fact, a period of municipal imperialism with the biggest cities acquiring growing space for the future. For example, the area of Chicago rose from 18 square miles in 1860 to almost 175 square miles in 1890, Saint Louis's territory increased from 14 square miles to 61 square miles during the same period, and the area of Cleveland almost quadrupled whereas that of Cincinnati tripled.[32]

Yet some of the newly populated areas remained outside the city limits and chose to establish themselves as separate municipalities. Thus in the late nineteenth century the Midwest witnessed the first stages of a phenomenon that would transform metropolitan America. Independent suburban governments were beginning to develop, governments which in future decades would surround the central city and block its opportunities for territorial expansion. These communities especially formed around the stations of the commuter railroads leading into the largest cities. Such sites offered the advantages of small-town living yet enjoyed ready access to the jobs, shopping, and cultural activities of the big city. The new suburban communities boasted of a quieter, more wholesome existence, and they created village governments dedicated to maintaining this separate and superior way of life.

Among the earliest midwestern suburban towns were those along the railroads leading north from Cincinnati. For example, the village of Wyoming became a favorite retreat for well-to-do Cincinnatians who wished a residence removed from the city's smoke and tumult. In 1882 a Wyoming resident lauded the village's "suburban situation . . . so happily blending city and country." "While we have not all the advantages of either," he observed, "we avoid most of the discomforts of both."[33] Moreover, Wyoming citizens took action to preserve their haven from the intrusion of unsavory newcomers or unwanted forms of development. Fearing that an auction sale of nearby land "would risk the placing of lots in undesirable hands," in 1874 village residents combined to purchase the tract and offered it for resale. Yet they reserved "the right of deciding upon the desirability of selling to parties who [might] apply."[34]

In the Chicago area outlying municipalities were also appearing. By the 1870s and 1880s the North Shore suburbs stretching from Evanston to Lake Bluff were already attracting the families of harried businessmen who sought a better way of life than the Windy City could offer. Already by the 1870s Lake Forest was being acclaimed as the "culmination of landscape beauty" with "more elegant private residences than almost any other suburb" and a population of "cultured and wealthy people."[35] Other communities, however, refused to bow before the supposed superiority of Lake Forest. In 1890 the founders of Kenilworth advertised it as "the model suburban community" with "pure air, quiet green grass, forest shade, and all the comforts and delights of rural life."[36] Meanwhile, enthusiasts of Wilmette, Winnetka, and

Glencoe were also praising the wooded beauty and refreshing lake breezes of these communities which had the added advantage of being only an hour by train from the center of Chicago.

Wyoming, Lake Forest, and Kenilworth were residential retreats for urbanites seeking to escape from business and industry. But in the late nineteenth century developers were also laying out a number of industrial satellite towns on the fringes of the central cities. These municipalities offered cheaper plant sites than were available in the core city, and with the construction of beltline railroads, the transportation advantages of the satellite communities could equal those of the hub. A growing number of beltlines circled America's major metropolises, connecting the converging rail lines and allowing trains to bypass congested core areas. Along these railroads, factories soon appeared, landmarks of the outward flow of the metropolis.

As early as 1869 meat packer George Hammond located his plant just east of Chicago, in the northwestern corner of Indiana, and around his establishment grew the city of Hammond. Boosting the fortunes of the community was the Chicago and Calumet Terminal Railroad, a beltline which began operation in 1888.[37] This line was even more significant for adjacent East Chicago, Indiana. Founded in 1888 along the beltline, East Chicago supposedly was destined to rival the great industrial centers of Britain, its promoters referring to it as the "Sheffield" of America. Though it never lived up to such exaggerated claims, only two years after its founding East Chicago already boasted of 1,255 residents, an oil tank factory, a railroad car wheel works, and a plant producing hay balers and other farm implements.[38]

Across the state border in Illinois developers were laying out Chicago Heights along the Elgin, Joliet and Eastern beltline railroad. Land sales began in 1891, and within the first two years fourteen thousand lots were put on the market.[39] To ensure the success of their town, the promoters of Chicago Heights offered special deals to manufacturers willing to locate in the nascent community. For example, they induced Inland Steel Company to construct its plant in Chicago Heights by giving the steelmaker six acres of land and $20,000 to erect factory buildings.[40] Such inducements were not uncommon in the emerging satellite cities. In the 1890s the city council of Hammond adopted an ordinance granting a five-year tax exemption and extremely low water rates to new factories.[41] Likewise, in 1891 the promoters of the industrial suburb of South Milwaukee lured the Bucyrus-Erie Company by promising it fifteen acres of land and $50,000 to pay for the building of a new factory.[42]

Despite such attractive offers and the sylvan lure of communities like Wyoming and Lake Forest, in the 1890s the suburban municipality seemed to pose little threat to midwestern central cities. Chicago, Milwaukee, and Cincinnati continued to expand and still had ample space within their boundaries for new homes and factories. Moreover, because of superior municipal services in the central city, many outlying residents were casting their ballots in favor of annexation. If one wanted an ample water supply and an effective fire department, the central city generally remained the best place to live and do business.

Yet the metropolitan population was reaching outward, and suburban towns were proliferating. From Waukegan on the north to East Chicago on the south, a continuous line of communities stretched for fifty miles along the shores of Lake Michigan. A traveler would still find many empty spaces along the lakefront, but the satellites were increasing in number and attracting residents and industry. Though Chicago boasted of the tallest buildings in the world, the metropolis was expanding at such a pace that even from the roof of the towering Masonic Temple the perimeter of settlement to the north and south was barely visible.

Cultivating the Midwestern Metropolis

With smoke-belching factories, bruising labor violence, lofty hives of office drones, and acres of shabby frame working-class dwellings, the midwestern metropolises often seemed ugly, frightening places. Unquestionably, midwestern cities had achieved material success, but outsiders and residents alike contended that in the pursuit of wealth these heartland urban centers had lost their souls. In the eyes of many observers, city life appeared devoid of beauty, good taste, and traditional standards of decency. Vulgar salesmen in shiny suits, tobacco-spitting politicians with their hands in the taxpayers' pockets, and rootless immigrants with a propensity for beer and bombs, these were the creatures populating the expanding heartland cities. With more money than humanity, more conflict than culture, Chicago, Cleveland, and Detroit were possibly nurturing future generations of barbarians without appreciation for the supposedly finer things of life.

Many Americans of the late nineteenth century viewed eastern cities as well as their midwestern counterparts as soulless congregations of fiercely competitive worshippers of Mammon. But because of their recent emergence from frontier status, midwestern cities were especially sensitive to the complaint that they lacked culture, refinement, and civilizing influences. The heartland hubs were regarded as nouveau riche with all the negative connotations attached to that term. During the late nineteenth century, then, Midwesterners sought not only to dispel the ugly pall supposedly hanging over all urban life; they also endeavored to prove to Easterners that they had truly emerged from the wilderness and were as civilized as New York or Boston.

In the minds of many Americans art and music were among the chief means for both curbing the barbarism of urban life and demonstrating to the remainder of the world that the meat-packing and metal-working centers were cultured and refined. Such higher culture was especially important in cultivating the middle and upper classes, those people who seemed inordinately obsessed with the pursuit of cash yet who were expected to put on a good front for the ambitious midwestern cities. They at least should benefit from the appreciation of art and music; they at least should become as cultured as their eastern counterparts. Thus during the 1870s and 1880s many Midwesterners sought to cultivate the arts in order to uplift urban existence and upgrade the reputation of their hometowns. Before the Civil War, Cincinnati had sought to prove that civilization existed west of the Appalachians. Now other midwestern cities also joined in the battle to revise the heartland's image as well as improve the quality of urban living.

Chicagoans emerged in the forefront of this cultural campaign. In 1882 some wealthy citizens organized the Art Institute, a museum intended to rival those of New York and Boston. The guiding spirit of this institution and president of the board of trustees from 1882 to 1924 was Charles Hutchinson, a wealthy grain trader and banker. Like many of his fellow Chicagoans, Hutchinson believed that art could provide a respite from the "busy material life." "[Art] may . . . turn our thoughts away from so much that is of the earth earthy," the philanthropic banker argued, "and lead us to contemplate those eternal truths which after all most concern the children of God."[43] Moreover, as a resident of the most earthy of American cities, Hutchinson felt a special need for the uplifting influence of painting and sculpture. "We live in a materialistic age," he told a gathering in 1888, "and—I fear we must admit here in Chicago—in one of the most barren cities."[44]

From personal experience Hutchinson knew how grasping and barren Chicago was. His own father was a legendary hard-drinking grain speculator known for his ruthlessness. He refused to allow Charles to attend college and was contemptuous of his son's interest in art. Responding to Charles's purchase of a French painting of a sheepfold, the elder Hutchinson purportedly exclaimed: "A son of mine! He paid $500 a piece for five painted sheep and he could get the real article for $2 a head!"[45] The elder Hutchinson was the type of man who had made Chicago the hog-slaughtering capital of the world. Now his son wanted to civilize it.

Charles Hutchinson and other Chicagoans knew that a distinguished art museum could establish their city's reputation as a truly mature metropolis rather than an overgrown and gawky factory town in the provinces. In 1892 a Windy City literary journal observed: "Chicago has put all the energy of this half-century of her adolescence into the development of a material body." Now, however, the Illinois metropolis needed to cultivate "the higher powers" which "unfold later in all normal life." "Already the signs are clear that the season of mere physical life is over," this journal concluded, "and that the life of the soul calls for exercise and nourishment."[46] In other words, Chicago was grown up, and it was about time it acquired some polish, learning, and taste.

The Art Institute flourished during the 1880's, but it did not have a monopoly on the public display of paintings and sculpture. Further contributing to the supposed refinement and cultivation of Chicago's populace were the annual exhibitions at the Interstate Industrial Exposition. Held annually from 1873 through 1890, the exposition was a trade fair designed to promote Chicago as a commercial and manufacturing hub. But the managers also included a display of canvases, statues, and objets d'art. According to one art critic, this Chicago exhibition "came to be representative of what the country had produced in art during the year—more widely representative than any other exhibition held in the East or West." "Among the American artists in France," observed the critic, "this show came to be known as the American salon." In fact, in 1885 a New York commentator noted that the Windy City had "anticipated New York, Boston and Philadelphia" in exhibiting the latest significant American art.[47] For those boosters seeking cultural distinction for Chicago, this was a prized coup.

When it came to the fine arts, Cincinnati's citizens were not far behind their compatriots in Illinois. In 1867 an article in the prestigious *Atlantic Monthly* had said of the Queen City: "There is a great sum of physical life there, but much less than the proper proportion of cultivated intelligence."[48] Stung by such rebukes and continuing their antebellum struggle to prove that culture could flourish west of the Appalachians, in the 1870s and 1880s Cincinnatians sought to fashion their city into the "Paris of America." The Queen City had fallen behind Chicago in commerce and industry, but it still might take advantage of the cultural headstart it had built up during the antebellum era and establish itself as a hub of painting, sculpture, and art in general.

Women led the crusade for the cultivation of the visual arts in Cincinnati. Such applied arts as china painting, needlework, and woodcarving first attracted the Cincinnati females. But they sought to foster the fine as well as the applied arts through the creation of a museum and adjacent art school. For them art not only would restore the regal bearing of the Queen City, it would also cultivate and refine the taste of an untutored urban population. In 1880 Elizabeth Perry, the president of the Women's Art Association, recognized the proposed museum's favorable impact on local aesthetics when she referred to its expected role in "the education of the eye and hand." In addition, she felt it would achieve a spiritual uplift, providing instruction for "the mind and heart." And she did not neglect the museum's role in boosting Cincinnati, claiming that as a result of its aesthetic and spiritual benefits "the prosperity and attractiveness" of the city might "be greatly enhanced."[49] As early as 1878 Perry and her association organized a temporary exhibition of art that enhanced the Queen City's repute. Reviewing the exhibit, a New York newspaper proclaimed: "Boston, New York, and the other cities of the East, will have to look to their laurels. . . . It really looks as if Cincinnati were, perhaps, destined to be the art city of the continent."[50] When in 1886 a permanent museum building finally opened, local boosters hoped that this destiny actually might be realized.[51]

Other midwestern cities also looked to art to educate the eye, uplift the heart, and boost the reputation. Inspired by the popularity of a temporary exhibition which attracted 135,000 visitors, in 1884 wealthy Detroit residents decided to create a permanent institution for the cultivation of culture, founding the Detroit Museum of Art. Five years later the owner of a local newspaper donated eighty paintings by old masters, but only after the appointment of a new director, Armand Griffith, in 1891 did attendance at the museum soar. The charismatic Griffith promoted the institution with missionary zeal, conducting popular Sunday afternoon lectures aimed at molding the taste of his midwestern flock and imposing an aesthetic discipline.[52]

Wisconsin urbanites were not far behind their Michigan counterparts in the pursuit of refinement. As early as 1873 a Milwaukee literary journal lauded the creation of a local gallery for the sale and display of paintings and sculpture. Noting the role of art in curbing bestiality in the city, the journal claimed: "Such institutions tend to lessen the necessities for enlarging our prisons and increasing the number of men on the police force." Moreover, like cultural boosters elsewhere in the Midwest, the publication praised local art devotees for "promoting those refining influences, and cultivating that taste for Art in its highest developments, so necessary to a city just emerging from the embryonic stage of a large commercial back-woods town, into the status of one of the principal metropolitan cities of the country."[53] As elsewhere, in Milwaukee art was intended to civilize and refine while at the same time advertising to the world the maturity of the formerly frontier community. In 1888 meat packer Frederick Layton endowed an art museum for Milwaukee and bestowed on it his collection of nineteenth-century European and American paintings.[54] When this institution opened its doors, the Wisconsin metropolis joined Chicago, Detroit, and the Queen City in the race for cultural supremacy.

Though the experiences of Detroit and Milwaukee were not identical to those of Chicago and Cincinnati, underlying the development of art museums in each city were the common themes of cultivation and promotion. Urban taste and behavior needed to be cultivated and refined; crass materialism needed to yield to an appreciation for supposedly higher values. A philanthropist like Hutchinson, a devotee of applied arts like Perry, a preacher of culture like Griffith, and the meat-packing Layton all agreed with this imperative for civilizing the city through the appreciation of art. But art also was a means of promoting each of the major midwestern cities, of proving to Easterners and Europeans that the heartland hubs were no longer a collection of bumpkins far removed from the cultural currents of Western civilization. The art museum would supposedly smooth each city's rough edges, but it would also stand as visible proof of each city's maturity.

Equally important in the cultivation and promotion of the midwestern city was music. No figure was more dedicated to refining the musical tastes of the Midwest than the great conductor Theodore Thomas. The German-born Thomas regarded himself as a "musical missionary" traveling with his orchestra throughout the country and introducing benighted audiences in Chicago, Cincinnati, and dozens of other cities to the glories of classical music. Thomas like Hutchinson regarded art as an uplifting force liberating the viewer or listener from the harsh grip of materialism. Thus he praised Chicago's cultural philanthropists for "establishing something ennobling and refining in [the] great Western metropolis, to temper the influences of the daily struggle of life and to lighten its sordid cares." And Thomas wrote of "a deeper joy and a nobler spirituality to be gained from familiarity with the higher art forms."[55] In the words of one historian, "For Theodore Thomas music was more than entertainment, it was spiritual enrichment."[56]

As a dedicated preacher of the gospel of good music, Thomas also disciplined his audiences and forced them to show proper homage to high Art. Arriving late or talking during a concert was intolerable, and the maestro might well stop a performance and turn his angry gaze on the offending party. When performing in Cincinnati in 1873, he insisted that no one be admitted after the orchestra had sounded the first notes of Handel's *Te Deum*. Tardy concertgoers might shuffle from the door to their seats during the playing of popular songs or works by a lightweight composer like Offenbach, but Handel's music deserved better. "When you play Offenbach or Yankee Doodle, you can keep your doors open," Thomas told Cincinnatians. "When I play Handel's 'Te Deum,' they must be shut."[57]

Cincinnatians obeyed Thomas's wishes, for the great conductor not only provided spiritual uplift, he also was a basic element in the Queen City's grand plan to become the Paris of America. In fact, in the 1870s Cincinnati boosters did seem to be establishing the Ohio metropolis as the nation's musical capital. This was largely owing to the city's biennial "Music Festival," an extravaganza directed by the renowned Thomas. In 1868 and 1872 the band leader Patrick Gilmore had organized Boston's musical jubilees, including on the program red-suspendered firemen playing the "Anvil Chorus." A Chicago publication referred disdainfully to Gilmore as a "leader of street music," "a sensationalist by nature" who could "combine anvils, but not instruments."[58] Thomas wanted something of a higher quality at the Cincinnati festivals, and his Queen City backers were especially eager to establish their cultural superiority over the supposedly refined city of Brahmins.

In the first festival of 1873 they succeeded gloriously. Thousands descended on the city to hear the 108-piece Thomas Orchestra and the almost-eight-hundred-member chorus including Cincinnati's finest singers. According to a Milwaukee journal, "So numerous were the arrivals in the city, that the hotel and other accommodations were soon speedily taken up."[59] Enthusiasm mounted with each of the eight concerts of the festival. After the performance of Beethoven's *Ninth Symphony,* the audience of six thousand stood cheering, waving handkerchiefs, and tossing hats, and at the close of the seventh concert an observer reported that "the enthusiasm was intense" as the audience called for Thomas who "bowed his acknowledgement, and retired amidst the wildest plaudits."[60] Out-of-town publications heaped praise on the Queen City. The *Chicago Tribune* proclaimed Cincinnati "the first musical city of the West" and reveled in the triumph of a heartland city over the high-toned East. "Poor Boston!" chortled one correspondent in the *Tribune;* "Who shall recover her laurels? Westward the star of musical empire has taken its way, and it will never go back."[61]

Though some of the later festivals did not have the electrifying effect of Cincinnati's first musical extravaganza, Thomas continued to lead the biennial event, and in 1884 the program of the sixth festival proudly proclaimed its five predecessors "the most memorable musical affairs this country ha[d] ever seen" and labeled Cincinnati "the festival city of the United States."[62] Cincinnati seemingly had succeeded in realizing the twin goals of cultivation and promotion. The Queen City had experienced what one concertgoer called "the civilizing and enlightening powers of music."[63] Moreover, it had established itself as a cultural center and in the process had tweaked the uptilted nose of Boston.

During the late 1870s Queen City boosters attempted to consolidate their cultural triumph by making Cincinnati the focus of musical education in America. Thus in 1878 they convinced Theodore Thomas to become director of a new College of Music in the Queen City. The editor of the *Cincinnati Daily Gazette* proclaimed that this project would make his hometown "the great musical center of the world," and other Midwesterners delighted in the fact that their region had once again triumphed culturally over the haughty East.[64] According to the *Indianapolis Journal,* Thomas was accepting the Cincinnati appointment because he found in the Midwest "more devotion to art than in the older and so-called more cultural communities of the East."[65] Easterners deplored the loss of Thomas who until then had resided in New York City between his many national tours. "While we begrudge to Cincinnati her acquisition, we cannot help congratulate her," wrote a Boston editor.[66] A New York newspaper called Thomas's move "the greatest musical calamity" ever to befall Gotham.[67]

Cincinnati's triumph, however, was shortlived. In 1880 after a clash with the college's board of directors, Thomas resigned his post and left the Queen City. Now eastern periodicals belittled the fallen musical capital, with the *New York Times* labeling Cincinnati "a trading and pork butchering emporium" and referring to Thomas's battle with "the infidels in the city of the unclean beast."[68] Even a Chicago journalist ridiculed Thomas's "Quixotic mission . . . to attempt to establish classical music amongst the pork-packers of Cincinnati."[69]

But Thomas had not given up on pork packers. For Chicago was now the greatest hog-butchering city in the world, and that was Thomas's next midwestern destination. While retaining New York as his base, during the 1880s Thomas directed the Chicago Biennial Musical Festival, the Windy City's attempt to emulate Cincinnati's earlier success. Moreover, beginning in 1877 he annually conducted summer garden concerts in the Illinois metropolis.[70] Then in 1891 wealthy Chicagoans pledged sufficient funds to create the Chicago Symphony Orchestra and convinced Thomas to forsake New York and assume the conductor's baton in the Windy City.[71] Until his death fourteen years later, Thomas and his musicians performed in the giant hall of Adler and Sullivan's Auditorium Building. Having permanently secured Thomas, Chicago had finally won from Cincinnati cultural as well as commercial supremacy in the Midwest.

Music proved especially popular in midwestern cities in part because of the large German population. With a strong musical tradition in their homeland, Germans dominated the development of orchestras and choruses in America. Theodore Thomas and most of his musicians were German; in fact, the language spoken at rehearsals of Thomas's orchestra was German. Yet the motives of Thomas and his backers were different from those of the many German immigrants who joined choral societies and local bands. The maestro and the native-born Americans who financed his missionary efforts sought to impose culture on the city, to refine and cultivate the urban populace and teach them not to shuffle or talk during concerts but instead to pay silent homage to the higher nonmaterial elements of life. Most German immigrants, however, were attempting to preserve their native, and supposedly superior, culture in the often hostile environment of the midwestern city. Music would perpetuate German culture and maintain Teutonic civilization in a land of Yankee Philistines.

In every midwestern city a long list of German singing groups and musicians sought to preserve this heritage. Milwaukee's leading organization was the *Musikverein* or Musical Society founded in 1850 "to further musical appreciation and education by the rendition of new and old music of intrinsic value."[72] By 1899 it had presented 386 concerts performed by Milwaukee's finest singers and instrumentalists as well as out-of-town guest artists.[73] The group's chorus represented Milwaukee in the national *Saengerfests* held at various locations during the late nineteenth century. In fact, in 1885 the Milwaukee *Musikverein* hosted the twenty-fourth *Saengerfest* of the North American *Saengerbund,* organizing a festival with an orchestra of one hundred musicians and a chorus of twenty-five hundred voices. In a poem written for this festival, a German Milwaukeean expressed sentiments characteristic of the age when he warned: "To the looming abyss of spiritual chaos/ This great nation drifts in its material lust." But the *Saengerfest* like Cincinnati's Musical Festival or Chicago's Art Institute would supposedly save the nation and its cities from this disastrous drift and allow the "Muses and their tempting golden songs" to prevail.[74]

During much of the late nineteenth century the music society's director was Eugen Luening, a Wagner student dedicated to the Teutonic musical heritage. He organized the Luening Conservatory to train musicians for the *Musikverein* and to prevent the loss of "such growing talent to the English [singing] societies."[75] Moreover, in 1890 he aroused a furor when he commented on "Yankee superficiality" at a Musical Society banquet. "The Germans alone were truth-loving," Luening supposedly said, "and must organize a federation to antagonize Yankee characteristics."[76] Like Hutchinson, Perry, and Thomas, Luening perceived the need for pursuing higher truths in the midwestern city and liberating its residents from material lust. Yet unlike the others, he felt that this pursuit required a defense of superior German characteristics and the benefits of German culture.

Elsewhere Germans also attempted to preserve the vaunted cultural attributes of their fellow immigrants. In Toledo Louis Mathias organized the Germania Music Association and attempted to maintain high musical standards. "Louis Mathias hated what he called 'cheap music,'" wrote one admirer of the Toledo maestro; "he refused to conduct or to play anything which could be called common or banal."[77] As early as 1843 Columbus Germans formed the *Liederkranz* singing club, praised two years later in the local German newspaper for "serving the worthy cause of preserving German culture in the West."[78] After the Civil War a newly organized *Liederkranz* resumed the efforts of its earlier namesake, performing an occasional opera as well as two concerts per year. Rivaling this society was Columbus's *Männerchor* singing club, its members described in 1873 as "successful missionaries of song and faithful worshipers of that divine art."[79] And the *Germania Gesang Verein* was yet another choral society in Ohio's capital city.[80] Meanwhile, during the 1870s the Germania Orchestra, consisting solely of German musicians, was the principal source of instrumental music in Cleveland.[81] In one Midwest outpost after another German singing masters and conductors mobilized the Teutonic community for competition in the *Saengerfests* and endeavored to keep alive the music of the fatherland.

Throughout the Midwest, then, exposure to the higher arts was supposedly cultivating some degree of refinement and appreciation among urban dwellers. In cities like Cincinnati and Chicago local boosters even dared to make claims of cultural superiority over the urban centers of the East. Yet in this striving for paintings and sculpture and the frantic efforts to secure Theodore Thomas and organize gargantuan choruses, there was evidence of the continuing sense of cultural inferiority in the Midwest. Indeed, Cincinnati and Chicago did protest too much, flaunting their cultural achievements more brazenly than would a city secure in its sense of superiority. Boston and New York were still the cities to beat in the cultural sweepstakes, and Midwesterners were well aware of this.

Moreover, the midwestern cities did not match the East or Europe in the creation of art as opposed to its display or performance. Cincinnati performed great music, but it did not nurture any great composers. Under the leadership of the distinguished local painter Frank Duveneck, Cincinnati's Art Academy did educate a number of reputable painters, though most left town to continue their training in Europe and find their fortunes beyond the heartland. With an ingrained perception of the East and Europe as the exclusive sources of truth and beauty, Cincinnatians proved poor patrons of their local artists. "Wealthy Cincinnatians purchase abroad," complained Duveneck in 1881; "home artists are not thought of, and if an artist comes among them he is nothing."[82] Likewise, Chicago may have hosted the "American Salon," but the paintings in the exhibition were largely imports from the East and Europe.

Midwesterners were reluctant to invest in canvases produced in their home region, and painters, sculptors, and composers did not find inspiration along the banks of the Ohio River or the shores of Lake Michigan. Urban Midwesterners were cultivating their cities by importing refinement from the outside world, for, according to prevailing opinion, civilization was not a home-grown commodity of the heartland. The typical midwestern city was the Birmingham, not the Paris, of America.

Sports and Saloons

For those uninterested in art and music, the midwestern city offered other diversions. Chief among these, especially for the male population, were sports and the saloon. Whereas the museum and concert stirred both male and female enthusiasm and attracted primarily the upper half of the social stratum, the baseball stadium and the corner tavern were primarily male preserves with a broader class appeal. The saloon, in fact, was known as the workingman's club, a refuge for lower-class males from the grim realities of the factory and the home. More affluent men also lined up at the bar, but the saloon held a special place in the life of the worker with few options for amusement. Thus while Hutchinson and Thomas were attempting to uplift the midwestern soul with painting and symphonies, millions of midwestern urban dwellers were downing a few beers at the tavern and consulting the baseball scores in the newspapers. Though many were eager for the Midwest to snare the greatest conductor, others were more concerned about getting a good first baseman for the local team.

Because of their lingering sense of inferiority, midwestern cities were inordinately motivated to excel in sports during the late nineteenth century. Just as museums and music festivals supposedly demonstrated the maturity of heartland hubs so did a winning baseball team. In every American city urban dwellers wanted to see their team win, but for fans in Cincinnati or Chicago a victory over New York or Boston was especially welcome. Such wins proved once again that the midwestern urban centers had actually entered the constellation of big cities and were equal to the eastern metropolises.

As in the fields of music and art, in the promotion of baseball Cincinnatians stood in the forefront. In the late 1860s a group of Queen City entrepreneurs decided to put together the greatest baseball team in the country by luring the best players with offers of salaries. Until then baseball was largely a game of amateurs with only some players receiving pay, but now Cincinnati decided to break the rules and create the first all-professional team. The plan worked, for in its first season in 1869, this paid team won sixty-five games and lost none, scoring 2,395 runs during the season compared with 575 for its opponents. And the following season it won its first twenty-seven contests including three with scores of 100–2, 104–9, and 108–3.[83]

Especially exciting were the victories over eastern teams which had formerly dominated baseball and had regarded midwestern clubs as second-rate upstarts. In 1868 a leading sports journal observed: "Although the East has heretofore been the great baseball playground of the country, the West is making rapid strides and bids fair to outstrip the East."[84] During the following two years Cincinnati did in fact put the haughty Atlantic seaboard in its place, and Queen City fans reveled in the victories. When the Cincinnati team beat the New York Mutuals, a Queen City newspaper reported: "We are tossing our hats tonight, and shaking each other by the hand. We are the lions, and baseball men are looking curiously at us as the club over whose grounds . . . will soon float the . . . emblem of the world championship."[85]

Leaders elsewhere also realized that winning teams like museums and orchestras could promote a city's reputation and boost its image. For example, even in the relatively small city of Rockford, business chieftains of the 1870s recognized that the local team had done much "to spread the fame of Rockford far and wide." According to these local notables, "It would be to our pecuniary advantage to put our hands deep down in our pockets . . . to maintain a first class club."[86] William A. Hulbert, the owner of the Chicago club and founder of the National League, was likewise a devoted local booster who, according to one of his players, "never spoke of what *he* would do, or what *his* club would do, but it was always what *Chicago* would do."[87] Baseball was one event in the multifaceted contest for urban supremacy in America, and in the minds of Hulbert and others the team's victory was a victory for the Illinois metropolis as a whole. Moreover, a player was expected to rally to the defense of his home region rather than forsake it for the rival East. In the 1870s, Chicago's Hulbert told an Illinois-born pitcher: "You've no business playing in Boston; you're a Western boy, and you belong right here."[88] Baseball was becoming a badge of pride for the midwestern city and to root for an opposing club or play for Boston or New York was regarded as blatant disloyalty. Cincinnati had to compensate for its loss of commercial supremacy by offering the best in baseball as well as the best in Beethoven and Brahms. Already boasting of the tallest buildings, biggest packing houses, the "American Salon," and Theodore Thomas, Chicago also sought the world championship in baseball. The emerging national pastime was not simply a game; it was a means for advertising to the nation that Rockford, Cincinnati, and Chicago had arrived.

A source of less boasting among midwestern leaders were the region's numerous saloons. The Midwest pioneered professional baseball, but it also was in the forefront of beer production and consumption. This was in part because of its large German population. Germans took pride in their *gemutlichkeit,* an untranslatable term connoting camaraderie, conviviality, and good times. Basic to *gemutlichkeit* were ample kegs of foaming lager beer. Drinking like music was, then, part of the German way of life, and just as many Teutonic newcomers viewed Yankees as tone-deaf barbarians so they regarded native-born opponents of alcohol as "water simpletons" without any comprehension of the good things in life.[89]

Drinking was not only a German avocation, it also provided many jobs for immigrants from Central Europe. In 1880, 43 percent of all saloonkeepers and bartenders in Chicago were of German birth whereas only 16 percent of the total work force were German natives. Likewise, only 11 percent of Indianapolis's employed population was German born, yet 60 percent of the local brewers and maltsters hailed from Germany.[90] Moreover, immigrants like Pabst and Busch achieved their fortunes in the New World by quenching the thirst of imbibers. In other words, alcohol meant money for thousands of midwestern Germans.

Though many Midwesterners viewed drinking as a national tradition and a source of livelihood, others regarded it as a sin and the root of manifold social evils. This latter view was especially prevalent among native-born women who made the Midwest the center of temperance agitation in the late nineteenth century. In 1874 in the small towns of Hillsboro and Washington Courthouse, Ohio, women marched on local saloons where they prayed and sang for the redemption of the alcohol-guzzling patrons. Their efforts sparked interest in the largest cities of the Midwest where similar crusades followed during March and April 1874. In Cincinnati at least five hundred women invaded saloons where they knelt in prayer, read Bible verses, and sang hymns.[91] Meanwhile, in Chicago two hundred women marched on city hall to present a petition with sixteen thousand signatures protesting a proposal to rescind the law prohibiting Sunday liquor sales. A local newspaper reported: "A glance at the faces [of the women] was sufficient to assure an onlooker that they were terribly in earnest in what they were undertaking."[92]

In Cleveland, however, the female crusaders met violent opposition. According to one nineteenth-century account, as the women proceeded from one saloon to another an angry mob dedicated to drink "hooted, sang obscene songs and made offensive and profane remarks." When the temperance crusaders knelt to pray before a saloon, "the hoodlums pressed closer upon the women." In fact, "one walked upon their dresses, as they kneeled; another thrust a tobacco quid into the open mouth of a woman while she was praying." Finally a dozen men rushed at the foes of alcohol, one shouting, "I'd shoot the _____"; in the mayhem one woman was struck in the side by a man's fist and another was kicked. Moreover, in the short run the temperance crusade backfired. In the upcoming election friends of the saloon triumphed supposedly because of "the prejudice and feeling which the crusades aroused among the Germans, and others of the foreign population."[93]

Yet the crusades did not cease. Instead, female foes of alcohol decided to form a permanent organization, the Woman's Christian Temperance Union

(WCTU), which held its first national convention in Cleveland in November 1874.[94] Though the WCTU attracted members throughout the nation, it remained based in the Midwest, in the 1880s establishing its national headquarters in Chicago. And its leading figure was Frances Willard of the Chicago suburb of Evanston. Moreover, the WCTU continued to impose its moral influence on midwestern cities. For example, in 1894 it convinced the Chicago public schools to recognize Temperance Day, and the city's classes adjourned so that thousands of children could march in a temperance parade. The delighted WCTU president viewed this as evidence of "the solidifying of public opinion in favor of steady habits, and the creation of a new atmosphere with more moral ozone in it."[95]

Many Germans, though, regarded such "reform" efforts as puritanical oppression imposed by narrow-minded spinsters. Thus liquor was splitting the population of heartland cities. On the one hand, thousands of concerned and devout Christian women felt that the saloon was a plague on the city, blighting the lives of the working class. On the other hand, thousands of immigrant males viewed it as a balm for the urban dweller, enriching the otherwise bleak existence of workingmen in Cleveland or Chicago. Moreover, by the early 1890s, the conflict between drinkers and temperance crusaders remained unresolved, a persisting battle that would continue for decades to come.

By the last years of the nineteenth century, however, conflict seemed one of the chief characteristics of midwestern urban centers. They were bastions of industrial capitalism where many manufacturers were making fortunes in meat, metals, beer, and buggies. But they were also hotbeds of labor radicalism, and the greatest midwestern city was an anarchist stronghold and the scene of the nation's most violent strikes. In fact, Chicago was both heaven and hell for the industrialist, a paradise for making money but a hades for labor relations. At the same time the heartland hubs included diverse ethnic groups, each with its own deeply felt moral and cultural traditions. Poles fleeing from German oppression in their homeland migrated to Milwaukee where they lived a short distance from Germans proud of their national heritage. Teetotaling native-born Americans had to share the urban area with immigrants thirsty for strong drink. With their polyglot populations, Chicago, Cleveland, and Detroit each seemed to rest on an uneasy foundation.

In many ways the heartland was not only a region of conflict but also of contradiction. Fiery socialists spoke at street corners and printed inflammatory newspapers, yet no other urban areas in the world could claim such a high proportion of property owners. It was a region of the tallest buildings and the most single-family homes, with cities that reached upward but also stretched outward. It was a region that boasted of its industrial success and welcomed fascinated visitors to its fast-paced slaughtering houses. Yet midwestern cities also wanted to prove their refinement and cultivation and remained sensitive about their reputation for crass materialism.

Conflict and contradiction thus underlay Chicago, Cincinnati, Saint Louis, and the lesser urban hubs of the heartland. The midwestern city was increasingly at the center of social and economic development in America and no longer at the edge of commerce and civilization. But as yet the heartland city remained a volatile hodgepodge, a collection of people that had grown rapidly but was not sure where it was going or perhaps even where it wanted to go.

UNION RAILWAY STATION, INDIANAPOLIS, INDIANA.
Interior View of General Reception Room.

8. Grand depots, such as this one in Indianapolis, testified to the preeminence of the railroad in midwestern life during the late nineteenth century. Indiana State Library.

9. McCormick's giant reaper works in Chicago was one example of midwestern industrial success in the late decades of the nineteenth century. Chicago Historical Society.

10. Euclid Avenue was Cleveland's most fashionable thoroughfare, where the wealthy displayed their material success. Ohio Historical Society.

11. Chicago entrepreneurs constructed modest cottages for the working class and appealed to German-Americans through bilingual advertisements. Chicago Historical Society.

12. Germans found *gemütlichkeit* in Sunday outings to beer gardens, a practice deeply offensive to many native-born Americans dedicated to keeping the Sabbath holy and sober. Ohio Historical Society.

13. Constructed in the 1880s, Cincinnati's Art Museum and Art Academy sat in Olympian isolation on the hilltops of Eden Park, symbols of the cultural aspirations of the city. Ohio Historical Society.

14. As seen in this illustration from 1893, the Cincinnati Art Museum was the scene of many social affairs where Queen City strivers sought to prove their culture and refinement. Ohio Historical Society.

4.

Automobiles and Reform
The Midwest Leads the Nation

Early in the morning of June 4, 1896, Henry Ford started the engine of his first automobile, headed out of the little brick shed at the back of his double house in Detroit, and drove down Grand River Avenue to Washington Boulevard.[1] The Midwest was never the same again. A new era of technology had dawned during which the states of the Old Northwest would lead the nation. In the course of the next two decades, Detroit would become the world's center of automobile production, and the rest of the Midwest would be transformed into a workshop providing parts, tires, machine tools, and steel for the booming Motor City. The entire region seemed to be bursting with ingenuity and invention, and in thousands of backyard sheds mechanically minded Midwesterners tinkered with new devices to revolutionize American life. Some failed and some gave birth to industries enriching the cities of the heartland. In any case, no longer was the Midwest primarily an importer of technology from the East; no longer was it attempting to catch up with the industrial might of the Atlantic seaboard states. The first decades of the twentieth century represented a golden age for midwestern manufacturing, an era when the heartland won all prizes for industrial innovation and achievement.

Yet it was also a period when urban Midwesterners experimented with new political and social institutions aimed at improving city life. Not only did the heartland boast of thousands of backyard mechanics, it was home as well to an army of people committed to tinkering with the laws governing midwestern cities and eager to fashion better machinery for urban rule. At the same time, in the city slums middle-class reformers were seeking to fix the flaws in the social mechanism of the Midwest. In the minds of political and social reformers alike the midwestern city fell far short of perfection. But these crusaders felt that the heartland hubs could be redeemed and could become models for the rest of the nation and the world. Chicago, Detroit, and Cleveland had nurtured great industry and worked miracles of production unprecedented in the history of the world. Supposedly they should likewise be able to conjure magic among the poor and in the corridors of city hall.

With the continuing rapid growth of midwestern cities, the need for political and social reform seemed to mount. As seen in Table 4, between 1900 and 1920 Chicago added one million people to its population, Detroit more

TABLE 4

Largest Midwestern Cities, 1900 and 1920

1900		1920	
City	Population	City	Population
Chicago	1,698,575	Chicago	2,701,705
Saint Louis	575,238	Detroit	993,678
Cleveland	381,768	Cleveland	796,841
Cincinnati	325,902	Saint Louis	772,897
Detroit	285,704	Milwaukee	457,147
Milwaukee	285,315	Cincinnati	401,247
Indianapolis	169,164	Indianapolis	314,194
Toledo	131,822	Toledo	243,164
Columbus	125,560	Columbus	237,031
Grand Rapids	87,565	Akron	208,435
Dayton	85,333	Dayton	152,559
Evansville	59,007	Grand Rapids	137,634

Source: Bureau of the Census, *Fourteenth Census of the United States—Population 1920* (Washington: Government Printing Office, 1921), pp. 82–86.

than tripled in size, and Cleveland more than doubled. The river cities of Saint Louis and Cincinnati grew less rapidly than the more northern urban centers where the impact of automobile production was marked. But every major city posted gains, and the number of communities in the Old Northwest plus Saint Louis with over 100,000 population rose from nine in 1900 to thirteen in 1920.

Thus midwestern urban centers continued to attract the talents and labor of thousands of newcomers. In the early twentieth century the pot of gold was not at the end of the rainbow but in Detroit, Akron, Flint, and the other booming heartland cities. In these communities the midwestern miracle of economic growth continued; these cities were the industrial marvels of the nation. Yet at the same time social and political problems persisted, challenging the ingenuity of urban dwellers throughout America's interior valley.

The Automobile Revolution

Though thousands of midwestern workers continued to earn paychecks from packinghouses, tanneries, and furniture factories between 1895 and 1920, increasingly automobiles were to become the lynchpin of the heartland economy. The gasoline-fueled internal combustion engine propelled the twentieth-century Midwest, and the region's fortunes became dependent on the rise and fall of motor vehicle sales. Like an addict, the Midwest would experience economic euphoria when injected with a heavy dosage of auto

sales. But when consumers refused to purchase, wracking economic with-
drawal ensued. By the close of the century's second decade, communities
across the heartland were hooked on the narcotic of motor vehicle production.

This was especially true of Michigan's cities. As early as 1904 Michigan
already led the nation in the production of automobiles and their parts, and
by 1909 it accounted for 34 percent of the wage earners in the auto industry
and 36 percent of the value added by manufacture. Michigan grabbed an
even larger share of the American auto industry during the next decade,
with 51 percent of the wage earners in 1919 and 58 percent of the value
added.[2]

Other midwestern states, however, shared in the boom. Ohio consistently
ranked second in auto production and in both 1909 and 1919 Indiana was in
fourth place whereas Wisconsin ranked sixth in value added in 1909 and
fifth ten years later. Overall, at the close of the second decade of the twentieth century the five states of the Old Northwest accounted for 79 percent
of the wage earners in the American auto industry and 81 percent of the
value added by manufacture.[3] In other words, the production of motor vehicles was a midwestern industry as characteristic of the heartland as the
planting of corn.

Automobile production took root in the Midwest largely because the region's industrial heritage was particularly conducive to the manufacture of
motor vehicles. During the late nineteenth century thousands of machine
shops and foundries operated in midwestern cities, many of them fashioning
steam engines. Traditionally less reliant on waterpower than the Northeast,
from the steamboat days the Midwest had specialized in fuel-dependent
mechanisms. Thus it had an abundance of experienced mechanics and metal
workers who could readily adapt to the demands of the new industry and
fashion the parts necessary for automobiles. Moreover, Detroit specifically
had taken a lead in producing gasoline engines for motor launches on the
Great Lakes, and consequently that city enjoyed a headstart in mastering
the technology of the internal combustion engine.

Not only did the machine shops of the Midwest nurture the nascent auto
industry, so did the region's many carriage, buggy, and wagon works. Owing
in part to their proximity to the timber resources of the Upper Midwest,
heartland wagon works had ranked among the nation's largest producers of
vehicles in the 1880s and 1890s. Since the first automobiles were basically
engines mounted on buggies, many of these factories readily took up the
production of automobile bodies. They already had the necessary know-how
in vehicle fabrication, and they parlayed this advantage into success in auto
manufacturing. For example, J. H. Whiting of the Flint Wagon Works expanded into auto production, establishing the Buick plant in his hometown.
Fellow Flint resident William Durant of the Durant-Dort Carriage Company
took over Buick and founded General Motors. In 1902 South Bend's Studebaker carriage and wagon company ventured into automobile manufactur-

ing, exploiting its existing marketing network for the sale of autos as well as wagons. In 1890 the carriage and wagon industry was the chief manufacturing employer in Toledo; thirty years later automobile factories led in employment.[4] Across the Upper Midwest the ready supply of carriage builders provided a firm foundation for automobile manufacturing and contributed to the region's dominance of the new industry.

Nowhere was the impact of the automobile revolution greater than in the motor capital, Detroit. As the largest Michigan city, it attracted mechanics from throughout the state who were eager to try their hand at automaking. The first mass-produced automobile with general public appeal was the Oldsmobile, the creation of the Lansing machinist Ransom E. Olds. Olds's father operated a small steam engine factory in the state capital where the inventive son fashioned his first horseless carriage. Eager to profit from his vehicle, Olds secured needed financial backing from a wealthy Detroiter who insisted that the Oldsmobile be produced in Detroit. Consequently, in 1899 Ransom E. Olds opened the Olds Motor Works on the city's east side. After a fire in 1901, Olds and his company's operations moved back to Lansing, but meantime others were embarking on similar ventures.[5] Detroit's Leland-Faulconer machine shop headed by Henry Leland manufactured engines for Olds. Yet in 1902 Leland decided to launch his own automobile, the Cadillac.[6] Then in 1903 Henry Ford founded his auto company in Detroit, and that same year the Packard automobile operations moved from Warren, Ohio, to the Michigan metropolis. By 1904 the automobile industry already employed twenty-two hundred Detroit workers.[7]

Five years later this figure was up to 17,400 and by 1919 the state labor department reported 140,000 auto workers in Detroit. Forty-five percent of all industrial employees in the city were engaged in the production of automobiles or automobile accessories.[8] During the decade and a half between 1904 and 1919 the automobile industry had taken off and overwhelmed Detroit. Modest machine shops had given way to huge plants sprawling across the Michigan landscape. In 1910 Henry Ford moved into his gargantuan plant in the Detroit suburb of Highland Park. Four stories tall and the length of three football fields, at the time of its construction it was the largest structure under one roof in Michigan.[9] Four years later a writer in a national magazine described a visit to the Ford plant with "its endless rows of writhing machinery, its shrieking, hammering and clatter, its smell of oil, its autumn haze of smoke." This observer felt he "was not in any factory, but in a Gargantuan lunatic asylum where fifteen thousand raving, tearing maniacs had been given authority to go ahead and do their damnedest."[10] Workers had to do their damnedest to keep up with demand, for from 1916 to 1917 Ford was selling two thousand cars daily.[11] Meanwhile, two machinists from Niles, Michigan, John and Horace Dodge, were building an even larger auto plant in the Detroit suburb of Hamtramck. With an assembly building two hundred feet longer than the Highland Park behemoth, by 1920 the Dodge brothers provided employment to about twenty thousand workers.[12]

Automobile factories could attract workers in part because they paid higher than average wages. In fact, in 1914 Henry Ford made headlines when he introduced the five-dollar-a-day minimum wage, thus doubling his workers' pay. At the same time, Ford adopted the eight-hour work day, instituting a policy long demanded by laborers. The Ford Company proclaimed this "the greatest revolution in the matter of rewards for its workers ever known to the industrial world." "It is the most generous stroke of policy between captain of industry and worker that the country has ever seen," agreed a Michigan business journal.[13] With twice the wages offered in other industries and a shorter work day, Ford's Highland Park plant seemed to promise all that workers could want, and it became a magnet for job-seekers. Automobile manufacturing was to be a high-wage industry, and the consequences were to be seen in the cash register tills of stores and shops throughout the urban Midwest.

Ford, Dodge, and the rest, however, not only generated money and jobs, they also spurred rapid population growth. Whereas the population of Detroit more than doubled between 1910 and 1920, the impact on Highland Park and Hamtramck was even more marked. During the second decade of the twentieth century, the number of inhabitants in Highland Park rose more than elevenfold from 4,120 to 46,499, and the headcount of Hamtramck soared fourteenfold from 3,559 to 48,615. In 1900 the municipality of Hamtramck had not even existed; twenty years later it was Michigan's sixth largest city, having surpassed such long-established centers as Jackson and Kalamazoo.

Many of the newcomers pouring into Detroit and its environs were foreign born. In 1914 one commentator wrote of the "savage-looking foreign population" operating the machinery at the Ford plant; two years later a magazine article observed: "Every third man you meet in Detroit was born in a foreign country."[14] Especially numerous were the Poles, who by 1920 outnumbered Detroit's German-born inhabitants by almost two to one. The industrial suburb of Hamtramck became a mecca for Polish immigrants, and in 1920 one-third of that community's population was of Polish birth.[15] The Polish social centers, known as *Dom Polskis,* erected in the Detroit area during the second decade of the twentieth century were landmarks to the ethnic consequences of the automobile age. Formerly Germanic Detroit was acquiring an increasingly Slavic complexion as newcomers from Poland found work assembling Dodges and Cadillacs.

Elsewhere in Michigan the expanding automobile industry also resulted in rapid urban growth. Lansing became the headquarters for Oldsmobile, and after severing ties with his namesake vehicle, Ransom Olds created a second auto corporation in his hometown, the Reo Company, which manufactured both cars and trucks. Other less successful auto works offered a temporary boost to the Lansing economy. For example, the ill-fated Bates Automobile Company attempted to drum up customers with the slogan, "Buy a Bates and Keep Your Dates."[16] The Bates failed, but with Oldsmobile and Reo as well as a number of firms supplying parts to auto manufacturers, Lansing became a boomtown. Between 1900 and 1920 the capital city's population soared 248 percent from sixteen thousand to over fifty-seven thousand.

Even more spectacular was the boom in Flint, the birthplace of General Motors. With both Buick and Chevrolet plants, Flint attracted thousands of workers, its population rising from thirteen thousand in 1900 to almost ninety-two thousand twenty years later. "Lodgings were at a premium," a contemporary account reported, "some of the keepers of large boarding houses in the factory district renting their beds to first day and then night 'shifts'."[17] One resident said of Flint: "They sleep them so thick that their feet hang out the windows."[18] From 1909 to 1910 an estimated one thousand people lived in tents in the woods and along the river banks adjacent to the auto factories.[19] At the beginning of the century General Motors founder William Durant laid out the Oak Park subdivision on the north side of Flint; fifteen years later thousands of workers crowded into this neighborhood surrounding the largest industrial plants.[20]

Some cities outside of Michigan shared in the exhilarating economic impact of the automobile boom. Across the border in Toledo the Willys-Overland Company became the dominant manufacturer. In fact, by 1915 Willys ranked second in automobile sales, surpassed only by Ford.[21] Likewise, Studebaker was successfully making the move from carriages to automobiles and thus provided continuing prosperity for South Bend. In 1916 former General Motors president Charles Nash purchased the Jeffery auto company of Kenosha, Wisconsin, and began producing the Nash automobile. Between 1916 and 1920 auto and truck production in Kenosha increased sixfold, and in the latter year Nash employed over four thousand workers.[22] Meanwhile, Kenosha's population rose almost 300 percent from 11,606 in 1900 to 40,472 in 1920.

Cadillac, Oldsmobile, Buick, Willys, and Nash all spelled economic boom for Detroit, Lansing, Flint, Toledo, and Kenosha. But communities that never produced a successful make of automobile also shared in the good times. Automobile plants consumed millions of tons of steel, demanded a seemingly endless supply of rubber tires, and purchased parts, accessories, and machine tools from contractors throughout the Midwest. Henry Ford and William Durant thus produced economic ripples that spread outward to cities from eastern Ohio to Illinois. In other words, Detroit's newfound wealth proved a bounty to a myriad of midwestern manufacturers.

Perhaps no city outside of Michigan benefited as much from the auto boom as Akron. Since 1871 B. F. Goodrich had produced rubber goods in the Ohio city, but the center of American rubber manufacturing in the late nineteenth century was in New England where factories made rubber boots and soles. With the advent of the automobile, however, the demand for rubber tires soared, and auto manufacturers preferred to buy from suppliers closer at hand than New England. Only 120 miles from Toledo and 180 miles from Detroit, Akron had an advantage over eastern producers and quickly profited. The Akron firms of Goodyear, Firestone, and Goodrich became the three largest tire manufacturers in the nation, and together these companies transformed their hometown into an economic miracle. By 1920 these giants and lesser Akron competitors employed seventy-three thousand rubber workers who produced 41 percent of the nation's rubber products and, according to the chamber of commerce, "more than half of the tires of the United States and the world."[23] Moreover, the city's population rose fivefold between 1900 and 1920, and stories of landlords renting beds in shifts circulated in the rubber capital just as they did in Flint. Reporting on the rush of workers to the Ohio city, a national magazine published an article entitled "Akron—Standing Room Only."[24] Though housing shortages plagued the community, in the minds of most Akron residents the advantages of the boom outweighed the disadvantages. Akron boosters proclaimed their community "the City of Opportunity" and referred to it as "the 'wonder city' of America."[25] Workers had good reason to flock to the rubber capital, for in 1917 a leading businessman observed that it was "well known that Akron [was] considered a high-wage town."[26] As a symbol of their relative wealth, most rubber workers reportedly wore silk shirts and often sported felt beaver hats.[27]

Thousands of these migrants to Akron were from Appalachia. So many people from the hills engulfed the rubber city that it was derisively labeled "the capital of West Virginia."[28] In fact, a candidate for governor of that Appalachian state once made a campaign speech in the Ohio city hoping to influence potential voters who might return to their native soil to cast their ballots.[29] Regarded as ignorant yokels by many of their fellow workers, the West Virginians were the butt of endless jokes and won the derogatory nickname of "Snake Eaters." One story that circulated in Akron told of a West Virginian who was given his first banana to eat. He proceeded to consume the peel and dispose of the remainder. "It's mighty good," he told his colleagues, "but there's an awful lot of core."[30] Thus Appalachian newcomers confronted prejudicial stereotypes that were to hamper their advancement in the urban Midwest. Yet the Akron rubber workers were just the first wave of a mass migration of white Southerners to the Midwest that would continue intermittently throughout the first two-thirds of the twentieth century. Just as the Poles of Detroit were changing the cultural and ethnic composition of the midwestern city so would the army of migrants from the South.

Twenty miles south of Akron, the city of Canton was another beneficiary of the automobile revolution. In the 1850s the German immigrant Henry Timken had founded a carriage factory in Saint Louis. There he invented a successful buggy spring and developed an improved roller bearing for wagon axles. By the turn of the century the farsighted Timken and his sons recognized that their company would benefit if it relocated closer to the manufacturers of steel used in the bearings and nearer the burgeoning automakers who could be lucrative customers for Timken axles. The Timkens selected

Canton as the site of their new plant, for it lay astride the steel belt stretching from Pittsburgh to Cleveland and was considerably closer to the automobile builders of Ohio and Michigan than was Saint Louis. The Canton plant opened in 1902 with thirty to forty workers, by 1909 it supplied axles and bearings to sixty-six motor car manufacturers, and ten years later it had nearly thirty-five hundred employees on the payroll.[31] Meanwhile, the population of Canton had almost tripled, rising from thirty-one thousand in 1900 to eighty-seven thousand in 1920.

While the Timkens were the great benefactors of Canton's economy, in Dayton a young engineer named Charles Kettering injected new vigor into that city's business life. Kettering had come to Dayton to work for National Cash Register, but with the support of that company's general manager Edward Deeds he devoted much of his time to developing an electric ignition for automobiles. In 1909 Deeds and Kettering convinced Cadillac's Henry Leland to purchase their ignition system, and to manufacture the invention they formed the Dayton Engineering Laboratories Company, known by the acronym "Delco." Then in 1911 Kettering sold Cadillac the first electric self-starter, which eliminated the need for manual cranking of the engine. By 1913, only four years after its inception, Delco already employed fifteen hundred Dayton residents and was expanding at a breakneck pace.[32]

Throughout the Midwest cities boasted of similar success stories. Toledo's glass industry was to prosper selling windshields to Detroit, and an Indianapolis company claimed to be the world's largest producer of shock absorbers.[33] In Milwaukee A. O. Smith founded a company that would become the nation's chief manufacturer of steel automobile frames.[34] Likewise, during the early decades of the twentieth century Rockford's machine tool factories began to overshadow that community's furniture plants as automakers spent millions of dollars on machinery to produce their vehicles. As early as 1914 the Ford company owned about fifteen thousand machines, and it was constantly seeking new equipment to increase productivity and reduce costs.[35] In Ohio, Indiana, and Illinois workshops sought to meet the automakers' needs, and if these firms won the desired contract with Detroit, the result was thousands of new jobs.

Basic to the expansion of midwestern industry was steel. The auto factories of Michigan, Ohio, and Indiana, the farm implement manufacturers of Illinois, and machinery makers throughout the Midwest all consumed vast quantities of this commodity. Recognizing the rising demand in the heartland, the nation's largest steelmaker, U.S. Steel, decided to expand its midwestern operations. The result was a new steel city which rivaled Detroit and Akron as a testimonial to midwestern industrial growth. Along the shores of Lake Michigan in northwestern Indiana, the steel company created the city of Gary, yet another example of the economic dynamism of the heartland in the first decades of the twentieth century.

When development of the new town began in 1906, its site was just an expanse of sand punctuated by scrub oaks. Four years later Gary housed seventeen thousand people, and with mammoth blast furnaces as well as the world's largest steel rail mill it was on its way to becoming the "Pittsburgh of the West."[36] During the next decade the fast-paced growth continued so that by 1920 the population surpassed fifty-five thousand. In 1909 a national magazine labeled it "the magic city" and noted: "The rapidity of construction is one of the most amazing things connected with the enterprise."[37] Others agreed. "Never before in the history of the material development of the American continent," boasted a local observer in 1908, "has an industrial enterprise of such gigantic proportions been conceived and put into execution, and carried out, as the marvelous enterprise now building at Gary, Indiana."[38] The steel company itself immodestly proclaimed its creation "the eighth wonder of the world."[39]

Intended to be the "model industrial city of the world," Gary, however, fell far short of the ideal.[40] As in Akron and Flint, workers in early Gary confronted a housing shortage, and many unskilled, immigrant laborers found shelter in "barrack-like shacks" on the city's south side. Even an admirer of the supposedly model community admitted that the area known as "The Patch" contained "structures that would not be tolerated in other parts of the town."[41] Moreover, drinking seemed to be the chief form of recreation in the steel city; by 1911 Gary had 238 saloons, or approximately one for every eighty-eight inhabitants.[42] Yet Gary remained an industrial wonder, even though it would win no prizes from the WCTU. In 1920 the city directory proudly proclaimed Gary "the Greatest and Most Prosperous City for Its Age, with Wonderful Results Accomplished and Growing Greater Day by Day."[43]

The automobile may have been transforming the midwestern economy during the first two decades of the century, but at the same time an alternative mode of transportation also captured the imagination of heartland investors. For this was the era of the electric interurban railroads, and nowhere in the country were there more interurban lines than in the Old Northwest. Ohio ranked first in the nation in interurban mileage, and Indiana was second. Together the five states of the Old Northwest accounted for more than 40 percent of the nation's total interurban network.[44] Throughout the Midwest the electric railroads linked scores of county seats and ensured rapid transportation between the small town and the big city.

With a relatively dense rural population and an abundance of small-town residents eager to escape the confines of their Main Street existence, the Midwest seemed well suited for the interurban business. The electric traction lines built during the first two decades of the twentieth century provided faster and more frequent service than the steam railroads, thus enabling residents from the hinterland to descend on city stores and offices at any time of day and return to their country homes at their leisure. By 1909 an Illinois interurban company offered 106 trains each day to and from Springfield, and two years later the interurban lines scheduled 140 trains daily in or out of Columbus, Ohio.[45] In 1910 busy Indianapolis boasted of over 400 interurbans arriving and departing every twenty-four hours.[46] These new lines promised to bring more shopping dollars to the heartland's larger cities, and consequently urban boosters throughout the region viewed them as devices for further accelerating the growth of their hometowns. "When those new electric roads commence to be built," wrote a contributor to a Lansing newspaper, "I shall be very much surprised if the old town doesn't experience something strangely like a boom." Small-town observers agreed that the interurbans would further concentrate business in the larger centers. Commenting on an impending electric traction line, the newspaper in little Portland, Michigan, predicted: "The time is fast approaching when . . . small towns . . . will be like the four-corner settlements of thirty or forty years ago in this state." Supposedly all the trade would "go away from small places like Portland and Mason and go to Lansing."[47]

Yet by the middle of the second decade of the twentieth century, the interurban boom was already over. Overbuilding by enthusiastic speculators produced red ink in the ledgers of many interurban companies. Moreover, the automobile was soon to win the race for popularity among the public. As more Midwesterners bought Model T Fords, fewer were attracted to the electric rail lines. During the early twentieth century the Midwest led the nation in both automobile production and interurban traction. Ultimately, however, the heartland was to cast its lot with the automobile and allow the interurbans to disappear.

The future of the midwestern city, then, rested increasingly with gasoline-fueled motor vehicles and their accessories. As millions of Americans purchased their first automobiles midwestern fortunes soared; automania was the key to urban growth in Detroit, Akron, Flint, and Lansing. Yet dependence on the automobile industry could also prove the bane of these communities, leaving them vulnerable to fluctuations in auto sales. By the close of the second decade of the century the rubber companies accounted for 81 percent of the industrial employees in Akron.[48] Akron was a maker of tires and little more. Likewise, Flint was the property of General Motors and its future depended on Buick sales. Automobiles could spell prosperity and high wages for thousands of Midwesterners, but they could also mean layoffs and economic instability.

Reforming City Government

The Midwest led the nation not only in industrial advances but in the effort to right the wrongs of city government. Throughout the country many perceived American city government as corrupt, wasteful, a perversion of democracy, and just plain bad. During the late nineteenth century city administrations could claim great achievements, having created fine libraries, laid out handsomely landscaped parks, maintained first-rate fire departments, and constructed water and sewer systems that were marvels of engineering. But most observers chose to overlook these successes and focus instead on the failures. Rumors of corruption and ballot-box stuffing were widespread, and virtually everyone assumed that public utility companies were bribing city officials and cheating urban consumers. Moreover, the plebeian sons of immigrants who occupied offices in city hall and sat in places of honor in the council chambers were an affront to the sensibilities of many middle-class observers who believed that breeding and civic virtue went hand in hand. Likewise, the whiskey-swilling, vote-buying neighborhood ward leaders who based their petty political domains in the corner saloon seemed a poor foundation for urban government. Sober, chaste middle-class reformers could no more stomach these unworthy participants in American politics than they could imbibe hard liquor. Though claiming to speak for the people, ward leaders were supposedly selling urban democracy to the highest bidder.

In Baltimore, New York City, and San Francisco as well as Cleveland, Detroit, and Chicago such attitudes prevailed among reform-minded citizens. Yet in the heartland the reform spirit was especially strong. This was in part because of the region's emerging political ethos. In the minds of Midwesterners, the interior valley was the most American of the nation's regions and the standard bearer of American principles. In 1893 the Wisconsin historian Frederick Jackson Turner presented his frontier thesis which identified the trans-Appalachian West as the nurturing ground of democracy. This notion reflected midwestern thinking at the turn of the century. The Midwest was seen as the valley of democracy and the homeland of that greatest American democrat, Abraham Lincoln. As opposed to the effete, aristocratic East and decadent, caste-ridden South, the Midwest was the true embodiment of the American political dream, a region where a rail-splitter could become president and where government was actually supposed to be of the people, by the people, and for the people. In the cities as well as the countryside that dream had to be preserved. If the hope of democracy could be realized in an urban setting, this realization would most likely take place in the Midwest. For in the heartland the roots of American principles reached deeply into the rich soil and supposedly nowhere did the nation's civic ideals grow taller or stronger.

The Midwest was in the forefront of the American dream materially as well as spiritually. As the economic miracle of the nation, it seemed a fertile breeding ground for governmental wonders. Midwesterners had transformed a wilderness into a region of great cities and towering skyscrapers in the span of a single lifetime. Why, then, could they not complete the transformation and realize the highest goals of city government? With a "can-do" spirit prevailing not only in Chicago but also in other models of urban success like Cleveland, Detroit, and Milwaukee, the imperative for upgrading urban rule was especially strong.

Considered from the more pedestrian standpoint of incidence of taxpaying, midwestern cities further seemed especially prone to reform campaigns.

With an unusually high percentage of homeowners, the heartland hubs had more property-tax payers among the electorate, persons inordinately sensitive to claims of corruption and waste in government. In contrast, the largely rent-paying citizenry of New England's cities never developed a strong urban reform tradition. To the thousands of small homeowners in Toledo and Detroit who daily read in the newspapers of the squandering of their tax dollars, reform was not just a matter of realizing the American political dream. It was an issue that struck at their pocketbooks.

The ethnic composition of Midwestern cities also made them susceptible to reform. For Irish immigrants the purportedly corrupt system of urban politics was a ladder of social mobility, an appreciated means for bettering themselves. In the Midwest as compared to the East, however, the Irish were less prevalent, and the immigrant population's predisposition for traditional ward politics was accordingly weaker. Midwestern Germans were more willing to line up behind crusaders urging honesty and efficiency in city government, especially when the reformers cited German cities as proud models of good government. If the reform message included attacks on beer and social imbibing, Germans might well bridle, but otherwise they proved more amenable to the gospel of political reformation than the Irish of the East.

The region's self-designation as the promised land of democracy combined with its boundless confidence and its Germanic homeowning electorate thus made it ripe for reform messages. If better city government was to be achieved, Midwesterners seemed destined by belief and circumstances to achieve it. In politics as in manufacturing, Midwestern cities were primed for success.

Leading the urban crusade in the Midwest was a trio of reform mayors who aroused their cities from political apathy and won accolades from like-minded persons throughout the country. From 1890 to 1897 Hazen Pingree established a reform agenda as mayor of Detroit and equally dedicated were Samuel M. Jones, mayor of Toledo from 1897 to 1904, and Tom L. Johnson, Cleveland's chief executive from 1901 to 1910. Each pursued his goals with a religious fervor, conceiving of himself as a crusader against manifold and powerful social wrongs. For them city government was not just a matter of municipal housekeeping with the mayor ensuring that the books balanced and the garbage was collected. Instead, in the minds of Pingree, Jones, and Johnson the mayor's office was the command center for an all-out assault on the obstacles in the path of achieving the highest ideals of urban democracy. Lincoln had emancipated the slaves and advanced toward the goal of a just democracy; now Pingree, Jones, and Johnson sought to emancipate the city and realize equity and justice in the metropolis.

Though each was a prosperous businessman who had profited handsomely from capitalism, these mayors shared a common hatred for corporate privilege, especially the privilege of public utility corporations. In their minds, the utilities bred corruption and exercised unjustifiable power over the consumer. To secure the right to service urban dwellers, these gas, electric, and streetcar companies reportedly offered ample bribes to city council members. Moreover, mergers and consolidations had eliminated competition among the corporations, leaving many major metropolises with one dominant trolley company or a single electric utility. With monopoly control over gas, electricity, and streetcar transportation, such companies became hated symbols of corporate abuse. Pingree, Jones, and Johnson sought to curb this abuse by favoring municipal ownership of utilities.

In 1897 Pingree summed up an article of faith basic to all three mayors when he wrote: "The time is coming when municipal monopolies will be owned by the people."[49] During his administration the Detroit executive sought to realize this goal by creating a municipally owned electric light plant. A state constitutional provision, however, prevented him from securing city ownership of the streetcar lines. Instead, he organized a new streetcar company in competition with the existing transit network. The new streetcar lines charged only three cents per ride as compared to the five-cent fare on the existing lines. Thus Pingree hoped to force a reduction in fares citywide and loosen the grip of the former transit monopoly on vulnerable Detroiters. Not only did the mayor aim to lower rates, he also sought to eliminate the principal source of bribery in local government. According to Pingree, the public utility corporations, "having a direct interest in municipal legislation and administration," were "the chief, if not the only source, of corruption in the city governments of America."[50]

Toledo's Jones agreed wholeheartedly. In 1899 he wrote: "Every wire, every pole, every conduit, every rail—everything permanently in or on the streets should be for the common benefit of all the people, not for the private benefit of a few." Thus he ran on a platform specifically dedicated to "public ownership of all public utilities." "Equal opportunities for all and special privileges to none" was Jones's popular stance.[51] Yet Jones proved less successful than Pingree. Toledo's aldermen rejected a proposal for a municipal electric plant, and Jones died in the midst of a struggle with the city council over the extension of the streetcar company's franchise. On the morning after the mayor's death, the transit company stock soared twenty-four points.[52]

Mayor Tom Johnson carried on the same battle, also with only limited success. A wealthy streetcar magnate, Johnson led Detroit's transit company during the 1890s and played the role of greedy archenemy in Mayor Pingree's crusading scenario. Attacking Pingree's three-cent fare, Johnson warned: "This is a fight for gore, and it will be carried right along to the finish."[53] By the turn of the century, however, the combative transit magnate had decided to emulate his foe rather than defeat him. Reestablishing himself in Cleveland, Johnson soon sought to win laurels as that city's reform hero, and basic to his new campaign was a hatred for the very type of business that had made him rich. In 1901 he proclaimed: "The public utility corporations are a bunch of thieves. I ought to know. I was one of them."[54]

For the next eight years Johnson battled the public utilities, and in his autobiography he wrote that "the greatest movement in the world" was "the struggle of the people against Privilege."[55] Though he failed to achieve municipal ownership during his administration, he began agitation for a city-owned electric light plant, and that goal was finally realized five years after he left office. Moreover, his streetcar crusade resulted in some reduction in fares, but private investors continued to own the transit lines.

The attacks on public utilities were just part of a larger campaign to help the urban masses in their struggle to survive. Pingree, Jones, and Johnson all were self-styled defenders of the common people, sponsoring programs to aid the poor. During the depression of the mid-1890s Mayor Pingree sought to provide employment for the jobless by increasing the number of laborers engaged in municipal works projects, and he also introduced his potato patch scheme which won national attention. Under this program the city assigned half-acre plots to almost one thousand indigent families so that they could grow food and stave off malnutrition. Pingree proclaimed "the unqualified success of the experiment" which proved that "at least 96 percent of the people who [were] in destitute circumstances, as a result of hard times, [were] ready, willing and anxious to work."[56]

Underlying Jones's devotion to the welfare of the poor was his belief in government according to the Golden Rule. The Toledo mayor claimed that "Do unto others as you would have others do unto you" should be the guiding principle of city government, and thus he favored an administration that would "consider the rights of the weakest child in the city as being equally important with those of the greatest and wisest man." Moreover, unlike most businessmen of his era, Jones supported labor unions. "Organized labor," the mayor contended, "has done more than any other agency during the last twenty-five years to bring men to a better understanding of the purposes of government, the meaning of justice and liberty and what we have a right to expect as the fruit thereof."[57] Acting in accord with his rhetoric, Jones introduced an eight-hour workday in the water and police departments, convinced the council to establish a minimum wage for municipal laborers, urged the development of playgrounds and parks, and sponsored free concerts. To encourage hygiene among the poor, the Jones administration built public baths, and to aid indigent children, it was instrumental as well in the creation of kindergartens. Any needy visitor to the mayor's office with a convincing sob story could get aid from the generous city executive. At the end of one long day, Jones sighed, "I could wash my hands every day in women's tears."[58]

In Cleveland as well the city government showed a new solicitude for the masses. Johnson ordered the removal of all "Keep Off the Grass" signs from the city's parks and sponsored both free concerts and the creation of playgrounds. "When he was Mayor," one historian said of Johnson, "the people for the first time learned that they really owned the parks."[59] According to a young disciple of the mayor, "Cleveland became a play city" and "on Saturday and Sunday the whole population played baseball in hundreds of parks laid out for that purpose."⁶⁰ Meanwhile, Johnson, like Jones, opened public baths in the poor neighborhoods where bathtubs were a rarity. Though the local chamber of commerce attacked such facilities as socialistic, the Johnson administration built them.⁶¹

Pingree, Jones, and Johnson also won the favor of many working-class constituents by refusing to take harsh action against the saloons and their less fortunate patrons. These reform mayors believed that drunkenness was a symptom of the underlying evils of society, and that imbibers were victims rather than criminals. Thus when acting as police magistrate, the forgiving Jones dismissed many of the accused with a sermon on the ills corrupting society. The Toledo reformer complained: "The popular conception of 'good government' seems to be confined to the thought of restraining saloons, gambling houses and brothels." Yet what he understood by good government was "expressed in the word 'Brotherhood.'" Speaking before the League of Ohio Municipalities, Jones attacked the criminal justice system for oppressing the poor. "They have no money, they have no counsel," the mayor argued, "and for petty offenses that are not offenses at all when committed by the rich, they are fined, imprisoned, disgraced, and degraded."⁶²

Tom Johnson's director of charity and corrections shared this view, regarding "delinquent men, women, and children . . . as fellow human beings who had been deprived of the opportunity to get on in the world." According to this Cleveland official, offenders of the law should "be cared for by the society that had wronged them."⁶³

Such comments earned the midwestern mayors considerable derision and enmity. Ohio's Republican boss Mark Hanna labeled Johnson a "socialist-anarchist-nihilist" and dismissed Jones as a "moral crank."⁶⁴ During Jones's reelection campaign in 1903, Toledo's leading newspaper was so hostile toward the reformer that it refused even to mention the mayor's name.⁶⁵ Likewise, Detroit newspapers ridiculed Hazen Pingree's unorthodox ideas. Responding to the mayor's potato scheme, a Detroit cartoonist depicted his honor as a despot named "Tuber I" bearing a carrot for a scepter and a potato for an orb.⁶⁶

Yet in the minds of many observers both at home and nationwide, the trio of heartland executives represented the brightest hope of urban democracy. In 1905 Lincoln Steffens, the nation's leading muckraker, pronounced Tom Johnson "the best mayor of the best-governed city in the United States." Johnson himself aroused great expectations when he defined as his goal "to make Cleveland the first American city to get good government."⁶⁷ The crusading mayor sought to make Cleveland into "A City on a Hill," a beacon light for the rest of urban humanity.⁶⁸ Moreover, he conveyed his enthusiasm to a throng of devoted followers. According to Steffens, members of the Johnson administration had "a sense of pride and preoccupation" such as he "never felt in any other American municipal government."⁶⁹ The young reform councilman Frederic Howe extolled Johnson's efforts as "a moral crusade rarely equalled in American politics." In fact, Howe believed that in Cleveland "were all of the elements necessary to a great experiment in democracy."[70]

Steffens and others certainly viewed with disdain the corrupt governments of Saint Louis and Cincinnati, but along the shores of the Great Lakes city dwellers seemed to be leading the nation in the cause of urban reform. Nowhere were hopes higher and the rhetoric more confident and idealistic. In 1899 Mayor Jones proclaimed: "We are in the beginning of a time when, through the administration of love as law, we are to realize in a larger degree the kind of liberty that Lincoln believed in and died for."[71] Cynics could scoff, but in the opinion of many Americans Cleveland, Toledo, and Detroit were no longer oversized, backward factory towns. They were the vanguard of reform, guiding urbanites throughout the nation and the world toward the democratic ideal.

Moreover, in both Cleveland and Toledo disciples carried on the reform cause after Jones and Johnson left office. Following Jones's death, novelist Brand Whitlock won the Toledo mayor's seat and attempted to realize the ambitions of his idealistic predecessor. Whitlock relied less on the rhetoric of Christian evangelism than Jones, but his vision of the city was just as lofty. He regarded as "the great purpose of democracy" to create "free" cities that would "be better, kindlier places to live in," that would "offer to every man on equal terms the opportunity to live a beautiful life."[72] Like Jones, Whitlock was staunchly pro-labor and felt a special sympathy for the less affluent. "I'd rather have the love of the poor and of the working classes," he told a fellow reformer, "than all the gold the rich men in town have."[73] And he refused to bow to the demands of pious souls and close Toledo's saloons. In 1907 an outraged opposition newspaper claimed: "Mayor Whitlock's administration is so clearly in the interest of the saloon and wine room and against the home that citizens are in revolt and mothers and wives are praying for change."[74] But for Whitlock as well as Jones, liquor, gambling, and prostitution were petty issues compared to the problems of corporate privilege and big-business corruption of municipal government. Whitlock argued: "The failures and shames of the American city have not been the failures and shames of democracy, but they have been the failures and shames incident of a lack of democracy."[75] Democracy and not simply sobriety would make Toledo a model to the remainder of the world, and during his eight years in office Whitlock endeavored to achieve rule by and for the people.

Meanwhile, in 1911 Tom Johnson's law director Newton Baker was elected mayor of Cleveland and served for the next four years. Though less flamboyant and charismatic than his reform predecessor, Baker remained committed to the Johnson agenda. Like his mentor, Baker was dedicated to municipal ownership and claimed that the public utility companies had "consistently corrupted and depraved government" for fifty years.[76] Acting on this belief the new mayor established a municipal electric plant, thereby realizing one of Johnson's dreams. Pious Clevelanders, however, found Baker's regime wanting, especially when an irate husband discovered his wife in the embraces of the scantily clad police chief. Others charged that the mayor was transforming Cleveland from a "City on a Hill" to a "City in the Hole."[77] Nevertheless, reformers lauded Baker as a worthy successor to Johnson in maintaining Cleveland's leadership in urban reform.

Though Cleveland and Toledo were in the forefront of reform, leaders in other midwestern cities shared some of the same concerns as Jones, Johnson, Whitlock, and Baker. Specifically, the issue of municipal ownership of public utilities was controversial throughout the Midwest, igniting battles in one city after another. For example, attacks on the utilities proved popular in Chicago where streetcar magnates had long exercised inordinate authority over corrupt aldermen. Describing the power of streetcar boss Charles Yerkes, one alderman said, "You can't get elected to the council unless Mr. Yerkes says so."[78] In the 1890s a local magazine reported: "It has been an open secret for many months that the council is controlled by a gang of corruptionists and that municipal franchises are as clearly matters of bargain and sale as goods at a bargain counter."[79] Responding to this situation, the reform-minded Municipal Voters League succeeded in defeating a number of the so-called grafters. But during the first years of the twentieth century demands for public control mounted, culminating in 1905 in the election of Mayor Edward F. Dunne on a platform calling for immediate municipal ownership of the utilities.

Dunne fumbled through the next two years, offending more voters than he satisfied. With a penchant for naming idealistic reformers to city positions, the new mayor alienated many practical people. Local newspapers labeled his appointees as "freaks, cranks, monomaniacs, and boodlers" and complained that his administration included too many "long-haired friends and short-haired women."[80] To placate moralists Dunne ordered raids on saloons and in the process aroused working-class opposition. "He has closed the saloons and dance halls and everything," charged one angry worker; "he had sacrificed everything for municipal ownership."[81] Yet his sacrifices were not sufficient, for in a 1907 referendum Chicago voters approved a new franchise agreement with the privately owned transit company. The electorate appeared satisfied with the improved franchise terms, demonstrating a pragmatic preference for better service rather than an inflexible devotion to the principle of municipal ownership. Soon afterward Dunne lost a bid for reelection, ending a controversial two-year reign during which Chicago sported the title of "the most radical city in America."[82]

Smaller cities also became embroiled in the struggle over transit corporations. For example, in Wisconsin's capital city, the hometown of the great reform hero Robert La Follette, local streetcar service remained a topic of debate and diatribe through much of the early twentieth century. In 1905 New York capitalist F. W. Montgomery bought the Madison Street Railroad Company and exposed the once placid community to his imperious personality. Within a few years Madisonians were grousing bitterly about the slow, overcrowded, unheated, dirty cars and complaining of Montgomery's failure to extend service to new residential areas. According to one letter to the editor printed in 1908, "Our wives, sweethearts, sisters and grandmothers are treated little better than hogs [and] cars are crowded until men and boys have to cling to the edges and sides like chimney swallows."[83] Madison residents repeatedly took their complaints to the state railroad regulatory commission, which time and again ordered Montgomery to upgrade his service. But in 1918 the commission shocked Madisonians by allowing the hated transit magnate to raise fares by a penny from five cents to six cents. In response, cries for municipal ownership increased, resulting in a referendum on the issue in 1920. As in Chicago, however, the electorate opted for continued private control.[84] When faced with the possible expense entailed in purchase of the streetcar system, Madison taxpayers lost their nerve and sided with the status quo.

Not all midwestern urban reformers warmed at the notion of municipal ownership and not all adopted the stance of Pingree, Johnson, and Jones. Those demanding change in city government were, in fact, a diverse lot with different agendas. Some believed corporate privilege was the chief problem; others felt drink and vice were at the root of urban ills and not just symptoms of deeper social evils; and still others found the supposed solution in changes in the structure of city government that would ensure honest, cost-effective, nonpartisan rule. Yet in every city there was a perception that something was wrong and something had to be done about it.

For example, leading the reform crusade in the Motor City during the second decade of the twentieth century was the Detroit Citizens League. Founded in 1912 by the Brotherhood of Westminster Presbyterian Church, the league sought to rally Detroit's "best citizens" in the fight against corruption and immorality. Its president from 1912 to 1924 was the Cadillac chieftain Henry Leland, a devout, teetotaling Christian who in the course of his long search for salvation had been a Quaker, a Seventh Day Adventist, a Congregationalist, a Baptist, and eventually a Presbyterian. "I find I need the church to keep me headed right," Leland observed.[85] And he endeavored to keep his hometown headed right as well. This God-fearing automaker explained to a prospective member that the league intended to make war on "the saloonkeepers, the brewers, the royal arc of the boodlers and grafters and demagogues" who corrupted life in Detroit.[86] In the words of the league's executive secretary William Lovett, the organization sought to transfer "civic power from the saloon to the church, from the political haunts of the 'Vote Swappers' League to the executive offices of factory and mercantile establishments."[87] Through the league, Detroit's most upstanding business moguls aimed to give their city a thorough cleansing.

Overall the league's conception of reform differed markedly from the views of mayors like Jones or Johnson. Unlike these Ohioans, Leland was no friend of labor unions, and as a self-made man he believed that the traditional virtues of hard work, thrift, and sobriety would lead to worldly success.

Unadulterated democracy also was less appealing to Leland than to the mayors of Toledo and Cleveland. He once recommended a book because it pointed out "the radical difference between a Republic and a Democracy" and demonstrated the reasons for fearing the nation's "drift towards democracy."[88] Moreover, in contrast to Jones and Johnson the Cadillac magnate had no tolerance for saloons. The public utilities were suspect, but liquor was worse. William Lovett later explained: "Two corrupting influences of major importance were the street railway issue and the unchallenged power of the saloon." But according to this reformer, "The organized beer barons and liquor dealers were accepted as the most powerful factor in local politics."[89] Lovett lauded the departed Mayor Pingree as the fountainhead of reform in Detroit, conveniently ignoring the late crusader's leniency toward liquor.[90] Yet the Citizens League clearly did not believe that corporate injustice and public utilities were the root of all evil; the forces of personal immorality were an enemy of greater significance. In the mind of a leading league official, the goal of democracy was not the liberation of the masses or the destruction of privilege, it was "the tremendous task of making . . . great cities . . . into efficient engines of righteousness."[91]

If Detroit was to become an efficient engine of righteousness, it needed a new structure of government, and the Citizens League sought to achieve this through charter reform. The special target of reform ire was the city council composed of forty-two members, two being chosen in partisan elections from each of Detroit's twenty-one wards. William Lovett characterized the council as "a hopeless, log-rolling, wasteful, unintelligent aggregation of performing simpletons," and the *Detroit News* described the municipal lawmakers as "the largest troupe of clowns in captivity."[92] According to reformers, the ward-based council members served only the narrow interests of their individual wards and their political parties and as neighborhood representatives were unable to comprehend the broader problems of the city as a whole. A speaker at a league meeting contended that the ward politician lived, thought, and acted "chiefly in the selfish interest of the ward." "He does not belong to the city as a whole," this reformer argued, "yet today the real community problems are those of the whole city."[93]

To deal with these problems the league favored a new charter with a small nine-member council chosen at large in nonpartisan elections. In the opinion of one supporter of charter reform, this new system would attract "men with more brains than the average peanut politician" to municipal government.[94] The *Detroit Journal* favored the small-council plan, arguing: "A big business cannot be run by a multiplicity of managers. . . . Running Detroit is like running a big business."[95] Local labor unions balked at this change that would deny working-class wards a direct voice in the council and shift lawmaking authority to those affluent Detroiters who had a favorable reputation throughout the city rather than just a neighborhood following. Thus the *Detroit Labor News* labeled the small-council plan as the handiwork of "emissaries of big business" and predicted it would be the "death warrant for democracy."[96]

Yet in an advisory referendum in November 1917 Detroit voters approved the small-council idea by a margin of better than two to one, and the following June they endorsed a new charter creating a nonpartisan, nine-member, at-large council by an overwhelming vote of 32,690 to 4,587.[97] Though white-collar, middle-class neighborhoods voted most heavily in favor of the scheme, it won in working-class, immigrant areas as well. By 1918 the league had seemingly built a consensus for reform. One commentator observed simply that "the people were tired of a big ward elected council, continually playing peanut politics."[98]

Elsewhere in the Midwest, however, reformers believed more drastic structural changes were necessary. Elimination of ward representation and party labels was not enough. Instead, the entire traditional mayor-council framework of city government had to be discarded. In its place cities needed to establish a manager-council system, with policy determined by a small nonpartisan council and administration in the hands of a professional manager. Expertise and efficiency were the hallmarks of the great auto corporations transforming the midwestern economy. Why not apply the same principles to city government? Thus in numerous heartland cities leaders believed that hired managers trained in the principles of municipal engineering should take charge in city government and emulate the success of Ford or General Motors at the municipal level.

In the forefront of the crusade for city manager rule was Dayton. Under the firm but paternalistic guidance of National Cash Register chieftain John Patterson, the Ohio city pioneered this new form of government and established a nationwide reputation as a model municipality. Though a loyal Episcopalian and longtime Sunday school superintendent, Patterson was not as concerned with personal morality as Henry Leland. The saloonkeeper and brewer were not the focus of his scorn. Rather, incompetence and inefficiency were the targets of his attacks, and his solution for the ills of the city was businesslike administration. He was, then, not an evangelist of Christian socialism like Jones, not a battler against monopoly like Johnson, not a diehard moralist like Leland. He was preeminently a businessman who believed in the efficacy of business principles. Such principles had reaped profits for National Cash Register, and they could likewise benefit Dayton.

Patterson's reform efforts dated from 1896 when he spoke before the local board of trade on the topic of "What Dayton, Ohio, Should Do to Become a Model City." His prescription for his hometown was straightforward: Place municipal affairs on "a strict business basis . . . directed, not by partisans, either Republican or Democratic, but by men who are skilled in business management and social science." In Patterson's mind, "A city is a great business enterprise whose stockholders are the people." Thus its rulers should treat the "people's money as a trust fund, to be expended wisely and economically, without waste, and for the benefit of all citizens."[99] As early as 1896, then, Patterson offered his formula for model urban government, a formula that he would endorse for the rest of his life. It included a heavy dose of expertise mixed well with a thorough application of business methods.

Dayton, however, failed to reform itself, and by 1907 Patterson was threatening to move National Cash Register to another city unless local officials promised some changes. The city council agreed to some of Patterson's demands, and the cash register company remained in Dayton.[100] Yet by 1912 Patterson was heading a committee to initiate a charter campaign. Under his guidance the committee pushed for a city manager plan of government consisting of an expert administrator appointed by a nonpartisan commission or council of five members elected at large. As early as 1908 the city council of Staunton, Virginia, had hired a general manager to administer the community's government. But as of 1912 no major city had adopted such a plan, and the notion of city manager rule was just beginning to gain national attention. Thus Patterson and his colleagues were leading their hometown into the forefront of structural reform in the nation.

Natural disaster stirred many normally cautious Daytonians to follow the daring path charted by the cash register mogul. In 1907 Patterson had complained: "[An] earthquake ought to come and stir up Dayton and make some improvement."[101] Six years later a flood instead did the job. For in March 1913 heavy rains caused the local rivers to rise and engulf the center of the city, covering Main Street with eight feet of water. Four hundred people died, and $100 million of property was lost.[102] But in the midst of the crisis Patterson took charge of relief work and demonstrated to Daytonians how one man versed in business methods could bring order out of chaos. Patterson became a local hero, and two months later his pro-manager slate swept the election for commissioners to draw up a new charter. Then in August 1913, a manager charter won voter approval by a margin of better than two to one. Local Socialists denounced the plan, claiming it imposed business rule, denied representation to working-class wards, and concentrated power in the hands of an unelected, undemocratic administrator. But a large majority of Daytonians were ready to embark on an unprecedented experiment in municipal rule.

Dayton was not the only heartland city to embrace the new mode of government. Favorable reports of the so-called Dayton Plan convinced many other communities to make the switch to expertise and supposed efficiency. By March 1920, 177 American cities had adopted city manager government, with most of the adoptions concentrated in the Midwest, South, and California. Michigan led the nation with twenty-three city manager municipalities while the Northeast lagged behind with only eighteen converts in the entire region. Three of the four city-manager municipalities of over 100,000 population were in Michigan or Ohio. Only three years after Dayton accepted the scheme, Grand Rapids did so, and Akron implemented the plan in January 1920.[103]

Thus reform enthusiasm was stirring communities across the region. The style, diagnoses, and prescriptions of the various reformers differed markedly. Pingree, Jones, and Johnson discovered the source of urban ills in corporate privilege. For Leland and Lovett the chief culprit was the cancer of moral corruption. John Patterson believed the maladies of city rule arose from a failure to apply business methods. Yet each of these figures exemplified the wave of discontent that swept the Midwest and made some of the heartland hubs inspiring archetypes for troubled cities throughout the nation. From Cleveland to Detroit stretched a reform belt that attracted the attention of all those concerned about urban government. Dayton became a model city in the eyes of devotees of efficiency and expertise. And when engaged in its crusades against boodlers and streetcar tycoons, Chicago seemed the hope of the urban world. Ideas on urban government no longer were moving only from east to west, with midwestern communities mindlessly imitating the structures and policies of their older eastern counterparts. The Midwest had become a hub of municipal innovation and a guide for cities in New York as well as California.

The Heartland of Socialism

Jones, Johnson, Leland, and Patterson were not the only Midwesterners seeking to transform municipal government into a more effective instrument for achieving the model city. Throughout the Midwest, Socialists believed that they had the solution to urban problems and sought to translate their ideas into action through victories at the polls. In one city after another, Socialists raised the banner of change and claimed that they were the best alternative to the waste, incompetence, and corruption of the past. According to these enemies of capitalism, big business was the source of the problem not the solution. The answer was to eliminate the John Pattersons and Henry Lelands rather than to give them greater control over municipal government.

Nowhere in the country did this message prove so successful at the municipal level as in the Midwest. According to the leading historian of American Socialism at the local level, "The Midwest—particularly the industrial belt running from western Pennsylvania to the Chicago-Milwaukee urban area and up through the Wisconsin lakeshore counties—seemed to produce the most solid Socialist victories." Moreover, this area "supplied the bulk of the national party leadership."[104] Contemporary observers agreed, with one knowledgeable commentator in 1911 referring to the Midwest as "the stronghold of Socialism" and the "seat of power" of foes of capitalism.[105] Eugene Debs commanded the Socialist cause from his home in Terre Haute, Indiana, and he found many of his staunchest adherents in the other industrial hubs and railroad towns of the heartland. After the November elections of 1911, Ohio ranked second among the states in number of Socialist officeholders, Wisconsin was in third place, Illinois fifth, Missouri sixth, Michigan seventh, and Indiana fifteenth. Pennsylvania had the most Socialist officials, though one political analyst claimed that the Ohio results were "socialistically much more significant" because Socialists captured more major positions in the Buckeye state and a larger portion of the victories were in urban areas rather than villages.[106] The Midwest offered the greatest opportunities for Socialists, for this region was the heartland of the cause and in the vanguard of the fight against capitalism.

This was, in part, owing to the Germanic roots of the midwestern cities. During the late nineteenth century, Central Europeans crowding into midwestern metropolises had proved ready recruits to radicalism, and their children in the early twentieth century were not reluctant to vote for the Socialist ticket in city elections. The rhetoric of Socialism did not sound so alien to German ears. Consequently, when fed up with existing conditions, the German voter more readily embraced candidates bearing the Socialist label.

Milwaukee, the most German of midwestern hubs, was the site of the greatest Socialist successes. In the Wisconsin metropolis Socialists held the mayor's seat for decades, won representation in Congress, and placed their comrades in the state legislature. By 1911 Milwaukee alone accounted for more than one-eighth of all the Socialist officeholders in the nation.[107] No other American city proved so favorable to Socialist candidates, and during the second decade of the twentieth century it appeared to be the brightest hope of the anticapitalist crusade. No longer just a beer town, Milwaukee seemingly was destined to become the model for Socialism at the municipal level.

Leading the Socialist effort in Milwaukee was Victor Berger, a German Jew born and raised in Austria-Hungary. In 1881, at the age of twenty-one, Berger came to Milwaukee, obtaining employment as a teacher of German. He had imbibed Socialist doctrine while a student at the University of Vienna and in 1893 began publication of the Socialist newspaper *Wisconsin Vorwaerts,* which became the leading organ of Milwaukee radicals. Meanwhile, an informal group of German Socialists gathered under Berger's leadership, and the radical editor also established a close relationship with local trade union chiefs. Moreover, in 1895 he visited Eugene Debs who was then in jail for his role in the Pullman Strike. According to the imprisoned Hoosier, at this time Berger "delivered the first impassioned message of socialism" Debs had ever heard and "as a souvenir of that visit" the Milwaukeean presented him with a copy of Karl Marx's *Das Kapital.*[108] On leaving prison Debs became a Socialist, founding his Social Democratic Party in Chicago in 1897. Branch One of the party, however, was in Milwaukee, and Berger was its leader.

Between 1897 and 1910 Berger's Milwaukee Socialists gradually built up support and became a model for fledgling foes of capitalism elsewhere in the nation. The Milwaukee branch was especially noteworthy for its effective organization and its results-oriented approach to the cause. Ideological feuds were minimized and the focus was on winning votes. "It is quite likely," one observer wrote, "that there is less talking and more working for Socialism in Milwaukee than anywhere else."[109] Local party leaders refused to invite speakers who had not mastered "the knack of making Socialists rather than making trouble for those who [were] Socialists."[110] Moreover, Berger continued to pursue close ties with the unions, seeking to unite all working-class interests under the Socialist umbrella. Yet Milwaukee party members did not rely on working-class consciousness alone in their pursuit of victory. Instead, they were willing to emphasize the common woes of Milwaukeeans regardless of class. In its city platforms of both 1908 and 1910, the party said of Social Democracy: "All its measures benefit not only the wage-working class, but the whole people, and while the working people are the banner bearers in this fight, in the last analysis everybody—the merchant, the professional man and the small shopkeeper—will profit thereby."[111]

In 1910 the pragmatic, inclusive approach of Milwaukee's Socialists reaped ample rewards. In the April municipal election, Socialist Emil Seidel won the mayor's office, garnering 27,622 votes compared to 20,513 for the Democratic contender and 11,262 for the Republican. Moreover, the party secured a 21-to-14 majority on the city council and an 11-to-5 edge on the county board of supervisors. The following fall Milwaukee voters also sent Victor Berger to Washington as the first Socialist Congressman. During the municipal election campaign, Republican and Democratic opponents equated Socialism with bloody revolution and claimed that Berger's followers planned to raise the "red flag of bloodlust" over city hall. The "many headed reptile of Socialism" also supposedly "threatened the home, the religious beliefs of our people and their liberty before God and man."[112] Yet thousands of Milwaukee voters failed to heed such warnings and placed their confidence in Social Democracy.

Given the moderation of the Socialist party platform in the municipal election, the predictions of chaos and revolution appeared especially unconvincing. The platform attacked trusts, a stance shared by Republicans and Democrats as well as Socialists. It also called for municipal "ownership and management of all public service enterprises," a position similar to that of Jones, Johnson, and Dunne. Moreover, the Socialists favored a "fair wage" for municipal employees, such mundane conveniences as public toilets, and such money-saving reforms as the utilization of "garbage and waste matter in a modern scientific manner" so that it would become a "source of fertility and wealth." And in a provision bound to win votes in the beer capital, the Socialist manifesto promised: "The Social-Democratic party does not intend to curtail the few amusements and places of recreation that capitalism has left the working class. The saloon is still the proletarian's club house." Attacks on the economic status quo laced the document, and the Socialists announced forthrightly: "This capitalist system not only results in untold misery and suffering, but also in crime, prostitution and corruption."[113]

Rhetoric aside, however, the actual program of the Social Democrats was not significantly more revolutionary than the proposals advocated by reformers in Toledo, Cleveland, or Chicago.

Yet the victories in 1910 were expected to be just the first step in the Socialist onslaught in America. That year Victor Berger wrote: "We must now show the people of Milwaukee and the United States that the philosophy of international Socialism can be applied and will be applied to a local situation, and that it can be applied with advantage to any American city of the present day."[114] The Wisconsin metropolis was, then, intended to be the showplace of Socialism, a visible example of the benefits flowing from the anticapitalist cause. In August 1911 Milwaukee party leaders organized a conference for Socialist mayors and aldermen from throughout the country, seeking to educate them in the problems of actual government. Moreover, a contemporary observer reported that the Milwaukee comrades were "drawing up models for work and action and . . . planning a guidebook for the use of Socialists elsewhere."[115] As forerunners in the crusade, Berger and his colleagues were charting the course for city leaders throughout the nation to follow.

Mayor Seidel's reign, however, was shortlived. In 1912 the Republicans and Democrats combined behind fusion candidate Gerhard Bading, and together the forces of the traditional parties were able to oust the Socialists from the mayor's office. Four years later Socialist Daniel W. Hoan challenged Bading, whom the leading Socialist newspaper attacked as a good mayor "for the Street Railway Company and the Manufacturers and Munitions Makers Association."[116] A majority of Milwaukee voters seemed to agree, placing Hoan in the mayor's seat. He remained there for the next twenty-four years, and his lengthy tenure reinforced Milwaukee's reputation as the capital of American Socialism.

Yet during Hoan's long tenure Milwaukee failed to become a cooperative commonwealth or a people's republic. The mayor used socialistic language; responding to a suggestion that the King of Belgium visit Milwaukee, he proclaimed: "I stand for the man who works, to hell with kings."[117] But in his own account of "the Milwaukee experiment" Hoan seemed as dedicated to "a high degree of governmental efficiency" as to the goals of social and economic equality.[118] Like more conservative reformers he boasted of honesty and the elimination of waste, but throughout his more than two decades in office the streetcar lines remained in private hands, and Milwaukee was not in the forefront of the municipal ownership of utilities. In fact, in 1922 under the leadership of multimillionaire Mayor James Couzens, one of the founders of the Ford Motor Company, Detroit became the first major city to purchase its streetcar system. A Detroit auto mogul thus proved more successful in achieving public ownership than the Milwaukee Socialists.

More radical Socialists were critical of the "sewer socialism" of the Hoan regime, regarding it as a perversion of the once-revolutionary cause. Yet during Hoan's years in office Socialists remained in the minority in the

Milwaukee city council, and the majority forces of capitalism probably would have stymied any more radical municipal program. Thus the Socialists maintained some political power in Milwaukee and achieved "good government," but they did not usher in a revolution.

During the early years of the century's second decade, however, hopes were high for Socialism at the municipal level. In 1911 Socialists elected a mayor and councilman in Canton, two councilmen in Akron, four council members in Columbus, three in Dayton, and one in Toledo. Two years later they had four seats in Akron's municipal legislature and two council positions in Toledo.[119] By 1917 the Socialists took 35 percent of the votes in Toledo's mayoral contest and secured three seats on the city council. That same year they captured 17 percent of the ballots in Evansville and won 20 percent of the votes for mayor in Fort Wayne where they also elected an alderman.[120]

One of the most promising Socialist strongholds seemed to be the automobile center of Flint. With woefully inadequate housing for workers and municipal services lagging behind the demands of the exploding population, Flint was a hotbed of discontent with many voters looking for an alternative to the two traditional parties. Local Socialists capitalized on this unhappiness by agitating among union members, bringing in out-of-town speakers, and circulating a weekly newspaper which asked workers: "Is it not about time that you woke up and demanded to be treated like men and not like beasts?"[121] In 1911 union official John Menton ran as the party's mayoral candidate on a platform calling for the "collective ownership of all means of production and distribution" and examination of "all municipal questions . . . from the standpoint of the working class, and not from the standpoint of the Capitalist class."[122] To the surprise of Socialists and non-Socialists alike, Menton won, as did three of the party's candidates for city council.

During the next year Menton and his comrades faced obstacles to overcoming the city's problems. The non-Socialist majority in the city council stymied the mayor's initiatives and refused to confirm his Socialist appointees. Budgetary constraints also kept the Socialists from constructing needed sewers or paving streets. Menton did win council approval for an eight-hour workday for municipal employees, and his administration upgraded standards of health and safety inspection in the city. But the results were not dramatic, and foes jeered at "Socialist blunders."[123]

Meanwhile, the city's business leadership mobilized to oust the feckless radicals from city hall. Thus they created the Independent Citizens Party as an opposition umbrella under which both Democrats and Republicans could congregate. Moreover, the new organization donned the popular garb of reform, claiming to be a "nonpartisan" group which promised to apply "expert knowledge" and "business system" to municipal rule.[124] For their mayoral candidate the Independent Citizens chose Charles Mott, chief of the Weston-Mott Axle Works and one of the founders of General Motors. In the ensuing campaign Mott announced that he had "no radical ideas on city government" but advocated the "public improvements" Flint so sorely needed.[125] Yet according to angry Socialists, the auto mogul was the "Flint representative of Wall Street interests."[126]

On election day Mott swept the city, leaving Menton with only 37 percent of the vote. The Independent Citizens ticket even carried the First Ward in the city's working-class North End. Mott's strongest support, however, was among the middle class, who lined up solidly behind the symbol of business success. With Democrats and Republicans combined in a "nonpartisan" assault on Socialism, Menton and his comrades were doomed. In fact, the day after the election the *Flint Journal* was already dismissing the Socialist Party as a transitional group, significant chiefly for its role in facilitating the triumph of business reform. According to the local newspaper, "The People of Flint were suffering from the hookworm in their city affairs until the Socialists pricked them and awakened the electors to the fact that Flint ought to have a business administration and an efficient city government."[127] The workers had rebelled and ironically ushered in an era of rule by General Motors.

Elsewhere in the Midwest foes of socialism were adopting the same tactic to halt the wave of radicalism. As already noted, Republicans and Democrats united in Milwaukee to keep Socialist Emil Seidel from winning a second term. Moreover, in 1912 the state legislature mandated nonpartisan elections for Milwaukee, seemingly in an effort to diffuse the Socialist threat. Henceforth, Republicans and Democrats would not offer competing slates in the Wisconsin metropolis. Instead, Socialists faced nonpartisan contenders who drew both Republican and Democratic votes. As early as 1911 "progressive contingents" of Republicans and Democrats had joined forces in Columbus, Ohio, in a united challenge to the radical tide. "Unless something of a drastic nature is done, at once," a Columbus capitalist warned, "the Socialists will elect a mayor next fall."[128]

Meanwhile, in Dayton a restructuring of government answered the need to contain Socialism. At the beginning of the century's second decade, Socialists seemed destined to seize power in the Ohio city, and in 1910 a local newspaper warned it was "high time for some citizens, some businessmen, some newspapers, to awaken to a realization of danger," or Dayton might "follow the example of Milwaukee."[129] The two traditional parties did not form an alliance, but John Patterson's city manager plan kept the Socialists from office. Under the new scheme, at-large contests replaced ward-based elections. Socialists, however, could win majorities only in working-class wards; they could not carry the city as a whole. In the first election after adoption of the new charter, a nonpartisan "Citizens" slate captured all the seats on the governing commission, and the Socialists were shut out. Patterson himself was not an unbending foe of the Socialist Party. Each year he purchased subscriptions to the local party newspaper for his corporate headquarters and also bought full-page advertising space in the radical journal for National Cash Register products. At his death the Socialist newspaper praised him as "a progressive and a liberal" and claimed that local residents owed "Mr. Patterson a debt of gratitude for having made Dayton a better place in which to live."[130] Yet Patterson's political handiwork seemed to spell death to the local Socialist cause.

Dayton Socialists, however, were not willing to pass away without a fight. In the 1917 primary the Socialist ticket outpolled both the Citizens and Democratic slates and won almost half the votes cast. The ensuing run-off election between the Socialists and Citizens proved a bitter contest in which friends of the "nonpartisan" ticket attacked Socialists for the antiwar stance of their national leaders. The *Dayton Daily News* indicted the Socialists as "the party of pro-Germanism" whose leaders wanted "to see the Kaiser become the emperor of the world." "No man who believes in the principles of democracy can conscientiously vote the Socialist ticket," the Democratic newspaper editorialized, "for every Socialist ballot that is cast at this time becomes A BULLET FIRED AT AN AMERICAN SOLDIER."[131] On election day such diatribes took their toll. The Socialists lost with 43 percent of the vote. They did well in the city's German wards where antiwar sentiment was not unpopular but failed miserably in middle-class neighborhoods.

In 1921 Dayton Socialists were still able to capture 45 percent of the local vote, but five years later they attracted less than 10 percent of the ballots. By 1923 financial difficulties forced the party to sell its Socialist Hall to the Ku Klux Klan, and in 1924 the local party newspaper ceased publication.[132] Within less than a decade Dayton's Socialist movement retreated from the threshold of power, becoming a minor outcast on the local political scene.

Throughout the Midwest the Socialist heyday was shortlived. Charges of anti-Americanism appeared to hurt the Socialists in some communities during World War I and its aftermath, though among German-Americans the antiwar stance of the national party leadership was less repugnant than among voters of British ancestry. More importantly midwestern Socialists seemed better able to arouse class consciousness among the business class than among the workers. When the Socialist threat became apparent, business leaders and middle-class voters rallied to the capitalist cause, thwarting the radicals through fusion tickets and structural reforms. Working-class Midwesterners never seemed as united or mobilized in favor of Socialism as the middle class was in opposition. Moreover, in a number of communities, Socialist electoral triumphs reflected dissatisfaction with the status quo and a simple desire for reform rather than dedication to the Socialist manifesto. For example, one observer said of an Ohio Socialist victory: "It was a rebuke to the mayor . . . for the manner in which he had conducted the affairs of the office and a warning to the immoral not to try to get a position of public trust here, and a declaration that the hands of a clean man will be upheld regardless of his politics."[133] Thus reform-minded coalitions readily undermined the Socialists by offering clean, honest, and efficient government without the troubling radical rhetoric of the party comrades. If the voters wanted only reform, capitalists could offer it as readily as Socialists.

In the end, socialism failed to develop deep roots in the Midwest. Among voters educated in Central Europe it struck appealing chords, but for those imbued with the midwestern political ethos its message sounded off key. The egalitarianism permeating midwestern political mythology was the egalitarianism of Lincoln. It rebelled at privilege but cherished the individual pursuit of success, the rise from log cabin to White House. By the 1940s Milwaukee's Mayor Hoan had left the Socialist fold, and his friend and successor as mayor, Frank Zeidler, attributed this defection to "dissatisfaction with some of the national leadership" and to Hoan's "orientation toward Lincoln as an ideal."[134] Likewise, the poet Carl Sandburg had been a confirmed Socialist and served as Mayor Emil Seidel's private secretary. But after his Milwaukee sojourn Sandburg's devotion to democracy and "the people" led him from Socialism to the study of Lincoln, resulting in a six-volume biography of the rail-splitter.[135] For Sandburg and Hoan as well as for most other Midwesterners, Lincoln ultimately had more appeal than Marx. In the heartland an amalgam of egalitarianism and individual opportunity won more votes than the promises of proletarian triumph.

The Urban Laboratory

Not only were midwestern cities experimenting with everything from socialism to city manager rule, they also served as laboratories for social programs aimed at quelling class conflict and improving the lives of workers. Chicago was especially notable as a center of social experimentation. As the site of the Haymarket Riot and the Pullman Strike, the Windy City was notorious for its class strife and social unrest. Nowhere in the late nineteenth century were strikes more costly or more violent. Therefore Chicago seemed particularly in need of measures aimed at healing the wounds in the social structure. By the turn of the century the fast-growing metropolis of the Midwest was not simply the most spectacular monument to the success of American business; it was also a textbook case of the ills plaguing capitalist society.

Chicago's chief social reform figure was Jane Addams. Though Addams's Hull House was not the first social settlement in America, it was, the most famous and, owing to her writings, the best publicized. Founded in 1889, Hull House was a community center and an oasis of middle-class amenities in the immigrant slums of Chicago's near west side. It sponsored clubs for neighborhood residents, conducted a kindergarten, and operated a coffeehouse, a gymnasium, and an art gallery. Moreover, the settlement house offered classes in everything from Dante and Browning to cooking and millinery. An average of two thousand people each day took advantage of its facilities, seeking something better than the tenement or the saloon could provide. According to Addams, the complex of buildings known as Hull

House was a concrete statement to the often indifferent citizens of Chicago "that education and recreation ought to be extended to the immigrants."[136]

Addams, however, not only regarded the settlement house as a tool for helping the poor, it also was a means of enlightening the well-to-do. Middle-class men and women lived at Hull House and mixed with their less affluent neighbors. By extending their hands across the social gap separating the comfortable and the needy, these middle-class settlement house residents would supposedly acquire an understanding of the demands and concerns of the immigrant poor. In Addams's words, Hull House "was soberly opened on the theory that the dependence of classes on each other is reciprocal."[137] Neither class could profitably stand alone in hostile opposition to the other. Instead, each would benefit from building bridges across the yawning social chasm. Through class mixing, then, both elements of society would gain and overcome the dangerous rifts so evident in strike-ridden Chicago.

Yet clubs, games, and interclass conviviality alone would not heal the shattered city. Seeking to harness the power of the state in aid of the poor, Hull House residents became leading agitators for reform legislation and political change. Addams herself observed: "The policy of the public authorities of never taking an initiative, and always waiting to be urged to do their duty, is obviously fatal in a neighborhood where there is little initiative among the citizens."[138] Recognizing this, Hull House residents felt compelled to take the initiative on behalf of the immigrant poor and to force government officials to act. Thus Addams became garbage inspector for the ward, securing the removal of layers of refuse from some neglected streets and endeavoring to eliminate dead animal carcasses from all the neighborhood's thoroughfares. In addition, Hull House led an abortive effort to unseat the corrupt ward alderman, engaging in the rough and tumble of local politics. Addams claimed that during one campaign she "received many anonymous letters—those from the men often obscene, those from the women revealing that curious connection between prostitution and the lowest type of politics which every city tries in vain to hide."[139] Meanwhile, Hull House residents battled for passage and enforcement of an adequate child labor law and legislation limiting the working hours of women. Reflecting standards of morality characteristic of the age, Addams recited the experience of one "working girl" who craved "a drink to dispel her lassitude before her tired feet should take the long walk home" and "had thus been decoyed into a saloon" where she was given "knockout drops" and later "awoke in a disreputable rooming house—too frightened and disgraced to return to her mother." "Long and exhausting hours of work," Addams concluded sadly, "are almost sure to be followed by lurid and exciting pleasures."[140]

Underlying Addams's efforts was a firm belief in the Lincoln ideal that she shared with many of her midwestern contemporaries. Born in a small Illinois town west of Rockford, Addams became a Lincoln worshipper in childhood and devoted an entire chapter of her autobiography to the influ-

ence of the martyred president on her life and work. "In our early effort at
Hull-House to hand on to our neighbors whatever of help we had found for
ourselves," Addams wrote, "we made much of Lincoln."[141] She especially
emphasized how "he never forgot how the plain people in Sangamon County
thought and felt."[142] Though he rose to the highest office in the nation,
Lincoln was a man without social class who achieved the pinnacle of success
yet remained basically one of the common people. He was, then, the personification of the supposedly classless, socially undifferentiated Midwest of
Addams's childhood. Though from a wealthy family, Addams characterized
herself as "a western American who had been born in a rural community
where the early pioneer life had made social distinctions impossible."[143] At
Hull House she sought to overcome the social distinctions purportedly bred
in the industrial city and regain the Lincolnian democracy of the bygone
pioneer Midwest. For Addams, like Jones, Hoan, and Sandburg, Lincoln was
the personification of heartland democracy, and like her fellow midwestern
reformers she sought to transplant the Lincoln ideal in the troubled city.

To aid in the battle for urban democracy, however, social settlements also
turned to social scientific research. Many of the middle-class residents were
students at nearby universities who viewed settlement houses as their windows onto the working-class world. Hull House especially took a lead in
early research on slum dwellers, with settlement house residents dishing out
tea and sympathy to the less fortunate and receiving hard data on deficient
plumbing in return. During the 1890s and the early twentieth century, Chicago, in fact, became renowned as a center for social investigation, a mecca
for those seeking to engage in "scientific" study of the roots of urban ills.

Jane Addams and Hull House were not solely responsible for this reputation for social research and experimentation. Of equal significance was the
University of Chicago. Founded in 1892 to serve as a center of Baptist higher
education in the area west of the Appalachians, the University of Chicago
soon veered toward the course of secular evangelism. At the young university, scholars worked with Christian zeal to solve the problems of the world
not through prayer but through "objective" study and research. Like any
Baptist preacher, they realized salvation was possible, but statistical data and
scholarly papers were the bread and wine of their communion. Moreover, the
class-divided, strife-torn city of Chicago provided an ideal setting for their
endeavors. Nowhere were the examples of social sin more prevalent; nowhere could the blessings of social research prove more valuable.

Imbued with such a spirit, the university could boast of the nation's first
department of sociology. Heading it was Albion Small, a Baptist clergyman
turned professor and true believer in the healing properties of social research. In Small's mind sociologists not only needed to investigate but also
to apply their knowledge to the problems of the world. Small founded the
first sociological journal in the United States, *The American Journal of
Sociology,* and in its first volume he stated his activist manifesto: "I would
have [American scholars], repeal the law of custom which bars marriage

of thought with action. I would have them become more profoundly and sympathetically scholarly by enriching the wisdom which comes from knowing with the larger wisdom which comes from doing."[144] Small's colleagues at the University of Chicago agreed. "To assist us in the difficult task of adjustment to new situations," wrote a particularly religious Chicago sociologist in 1899, "God has providentially wrought out for us the social sciences and placed them at our disposal."[145]

Students and faculty alike recognized that God and humanity had made Chicago fertile ground for scholarly activists seeking to investigate the problems of industrial America. In 1893 Small's department of sociology boasted: "The city of Chicago is one of the most complete social laboratories in the world. . . . No city in the world presents a wider variety of typical social problems than Chicago."[146] Only a streetcar ride from Hull House, the University of Chicago was at the very hub of social reform excitement in the nation. Moreover, in 1894 a campus group known as the Christian Union decided to create another "laboratory of social service in the city," founding the University of Chicago Settlement.[147] Located in Chicago's stockyards district, like Hull House this adjunct of the university sought to create social unity in the divided metropolis. The "Young Citizen's Creed" of the university settlement began with the affirmation: "We believe that God hath made of one blood nations of men, and that we are His children, brothers and sisters all."[148] The head of the university settlement, Mary McDowell, was a product of the rural Midwest and like Addams was, in the words of her biographer, influenced by "the idealism with which she regarded Lincoln."[149] Deeply troubled by the Pullman Strike, McDowell claimed that incident "was only typical of a great world unrest which *must* be understood."[150] During the following decades, she and the students of Albion Small sought that understanding through the lessons taught at the settlement.

McDowell's settlement and Small's sociology department were not the only branches of the University of Chicago dedicated to social reform. Instead, the spirit of social activism and problem solving infected one department after another. While serving at Chicago between 1894 and 1904, the head of the combined department of philosophy and pedagogy, John Dewey, formulated his highly influential theories of progressive education, which he applied at the university's Laboratory School. In the political science department Professor Charles Merriam was not simply studying government but also engaging in it. He first chaired the committee on revenue and taxation of the City Charter Commission and then in 1909 won a seat on the city council. After two years as a reform alderman, Merriam ran as Republican candidate for mayor, losing the contest with 44 percent of the ballots. In 1909 Merriam noted: "The modern university has something which the community, including the business world, ought to know about and make use of."[151] Both Dewey and Merriam were attempting to tear the veil of ivy from the university and make sure the community knew about and used the knowledge generated by professors.

Two female Ph.Ds from the University of Chicago were attempting to do likewise. In the winter Sophonisba Breckinridge taught in the university's Department of Household Administration but over summer breaks she resided at Hull House. Her friend Edith Abbott was a part-time instructor in the sociology department and lived permanently at the famed social settlement. Both were scholars, but their residence at Hull House demonstrated that neither yearned for an ivory tower. Attributing to Breckinridge goals that also applied to herself, Abbott wrote of her colleague: "She [was] eager to do something that was really useful and unwilling to be absorbed into the quiet academic life."[152] With a commitment to objective investigation as well as social reform, they not only taught at the university but also associated themselves with an independent social work training institution, the Chicago School of Civics and Philanthropy. At this school they pioneered academic training in social work and conducted a series of influential investigations of such urban problems as slum housing, delinquent children, and truancy. In 1920 Breckinridge and Abbott finally secured the long-sought goal of affiliating their training academy with the University of Chicago. Renamed the School of Social Service Administration, it was the first graduate school in social work supported by a leading research university.

Abbott, Breckinridge, Merriam, Dewey, McDowell, and Small all believed that through research social scientists could discover the means for taming the brawling city. Together with Jane Addams they made Chicago a center of social reform activism and the city's chief university a model for the pragmatic pursuit of learning. In addition, they laid the groundwork for the world-famous "Chicago School" of sociology which developed during the 1920s under the renowned Robert Park. Urban sociology was as much a product of Chicago as were skyscrapers and farm machinery. Whereas Tom Johnson's Cleveland was a city on a hill for municipal reformers and Victor Berger's Milwaukee was the brightest hope for American Socialists, Jane Addams and her satellites at the University of Chicago were an inspiration for social reformers throughout the nation. By the second decade of the twentieth century, Chicago was an urban laboratory without peer.

Elsewhere in the Midwest social reformers followed the shining example of Jane Addams. Every major city had at least one settlement house which sought to narrow the gap between social classes and provide a better understanding of urban ills. In Milwaukee's Polish district the Wisconsin University Settlement endeavored "to carry on the usual lines of social settlement work and to furnish a sociological laboratory for the University of Wisconsin." According to its statement of purpose, "The settlement stands for neighborliness in the midst of crowded city conditions where the word 'neighbor' too often means less than it should."[153] Cleveland's Hiram House was founded in 1896 by students from Hiram College who intended the settlement "to become part of the life of its own ward becoming so by personal helpfulness."[154] A few years later the city's most famous multimillionaire, John D. Rockefeller, provided the money for Alta House, a settlement specifically for children. "May the spirit of the Christ Child dwell within this house, built primarily for the children," wrote Rockefeller at the time of the settlement's dedication ceremony, "and may that same spirit of love go out with each one who passes through its doors and be broadly disseminated in the surrounding homes."[155] Meanwhile, in Indianapolis the Flanner Guild was a settlement "for the industrial and moral uplift of colored girls and boys."[156] Some settlements were for blacks and others were for Poles; some emphasized sociological investigation and others the dissemination of the spirit of the Christ child. Yet all aimed to correct the flaws in the urban social fabric. Throughout the Midwest well-to-do and middle-income urbanites perceived troubling rents in that fabric, and like Jane Addams they felt compelled to attempt repairs.

Yet none of the heartland hubs rivaled Chicago as a laboratory for social experimentation. Nor did Philadelphia, Boston, or even New York City. Chicago was home of the most famous social settlement, the first department of sociology, the first sociology journal, and the first graduate program in social work at a major university. Just as Detroit was leading the nation in industrial technology, Toledo and Cleveland in municipal renewal, and Dayton in manager rule, Chicago was in the vanguard of social research and reform.

5.

In the Cultural Vanguard

In 1893 the World's Columbian Exposition opened in Chicago amid great hoopla. Intended to commemorate the four-hundredth anniversary of Columbus's landing in America, in fact it was more a celebration of Chicago's arrival among the ranks of the world's great cities than a tribute to the exploits of the Italian explorer. Known popularly as the Chicago World's Fair, it focused the world's attention on the Windy City and that never-bashful city showed all humanity that it was truly a magnificent metropolis. Everyone had known of its exploits as a meat packer, but now Chicago presented itself as a hub of culture and enlightenment. The fair's ensemble of gleaming white neoclassical buildings and monumental sculpture awed and thrilied millions of visitors. One critic told prospective fairgoers: "You will behold a sight which . . . has not been paralleled since the Rome of the emperors stood intact."[1] Proclaimed by another author "the most beautiful piece of architecture in the world," the art building contained eighty galleries as well as 108 alcoves for the exhibition of paintings from sixteen nations.[2] Moreover, the world congresses held in association with the fair attracted participants from every continent who delivered a total of 5,978 speeches or papers on every topic from "Women's Progress" to "Commerce and Finance" to "Sunday Rest."[3] For the six months of its existence, Chicago's exposition seemed the culmination of world civilization. An English novelist concluded: "Art and Music and Poetry belong to Chicago; the Hub of the Universe is transferred from Boston to Chicago."[4]

But once the fair closed, Chicago did not return to its unrefined groove and eschew art and literature for hog butchering and grain handling. Instead, the fair marked the beginning of an era of aesthetic innovation in the midwestern metropolis during which Chicago would take its place in the cultural vanguard of the nation and the world. For decades a sense of cultural inferiority had plagued Midwesterners who were ever doubtful of their region's ability to foster art and literature. During the antebellum era, sculptor Hiram Powers had abandoned Cincinnati for Florence, responding to the common prejudice that Tuscany could nurture artistic achievement whereas Ohio was good only for corn. After the Civil War both Cincinnati and Chicago had fought to secure the services of that missionary of highbrow music Theodore Thomas; if dubbed by his baton, a city supposedly would no longer be a porkopolis but a true metropolis. During the quarter century following the Columbian Exposition, however, many Midwesterners, most notably Chicagoans, recognized that the interior valley no longer needed to follow the cultural lead of the Atlantic seaboard and Europe. As the fair had proven, Chicago was a hub of brains as well as brawn destined to assume a leading place in the world of ideas as well as industry.

In the fields of architecture and literature, some Chicagoans not only rejected long-standing obeisance to Europe and the Atlantic seaboard but also rebelled against the artistic conventions of the traditional cultural centers. For these innovators the newness of Chicago and its removal from the cultural capitals of the past were not shortcomings but assets. In fact, many of the post-fair generation found fertile ground in the Midwest for a new aesthetic. They claimed to take their inspiration from the previously ignored beauty of the surrounding prairies, from the democratic idealism of the land of Lincoln, and from the material grit of the midwestern metropolis. Italy and New England were not the crucibles of culture for these Midwesterners. Instead, they turned to that epitome of freshness and modernity, Chicago.

The World's Fair was, then, the overture for a new age of cultural self-confidence during which Chicago transformed American planning, architecture, and literature. In 1893 the Windy City loudly proclaimed that it was a fresh force to be reckoned with, culturally as well as economically. Throughout the following quarter century, it would reiterate this proclamation, making the rest of the world take notice.

The New World of City Planning

What most impressed visitors to the world's fair was the White City, the collection of domed and pillared structures that housed the exhibits. Not simply the architecture of the individual buildings excited them but also the harmonious and complementary arrangement of the structures around the exposition's great Court of Honor. At the outset of construction, the fair's various architects had agreed to conform generally to classical guidelines and to maintain a uniform cornice line sixty feet about the ground. The resulting sense of unity contrasted markedly with the individualistic hodge-podge characteristic of the late nineteenth-century city where fifteen-story office towers abutted aging two-story commercial blocks and the rugged brown masonry of a Romanesque revival hulk stood next to a white, marble-sheathed Second Empire extravaganza. A leading architectural critic contended that the success of the fair was "a success of unity, a triumph of ensemble. The whole is better than any of its parts and greater than all its parts, and its effect is one and indivisible."[5] Another visitor to the exposition asked "Were ever composition, arrangement, variety, unity—those principles invoked by the artist in the creation of his canvas, and by the architect in the erection of his building—were ever these principles applied on so gigantic a scale?"[6] In an age of chaotic urban development, the White City seemed a marvel of harmony and order.

In fact, perhaps the fair's greatest impact was on American ideas about planning and the grouping of buildings. Chicago architect Peter Wight said of the exposition; "It will teach us that the beauty of our cities can be enhanced as much by careful consideration of the relation between building and building as by the superior excellence of individual but adjacent structures."[7] A decade after the fair's closing, a University of Chicago professor likewise contended: "The White City was . . . a prophecy of what we could do if we . . . added to individual excellence a common purpose."[8] According to these observers and many others, Chicago's exposition clearly demonstrated the advantages of cooperation and planning. For decades before 1893 park planners and local improvement associations had been laying the foundation of an urban planning movement.[9] But the Chicago World's Fair was a concrete embodiment of all that planning could achieve, and advocates of urban beautification repeatedly appealed to memories of its magnificence. The lesson of the fair was simple: rampant individualism bred ugliness; planning produced beauty.

One person who could not forget this lesson was the fair's chief of construction, Chicago architect Daniel Burnham. During the remaining two decades of his life he was to become the leading figure in American urban planning and was to pioneer comprehensive planning on a metropolitan scale. Throughout the first years of the twentieth century cities across the nation sought his services, aiming to achieve beautification through planning. Moreover, Burnham became known as the chief figure in the City Beautiful movement, which sought the transformation of the city through the creation of neoclassical civic centers, park systems, tree-lined boulevards and plazas with fountains and statuary. This Chicagoan was the spearhead of a cause spreading throughout the country, and because of him, the Windy City captured the attention of Americans entranced by the possibilities of urban planning.

Cleveland, however, was the first heartland city to take advantage of Burnham's planning talents in an attempt to recreate the beauty of the World's Fair. In 1895 the newly founded Cleveland Architectural Club, "inspired by the fine groups of buildings displayed at the Chicago Exposition," called upon architects to submit plans to a competition for the "grouping of Cleveland's public buildings."[10] This contest produced no immediate action toward the creation of such a grouping, but it aroused some local interest, and by the close of the decade the Chamber of Commerce had taken up the cause and appointed a Grouping Plan Committee. According to local boosters, the harmonious grouping of the city hall, county courthouse, public library, and post office would enhance Cleveland's reputation as a city on the cutting edge of urban beautification. "How would she [Cleveland] be known," asked one Clevelander in 1899, "if she were to so plan her coming public buildings as to present the eye of the traveller a reality, in imperishable material, of the past Court of Honor at the World's Fair." According to this proud citizen, "She would be known as the only city in the United States, having such an opportunity to grasp its import, to so wisely read the signs of the times, to see the necessity of solving the problem in no other way to meet the progress of the world."[11]

Mayor Tom Johnson heartily agreed, throwing his full support behind the Group Plan. He secured state legislation authorizing an expert commission to advise Cleveland on the planning of the proposed civic center. One of the three comissioners was Daniel Burnham, and together with his two colleagues, architects John Carrère and Arnold Brunner, he drew up a plan which they presented in 1903. The plan arranged Cleveland's public buildings around a grand mall, 560 feet wide, with sculpture-laden fountains at either end of this esplanade. A monumental rail depot was to stand at the head of the mall; thus the beautiful civic center would become the doorway to the city for visitors arriving by train. The commission also recommended that all the buildings be constructed of the same material, have a uniform height and width, and that the design of the structures be derived from "the historic motives of the classic architecture of Rome."[12] Harmony and compatibility were the desired goals. According to the commissioners, "The jumble of buildings that surrounds us in our new cities contributes nothing valuable to life; on the contrary, it sadly disturbs our peacefulness and destroys that repose within us that is the true basis of all contentment." "Let the public authorities, therefore, set an example of simplicity and uniformity," said Burnham and his colleagues, "not necessarily producing monotony, but, on the contrary, resulting in beautiful designs entirely harmonious with each other."[13] The civic center was, then, intended to be a lesson to private developers in the Ohio metropolis. The commissioners concluded: "An example of order, system and reserve, such as is possible here, will be for Cleveland what the Court of Honor of 1893 was for the entire country, and the influence will be felt in all subsequent building operations, both public and private."[14]

Johnson and his followers enthusiastically embraced the commissioners' scheme, and throughout the country critics commended Cleveland's municipal leaders for once again taking their place in the forefront of American urban development. One observer told Clevelanders: "You are fifty years ahead of most cities."[15] Another noted that "in addition to being one of the best governed cities in America," Cleveland was "fulfilling the dreams of its most altruistic inhabitants in carrying out a line of public improvements remarkable for their plan and scope."[16] In 1904 a national magazine praised Cleveland for pioneering "a new conception of the municipality." "Here is a city among the most radical in its democratic tendencies of any in the country," observed the periodical, "courageously authorizing the expenditure of from ten to fifteen million dollars in the development of an idea."[17]

In fact, the civic center was an integral part of the new vision of the municipality that was being tested in Johnson's Cleveland. Johnson and his followers were fighting what they perceived to be the individualistic avarice of streetcar magnates and corrupt councilmen. In their minds the city was

not an arena for the no-holds-barred pursuit of wealth but a community
where cooperative effort would ensure a better life for all people. The streetcars were to be the people's property, and the parks were to be a communal
backyard rather than pristine domains protected by "Keep Off the Grass"
signs. The civic center was the keystone of this vision. Its mall provided
a communal space for civic celebrations and its uniform cornice line and
harmonious design symbolized the rejection of individualism and competition. Johnson's disciple Frederic Howe wrote of his "architectonic vision of
what a city might be." "It was not economy, efficiency, and business methods
that interested me so much," Howe claimed, "as a city planned, built and
conducted as a community enterprise."[18] The Cleveland civic center was a
model of such a city. It was the physical embodiment of community enterprise. Though its architecture reflected a conservative devotion to the classical, its underlying plan expressed the democratic idealism of Cleveland's
reformers.

Cleveland's leaders only slowly realized the civic center plan, the federal
building being completed in 1910, the county courthouse two years later,
and the city hall in 1916; a grand railroad depot never was to grace the
mall. Meanwhile, Burnham was drafting plans for cities as far afield as San
Francisco and Manila. His greatest achievement, however, was his comprehensive plan for Chicago. Burnham had long dreamed of replanning his
hometown, and as early as 1897 he asked assembled business leaders,
"Should we not without delay do something competent to beautify and make
our city attractive?" Appealing to the assembly of mercenary minds, Burnham concluded on a practical note: "Beauty has always paid better than any
other commodity and always will."[19] According to novelist Hamlin Garland,
six years later Burnham spent a summer afternoon in the country regaling
his friends with "his vision of a great front park, harbors and lagoons, . . .
the civic centers and the great architectural plazas which were component
parts of his design." "It is all too fine, too splendid to come in our day,"
thought the skeptical Garland.[20]

Yet by the close of the first decade of the twentieth century, Burnham had
embodied his ideas in a formal published plan, and neither the city of Chicago nor urban America as a whole was ever the same again. In 1907 Chicago's prestigious Commercial Club commissioned Burnham and his
assistant Edward Bennett to prepare a plan of the metropolis, and after two
years of work they completed a sumptuous volume containing 142 illustrations depicting the Windy City as it could be. Burnham's oft-repeated credo
asserted: "Make no little plans; they have no magic to stir men's blood. . . .
Make big plans . . . remembering that a noble, logical diagram once recorded will never die, but long after we are gone will be a living thing, as-
serting itself with ever-growing intensity."[21] His plan for Chicago certainly
lived up to his belief in the grand scheme, for his scope was broad and
audacious. Burnham and Bennett did not confine themselves to the bound-

aries of Chicago itself, but provided a blueprint for future development for the entire region within a sixty-mile radius of the downtown Loop. From Kenosha, Wisconsin, on the north to Michigan City, Indiana, on the south, Burnham's plan outlined a regional network of highways, parkways, and forest preserves that would supposedly serve the needs of coming decades.

Within the city itself Burnham's plan reserved the lakefront for parkland, envisioning the creation of a communal front lawn for Chicago's residents. From Jackson Park on the south through Grant Park in the core of the city and Lincoln Park on the north side to the suburb of Wilmette, a green strand was to stretch twenty-five miles along the shores of Lake Michigan. Burnham's plan also suggested the broadening of certain existing streets and the creation of new diagonal boulevards. A number of these grand avenues were to radiate from a monumental civic center on the near west side where a giant domed city hall would symbolize the grandeur of Burnham's rebuilt city. Moreover, Burnham's vision of a perfect Chicago included a uniform cornice line, and in the plan's illustrations blocks of buildings of identical height extended off into the distance.

On a more practical note, the plan sought to cope with the city's transportation problems. According to Burnham, "Separate [rail] roads operating separate and independent rights of way to the separate and independent freight houses cannot do the work." Consequently, his plan proposed the development of "one common system for the handling of freight—a traffic clearing house."[22] Besides the central shared freight yard, Burnham urged the construction of three union passenger terminals to supplant the six existing depots and thereby ensure a more orderly and convenient transfer of people as well as freight.

Though it was to be criticized for its indifference to the problems of housing the poor and the miseries of slum life, Burnham's scheme was not oblivious to the social divisions tearing the city apart. In fact, in Burnham's mind beauty could tame the beast of social unrest, and his parks and boulevards, therefore, could be as efficacious in healing the wounds of class and ethnic conflict as Jane Addams's social settlements. In the 1890s he told the Merchants' Club that through a scheme of civic improvements and beautification Chicagoans would be taking "a long step towards cementing together the heterogeneous elements of our population, and towards assimilating the million and a half of people . . . who were not here some fifteen years ago."[23] The Chicago Plan's introduction likewise noted that the time had come "to bring order out of chaos incident to rapid growth, and especially to the influx of people of many nationalities without common traditions or habits of life."[24] Urban parks supposedly would offer an elixir to both the body and spirit of working-class Chicagoans, and the beauty of the renewed metropolis would engender a common civic pride that would cut across class lines and unite the fragmented urban society in a shared devotion to the city. According to Burnham, "Good citizenship is the prime object of good city planning."²⁵ In other words, planning was not simply intended to apply a more attractive veneer on the physical city; it was meant to redeem the souls of urbanites.

Even before it was published, Burnham's schemes for urban redemption won praise, and in the years following its presentation the plan received added applause. Anticipating the plan's appearance, in 1908 Professor Graham Romeyn Taylor wrote: "Chicago is now within a very few months of arriving at the precise moment which ushers in a new epoch in the city's history." According to Taylor, the "dawning realization that the future Chicago" might permanently wear "the mantle of 1893" had "taken form in a magnificent working plan and a powerful movement which every day gain[ed] momentum toward a glorious achievement."²⁶ In Germany Kaiser Wilhelm was also impressed. In 1911 the Berlin correspondent of a Chicago newspaper reported that the emperor was "thoroughly stirred up by the plans for the improvement and beautification of Chicago," and had "appointed a commission to prepare a similar plan for the city of Berlin." The Kaiser supposedly "declared several times that the Burnham plans were the most perfect and satisfactory that he had ever seen."²⁷

If local leaders were going to translate Burnham's ideas into actual improvements, however, they had to convince Chicago's citizenry and not just foreign potentates. With this in mind, the newly created Chicago Plan Commission hired Walter D. Moody to publicize and promote the plan. A former traveling salesman, Moody turned his considerable talents to "the scientific promotion of scientific planning."²⁸ Thus he prepared a ninety-page booklet titled *Chicago's Greatest Issue: An Official Plan* and distributed it free of charge to over 165,000 of the city's residents. Moreover, he sought to influence Chicago's children by introducing the study of city planning in the public schools. Burnham himself had said, "Children must grow up dreaming of a beautiful city," and Moody prepared a textbook that was intended to inspire such dreams.²⁹ This hustler for civic improvements also gave slide lectures on the plan to an estimated 175,000 people and prepared a film on the Burnham scheme which premiered in 1915 and played in fifty Chicago-area theaters. In 1919 Moody even had one Sunday designated "Plan of Chicago Sunday" and urged Chicago's clergy to preach on the merits of comprehensive planning.³⁰ "City planning work in all its practical essentials," Moody wrote, "is a work of promotion—salesmanship."³¹ During the second decade of the twentieth century, Moody forcefully demonstrated what he meant by these words.

Moody's efforts reaped some success. Chicagoans largely carried out Burnham's plans for a green lakefront and an outlying ring of forest preserves. In addition, the city implemented some of the proposals for street improvements, broadening Twelfth Street (later Roosevelt Road), extending Michigan Avenue northward, and constructing Wacker Drive along the river's banks. Yet the civic center remained an unrealized dream, and the city never constructed a grand plaza with radiating boulevards on the near west side. Moreover, Chicago's jagged skyline survived, the very antithesis of Burnham's utopia of uniform cornice lines.

These failures meant that Chicago would remain characteristically midwestern rather than a replica of Paris. Some commentators have criticized Burnham's reliance on European models, especially the Paris created by Baron Haussmann under Emperor Napoleon III. In fact, a leading planning historian has referred to Burnham's ideal Chicago as the "Haussmannized capital of the Middle West."[32] Indeed, Burnham's dream city was imitative rather than indigenous to the Midwest. Yet much of the plan was pure Chicago. Its very breadth and ambition was sure to appeal to boasting Chicago leaders who conceived of their city as the capital of audacity. When Burnham advised against making little plans, he was expressing not only a personal credo but the philosophy of his hometown as well. Moreover, the plan's concern about disorder and social fragmentation reflected Chicago's breakneck growth, polyglot population, and violent class conflict. Burnham recognized that this was the city of Haymarket and Pullman. And the plan commission's sales campaign distinguished democratic Chicago from the Paris of the Napoleons. In Chicago the business elite had to sell its plan to the people; no emperor could impose it. As Walter Moody well recognized, heartland urban planning drew on the merchandising skills of Sears, Roebuck as well as the aesthetic judgments of architects. Midwesterners huckstered public policy just as they sold Model T Fords.

Many Chicagoans succumbed readily to Moody's sales pitch, for during the early twentieth century Burnham and his accomplices were not the only Windy City residents eager to beautify their hometown. Writing of Chicago's "municipal art" movement, in 1905 one author claimed: "The civic conscience has awakened and the same lively enthusiasm that led to the building of a world city . . . is displaying itself in an effort to make the city a better place in which to live."[33] Eight years later Hamlin Garland observed that Daniel Burnham "and his laborers were . . . only a part of the story of Chicago's civic awakening" and wrote of "the new spirit which pervade[d] the city."[34] In other words, Burnham's work reflected the thinking of thousands of Chicagoans who shared his dream of recreating the White City on a permanent basis. While Burnham and the Chicago Plan Commission were formulating and selling their grand scheme, with less fanfare the city's Municipal Art League was seeking support for public sculpture as well as battling against the palls of smoke polluting urban skies and the ugly billboards blighting Chicago's landscape. A godsend for the league's cause was the wealthy lumber dealer B. F. Ferguson. When he died in 1905, Ferguson bequeathed a fund of $1 million, the income from which was to be spent for "the erection and maintenance of enduring statuary and monuments . . . in the parks, along the boulevards or in other public places, within the city of Chicago."[35] Like Burnham and the art league, Ferguson believed in uplifting his hometown through civic beautification and creation of a city that approximated the ideal of 1893.

Though Chicago was in the forefront of the new planning efforts and Cleveland could claim the first civic center, residents in other heartland cities shared the sentiments of Ferguson and Burnham. Urbanites throughout the Midwest felt that their cities had reached a new level of maturity that demanded a higher standard of civic life. The nascent frontier stage had passed, as had the decades of adolescent industrialization when the cities grew by leaps and bounds without sufficient thought of their future. Now the heartland hubs were large and prosperous and had the resources to garb themselves in amenities more suitable to their new station among the nation's cities. They needed refinements worthy of their rank but which also would engender loyalty to the city among the diverse population that had proved troublesome in the late nineteenth century. Midwestern cities needed improvements that would finally convince both outsiders and their residents of the greatness of the heartland metropolises.

Saint Louis had sought to be the site of the Columbian Exposition of 1893, but as was so often the case in the decades following the Civil War the Missouri metropolis came in second to Chicago. Eleven years later, however, Saint Louis did host the Louisiana Purchase Exposition, a world's fair that again dazzled visitors with an array of neoclassical palaces. Yet the Saint Louis exposition went Chicago one better and offered a "Model Street" lined with model municipal buildings erected by various American cities to house their exhibits. According to the official guide to the exposition, this section of the fair was intended "to create higher standards of street equipment and city arrangement by practical suggestions from experts and by comparison of methods in vogue in American cities."[36] A contemporary account described the street itself as "an exhibit of various kinds of road materials[,] . . . showing the finest examples of curbing and of paving made with asphalt, vitrified brick, wooden blocks, and other paving materials."[37] Located at the center of the model street was the Civic Pride Monument, a sculptural expression of the spirit emerging not only in Chicago but throughout the United States. American cities supposedly needed a hefty dose of civic pride and loyalty to unify their citizenry in the common battle for upgrading the urban environment. As planning created order out of chaos and beauty out of ugliness, this spirit of pride would infect not simply the elite but spread throughout the city to people of every class and ethnic group.

After the fair's closing Saint Louis leaders took action to apply some of the new ideas on planning and civic improvements to their own city. In 1905 the Civic League of Saint Louis selected a committee to consider the feasibility of drafting a comprehensive blueprint for the future development of the Missouri city, and two years later the league published the resulting plan which offered proposals for park, street, and riverfront improvements. Like Burnham, the Saint Louis committee emphasized the need "to realize the unity of . . . civic life by bringing together the different sections of the city" and the desirability of creating "civic orderliness and beauty" to supplant a "lack of unity and an absence of dignity and harmony."[38] But also

like the Chicago architect, it believed beauty was profitable."A city can not
. . . maintain a high commercial standing," the plan noted, "unless it main-
tains, at the same time, a high civic life."[39] A metropolis that looked great
would draw visitors and commerce; a town that appeared down at the heels
would lure few dollars.

The most innovative section of the Saint Louis plan proposed the creation
of neighborhood civic centers. Eschewing the idea of a single collection of
government buildings serving the entire city, the plan believed that neighborhood centers "would tend towards the development of better citizenship."
The neighborhood school, police station, branch library, and public bathhouse would cluster around a park and playground creating a focus for
the district and supposedly fostering "civic pride in the neighborhood."[40]
According to Dwight Davis, the chairman of the Civic Center Committee of
the Civic League, "It is in relation to the immigrant that the neighborhood
center would perform one of its most important functions."[41] These newcomers to the city seemed most vulnerable to the antisocial influences of crime,
drink, vice, and political radicalism that proved destructive of civic order
and unity. "Why not bring this same foreigner in contact with the best of
our civilization, and teach him that our government is maintained for his
welfare," asked Davis.[42] The neighborhood centers could achieve this end,
creating the civic loyalty so much admired by heartland planners at the
beginning of the twentieth century. With their polyglot populations and histories of conflict, midwestern cities needed to create ties to bind the many
diverse newcomers. Saint Louis reformers believed the neighborhood civic
centers would achieve this end.

Saint Louis failed to implement this scheme of neighborhood centers, but
elsewhere in the Midwest cities were grouping public buildings in the Burnham mode. Detroit accepted the plan of Burnham's lieutenant Edward Bennett for an eleven-building Center of Arts and Letters built around the
nucleus of a white marble library and a monumental art museum. Again this
was intended to be an object of pride and a gathering place for all Detroiters.
In 1909 a local newspaper described the existing museum as a place "where
all nationalities" met "on common ground" and the new structure would
supposedly perpetuate this communal function.[43] The city librarian favored
a municipal auditorium at the arts center, claiming: "It . . . will serve to
unify more than all other influences, the varied elements that go to make up
our population."[44] "Hardly a city or a town," wrote Toledo's Mayor Brand
Whitlock in 1912, "has not its commission and its plans for a unified treatment of its parks, for a civic center of some sort—in a word, its dream."
Whitlock sought to formulate such a dream for Toledo, for he believed that
building a civic center would "intensify the spirit of unity, the wholesome
spirit," which he claimed would nurture an all-important "city sense." This
was essential because the people had to be "inspired by a single ideal" and
everything else had to be "subsidiary to the achievement of this ideal."[45]
Financially-strapped Toledo failed, however, to build the city hall and sur-

rounding civic center which the mayor deemed so necessary to the community's spirit. Meanwhile, Milwaukee considered a series of plans for a civic center, yet that city also delayed and prior to the 1920s did not break ground for the first of its new civic temples.[46]

In capital cities urban beautification seemed especially appropriate, for there the shabby and unsightly not only brought shame upon the municipality but on the state itself. In 1907 and 1908 a commission consisting of two architects, one landscape architect, one sculptor, and a "civic advisor" drafted a plan for Columbus seeking to make that city "the most beautiful and best ordered State capital of the Union," and included in the scheme was a grand civic center constructed around the existing statehouse.[47] At the same time, Indianapolis was paying Kansas City landscape architect George Kessler to lay out a system of parks and boulevards to beautify the Indiana metropolis.[48] Madison hired the services of planner John Nolen, who claimed that the Wisconsin capital had "the best opportunity to become . . . a model modern American city" and "the hope of democracy."[49] Predictably, Nolen proposed a grand mall flanked by government office buildings which would lead from the capitol building to the shores of Lake Monona, where it would intersect with a grand esplanade adorned with fountains and statuary. "If properly carried out," Nolen believed, "this would contribute more than any one thing to the making of Madison a worthy Capital City for Wisconsin."[50] By 1918 Springfield likewise had a tentative plan, including a parkway lined "with beautiful architectural buildings, public and semi-public edifices, representing the art and culture of the middle west." Moreover, the two statewide organizations of architects both were committed to making Springfield "a state center worthy in every way of Illinois and the Middle West."[51]

In Madison, Indianapolis, Saint Louis, and Cleveland the rhetoric was much the same. The time had come to make the heartland cities orderly, unified, and beautiful. During the nineteenth century they had grown wealthy and successful; now they should look like it. And these urban centers should nurture a civic pride and loyalty which would bridge social divisions and inspire devotion to American government and principles among foreign newcomers. Chicago was preeminent in the planning movement, winning attention throughout the world as a leader of the cause. But the other midwestern cities followed suit. With the same willingness to experiment, reform, and create that motivated Samuel Jones, John Patterson, and Jane Addams, Midwesterners were embracing new plans for their communities and dreaming of a markedly better future. Beauty and order, equity and efficiency, all were on the agenda of heartland cities during this age of energy, ambition, and optimism.

The Prairie School

Though Daniel Burnham was in the vanguard of the city planning movement, he remained devoted to Old World models and the inherited tradition of classicism. He was a pioneer but hardly a rebel. Yet at the very time Burnham was drafting his scheme for Chicago, that city was home to a band of innovative architects who made the great planner look like a reactionary. Known as the Prairie School, they were Midwesterners and proud of it. Unlike earlier generations of heartland urbanites who had sought to civilize their region by importing the styles of Europe and the Atlantic seaboard, these architects refused to kowtow to the long-standing centers of culture and believed that the Midwest was giving birth to a new building art superior to that of the past. In the Prairie School's opinion, Chicago should teach the world and not obediently learn lessons shipped in from east of the Appalachians.

The most famous of the Prairie School architects was Frank Lloyd Wright. Born in rural Wisconsin, Wright attended school in Madison before moving to Chicago, where he became a draftsman and apprentice architect in the office of Adler and Sullivan. Wright acknowledged Louis Sullivan as his "master," and the leading student of the Prairie style has referred to Sullivan as "the spiritual leader of the school."[52] With his antagonism toward the inherited styles of Europe and especially the neoclassicism of the Columbian Exposition of 1893, Sullivan was an inspiration for younger architects like Wright who believed that Chicago and the Midwest had as much to contribute to art and civilization as ancient Greece or Renaissance Italy. Wright, however, would prove more daring and iconoclastic than his master. In the mind of the egotistical younger architect, Sullivan was John the Baptist; but Wright himself was the messiah redeeming American architecture.

In most latter-day accounts other Prairie School architects have remained in the shadows of the overpowering Wright. But in fact many young practitioners joined in the midwestern rebellion and contributed significantly to the cause. Like Wright, most of them were born or raised in the Midwest and received their professional training either in Chicago architectural offices or at heartland universities. For example, George W. Maher spent his childhood in New Albany, Indiana, before embarking on an apprenticeship in a Chicago architect's office. Walter Burley Griffin, William Drummond, and William Steele all studied architecture at the University of Illinois, and Griffin, William Gray Purcell, and John Van Bergen all grew up in Oak Park, Illinois, the Chicago suburb where Wright also resided. Griffin's wife, Marion Mahony Griffin, was a native Chicagoan who worked with her husband in Wright's office, though she received her university training in the East at Massachusetts Institute of Technology.

These architects not only shared midwestern roots but also found a common inspiration in the heartland landscape. They appreciated the beauty of the midwestern prairie, and their architecture was intended to complement the region's flat expanses. In 1908 Wright wrote: "We of the Middle West are living on the prairie. The prairie has a beauty of its own and we should recognize and accentuate this natural beauty, its quiet level." In order to do so, Wright favored an architecture of "gently sloping roofs, low proportions, quiet sky lines, suppressed heavy-set chimneys and sheltering overhangs, low terraces and outreaching walls sequestering private gardens."[53] The horizontal predominated in Prairie School structures and low overhanging roofs and horizontal ranges of casement windows were among their characteristic features. Moreover, they were relatively free of ornamentation. They were stark, clean, and ground hugging like the broad, uncluttered prairies of Illinois.

Yet for Wright and his colleagues the prairie represented more than a beautiful landscape. "The prairie served as a metaphor," architectural historian Richard Guy Wilson has written, "offering the promise of a new society and a new art, freed from stultified Old World and East Coast traditions."[54] For the Prairie School the midwestern plains were a symbol of liberation. They were open, fresh, and fertile; they were not the worn-out lands of Europe or New England with horizons blocked by age-old hedgerows or stone walls. And this new indigenous architecture of the Midwest was similarly unencumbered by boundaries and barriers inherited from the past. In 1906 George W. Maher complained that "the reactionary spirit in architecture" prevailed in the East where all seemed "steeped in precedent." "Little or no hope of an expressive art can evolve from our Eastern cities," Maher contended, "and if there is to be an art that is to indicate the trend of our national life, it must spring from the central portion of this country, or where traditional Europe has not yet laid upon us its heavy hand."[55] Nine years later William Drummond concurred: "Especially in the Middle West, life exhibits without a doubt a fullness of vision . . . such as has never before in history been true of any people of any other time or place." According to Drummond, in the territory west of the Appalachians, the typical client was more likely to protest "against the present tendency toward 'style' mongering," not caring "for templesque or cathedralesque or for any expression of 'style' intended to recall these by the use of derived forms."[56] The hand of the past rested lightly on the Midwest, and thus on the prairies would supposedly grow the architecture of the future.

According to Prairie School proponents, this new architecture, uncorrupted by European cultural baggage, was truly American. Like most of their heartland contemporaries, the Prairie School architects believed the Midwest to be the most American region of the nation, and they repeatedly identified their work as an expression of Americanism in stucco and brick. For Northwestern University in suburban Evanston, George Maher sought to design "buildings entirely typical of American effort" and create a campus "expressing Americanism in architecture, landscape, and flora, employing standards of beauty our own." He endeavored "to hold precedent subservient, as a means to the end and to look for . . . inspiration in surrounding life and environment."[57] In 1915 Prairie School architect John Van Bergen wrote an article titled "A Plea for Americanism in Our Architecture," noting in his essay that "especially Chicago and vicinity [had] produced a school of men" who had "been able to launch an architecture for and of the future America."[58] That same year a midwestern architecture journal discussed the domestic work of one Prairie School firm, commenting: "We . . . like to think that the houses of the average citizens in our part of the country, are just a little more American than those of our brothers on the Atlantic."[59] Eschewing the French chateau and the Gothic castle, the heartland innovators were building American homes, dwellings that were an indigenous creation of supposedly the most American of the nation's regions.

Prairie School practitioners believed that their architecture, like their native region, was not only truly American but also an expression of democracy. Like historian Frederick Jackson Turner and many Midwesterners of the period, they viewed the heartland as the cradle of the national ideology, and thus it naturally was to be the birthplace of democratic architecture. For the Prairie School advocates, democracy did not necessarily mean the communalism of Tom Johnson or Samuel Jones, but rather a liberation from the autocratic styles of the past and a new creative freedom for the individual. In 1908 Frank Lloyd Wright wrote: "Our ideal is Democracy, the highest possible expression of the individual as a unit not inconsistent with a harmonious whole."[60] In other words, these avant-garde Chicagoans believed that architects must be free to do their own thing, unrestrained by preconceptions or formulas. They must design for the situation at hand and not impose irrelevant pattern-book styles. A 1914 article on George Maher wrote of his belief in "a democracy in Art and Architecture" by which he meant "that buildings should be erected to fit the actual needs of the people who inspire them, adhering closely to the principle that each proposition should be different, dependent upon the needs and conditions presented."[61] Maher himself wrote of an architectural "expression born of democracy . . . not hindered to any extent by precedent or tradition" with "unfettered opportunity for an expression of the new."[62]

Individualism and freedom were not the only democratic elements of Prairie School architecture. Equally significant was the simplicity of the style. It rejected pretentious ornament and rich detail; nor did it tolerate turrets or towers that shouted wealth and money to the onlooker. Though the owners of Wright's houses certainly were of greater than average affluence, his low, stark structures were not small-scale European palaces for Americans with aristocratic pretensions. In 1918 Chicago architect Irving K. Pond said of the school: "The horizontal lines of the new expression appeal to the disciples of this school as echoing the spirit of the prairies of the great Middle West, which to them embodies the essence of democracy."[63] The simplicity of the rural Midwest was the Prairie School's ideal; this was the land of Lincoln, with a field for opportunity as level as the landscape. It was not a utopia of economic equality, but according to prevailing myth, it was a land where inherited barriers and traditions did not hold a person down. Simple, basic, and horizontal, Prairie School buildings seemed appropriate expressions of this midwestern ideal.

Thus the Prairie School architects agreed with Jane Addams and Tom Johnson: the heartland was in the vanguard of American democracy and on the front lines of the battle for a more enlightened and liberated world. While Johnson fought "Privilege" in the form of streetcar monopolists, Wright and his colleagues attacked the privilege of entrenched European styles. Addams and her co-workers viewed Chicago as a great social laboratory where right-thinking individuals could arrive at formulas for a better urban life. The iconoclastic achitects saw that same city as the crucible for a new American architecture similarly free of the ills of the past. The political, social, and aesthetic reformers agreed that the Midwest represented the best hope of the world, the region where all that was most desirable in Americanism would triumph. There democracy and all it entailed had the strongest chance for victory. In Chicago and the other heartland hubs Americans would supposedly find the answers for the future.

Addams and Johnson, however, were urban crusaders; the Prairie School architects in contrast were prophets of suburbia. The largest portion of their work was in the suburbs surrounding Chicago, with Wright's hometown of Oak Park possessing the richest collection of Prairie School structures. Louis Sullivan was the preeminent architect of Chicago's upward thrust, pioneering the design of downtown skyscrapers. Wright was the most distinguished architect of Chicago's outward thrust, building expansive, ground-consuming homes on the metropolitan outskirts. The Prairie School architects shared a typically midwestern devotion to the single-family, owner-occupied home, and these structures constituted the bulk of their work. They did not attempt to Manhattanize the prairie with apartment buildings or import the New England triple decker to the shores of Lake Michigan. While challenging design precedents, they remained loyal to the established midwestern tradition of the detached family home so evident in the late nineteenth century.

Moreover, those few Prairie School architects who also tried their hand at land use planning were dedicated to the preservation of open space and low-density development. For example, Walter Burley Griffin submitted designs for a number of small suburban or semirural projects in the United States. His scheme for the Trier Center Neighborhood in the Chicago suburb of Winnetka typically sought "to preserve for the neighborhood a maximum of the site's natural beauty and to secure that garden charm which alone justifie[d] living out in the suburbs." According to a midwestern architectural journal, "The architecture of the houses is reduced to a minimum of scale, height and obtrusiveness, considerations that have dictated masonry construction with its minimum of trim and accessory features and a maximum suitability to bower and embellishment with luxuriant growth not only over walls but roofs also."[64] Nature was to take precedence over buildings in Trier Center; the houses were to be unobtrusive and engulfed in foliage. Griffin's greatest achievement was the plan for the Australian capital of Canberra. True to Prairie School predilections it was an expansive, low-density community sprawling across the Australian hills.

Frank Lloyd Wright's ideal community also would be as broad and expansive as the prairie itself. Never a fan of urban life, as early as the 1890s Wright established a design studio in suburban Oak Park because he found the hubbub of Chicago too distracting. In 1902 in an address delivered at Jane Addams's Hull House, Wright pictured the city as a frightening and awesome creation, referring to it as a "monster leviathan" with "fetid breath," a "monstrous thing" of "ghastly" noise and "poisonous waste."[65] Later in the 1930s he turned to the problem of solving urban ills, submitting his plan for the utopian Broadacres City. An anti-city rather than a city, the Broadacres plan proposed a dispersion of population and a semirural lifestyle with a food garden for every family. Only fourteen hundred families would inhabit a typical sixteen-square mile tract, and low-density settlement and decentralization were the dominant themes of his scheme.[66]

Unlike Daniel Burnham, the Prairie School thus offered little help in reforming, as opposed to obliterating, the existing urban pattern of heartland America. These rebellious architects seemed at best indifferent to the urban core and at worst hostile. The suburban fringe was their domain; their turf was Oak Park not State Street or Michigan Avenue. Frank Lloyd Wright was Chicago's greatest contribution to world civilization. Yet like Frankenstein's monster, given the opportunity he would have destroyed the city that nurtured him.

The Prairie School practitioners not only built houses of startling originality and dabbled in community planning, they also experimented with new and daring designs for furniture. Like their architecture, their furniture was characterized by straight lines and relative simplicity, the only ornament being stylized floral motifs or abstract geometric forms. For their floral motifs, the Prairie architects most often chose a flower native to the region because, in the words of George Maher: "The leading flower of a neighborhood is nature's symbol of the spirit out-breathed there."[67] The Prairie School's architecture was supposed to conform to the configurations of the surrounding prairie landscape, and its interior decoration also was intended to be indigenous to the region rather than exotic or foreign. Wright's furniture and interiors were especially Spartan, and in the late 1890s a correspondent for *House Beautiful* wrote of the dining room of the architect's Oak Park home: "One's first impression . . . is of its simplicity—no rugs, no curtains, and only the necessary furniture."[68] With more concern for stark geometric beauty than utility, Wright did not necessarily produce furniture conducive to human comfort. He admitted: "I have been black and blue in some spot, somewhere almost all my life from too intimate contact with my own early furniture."[69]

Fortunately for their physical well-being, most Midwesterners did not rush out to order the avant-garde Prairie furniture. Though Wright won international fame and the Chicago rebels became renowned for their contribution to modern architecture, during the first two decades of the twentieth century the Prairie School's direct impact on the midwestern built environment remained minor. Outside the Chicago area Prairie School architecture was not common, and in cities like Cleveland, Cincinnati, Detroit, and Saint Louis it was almost as rare as in New York or Philadelphia. The Chicago architects led a rebellion against the long-standing tyranny of imported styles and tastes, but few Midwesterners joined in the insurgency. Instead, the more affluent heartlanders built colonial revival homes, Tudor manses, or imitation Renaissance palazzos and supported campaigns for neoclassic civic centers in the style of Daniel Burnham. Wright's clients were not the wealthiest or most influential figures of the day, nor were they the cultural leaders of their communities. Instead, Wright described his patrons as "American men of business with unspoiled instincts and untainted ideals."[70] They were most often mechanically minded managers or owners of moderate-sized manufacturing concerns. Chicago's industrial aristocrat Harold McCormick turned down Wright's plan for his estate, opting for a more traditional design. Wright and his Prairie colleagues basically remained heartland curiosities, attracting attention but failing to win support from the region's elite.

Nor did Wright and his fellow rebels win the choicest contracts for public or commercial structures. Governing boards invariably chose the classical or renaissance style for the art museums constructed across the Midwest during the early twentieth century. Midwesterners were still not confident enough of their own cultural worth to garb their palaces of art in native clothing. Imported goods remained the preference of those heartlanders who felt that Chicago would inevitably fall short of Athens, Rome, or Florence. Wright's grandest nonresidential structure built in the Midwest during the first two decades of the twentieth century was Midway Gardens, a large beer garden for the amusement of Chicago's populace. The task of designing more elevated monuments went to practitioners subservient to the inherited stylistic dogmas of Europe and the Atlantic seaboard.

By the end of the second decade of the twentieth century, the Prairie School had lost the battle for the loyalties of midwestern clients. Wright had left Chicago, retreating to rural Wisconsin, in part owing to the scandal surrounding his love affair with a client's wife. Griffin and his wife were in Australia building that nation's capital city, and the other Prairie architects were disheartened. In 1917 one of them lamented: "Clients, the wives of whom at least, have received their architectural education in magazines edited in Boston and New York, now have turned back to pretty Colonial or fashionable Italian. Where are Sullivan, Wright, Griffin, and the others?"[71] Six years later when surveying the architecture of Cleveland, a national magazine wrote: "The newer buildings are fine and are often very well done but it is a question whether they are in any way distinctive of Cleveland. They might have been built in any city."[72] The same could have been said for Detroit, Indianapolis, Saint Louis, and every midwestern metropolis. Despite the efforts of the Prairie School to create a distinctive heartland architecture, the most prominent structures in midwestern centers conformed to standard imported patterns.

Though Wright and his colleagues were not winning the battle against tradition, their heartland spirit of rebellion was also stirring new ideas in the field of landscape architecture. In fact, during the early twentieth century a Prairie School of landscape architecture emerged, its adherents dedicated to the Midwest's natural land forms and to the use of native plants rather than foreign exotics. Professor Wilhelm Miller of the University of Illinois was the chief publicist of the cause, writing a series of essays on the subject, including one in 1912 titled "How the Middle West Can Come into Its Own." In this article he noted that the Midwest was just entering the highest stage of gardening when heartlanders would begin to recognize that midwestern character was "more to be desired than all the finest plants in all the nurseries of the world." According to Miller, "The East is now busy copying England and Italy, while the Middle West is joyfully spending its millions in copying the East." But he hoped those living west of the Appalachians would see the folly of this devotion to alien flora. "Let 90 per cent. of your planting consist of Western material," he exclaimed.[73] Just as the innovative Chicago architects called for a liberation from the aping of imported styles, Prairie School landscapists called for a midwestern style of planting rather than the creation of bogus English lawns in Illinois and imitation Italian sunken gardens in Indiana.

An early practitioner of this indigenous style was Chicago's Ossian Simonds. Born in Grand Rapids, Simonds moved to Chicago in the late 1870s and began his lifelong work as landscape architect for Graceland Cemetery on the city's north side. In the course of his fifty-year career, he also designed parks in Springfield and Quincy, Illinois, and Madison, Wisconsin, as well as private estates and parks in Chicago's north shore suburbs. In his projects Simonds used primarily native plants, and an admiring Miller wrote of Graceland Cemetery: "The guiding spirit was that respect for the quieter beauties of native vegetation which comes to every cultured person." Simonds himself said: "In making a planting design for any given territory, one should seek to retain the local character, and this he can do very largely by using indigenous plants."[74]

But the most notable Prairie style landscape architect was Jens Jensen. A Danish immigrant, Jensen settled in Chicago in the 1880s and fell in love with the flora and natural landscape of the Midwest. Most of his work was in Illinois, Michigan, and Wisconsin, and he was so devoted to the Midwest that he proved reluctant to lay out an estate for Edsel Ford in Maine, claiming that he had little feeling for the eastern coastal landscape.[75] The outspoken Jensen was not reluctant to attack Eastern practitioners for their devotion to formal Italianate gardens. In Jensen's mind, the prairie was not simply a beautiful landscape; it also represented the rejection of imported tradition. As his biographer has observed: "The prairie, a type of landscape which did not exist in the East, was for him and for Wright a symbol of regional rebellion."[76]

Jensen began his landscape career in the employ of Chicago's West Park Commission, and he did some of his finest work for that body. But he also designed the park system of Racine, Wisconsin, and was instrumental in the creation of the Cook County Forest Preserve, the sylvan ring encircling Chicago envisioned in Burnham's plan of 1909. Moreover, his private work included landscaping for some of the homes designed by Prairie School architects. Like these architects, Jensen emphasized the horizontal in his plantings. Thus he had a fondness for the horizontal branches of the native crabapples and hawthorns and the horizontal lines of stratified rock. Moreover, he planted prairie flowers that less imaginative gardeners regarded as common weeds. Seeking to give city dwellers an idea of the natural Illinois landscape, he created a prairie river in Chicago's Humboldt Park. At Columbus Park he maintained an expanse of open prairie and made sure that urbanites could view the setting sun over the flatlands, "one of Nature's most dramatic expressions, yet a strange phenomenon to most people of . . . great cities."[77] In this same park, Jensen constructed a swimming hole with stratified limestone ledges, repeating the horizontal lines of the prairie. Later in life he wrote of his "early desire to bring to the city dweller a message of the country outside his city walls."[78] In the parks on Chicago's west side he largely achieved this goal.

For Jensen and like-minded landscapists as for the innovative architects, this new Prairie style was a visual manifestation of the democracy and Americanism of the Midwest. Though Wilhelm Miller noted that America had "contributed no new principles of design in any fine art," "the work of these Middle-Western landscape architects" impressed him "as being new and American." In his opinion, it was an "American mode of design."[79] One of Jensen's trademarks was the council ring, a circular stone bench which symbolized for the great landscape architect the spirit of democracy. "It is really democratic in its conception," Jensen wrote. "Here one is no more than the other," he explained, for all sat in a circle, none enjoying a seat of prominence at the head of the assembly.[80] Appropriately his Lincoln Memorial Garden in Springfield, Illinois, was planned around eight such rings, democratic landmarks in a park dedicated to the Midwest's mythic giant of democracy. Throughout his career Jensen attempted to create a democratic, American alternative to the great aristocratic parks of Europe. "Pomp and pose are an inheritance from enslaved peoples," he argued; "their expression in architecture is beyond the comprehension of common people and foreign to democratic thoughts."[81] Simple and native, the Prairie style was supposedly well suited to the nation's most democratic and American region.

Yet Jensen's initiatives like those of Wright failed to convince most Midwesterners. Wealthy heartlanders generally opted for Italianate gardens rather than prairie plantings, and imported styles of landscaping remained fashionable, just as did neoclassical columns, neocolonial woodwork, and renaissance facades. Jensen did win the Ford family's lucrative patronage, but he remained an outsider among American landscape architects. His dogmas did not become the establishment credo. Moreover, Chicago's park authorities failed to maintain his carefully wrought landscapes. In Columbus

Park his open prairie became a golf course, and a utilitarian concrete tank replaced Jensen's swimming hole. Like Wright, Jensen was never fond of the city, at one point claiming that it destroyed beauty and crowded "the landscape with ugly brick boxes in which people [were] packed like sardines."[82] Finally in the 1930s he retreated to northern Wisconsin, abandoning the prairie metropolis for the wooded shores of Lake Michigan.

For a few short decades, however, innovators like Jensen and Wright had made Chicago the center of aesthetic unrest in the nation. In 1912 a national magazine described the "insurgent architecture" of the Midwest, referring to the region as "a new country settled by progressives" who knew "little about and care[d] nothing for 'precedent.'"[83] In other words, the heartland was in the vanguard; it was the region where Americans had finally dared liberate themselves from the past. It had shed the dull imitation so prevalent in the East and placed itself on the cutting edge of culture. Wilhelm Miller claimed that "the horizontal line of the prairie ha[d] become a symbol of aspiration."[84] For Jensen, Wright, and their like-minded colleagues, it certainly was. It symbolized the aspiration to break free and create, in the hope of fashioning an American and democratic culture in the nation's heartland.

"Parnassus on the Prairie"

In 1917 the Baltimore-bred critic H. L. Mencken proclaimed Chicago "the most civilized city in America." "Find me a writer who is indubitably an American and who has something new and interesting to say," Mencken wrote, "and nine times out of ten . . . he has some sort of connection with the abbatoir by the lake." Chicago authors expressed "the authentic bounce and verve of the country and the true character and philosophy of its people."[85] Three years later he reiterated his praise, claiming: "With two exceptions, there is not a single American novelist . . . deserving a civilized reader's notice—who has not sprung from the Middle Empire that has Chicago for its capital. . . . Go back for twenty or thirty years, and you will scarcely find an American literary movement that did not originate under the shadows of the stockyards."[86]

The iconoclastic Mencken delighted in needling the stuffy eastern establishment, and his praise of Chicago was an exquisite means for achieving this end. Yet Mencken expressed much truth in his tributes to Chicago. During the quarter century following the Columbian Exposition Chicago shed its provincial image and strode boldly to the forefront of the literary world. In literature as in architecture, it acquired a reputation for insurgency and became the center of rebellion against the hidebound literati of the Atlantic seaboard. Moreover, the Chicago offensive was seen as a war for American independence. Mencken, like the Prairie practitioners, perceived Chicago's creations as a flowering of Americanism in the arts. Once again the Midwest and its capital were seen as more truly American than any

other locale in the nation. In literature as in architecture, the honest-to-god
Americans of the heartland were thumbing their noses at effete, European-
ized Easterners and molding an indigenous culture.

This spirit of creativity and rebellion attracted some of the brightest and
most original young minds from throughout the Midwest. Farm girls and
office boys with literary pretensions headed for the Illinois metropolis to
participate in the cultural ferment and achieve their fame as great American
bards. Writing of this period, one author referred to Chicago as "Montmartre
in the Midwest" and "Parnassus on the Prairie."[87] "Nearly all the bright
young Indianians have gone to Chicago for a semester or two," Mencken
wrote, "and not only Indianians, but also the youngsters of all the other
Middle Western States."[88] Especially during the halcyon days of the second
decade of the twentieth century, Chicago lured the best of the heartland-
bred writers. For a time the Windy City was the place to go.

Chicago appealed to writers in part because it seemed so representative
of American society. With its reputation for being typically American, the
Windy City appeared to encompass all that was wrong with the nation as
well as all that was right. In fact, its rapid growth and spectacular commercial
success seemed to magnify the blemishes of American life, making them
more frightening but also more easily examined. It was a microcosm of
America in which the costs and benefits of American materialism were writ
large. Like the sociologists at the University of Chicago and at Hull House,
Chicago writers found the city a fascinating social phenomenon. The social
scientists used statistics and surveys to dissect it, whereas the writers used
verse and prose. But for both Chicago was an ideal specimen of modern
America which could not be ignored.

Chicago was, then, not only the writers' address, it was one of their chief
characters. In novels and poems it loomed as a powerful symbol of the
modern industrial world. It was both impressive and repulsive, an awesome
giant compelling a perverse admiration while at the same time deserving
censure. In one novel after another, it was heartless and cruel, a wrecker of
fortunes and a debaucher of morals. Its corruption and economic inequities
threatened democracy; its greed and materialism endangered civilization.
Yet almost in spite of themselves, Chicago writers were in awe of the place.
Like its fast-paced slaughterhouses, in prose and verse Chicago was brutal
but spectacular.

The Columbian Exposition of 1893 spurred a new sense of cultural confidence in the Windy City and ushered in an age of literary prominence. In
the minds of many Midwesterners, the World's Fair announced that the
nation's interior had emerged culturally, and its greatest city intended to
supplant New York and Boston as the hub of arts and letters. Recently
returned to the Midwest after a sojourn in Boston, Wisconsin-born Hamlin
Garland predicted the impending literary triumph of the interior in his 1894
collection of iconoclastic essays titled *Crumbling Idols*. Garland proclaimed:
"Centres of art production are moving westward: that is to say, the literary

supremacy of the East is passing away." "The rise of Chicago as a literary and art centre is a question only of time, and of a very short time," the heartland prophet announced; "for the Columbian Exposition has taught her her own capabilities in something higher than business." Reiterating the common theme that only the heartland could produce a truly American culture, Garland claimed: "New York, like Boston, is too near London. It is no longer American." "The interior is to be henceforth the real America," he contended; "from these interior spaces . . . the most vivid and fearless and original utterance of the coming American democracy will come." Previously the area west of the Appalachians "reckoning itself an annex of the East" had "imitated imitations," but now a national literature supposedly was to develop, and Chicago was to be the source of this American literary tradition.[89]

Garland's harangues against the convention-bound, derivative East expressed an emerging midwestern belief in the heartland's destiny that architects like Wright and landscapists like Jensen were to share. But eastern journals scorned Garland's declaration of independence. "The book should have been printed on birchbark and bound in butternut homespun," wrote a critic in Boston's *Atlantic,* "and should have had for cover design a dynamite bomb, say, with sputtering fire-tipped fuse, for the essays which it contained were so many explosions of literary Jingoism and anarchy."[90] The feisty Garland had ignited a noisy blast in the heartland revolt but the East did not seem intimidated by the midwestern rebel.

Chicago in the 1890s, however, was developing a literary culture of some renown. In her "Chicago letters" published in the New York-based *The Critic,* Lucy Monroe reported on the local literary scene to a national audience. Newspaper columnist-poet Eugene Field likewise offered a lively commentary on the city and its culture, and fellow Chicago journalists George Ade and Finley Peter Dunne were beginning to establish their national reputations as humorists. Garland and his brother-in-law sculptor Lorado Taft joined with other local artists and persons of letters to found the Little Room, an informal club designed to foster artistic inspiration through association and conversation. It was no national academy, but its members viewed it as the hub of the burgeoning artistic life of the city.

Meanwhile, Chicago was achieving further cultural distinction as the headquarters of the most innovative American literary journal of the 1890s. In 1894 two young Harvard men, Hannibal I. Kimball and Herbert Stone, moved the newly created *Chap-Book* from Cambridge, Massachusetts, to the Windy City. For the next four years their "little magazine" offered a relief from the suffocating conventionality of most literary journals of the day. The Chicago publication was dedicated to the free expression of views, and Stone and Kimball claimed it represented "the strongest protest . . . in America against the habit of promiscuous over-praise" which was "threatening to make the whole body of American criticism useless and stultifying."[91] It also was an outlet for the work of such distinguished European and American writers as Robert Louis Stevenson, H. G. Wells, Paul Verlaine, Henry James, and Stephen Crane as well as a number of young, less noteworthy aspirants for literary glory. According to one contemporary, "Young writers in Chicago and the West . . . found in the *Chap-Book* a medium which was suited to the virility and independence of their westernism, but at the same time was so cosmopolitan an exponent of literary expression from various parts of the world as to make for the broadening of their striving toward artistic expression."[92] In other words, Stone and Kimball offered a journal infected with the spirit of heartland rebellion but which also introduced the region's writers to the latest literary fashions from the outside world.

Though never a regional journal, the *Chap-Book* was intended to promote Chicago's position as a cultural center by demonstrating "that a good literary magazine could be published in the West."[93] Hamlin Garland described Stone and Kimball as "missionaries of culture" and when "each in a long frock coat, tightly buttoned, with cane, gloves and shining silk hats, paced side by side down the Lake Shore Drive they had the effect of an esthetic invasion." According to Garland, with the arrival of the two young editors "culture on the Middle Border had at last begun to hum!"[94] During its short existence the *Chap-Book* did, in fact, draw many eyes to Chicago. A flock of envious imitators created little magazines in cities throughout the country, hoping to recreate the literary vitality that was stirring the midwestern metropolis. H. L. Mencken called the Chicago-inspired craze for small literary journals "the pianissimo revolt of the nineties."[95]

During the 1890s a number of writers were also drawing attention to the Windy City by producing what became known as Chicago novels. Hamlin Garland, Henry Blake Fuller, and Robert Herrick were the most prominent creators of these commentaries on Chicago society. Fuller, like Garland, was a native Midwesterner, born and raised in Chicago and the genteel survivor of a pioneer family of declining fortunes. In contrast, Herrick was a native of Cambridge, Massachusetts, and a Harvard graduate recruited to teach English at the University of Chicago. From his ivy-covered perch on Chicago's south side, Herrick proceeded to examine and interpret the strange giant that had become his home.

In the Chicago novels of these and later authors, the midwestern metropolis is a rough, loud, overpowering arena for the pursuit of individual ambition. Fuller's 1893 novel *The Cliff-Dwellers* deals with those who work in a Chicago skyscraper and become dehumanized "money machines" as they strive for wealth within the soaring man-made cliff. Fuller describes Chicago businessman Erastus Brainard as "merely a financial appliance—one of the tools of the trade" who lives for nothing but business. "He wrote about nothing but business," Fuller explains, "his nearest relative was never more than 'dear sir' and he himself was never otherwise than 'yours truly;' and he wrote on business letterheads even to his family."[96] This business automaton is well suited to the Windy City, for in the Chicago novels the Midwest's greatest metropolis is a perfect playing field for creatures of avarice. "The thousands of acres of ramshackle that made up the bulk of the city," Fuller writes, "seemed . . . to constitute a great checker-board over whose squares of 'section' and 'township' keenness and rapacity played their daring and wary game."[97] In Fuller's *With the Procession* (1895) Chicago is likewise presented as "the only great city in the world to which all its citizens have come for the one common, avowed object of making money."[98] John Wilbur, the protagonist of Herrick's *The Gospel of Freedom* (1898), yields totally to the Chicago spirit of money making. Herrick says of Wilbur: "Strife for advancement summoned all his virility, and the sense of rapid success exhilarated him."[99] In *The Common Lot* (1904) a Herrick character claims that Chicago throttles "the finer aspiration of men like a remorseless giant, converting its youth into ironclad beasts of prey answering to one hoarse cry, 'Success, Success, Success!'"[100]

The protagonist of Hamlin Garland's *Rose of Dutcher's Coolly* (1895) is a woman who comes to Chicago not seeking money but rather fame as a poet. Once again Chicago represents the opportunity for fulfilling worldly ambitions. Garland's novel also includes a common element in Chicago literature—the young Midwesterner who comes to the metropolis and finds it both alluring and appalling. For Rose Chicago embodies both the wonderful and the terrifying: "In all the city she saw the huge and fierce. She perceived only contrasts. She saw ragged newsboy and towering policeman. She saw the rag-pickers, the street vermin, with a shudder of pity and horror, and she saw the gorgeous show windows of the great stores."[101] Such impressions are basic to Chicago novels. The city is a monument to the materialism of the industrial age, displaying both the riches and the poverty nurtured by rapacious capitalism.

In the early twentieth century Theodore Dreiser, the greatest Chicago novelist, reiterated these themes. Whereas Fuller was a genteel realist who tempered his fealty to truth with a sense of decorum, Dreiser, both in his writing and his private life, defied prevailing standrds of taste and propriety. Yet in his novels Chicago played much the same role as in the works of the more restrained realists of the 1890s. Like Garland's Rose, Dreiser's chief character in *Sister Carrie* (1900) is a young woman from rural Wisconsin for whom "the approach to a great city for the first time is a wonderful thing." Yet when seeking a job, Carrie finds the city's "great business portion" grows "larger, harder, more stolid in its indifference." She feels "her own helplessness without quite realizing the wisp on the tide" that she is. According to Dreiser, "The entire metropolitan centre possessed a high and mighty air calculated to overawe and abash the common applicant, and to make the gulf between poverty and success seem both wide and deep."[102]

In Dreiser's work Chicago remains the stereotypical hub of materialism. "Its many and growing commercial opportunities gave it widespread fame," Dreiser writes in *Sister Carrie,* "which made of it a giant magnet, drawing to itself from all quarters, the hopeful and the hopeless—those who had their fortunes yet to make and those whose fortunes and affairs had reached a disastrous climax elsewhere." Though no robber baron, Carrie herself is a materialist who on seeing the city's office towers can "only think of people connected with them counting money, dressing magnificently, and riding carriages."[103] In Dreiser's *The Titan* (1914) Chicago is the arena for the triumphs of grasping streetcar magnate Frank Cowperwood. On his arrival in Chicago, Cowperwood is thrilled by the "seething city in the making" and "something dynamic in the very air" appeals to him. "The city of Chicago, with whose development the personality of Frank Algernon Cowperwood was soon to be definitely linked!" exclaims Dreiser when the striving capitalist disembarks in the Illinois metropolis.[104] And in fact, the personalities of Chicago and Cowperwood have much in common. Both are sometimes heartless empire builders, magnificent if judged by the standard of material success but tainted by corruption. For Cowperwood and Chicago it is love at first sight, and rightfully so, for man and city are a perfect match.

Thus in one novel after another Chicago was a powerful character, a model of material success attracting the ambitious and bestowing upon some wealth and upon others misery. In the late nineteenth and early twentieth centuries, the Windy City captured the literary imagination and became the prevailing symbol for industrial America. Dreiser, Garland, Herrick, and Fuller all viewed the midwestern metropolis as embodying the very essence of the national struggle between Mammon and humanity.

Yet by the turn of the century these prominent novelists found Chicago more appealing as a subject than as a center for creative activity. Despite the Little Room, the *Chap-Book,* and the companionship of Henry Blake Fuller, Chicago proved a disappointment to that prophet of its literary greatness Hamlin Garland. "New York allured me as London allures the writers of England," admitted Garland, and in the early twentieth century he privately remarked to Fuller: "As soon as I can afford it I intend to establish a home in New York." "I'd go further," Fuller answered. "I would live in Italy if I could."[105] Never happy in his adopted city, Herrick likewise kept his eyes turned to the East, and following the breakup of his marriage returned to New England. Dreiser had lived in Chicago for a short time as an adolescent, and later as a young man he began his career as a newspaper writer there. Later in life he wrote of the early inspiration he derived from Chicago, a city which "seethed with a peculiarly human or realistic atmosphere."[106] But as an adult novelist he never made the Windy City his residence, using New York instead as his base. Dreiser was actually a Chicago novelist in absentia. For too many literary figures, Chicago was a good place to write about, but they did not want to live there. In the 1890s Chicago boasted of its literary achievements and did seem on the road to enduring status as a cultural capital. Ten years later, in the minds of Garland and others, its artistic destiny remained uncertain.

During the second decade of the century, however, this changed. For a few short years Chicago became not only a metaphor but a mecca, which drew a fresh crop of innovative young minds from throughout the Midwest.

Among others Floyd Dell arrived from Davenport, Iowa, Ben Hecht from Racine, Wisconsin, Sherwood Anderson from Elyria, Ohio, Vachel Lindsay from Springfield, Illinois, and Carl Sandburg from Galesburg, Illinois, via Milwaukee. A bohemia of artists and writers developed around 57th Street on the city's south side and the unofficial center of this colony was the studio of novelist-critic Floyd Dell and his wife Margery Curry.[107] On the near north side the area known as Towertown also took on bohemian airs with the Dill Pickle Club, run by ex-safecracker Jack Jones, attracting a loyal literary clientele. When feeling generous, Jones would pay struggling writers to recite their poetry, though there was a limit to his devotion to literature. He told Sherwood Anderson, "I give them the high-brow stuff until the crowd grows thin and then I turn on the sex faucet."[108] Both on the south side and in Towertown a heady feeling of creativity and experimentation seized the Windy City writers during the century's second decade. According to Anderson, it was a "time in which something blossomed in Chicago and the Middle West." "Something which had been very hard in American life was beginning to crack," Anderson wrote, "and in our group we often spoke of it hopefully. . . . Something seemingly new and fresh was in the very air we breathed."[109]

Yet there was continuity with the past, and the Chicago novels of this period repeated some of the same themes found in earlier works. For example, in Sherwood Anderson's *Windy McPherson's Son* (1916) Chicago has an inevitable attraction for the novel's protagonist who has "the cold, quick business stroke of the money-maker." Like so many characters in Chicago novels, he comes from a small midwestern town and dreams of "himself going on and on, directing, managing, ruling men" and eventually "grey, stern and capable, sitting at a broad desk high in a great stone building."[110] In Anderson's *Marching Men* (1917), "the word regarding the making of money" in Chicago "runs over the land like a wind among the corn," attracting young men with "no dream, no tradition of devotion to anything but gain."[111] Chicago remains, then, the holy city for worshippers of profit. Moreover, as in earlier works it is huge, tough, disorderly, and overwhelming.

Chicago writers of the second decade, however, appeared more daring than some of their predecessors. Though tame by later standards, their works, for example, dealt more openly with sex than the genteel novels of the nineteenth century. "We had the notion that sex had something to do with people's lives," Anderson wrote, "and it had barely been mentioned in American writing before our time." Yet for "bringing sex back to . . . its normal place in the picture of life," Anderson and his colleagues were called "sex-obsessed."[112] In Floyd Dell's *The Briary Bush* (1921) a character much admired by the protagonist argues that literature is "a kind of social dynamics. It had been used to build up through the ages a vast system of 'taboos'—and now it was being used to break them down again."[113] Dell believed that the Chicago writers were playing a vital role in this breaking down process. Actually sex was not new to Chicago literature; both Gar-

land's *Rose of Dutcher's Coolly* and Dreiser's *Sister Carrie* had been condemned as obscene by conservative critics.[114] But the writers of the second
decade viewed their naturalistic depiction of human emotions as one of the
hallmarks of their rebellion.

In the field of poetry the spirit of rebellion was also pronounced. In fact,
during the second decade of the twentieth century Chicago became the
unchallenged center of modern poetry in America. This was largely owing
to the efforts of Harriet Monroe. The daughter of a prosperous Chicago
lawyer, Monroe was a genteel poet in the nineteenth-century tradition who
gained some fame for her "Columbian Ode" read by a chorus of five thousand voices at the dedication of the 1893 World's Fair.[115] As a habitué of the
Little Room she had close connections with the city's leading literary and
artistic figures. Moreover, family ties ensured her place in the Windy City'
cultural world; her sister authored the "Chicago letters" column in *The
Critic,* and her brother-in-law was John W. Root, the famed architect and
partner of Daniel Burnham. Not necessarily avant-garde in her tastes, as art
critic for the *Chicago Tribune* she aroused the ire of Frank Lloyd Wright
because she failed to fully appreciate his nontraditional designs.[116] Yet by
1911 she was disgusted by the sterility of American poetry and by the desic-
cated eastern practitioners who dominated the nation's verse. "Innovations
were sporadic," she later remarked, "and contrary to the general practice
and prejudice of the time."[117]

Consequently, in 1911 Monroe began soliciting funds from wealthy Chicago acquaintances for the support of a magazine solely devoted to the
promotion of poetry. Longtime cultural philanthropist Charles Hutchinson
assured her, "You may count on me as long as I live."[118] Others were also
generous, and in 1912 Monroe published the first issue of her journal named
simply *Poetry.*

Though *Poetry* was not a regional journal, Monroe was a steadfast Chicagoan and Midwesterner dedicated to the promotion of her hometown as a
cultural center and to the poetic expression of her fellow heartlanders. Thus
she took special pride in "discovering" and publishing the innovative works
of such heartland writers as Edgar Lee Masters, Carl Sandburg, and Vachel
Lindsay. These poets often wrote on midwestern themes and expressed
themselves in a bold, simple style that conformed to the heartland image of
democracy and Americanism. Both Sandburg and Lindsay were self-styled
poets of the people with a Lincolnesque devotion to verse of the people, by
the people, and for the people. In fact, Lindsay traveled throughout the
country as a modern troubadour reciting his poems to whomever would
listen.

Such effrontery to intellectual elitism was bound to stir some praise but
much criticism. One critic found Lindsay's "General William Booth Enters
into Heaven" to be "daring and shocking and upsetting."[119] Celebrating the
gritty, horny-handed vitality of the "City of Big Shoulders," Sandburg's "Chicago" came under especially heavy attack from genteel observers who

viewed it as "nothing less than an impudent affront to the poetry-loving public."[120] The generally mild-mannered Monroe responded sharply, proudly proclaiming: "We have taken chances, made room for the young and new, tried to break the chains which enslave Chicago to New York, America to Europe, and the present to the past."[121] A grateful Masters expressed the feeling of his midwestern colleagues when he wrote Monroe: "Hold on to the magazine. It has done more for Chicago authors than anything we've had."[122]

Monroe stirred the literary world not only by publishing the work of midwestern rebels but also by providing a forum for some of the latest European verse. Her European editor was the American-born émigré Ezra Pound who vigorously sought to impose his stamp on the Chicago journal. *Poetry* published Pound's work but also T. S. Eliot's "Love Song of J. Alfred Prufrock" as well as the poems of William Butler Yeats, H. D., and Richard Aldington. A Philadelphia newspaper headlined an editorial on Monroe's journal "Poetry in Porkopolis" and ridiculed the midwestern metropolis's literary pretensions by observing: "Chicago loves poetry. It uses the proceeds of pork for the promotion of poetry."[123] Yet neither the dull burg on the Schuylkill nor its northern neighbor on the Hudson could boast of any literary magazine equal to *Poetry*. Through the efforts of Harriet Monroe Chicago did indeed capture the rapt attention of the American and European avant-garde.

Other Chicagoans were also trying their hand at literary journalism. Floyd Dell edited the *Friday Literary Review*, using it as a pulpit for criticizing the genteel traditionalists. A characteristic essay by Dell argued: "The poets have always preached the gospel of disorder. The novelists from Fielding to Galsworthy have spoken in behalf of the man at odds with society."[124] In 1911 Margaret Anderson left Columbus, Indiana, for Chicago where she founded the *Little Review* and earned a well deserved reputation as an extravagant free spirit. In her autobiography she wrote: "I have never been able to accept the two great laws of humanity—that you're always being suppressed if you're inspired and always being pushed into the corner if you're exceptional. I won't be cornered and I won't be suppressed."[125] The *Little Review* reflected this attitude of irrepressible rebellion and this devotion to absolute freedom. Besides publishing contributions by leading literary figures, it carried Anderson's controversial editorials. In February 1915 she announced that her journal "existed to create some attitude which so far is absolutely alien to the American tradition." The following month Anderson criticized a recent lecture on sex for failing to approve explicitly of "free love, free divorce, social motherhood, birth control, and the 'sex' morality of the future." And in December 1915 she concluded an editorial by asking: "For God's sake, why doesn't someone start the revolution?"[126]

With Margaret Anderson and Harriet Monroe as well as Sherwood Anderson and Carl Sandburg, Chicago seemed as much a center of literary insurgency as it was a focus of architectural revolt. During the second decade of the twentieth century, it had become an intellectual hub that momentarily at least made New York seem dull by comparison. Writers were breaking free of the past in hope of creating an American literary tradition in that supposedly most American of regions, the Midwest. In 1917 the city's greatest outside admirer H. L. Mencken summed up the irreverent, antitraditional American feeling that pervaded the Windy City literary scene when he wrote: "[Chicago] is not London-and-Harvard. It is not Paris-and-buttermilk. It is American in every chitling and sparerib, and it is alive from snout to tail."[127] The long-sought cultural independence from the East apparently had arrived, and in the minds of the novelists, essayists, poets, and literary hangers-on clustered along the shores of Lake Michigan, Chicago was a city whose intellectual horizons were as broad and open as the heartland prairies.

But Chicago's literary heyday proved relatively shortlived. As early as 1913 Floyd Dell left for New York City, four years later Margaret Anderson and her *Little Review* had joined him in Gotham, and in 1922 Sherwood Anderson abandoned Chicago for good. In 1928 Carl Sandburg moved his family from the hog butcher of the world to a goat farm in Michigan, and in 1936, 75-year-old Harriet Monroe died while traveling in Peru. As late as 1923 Ben Hecht's *Literary Times* could still refer to New York as "the national cemetery of arts and letters" where cultural journals talked "about Art as if it were their dead grandmother."[128] Yet two years later Hecht had migrated to that cemetery, and in 1926 Mencken's *American Mercury* carried an article bearing the title "Chicago: An Obituary" which listed thirty-six writers who had moved from the Windy City.[129] In 1940 a compendium titled *Contemporary American Authors* surveyed the nation's literary talent, but not one novelist, critic, short-story writer, or historian then resident in Chicago won inclusion in the work.[130] This survey might have unfairly omitted some deserving Chicagoans, but clearly the Illinois metropolis was not the literary force it once had been.

Chicago's literary boom of the second decade of the twentieth century was in the words of Sherwood Anderson a "Robin Egg's Renaissance" that "fell out of the nest." "Had we stayed in the home nest," Anderson wrote, "in Chicago, where it all began for so many of us, the Robin's Egg might have hatched."[131] Anderson and the others, however, scattered abroad, and the intellectual momentum was lost. Chicago continued to fuel the literary imagination of its former residents, and such novelists as Dreiser and Dell continued to use the city as a setting for their works long after they had moved away. To a large degree, Chicago played the same role for the authors as it played for the characters in their books. It was the way station to success; the place where young small-town Midwesterners came to find fame and fortune. Once they had profited from the tough, lively giant on Lake Michigan, they moved on. In fiction and in life, Chicago spelled opportunity; it was a place to fulfill one's ambition but having done so one could depart for pleasanter or more refined climes.

Yet during the early twentieth century when Jane Addams presided at

Hull House, Daniel Burnham made big plans, Frank Lloyd Wright designed tradition-defying buildings, Harriet Monroe breathed life into American poetry, and a corps of creative writers gathered at Floyd Dell's studio, Chicago was a city of extraordinary vitality. The Windy City and the Midwest in general was at high noon, having achieved an industrial, political, and cultural zenith. The heartland was truly the heart of the nation, the place where the action was in all areas of life. Moreover, for a short, thrilling moment it seemed that Anderson's egg of renaissance was actually going to hatch, producing progeny of distinction for decades to come.

15. Hull House, pictured here about 1910, was the center of social reform in Chicago. Chicago Historical Society.

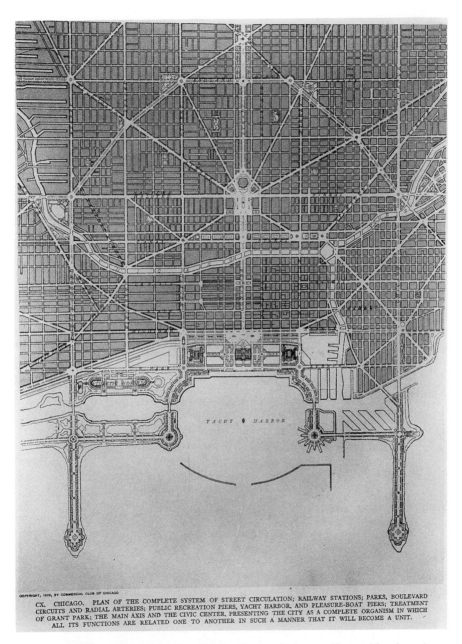

CX. CHICAGO. PLAN OF THE COMPLETE SYSTEM OF STREET CIRCULATION; RAILWAY STATIONS; PARKS, BOULEVARD CIRCUITS AND RADIAL ARTERIES; PUBLIC RECREATION PIERS, YACHT HARBOR, AND PLEASURE-BOAT PIERS; TREATMENT OF GRANT PARK; THE MAIN AXIS AND THE CIVIC CENTER, PRESENTING THE CITY AS A COMPLETE ORGANISM IN WHICH ALL ITS FUNCTIONS ARE RELATED ONE TO ANOTHER IN SUCH A MANNER THAT IT WILL BECOME A UNIT.

16. Daniel Burnham's plan for Chicago imposed elegant diagonal boulevards on the city's grid as well as providing for a new civic center plaza (center) and a yacht basin (bottom center). Chicago Historical Society.

17. A rendering of Burnham's proposed Chicago civic center, with the union station in the foreground and domed city hall in the background. Chicago Historical Society.

18. This demonstration in support of the Chicago Plan, complete with a brass band, is representative of the sales techniques of Walter D. Moody. Chicago Historical Society.

19. With its horizontal lines and low, overhanging roof, Frank Lloyd Wright's Robie House was a classic expression of the architectural style of the Prairie School. Chicago Historical Society.

20. Pictured here in 1950, Gary's U. S. Steel plant, and the mass of Detroit-made automobiles in the parking lot, exemplified the industrial might of the Midwest during the first two-thirds of the twentieth century. Chicago Historical Society.

21. Gary's blast furnaces were a symbol of the continuing vitality of midwestern manufacturing during the midcentury. Indiana State Library.

22. In 1950 Chicago was the center of radio and television manufacturing. Shown here is the Zenith Radio Corporation plant. Chicago Historical Society.

6.

After the Heyday

From the late 1890s to the close of the second decade of the twentieth century, an exciting energy had pervaded the heartland cities, making them the envy of the world. They were the birthplace of the automobile revolution, an industrial and technological transformation that put dollars in the pockets of workers and capitalists alike and which freed millions of Americans from the plodding horse and buggy and the crowded streetcar. Midwestern hubs were also hotbeds of political reform where idealists sought to create good government and achieve the goal of urban democracy. Moreover, the great social laboratory of Chicago seemed to promise solutions to problems plaguing urban centers throughout the world. That same city was on the cutting edge of planning, architecture, and literature. Ford, Johnson, Addams, Wright, and Monroe all dreamed of a great new world, and they sought their wonder-working transformation in the cities of the heartland. Together they presided over the heyday of the midwestern cities.

After World War I the heartland centers remained wealthy hubs of manufacturing and commerce, but they no longer captured the imagination as they once did. The heyday had passed, and Chicago, Cleveland, Detroit, and Saint Louis settled into a period of maturity. They still demonstrated considerable life but were troubled by the first signs of deteriorating health. Between 1920 and 1945 economic depression and labor conflict took especially heavy tolls in the industrial Midwest. At the same time, the rhetoric of political reform grew stale, and expectations for utopian government on the shores of Lake Erie waned. Sherwood Anderson's Robin's Egg Renaissance never hatched, and the practitioners of the Prairie School grew older and more discouraged, having failed to secure the triumph of their heartland aesthetic. The quarter century from the close of World War I to the end of World War II proved a less than exhilarating postlude to the golden quarter century following the Columbian Exposition of 1893.

This transition to a state of troubled maturity was evident in the population figures for the period. In the 1920s cities like Detroit and Flint continued to post impressive population gains, and the other midwestern centers also recorded healthy increases. Yet the nation's boomtowns were now in the Sunbelt. During the 1920s the five fastest growing metropolitan districts were Miami, Los Angeles, Oklahoma City, Houston, and San Diego; of the twenty-five metropolitan areas with the greatest rate of population increase,

TABLE 5

Most Populous Midwestern Cities, 1930 and 1940

City	1930 Population	1940 Population	Percentage of Change
Chicago	3,376,438	3,396,808	+0.6
Detroit	1,568,662	1,623,452	+3.5
Cleveland	900,429	878,336	−2.5
Saint Louis	821,960	816,048	−0.7
Milwaukee	578,249	587,472	+1.6
Cincinnati	451,160	455,610	+1.0
Indianapolis	364,161	386,972	+6.3
Toledo	290,718	282,349	−2.9
Columbus	290,564	306,087	+5.3
Akron	255,040	244,791	−4.0
Dayton	200,982	210,718	+4.8
Youngstown	170,002	167,720	−1.3

Sources: Bureau of the Census, Censuses of 1930 and 1940 (Washington: Government Printing Office,1932 and 1942).

only three were in the Old Northwest, whereas eighteen were in the states of the former Confederacy plus Oklahoma and California.

The data for the 1930s were even less encouraging for the Midwest. As seen in Table 5, five of the twelve largest cities in the industrial Midwest lost population, with Cleveland, Saint Louis, Toledo, Akron, and Youngstown all recording losses for the first time in their histories. During the sluggish depression decade, the population of the nation as a whole rose 7.2 percent, but not one of the twelve largest heartland cities could even match this national average. Moreover, lesser midwestern hubs also proved less than dynamic in their growth. Nine of the twenty midwestern cities having over 100,000 inhabitants in 1930 lost population during the following decade, with Grand Rapids, Flint, Evansville, and South Bend joining Cleveland and the others in the loser's column.

In part, this was owing to the failure of heartland cities to annex additional territory. Chicago, Cleveland, and Cincinnati were finding it increasingly difficult to add acreage to their municipal domains, and consequently a large portion of new residential construction was beyond the central-city boundaries. In fact, the total land area of the twelve largest heartland cities rose only 4 percent during the 1930s, with only a 2-percent increase for the top six midwestern central cities.

Yet even the figures for the metropolitan areas, including both central cities and suburbs, testified to below average growth in the urban Midwest. The 1940 census identified thirty metropolitan districts in the Old Northwest plus Saint Louis, and of these thirty only four grew at a faster pace than the national average for metropolitan districts. Twenty-six increased at a slower rate or in the case of Toledo actually lost population in the metropolitan area as a whole as well as in the central city. Moreover, the four that topped the national average were the smaller metropolitan areas of Madison, Evansville, Lansing, and Peoria. The Chicago, Cleveland, and Cincinnati metropolitan areas each posted a population gain of less than 4 percent. By comparison, of the forty-two metropolitan districts in the former Confederacy plus California, thirty-seven grew at a rate greater than the national average for metropolitan areas. Only five increased at a slower pace or dropped in number of inhabitants. The figure for Miami and suburbs soared 90 percent, for metropolitan Houston the rise was 51 percent, and the population of the sprawling Los Angeles metropolitan area increased 25 percent.

Already, then, a pattern of Sunbelt urban growth and midwestern metropolitan sluggishness was apparent. This was a phenomenon that was to become an established fact of American life for the remainder of the century, and it resulted in a shift in the midwestern regional consciousness. Traditionally, Midwesterners had seen the Northeast as their preeminent rival; Chicago and Cleveland had long sought to upstage New York and Boston. The South was a primitive land that posed no economic or cultural threat, and the West was a sparsely populated market for midwestern goods. Gradually, though, the South and West would become the new focus of midwestern regional anxieties. These were the areas that increasingly seemed to be robbing the heartland of its wealth and profiting from its misfortunes.

During the period 1920 to 1945, however, there was still a good deal of life left in the mature midwestern cities. They remained great manufacturing centers and were still at the heart of the nation's economy. Advertisements in national magazines warned readers that prices for the advertised product might be "slightly higher west of the Rockies," for that territory remained remote from most of the country's great factories. Nevertheless, by the 1930s Americans no longer viewed the Midwest as a land of unequaled opportunity nor did novelists continue to use Chicago as a metaphor for the American dream of material success. Now golden California represented the fulfillment of American aspirations. In 1900 Sister Carrie had gone to Chicago; had the novel been written forty years later she would have gone to Hollywood. The course of empire was moving westward and southward, and it seemed, for the first time, to be passing beyond the Midwest.

The Urban Economy

In 1930 and in 1940 as in 1920 the automobile dominated midwestern industry. No new products challenged its supremacy, and in one city after another thousands of workers depended on motor vehicles and their accessories for their livelihood. Henry Ford, Ransom Olds, Henry Leland, and

William Durant had firmly planted the motor vehicle industry in the Midwest, and during the 1920s and 1930s its roots reached ever deeper into the region's urban economy.

Detroit remained the auto capital, the city's name becoming a synonym for the American motor industry. In 1929, 54 percent of the industrial wage earners in Detroit and environs were engaged in the manufacture of motor vehicles, bodies, and parts. By 1939 this figure had risen to 62 percent. In 1940 one observer commented: "Detroit's changing social moods can be read in statistics of automobile production. When the industry can build and sell 4,000,000 cars or more a year, . . . every one in Detroit feels buoyant." Yet "cut production in half," and no one tied to the city's all-important industry could be "even moderately cheerful."[1] Autos alone determined Detroit's fortunes; the moods, hopes, and anxieties of the entire metropolis were simply by-products of that one industry.

Elsewhere in Michigan the automobile wielded equal power. The state's third largest city, Flint, was the domain of General Motors, and by 1936 more than two-thirds of the gainfully employed in that community were on the General Motors payroll. In the late 1930s a local cleric observed succinctly and accurately: "Flint is decidedly a Company Town."[2] With its furniture industry, Grand Rapids, Michigan's second largest city, enjoyed greater freedom from the sway of the motor vehicle, but even there auto manufacturing was gaining a strong foothold. By 1929 the city's largest employer was the Hayes Body Corporation, which produced auto bodies for Chrysler, Willys-Overland, and Reo, and in 1935 General Motors opened a stamping plant in the community.[3]

Outside Michigan auto manufacturing also paid the bills in many households. In terms of value added by manufacture, in 1929 motor vehicles and their bodies and parts ranked first among the industries in both the Cleveland and Milwaukee industrial areas. As defined by the census bureau, the latter district included Kenosha, where Nash continued to turn out tens of thousands of autos each year. Moreover, in the Indianapolis and Dayton metropolitan districts the motor vehicle industry placed second in value added. In Studebaker's hometown of South Bend more than half the factory workers were engaged in the manufacturing of motor vehicles, and Toledo was almost as dependent on automaking as Flint and Detroit, with the Willys-Overland automobile company providing 41 percent of the city's entire payroll in 1925.[4] Like Flint, Toledo during the 1920s was virtually a single-company town under the control of John Willys and his corporation. "It took the greater part of the auto industry to refashion Detroit," wrote one industry expert, "whereas, the development of Toledo was almost a one-man job."[5] In the 1930s Willys-Overland fell on hard times and its role in Toledo's economy diminished, but auto-related industries remained the mainstay of the community. By 1939 Toledo was the center of the automotive electrical equipment industry, accounting for 22 percent of the nation's total production in this field.

Overall, the Old Northwest continued to manufacture an overwhelming proportion of the nation's motor vehicles, with Michigan, Ohio, Indiana, and Wisconsin ranking first, second, third, and fifth respectively in auto production. In 1929 the region accounted for 76 percent of American wage earners in motor vehicle manufacturing, and ten years later this figure had risen to 84 percent. No one could deny that the Midwest was still the heartland of American automobile manufacturing.

Much of the region's other industry was dependent on the fortunes of auto manufacturers. Though not actually fabricating vehicles, factories throughout the region supplied automakers. Detroit was their best, and sometimes their only, customer. For example, Cleveland remained a great steelmaking center, and as early as 1919, 50 percent of the steel manufactured in the Ohio metropolis went to the motor vehicle industry.[6] During the interwar years Cincinnati claimed to be "the recognized world center for machine tool production," and in 1929 it accounted for 13 percent of the nation's wage earners in this industry.[7] With its yearly model changes, Detroit demanded an ever changing inventory of new machine tools, thus keeping the Cincinnati works humming.

Akron's tire industry was even more closely linked to Detroit. More autos meant a demand for more tires, so when Detroit prospered so did Akron. Moreover, the high wages paid by the rubber companies discouraged other industries from locating in the community, keeping it in bondage to one product. In 1929, 79 percent of Akron's wage earners worked in the rubber plants, and rubber was all that counted in the local economy. At the close of the 1930s novelist Ruth McKenney wrote of the Ohio city: "The town stinks and throbs and sometimes gets rich and more often goes on relief with Rubber. Rubber is the first and last fact of life to the people of Akron."[8]

During the 1920s and 1930s, however, Akron's share of the nation's tire output declined because of the rubber companies' efforts to decentralize production. Ohio was home to 66 percent of the nation's tire workers in 1929, but ten years later this figure was down to 55 percent. Goodyear pioneered decentralization, opening a plant in Los Angeles in 1920. By the close of the decade three other rubber companies had followed suit, making the California metropolis the second largest rubber manufacturing center in the United States. In 1929 Goodyear established a factory in Gadsen, Alabama, again opting to invest outside of Akron.[9] These moves did not bode well for the Ohio city. It remained a community almost wholly dependent on rubber, but gradually tire makers were seeking factories elsewhere.

Akron, Cleveland, Dayton, Indianapolis, Milwaukee, and a score of others all remained in Detroit's industrial sphere of influence, both suffering and prospering with the Michigan metropolis. In one community after another residents claimed that when Detroit sneezed, their city caught pneumonia. But when Detroit was fat and happy so were all its industrial satellites. The auto was king in the Midwest, and during the 1920s and 1930s it seemed secure on its throne.

There were, however, a few notable exceptions to its domain. Chicago never had achieved success as an automobile manufacturing center and thus was less vulnerable to the side effects of decreased sales of Fords or Chevrolets. Ford maintained an assembly plant on the far south side, and the metropolitan area could boast of some truck manufacturers as well as the makers of headlights, speedometers, radiators, and an assortment of other accessories.[10] But meat packing, steel making, furniture manufacturing, and railroad car construction and repair still employed far more workers in Chicago and environs than did the motor vehicle industry. The Windy City remained the nation's greatest provisioner of meats, and the completion of the American Furniture Mart building in 1924 and the gargantuan Merchandise Mart in 1930 made it the undisputed hub of America's wholesale furniture trade.[11] Meanwhile, the city's Wrigley Company was selling Americans on the advantages of chewing gum. Chicago was a city of diversity, not enslaved to one product or dependent on the sales of a single item.

Though the Windy City failed to corner the automobile trade, it was profiting from the new technology of the twentieth century. During the 1920s and 1930s it was the recognized center of the electrical equipment industry and ranked first in radio manufacturing. "Many of the Chicago [radio] plants are running night and day," reported a local journal in 1922, "and are still behind in filling orders." By 1928 Chicago was the source of approximately one-third of the nation's radios, and at the close of the 1930s the Chicago area accounted for 24 percent of all American wage earners engaged in the manufacture of radios, radio tubes, and phonographs.[12] So long as families in New York, Texas, and California continued to tune in to their favorite radio programs each night, Chicago seemed destined to profit.

The other great midwestern metropolis that remained outside the automobile's industrial domain was Saint Louis. Like Chicago and unlike Detroit, it was a community of diverse manufactures. Meat packing and iron and steel making were major industries, but in both 1929 and 1939 shoe manufacturing led in the number of wage earners. Saint Louis was the "Shoe City," the headquarters of the nation's largest footwear manufacturer, International Shoe Company, as well as the third largest, Brown Shoe Company. By 1934 Saint Louis manufacturers boasted of producing one-fifth of all the shoes in the country.[13] During the interwar period, however, Saint Louis shoe moguls were shifting much of their production to plants in impoverished small towns scattered through southern Illinois, Missouri, Kentucky, Tennessee, and Arkansas. Such towns enjoyed an abundant supply of low-wage labor, offering manufacturers a welcome alternative to more expensive urban workers. By 1928 the five leading Saint Louis shoe manufacturers had opened factories in fifty-six small communities within a two-hundred-mile radius of the Missouri metropolis.[14] These plants employed over thirty thousand workers, as compared to only eleven thousand wage earners in the shoe industry in the Saint Louis metropolitan area.

Thus Saint Louis's leading industry was migrating from the city to less expensive rural areas. This was a phenomenon that would increasingly plague midwestern urban centers. Corporate headquarters would remain in Saint Louis and the other heartland hubs, but the corporations' factories would depart. If industrialists could find cheaper labor in small towns, the South, or even abroad, they would abandon their urban plants and head out of town, leaving heartland urbanites jobless. Already workers in Saint Louis shoe plants were witnessing this threat to urban manufacturing; in future decades employees throughout the Midwest would become well aware of the eroding influence of cheap labor elsewhere.

Shoemaking, however, was of little concern to most heartlanders, for their region was primarily dependent on the internal combustion engine and big-ticket durable goods. Automobiles and trucks from Detroit, Flint, Toledo, South Bend, and Kenosha were the mainstays of much of the midwestern economy. Even where the automobile was not so entrenched, other heavy durable goods prevailed. In the Milwaukee area the largest manufacturing corporation was Allis-Chalmers, the producer of agricultural, industrial, and electrical machinery, including million-dollar hydraulic turbines.[15] Racine's J. I. Case Company turned out tractors, Columbus's Jeffrey Corporation built mining machinery, and Youngstown Sheet and Tube produced the steel necessary for all of these. The Midwest created goods for the big spender: the consumer eager for a shiny new car and the industrialist ready to expand and install millions of dollars of new machinery.

Because of the heartland's focus on expensive durables, it was especially sensitive to the fluctuations of the economic cycle. If the economy turned bad, consumers quickly shelved plans to purchase a new automobile; the old one was always good for a few thousand additional miles. Likewise, if demand was down, manufacturers immediately cut back on machine tool orders. When agricultural prices plummeted, farmers were not likely to rush to their J. I. Case dealer for a new tractor. In good times and bad, people bought sausage and shoes, but Midwesterners had increasingly invested their labor and capital in products that were not wanted when depression loomed. Consequently, economic depressions struck especially severe blows in the heartland. Cleveland, Detroit, and Milwaukee were on an economic roller coaster of unequaled danger. Nowhere were the plunges so sharp or the ascents more abrupt.

This was evident in the short depression of 1920 and 1921. Throughout the nation business slumped, but the Midwest suffered a most precipitous drop that emptied the pockets of many urban heartlanders. In March 1920 the automobile industry produced a record 220,000 cars; by January 1921 the monthly output had plummeted to 20,000. In December 1920 Henry Ford halted all production at his plants, laying off his labor force of 60,000 persons, and that same month the giant Dodge factory was operating only two days a week.[16] Meanwhile, at Akron's Goodyear plant, tire production dropped from a daily average of 33,000 to only 5,000.[17] As a result of the debacle, General Motors founder William Durant was forced from command of the giant automaker, Goodyear founder F. A. Seiberling likewise lost control of his corporate creation, and Toledo's Willys Corporation went into receivership.

The impact on workers was sharp and quick. By October 1920, 54,000 jobless auto workers walked the streets of Detroit.[18] The number of wage earners in Cleveland's automobile plants fell from 25,749 in July 1920 to 8,518 in December 1921; in Toledo the number plunged from 18,935 in January 1920 to 2,264 one year later.[19] Akron's tire factories employed 80,513 wage earners in April 1920 but less than 22,000 in January 1921.[20] Boomtowns that had known unprecedented growth and prosperity during the previous decade now became visible reminders of the fickleness of an auto-based economy. "Akron, after many years of abundant prosperity . . . which directed the attention of the country to us, is now passing through its first slow period in more than a dozen years," admitted the president of the Akron Chamber of Commerce in early 1921. But he denied the truth of stories claiming that a "large percentage of [Akron's] population" had "left the city" and claimed that the city was "only making its contribution to the readjustment which [was] absolutely necessary" before Akron went "forward into a period of sane development."[21] By the summer of 1921 his views seemed justified, and the chamber of commerce was boasting that Akron had "recuperative powers which were not dreamed of" a year before.[22] Yet the shortlived downturn powerfully demonstrated the vulnerability of the Midwest's industrial economy.

Even during the prosperous years of the mid-1920s the auto industry suffered from pronounced and unpredictable seasonal fluctuations that meant layoffs for thousands of workers. A 1928 study of industry in Ohio noted "the extremely irregular character of the seasonal fluctuations in employment" in auto manufacturing which reflected "the inability of the industry to adjust its production schedules to demand conditions."[23] In the best of times, auto sales would dip for a few months and then soar, forcing automakers to contract and expand in rapid succession. For example, in Toledo, the number of auto workers rose from 11,778 in January 1925 to 17,986 in May of that year and then back down to 12,939 in August.[24] That same year in the nation as a whole, the number of auto workers in the worst month was 76 percent of the number in the best month; by comparison the number of wage earners in the cotton goods industry in the slowest month was 93 percent that in the busiest.[25] Demand for textiles was steady, ensuring greater employment stability in the cloth-producing states of New England and the Southeast. But in the auto empire of the heartland instability was the norm, and no one was able to smooth the jagged graphs of sales and production. In 1938 a General Motors economist admitted: "The answer to the problem of stabilizing the demand for auotomobiles still lies in the unknown future." "Certainly it lies largely beyond the present powers of the automobile manufacturers," he concluded, "so long as free citizens continue to have the right to make their own choices of values and, what is more important, to change those choices without advance notice to the producers."[26]

During the early 1930s consumers exercised this freedom of choice with a vengeance, forcing the automobile industry to its knees. Auto and truck production plunged from over 5,600,000 vehicles in 1929 to 1,431,000 in 1932; during this same period tire output fell 40 percent.[27] Lansing's Durant Company ceased production in 1932, and four years later that city's Reo Motor Company abandoned the passenger car field and restricted itself to the making of trucks and buses.[28] In 1933 Toledo's Willys company again went into receivership as did South Bend's Studebaker Corporation.[29] Production at Kenosha's Nash Motors plant plummeted from almost 117,000 cars in 1929 to less than 15,000 in 1933, and Hamtramck's Dodge Main factory turned out 250,000 autos annually in the late 1920s but only 28,000 in 1932.[30] By 1932 auto buyers were a rare species. From the beginning of July to the end of September that year, 9,068 automobiles were sold in Chicago whereas 10,199 were stolen.[31] Thieves were doing a better business than dealers.

The hardships resulting from economic disaster were especially evident in automobile communities, but they were felt in other cities as well. Even before the stock market crash in October 1929, a growing number of auto workers found themselves jobless, and the number of Michigan wage earners in the industry fell 42 percent between April and December 1929.[32] The drop continued, and in Flint alone employment at General Motors plunged from 56,000 in mid-1929 to under 17,000 three years later.[33] In Milwaukee County the number of employed wage earners declined 44 percent, falling from 117,658 in 1929 to 66,010 in 1933.[34] In the contest for gloomy statistics, Cincinnati proved almost as successful, losing 41 percent of its wage-earning jobs during this same period.[35]

Throughout the Midwest, heartlanders suffered the grim consequences of joblessness. In Fort Wayne foreclosures on mortgages soared from a yearly average of about 70 in the late 1920s to 612 in 1932.[36] One-fifth of Milwaukee's population was on relief by April 1933, and the city was able to collect less than 50 percent of the levied property taxes from its hard-pressed citizenry.[37] As early as January 1930, a social worker visiting Detroit reported that "more of the automobile workers were found among the men and women shuffling dejectedly at the public and private employment offices."[38] One discouraged Detroit job seeker exclaimed: "Only God knows and sometimes I think even God don't know much about hunting a job."[39] In 1932 Milwaukee's Socialist mayor Daniel Hoan told the city council: "We are in the midst of a world-wide economic and social revolution that will not cease until the present industrial system, called Capitalism, is entirely replaced by the next stage of human development which is called Socialism." According to Hoan, Midwesterners were experiencing "but the death agonies of a dying system, and the birth pains of the building of a new and better world."[40] For those in Detroit, Fort Wayne, and Milwaukee who were losing their jobs, their homes, and their self-respect, this supposed death of capitalism was a long and arduous ordeal, and they saw little evidence of the better world to come.

Moreover, the economic decline in the Midwest was more prolonged and lasting in its effects than in the nation as a whole. Of the thirty-three major industrial areas identified in the 1939 census of manufactures, eleven were in the Old Northwest plus Saint Louis. Whereas the number of wage earners in the nation as a whole fell 5.8 percent between 1929 and 1939, in nine of these eleven midwestern centers the decline was even more marked. In the Cleveland, Saint Louis, Cincinnati, and Indianapolis industrial areas the drop was over 10 percent, whereas in Milwaukee the number of wage earners in 1939 was almost 30 percent less than in 1929, and in Akron and Toledo the decline was about 40 percent.[41] In fact, of all the nation's major manufacturing centers, these latter two recorded the sharpest fall in number of industrial workers. By contrast, in the Los Angeles area the number of wage earners rose approximately 25 percent between 1929 and 1939. Los Angeles had not escaped the depression of the 1930s, but its economy had shown greater resiliency than that of the midwestern hubs and had recovered sufficiently to record a healthy growth for the decade. Ironically, however, the rubber capital had not bounced back, and neither had most of the other heartland centers.

Sluggish sales and persistent layoffs were not the only problems plaguing midwestern industry. Equally troublesome was the emerging labor unrest, as unions sought to organize the great factories and management resisted. Chicago had been renowned as a hotbed of labor radicalism in the late nineteenth century, and socialism had won a temporary following among heartlanders in the early twentieth century. But the giant auto, rubber, and steel plants of the Midwest had escaped unionization, and chambers of commerce in one community after another had boasted that their city was an open-shop town. One of the attractions of Detroit for automakers had been its reputation as an open-shop stronghold, and until the 1930s General Motors, Ford, and the others had successfully kept unions from gaining control over the local labor force. Yet all this changed in the 1930s, as the industrial Midwest became a bastion of big labor and won an unenviable reputation for poor labor relations and union-management violence.

Encouraged by New Deal legislation favorable to their cause, unions mobilized during Franklin Roosevelt's first two terms, and strikes erupted throughout the heartland. In 1934 at least 107 strikes involving more than twenty-seven thousand employees broke out in Milwaukee. The most disruptive was that against the Milwaukee Electric Railway and Light Company, but that year it seemed as if everyone was ready to walk off the job in the Wisconsin metropolis. Students at the Dover Street grade school even struck, demanding shorter hours and no homework.[42] In 1934 and 1935 Toledo witnessed twenty-two strikes involving thirteen thousand workers, and the work stoppage at the Electric Auto-Lite Company resulted in a pitched battle between strikers and the Ohio National Guard that left two men dead.[43] In 1936 labor agitators closed Akron's Goodyear plant for five weeks, idling almost fourteen thousand employees. "The present issue is one of defiance of duly constituted government to protect a man in his right to work," announced Goodyear's president, but the mayor's chief concern was "the peaceful settlement of the strike before violence and before heads [were] broken and men put in hospitals."[44]

Before 1937 the unions won only partial victories in the battle for recognition; management would negotiate with the unions but not recognize them as the sole bargaining agent for the workers. In 1937, however, an unprecedented wave of labor action would strengthen the hand of union leaders, and by the close of the decade the success of the unionization crusade was ensured. The high point of the agitation in 1937 was the famous sit-down strike against the General Motors plants in Flint. Action against General Motors actually began on December 28, 1936 when seven hundred of the seven thousand workers at Cleveland's Fisher Body plant sat down on the job and refused to leave the factory, thereby halting production. Two days later a group of employees at the Fisher Body Division of General Motors in Flint did likewise, beginning a forty-four day occupation of the automaker's plants. Members of the United Automobile Workers union led by the Reuther brothers demanded that General Motors recognize their organization as the exclusive bargaining agent for the company's production employees. For weeks Flint remained tense, with periodic outbreaks of violence. In the "Battle of the Running Bulls," city police used tear gas and riot guns against strikers who responded by hurling automobile door hinges, bottles, and stones. Sixteen civilians and eleven law enforcement officers were wounded in the fray.[45] In February 1937, an observer described Flint as "an armed camp" with "more than 4,000 National Guards . . . , including cavalry and machine gun corps." "A night visit to the big Chevrolet plant and Fisher Body #2," she wrote, "reminds one of an American sector in war time France."[46] Finally General Motors agreed to recognize the United Automobile Workers as a bargaining agent, though not necessarily the sole one, and production resumed.

But the Flint stoppage initiated a wave of sit-down strikes, disrupting business throughout the Midwest. A management spokesman claimed that between November 1, 1936, and December 31, 1937, Detroit alone was the scene of 325 sit-down strikes involving not only factories but other concerns as well.[47] Sit-downers occupied the city's Statler and Book-Cadillac hotels, and in March 1937 strikers took possession of the Chrysler facilities for eighteen days, including the giant Dodge Main. Meanwhile, workers sat down at the Hudson automobile plants, occupying them for five weeks. "Sitting down has replaced baseball as a national pastime," remarked a Detroit newspaper reporter, "and sitter-downers clutter up the landscape in every direction."[48] A national magazine commented ominously: "Detroiters last week were getting an idea of what a revolution feels like."[49] In testimony before Congress a representative of the Automobile Manufacturers Association referred to the flurry of sit-down stoppages as a "wave of lawlessness and violence which . . . engulfed Detroit commercial life."[50] Once a monument to American capitalism, the Motor City was apparently becoming a symbol of the breakdown of the vaunted economic system.

Elsewhere in the heartland, however, labor unrest also captured the headlines. Ohio's National Guard was called to duty in Cleveland during the explosive strike against Republic Steel during the summer of 1937. On June 7, 1937, workers in Lansing called a one-day general strike, though when union members attempted to extend the stoppage to adjacent East Lansing, students at the state college came to the defense of management and tossed labor agitators into the Red Cedar River.[51] Yet employers and the Michigan State students were fighting a losing battle. Pressure from the federal government's National Labor Relations Board combined with strike action by labor organizations were forcing midwestern management to yield to the demands of the United Automobile Workers, the United Steel Workers, and the United Rubber Workers. In December 1939 the *New York Times* recognized this marked change when it observed of the motor capital: "The pendulum, which once swung so far to one side that this city came to be known by employers as the model open-shop or non-union community in the country, has now swung in the other direction. Labor now regards Detroit as one of the best organized cities in the nation."[52] By the beginning of the 1940s unions had conquered not only the Motor City but the entire industrial heartland.

In the process, however, the Midwest had acquired a threatening blot on its economic record. The news from Flint, Detroit, Cleveland, Milwaukee, and elsewhere had given the heartland a reputation for poor labor relations; in the future, industrialists would invest in the Midwest at their own risk. In 1940 one student of Detroit wrote: "A new incentive now exists for manufacturers to decentralize the work of materializing Detroit's energy into motorcars." Because "cities of lesser population" beckoned with "lower rents, promises of lower living costs, and hints of greater satisfaction for workingmen," he believed that it was "a safe guess" that future expansion in the auto industry would "take place elsewhere at a faster rate than in the corporate limits of Detroit and its sister cities of the automobile belt."[53] Akron boosters likewise feared decentralization of the rubber industry to communities with cheaper, more docile labor. In 1938 B. F. Goodrich threatened to take five thousand jobs out of Akron if its workers refused to accept a wage cut. Goodrich employees did not yield, and the company failed to follow through on its threat.[54] But the local chamber of commerce turned pale, recognizing that the rubber companies were already gradually shifting production elsewhere. Some day perhaps Goodrich, Goodyear, and Firestone would get so fed up with the high wages and labor strife of the rubber capital that they actually would leave town. This was the nightmare that kept Akron's chamber of commerce leaders awake; and in other heartland communities with labor troubles, similar bad dreams disturbed the sleep of loyal boosters.

During the early 1940s, however, fears of industrial decline were momentarily forgotten as World War II brought new prosperity to the Midwest. With its concentration of metal-working industries engaged in the manufacture of vehicles and machinery, the heartland proved invaluable to the American war effort and won a hefty share of lucrative defense contracts. Evansville produced amphibious landing craft and airplanes, and because of this war business the local labor force soared from twenty-one thousand to sixty-four thousand workers.[55] Indianapolis manufactured airplane engines and boasted of the largest aircraft propellor plant in the nation. By 1942 the federal government was classifying Indiana's capital city as a "labor shortage area," something that depression-stricken Hoosiers a few years before never would have imagined.[56] Rockford took pride in its designation by a War Department official as "the most important city of its size in the country in terms of national defense."[57]

Meanwhile, Cleveland became the home of the Thompson Aircraft plant with twenty-one thousand employees and the giant Fisher Aircraft factory. From 1940 to 1944 employment in the Ohio metropolis rose 34 percent, and the Federal Bureau of Labor Statistics remarked: "Cleveland is one of the Nation's industrial centers which has expanded most since the beginning of the war."[58]

Michigan, however, was the true arsenal of democracy, exceeding the other heartland states in the dollar value of its war production. With only 4 percent of the nation's population, Michigan garnered more than 10 percent of the defense contracts.[59] In Lansing, Oldsmobile manufactured 48 million rounds of ammunition, 140,000 tank cannons and aircraft machine guns as well as almost 350,000 aircraft engine parts.[60] Residents of the Michigan capital proudly proclaimed that everyone was joining in the production effort. "A trip through Lansing war plants today reveals many startling changes, especially in personnel," wrote a local newspaper in 1943. "Men who formerly operated retail business establishments, salesmen, gas station attendants, housewives, clerks, and people from many of the professions are working together along assembly lines."[61] But Lansing's contribution was minor compared to that of Detroit. The Motor City surpassed every other American metropolis in its wartime production, and total employment in the Detroit area more than doubled from 396,000 in 1940 to 867,000 in November 1943.[62] Detroit was again a boomtown, overcrowded with a restless, shifting population. Following a visit in October 1943, a reporter for *Daily Variety* described the Motor City as "the hottest town in America," "where they stand in line for a glass of beer . . . where the sidewalk madonnas get too much opposition from home talent . . . and where everybody has two sawbucks to rub against each other."[63]

The much publicized symbol of the Detroit area's awesome productive capacity was Henry Ford's mammoth bomber plant at Willow Run. Thirty miles west of the Motor City, Willow Run's main building covered sixty-seven acres and its final assembly line stretched more than a mile in length. Charles Lindbergh described the factory as "a sort of Grand Canyon of the mechanized world."[64] At peak production the plant employed over forty-two thousand workers, and adjacent to it was a fifteen-building dormitory complex accommodating more than seven thousand persons.[65] Willow Run visibly testified to the fact that the Midwest remained the heartland of American manufacturing. It seemed a concrete repudiation of the region's depression-era failures.

Yet while thousands of workers manufactured aircraft at Willow Run, others were doing likewise at the sprawling assembly plants of California. Los Angeles gained on Cleveland, Detroit, and Chicago in the 1930s and it continued to do so in the 1940s. Moreover, World War II spurred production and growth in such previously minor contenders for urban glory as San Diego and Phoenix. During the war years midwestern plants were humming, but the specter of postwar decentralization remained. Both their bondage to the volatile vehicle industry and their high-wage, militantly unionized labor force made the heartland cities economically vulnerable. Already shoe manufacturers were forsaking Saint Louis workers for cheap rural labor, and Akron industrialists were seeking plant sites beyond the Buckeye state. The war had put money in pockets that had long been empty. But possibly this was a short-term reprieve from a long-term problem.

The Changing Population

Visitors to Willow Run or the other midwestern defense plants would have found that the workers in the shops and along the assembly lines were different from their counterparts a generation earlier. They would hear fewer foreign tongues spoken in the factories, for the two world wars together with restrictive federal immigration laws enacted in the early 1920s had curbed the influx of newcomers from Europe. Whereas as late as 1910 the foreign born constituted 36 percent of Chicago's population, 35 percent of all Clevelanders, and 34 percent of Detroit residents, by 1940 this figure dropped to 20 percent for Chicago and Detroit and 21 percent for Cleveland. Yet those touring wartime plants would hear more southern drawls, for picking up the labor slack was an army of migrants from the South. In the years immediately before World War I Czechs and Poles had furnished the muscle for the foundries, packing houses, and auto plants of the heartland; by the close of World War II native-born blacks and whites from the southern states were filling an increasing number of the menial jobs in midwestern industry. Thus the midwestern cities were growing more American as the ranks of the native born swelled. Yet they were also growing more diverse as newcomers with different cultures and complexions continued to find a home in the heartland centers.

Especially noteworthy was the decline in German influence in the traditional Teutonic stronghold of the nation. Already before World War I ties to the fatherland were weakening as many of the older immigrants died and the influx of newcomers from Germany slackened. Yet even in 1910 Germans constituted the largest foreign-born group in Chicago, Cleveland, Saint Louis, Milwaukee, and Cincinnati. During the early years of World War I while the United States remained neutral, Germans throughout the Midwest demonstrated their continuing devotion to the fatherland by rallying behind the Kaiser and his empire, with some even volunteering for the Imperial army. The president of Chicago's Germania Club viewed Germany as the defender of civilization, claiming the conflict was a "war of the Teutonic race against the Slavic" to determine "whether the civilization of western Europe or the barbarism of Russia [was] to prevail."[66] Likewise, the heartland's German press depicted the war as "a battle to the bitter end between German civilization and the pan-Slavic, half-Asiatic, and thinly veneered barbarism of Russia."[67] Yet with the American declaration of war against Germany in 1917, such pro-German remarks became taboo. For thousands of heartland urbanites their ethnic origins now became a badge of opprobrium.

Responding to the nation's hatred of all things German, many heartlanders Anglicized their names, becoming Smith rather than Schmidt and Miller rather than Muller. German-American institutions likewise recognized the need to adopt new names. In Indianapolis *Das Deutsche Haus* became the Athenaeum and the *Maennerchor* temporarily became the Academy of Music.[68] Cleveland's German American Savings Bank shortened its name to American Savings Bank.[69] In Chicago the Germania Club became the Lincoln Club, German Hospital was now Grant Hospital, the Bismarck Hotel was transformed into the Hotel Randolph, and the Kaiser Friedrich Mutual Aid Society wisely adopted the new title of George Washington Benevolent and Aid Society.[70] The sentiments of some heartland Germans led to their incarceration. On the day President Wilson sent his request for a declaration of war to Congress, German-born Ernst Kunwald, conductor of the Cincinnati Symphony Orchestra, obediently performed "The Star-Spangled Banner" at the opening of a scheduled concert. Then he announced tearfully to the audience: "But my heart is on the other side." For the duration of the war Kunwald was interned as an enemy alien, and his concertmeister Emil Heerman was likewise arrested, though released into the custody of Cincinnati's Conservatory of Music.[71] To ensure no such incidents occurred in Chicago, the manager of that city's symphony orchestra warned the orchestra's German musicians: "If ever I hear the slightest disloyal or pro-German remark from anyone of you, I will report him not only to the orchestra society, but also the Department of Justice, to make him pay for his foolishness."[72]

Perhaps most damaging to the perpetuation of German culture in the heartland was the widespread attack on the German language. In both Chicago and Cleveland the school boards eliminated instruction of the German language in the elementary grades. Cleveland retained it in the high school curriculum because of "military necessity," and in some Chicago secondary schools pupils could continue to study the language, though few opted to do so.[73] Indiana's legislature outlawed instruction of the language in all public, private, and parochial schools, ensuring that German-Americans of the younger generation would not be taught their linguistic heritage.[74] Until World War I, German had generally been the most commonly studied foreign language in the Midwest, and public and parochial schools had helped second- and third-generation German-Americans to remain bilingual. But after World War I, French and Spanish became the preferred foreign tongues in the high school and college curriculum, as heartlanders cut their ties with the Germanic past.

During the decades following World War I some German-American organizations attempted to rekindle the Teutonic spirit in heartland cities. For example, in 1925 a German-language newspaper in Chicago reported on a local rally of some three thousand sons and daughters of the fatherland which supposedly demonstrated that "the German oak tree [was] still alive despite some devastating storms."[75] Yet in Saint Louis the German-language newspaper *Amerika* ceased publication in 1924, and its one-time competitor the *Westliche Post* closed down in 1938 after years of financial losses.[76] German-language theater attracted meager audiences, and the pro-Nazi German Bund groups active in Milwaukee and Chicago during the 1930s did not enhance the popularity of Teutonic culture among loyal American Midwesterners. Many persons of German ancestry refused even to acknowledge their roots in the wake of World War I. Thus only 112,000 Chicagoans claimed to be German born in 1920 as compared to 191,000 in 1914.[77] Death might have accounted for some of this decline, but changing attitudes toward Germany clearly led many to deny their origins.

Many of the newcomers to the heartland cities during the period 1917 to 1945 did not need to prove their American roots, for their ancestors had settled the South as early as the seventeenth century. Thousands of blacks and whites, however, had little to show for their centuries in the new world; they were impoverished and seemed to have little future in the economically backward states south of the Ohio River. Consequently, they flooded northward at the beginning of World War I and kept coming during the 1920s and the years of World War II. Midwestern factories hungry for labor appeared to offer economic rewards unavailable in the migrants' native region. Cleveland, Detroit, Chicago, and other heartland hubs may not have been paved with gold, but they could provide three meals a day to Southerners in search of something better than coal mines and cotton fields.

The influx of southern blacks was apparent in each succeeding census. Whereas blacks constituted only 2.0 percent of Chicago's population in 1910,

TABLE 6

Percentage of Blacks in Total Population in Largest
Midwestern Cities, 1910 and 1940

City	1910	1940
Chicago	2.0	8.2
Detroit	1.2	9.2
Cleveland	1.5	9.6
Saint Louis	6.4	13.3
Milwaukee	0.3	1.5
Cincinnati	5.4	12.2
Indianapolis	9.3	13.2
Toledo	1.1	5.2
Columbus	7.0	11.7
Akron	1.0	5.0
Dayton	4.2	9.6
Youngstown	2.4	8.7

Sources: Bureau of the Census, Censuses of 1910 and 1940 (Washington: U.S. Government Printing Office, 1913 and 1943).

in 1920 the figure was up to 4.1 percent, in 1930 to 6.9 percent, and in 1940 to 8.2 percent. As seen in Table 6, the black share of the total population increased most dramatically in the Great Lakes cities, rising six or sevenfold in Detroit and Cleveland. Of the major Great Lakes centers only Milwaukee remained virtually lily-white, with African Americans constituting a mere 1.5 percent of the population as late as 1940. In the southern half of the Midwest the African-American population had traditionally been larger, and the rise during the interwar years was less dramatic. The black share approximately doubled in Cincinnati and Saint Louis and increased two-thirds in Columbus and less than half in Indianapolis. Only Evansville, the most southerly of the midwestern cities with over 100,000 inhabitants, deviated from the regional trend and became increasingly white. Conforming to a pattern typical of such upper South cities as Louisville and Nashville, Evansville's blacks made up 9.0 percent of that city's population in 1910 but only 7.1 percent thirty years later.[78]

Most of the black newcomers to the Midwest were from such central southern states as Mississippi, Alabama, and Tennessee, having migrated due north. Some arrived en masse, suddenly boosting the local African-American population. For example, in late May 1917 "896 Negroes" in "sixteen railroad cars" disembarked in Toledo, a city that seven years earlier recorded a total black population of less than nineteen hundred.[79] Most often, however, African Americans arrived in small groups and individually, lured by letters from friends and relatives who had moved north earlier or enticed by glowing articles published by such midwestern black newspapers as Chicago's *Defender*. With a wide circulation in the South, the *Defender* printed an unceasing barrage of propaganda favorable to Chicago and unfavorable to the southern states. Comparing the climate of Chicago with the oppression of the South, the *Defender* proclaimed: "To die from the bite of frost is far more glorious than at the hands of a mob."[80]

Especially appealing to the African Americans was the new sense of freedom in the North. Though racial barriers certainly existed north of the Ohio River, the midwestern cities proved less restrictive than the caste-ridden rural South. When in 1920 the Chicago Commission of Race Relations asked recent black migrants what they liked about the North, almost all the respondents spoke of freedom.[81] According to one newcomer, in Chicago a black person could "go anywhere" and did not "have to look up to the white man, get off the street for him, and go to the buzzard roost at shows."[82] Unlike in the South, in the heartland cities blacks could sit next to whites on streetcars and exercise some political power by casting ballots. Summing up the sense of relative freedom associated with midwestern centers, one migrant said of life in Chicago: "A man could feel more like a man."[83]

While caste pushed blacks from the South, cash pulled them to the midwestern cities. In Chicago, Detroit, and Cleveland, one could find not only a modicum of freedom but also an escape from the menial service jobs traditionally reserved for urban blacks. Migrants did not need to earn their living as servants, waiters, or porters but could find work in factories. Whereas in 1912 blacks constituted only 1.5 percent of all employees at the United States Steel plants in Gary and South Chicago, by 1928 they represented 12.3 percent of these factories' work force.[84] According to one migrant, the steel mills during World War I "were hiring day and night. All they wanted to know was if you wanted to work and if you had a strong back."[85] Likewise, the black share of the work force in the Chicago meat packing industry rose from 3.0 percent in 1909 to 29.5 percent in 1928.[86] "A Negro could always get a job in the stockyards," remembered a railroad porter of the boom days of World War I and the 1920s. "They could go to the stockyards any day of the week and get a job."[87] A 1924 survey of twelve large foundries in Cleveland found that African Americans made up anywhere from 10 to 60 percent of the labor force at each of the establishments. Moreover, in these factory jobs many of the newcomers earned two or three times as much as they had in the South.[88] Yet in Chicago, Cleveland, and elsewhere, blacks remained concentrated in the least skilled, least paid factory jobs. In 1928 at the Gary and South Chicago steel works, only 4.7 percent of black workers were classified as skilled as opposed to 36.7 percent of all employees. Four-fifths of all the black steelworkers had unskilled positions.[89] Thus blacks were taking the place of the Poles and the Czechs in the dirtiest industrial jobs, having been relegated by white employers to tasks that required brawn but little brains.

Some jobs, however, were less backbreaking and offered a greater chance of fame and fortune. For example, among the black migrants to Chicago were a number of jazz musicians from New Orleans who searched for greener pastures after authorities closed the Louisiana metropolis's red-light and entertainment district of Storyville. Their arrival transformed the Windy City into the jazz capital of the world, and by the early 1920s Ben Hecht was calling Chicago "the jazz baby by the lake."[90] Louis Armstrong, "Jelly Roll" Morton, Bessie Smith, and many others performed at such south side hangouts as the Sunset Cafe, the Plantation, and the Dreamland. Many middle-class Chicago blacks looked down on jazz, and in 1928 the music correspondent for the *Defender* predicted: "Jazz is on the wane, and the better class of music is coming back into favor with the critical public."[91] But for a number of talented musicians the Chicago jazz world of the 1920s was an attractive alternative to laboring in the steel mills or packing houses.

Black newcomers to Chicago and other midwestern cities, however, met resistance from hostile heartlanders and faced racial intimidation. In 1917 the *Chicago Tribune* proclaimed bluntly, "Black man, Stay South!" and the following year black tenants moving into a white area on Chicago's south side received a letter warning: "We are going to BLOW these FLATS TO HELL and if you don't want to go with them you had better move at once."[92] Moreover, this was no idle threat, for from 1917 to 1921 Chicago was the scene of fifty-eight racially motivated bombings.[93] The Ku Klux Klan enjoyed a resurgence in the early 1920s, proving especially successful in winning Hoosier members. But Detroit-area membership also rose markedly from three thousand in the fall of 1921 to twenty-two thousand in 1923, and these devotees of white, Protestant rule attacked local blacks as well as Catholics and Jews.[94] "Nigger!" wrote the Klan to a black teacher in 1923, "You are being watched very closely. . . . KNOW YOUR PLACE in the future. This applies in the class-room as well as other places. Speak when spoken to and not OTHERWISE. You may be in the north, but there are still tar and feathers up here."[95] Even among other ethnic newcomers blacks could not necessarily find allies. In the late 1920s a Mexican migrant said of African Americans: "I have never liked them and try never to get work near the Negroes."[96] A Cleveland black newspaper summed up the dismay of many African Americans during the late 1920s when it editorialized: "Daily it becomes more apparent that the virus of southern race prejudice is bearing its malignant fruit in this cosmopolitan city of Cleveland."[97]

Racial tensions in the World War I era produced deadly riots in both East Saint Louis and Chicago. The East Saint Louis riot of July 1917 left at least eight whites and thirty-nine blacks dead, though contemporary estimates of black fatalities ranged as high as 250 or even 400.[98] Many blacks escaped across the Mississippi River to Saint Louis, and the African-American population of East Saint Louis dropped from an estimated 10,600 in 1917 to 6,800 in 1918.[99] Considering the continued hostility of many East Saint Louis whites, this decision to depart was probably a wise one. "The only trouble with the mob was that it didn't get niggers enough," observed a local white mailman in the wake of the riot.[100] Chicago's riot of 1919 resulted in the death of twenty-three blacks and fifteen whites and at least 537 other persons were injured.[101] For five days blacks and whites battled, until a fortuitous rainstorm finally dampened mob passions and the Illinois National Guard restored order. Yet few blacks left the Windy City; instead the migration northward continued.

During World War II the rapid increase in Detroit's black population heightened racial tension in the Motor City. Between 1940 and 1944 the number of African Americans in the Detroit metropolitan area soared from 170,552 to 259,490, and within the city of Detroit itself the number of whites actually dropped 2 percent, whereas the black population rose 41.5 percent.[102] Ford's River Rouge complex alone employed over 15,000 African Americans.[103] Protesting either increased black employment or management's decision to promote blacks, many white workers staged "hate strikes," such as the work stoppage at the Packard plant in June 1943.[104]

That same month full-scale rioting erupted in Detroit after a black youth gang roamed through Belle Isle Park picking fights with white picnickers. For the next thirty-six hours, white mobs confronted black mobs, eventually leaving twenty-five blacks and nine whites dead.[105] During the rioting Detroit's white police fired indiscriminately at blacks, causing civil rights lawyer Thurgood Marshall to charge that the record of police action read "like the story of the Nazi Gestapo."[106] But a national magazine blamed the deaths on "an old, ugly fact in U.S. life: prejudice and misunderstanding between the white and black races."[107]

Black migration and racial tension, however, were not unique to the Midwest. Thousands of African Americans moved to Philadelphia and Newark just as they migrated to Chicago and Cleveland, and in the summer of 1943 race rioting broke out in New York City as well as Detroit. What was distinctive about the Midwest was the magnitude of the white migration from the South during the period from World War I through World War II. In the Midwest unlike in the Northeast, white southern migrants far outnumbered black southern newcomers, creating a population pattern in the cities of the heartland different from that of the Atlantic seaboard. By 1950, 60 percent of all southern-born persons in the five states of the Old Northwest were white and 40 percent were nonwhite. In the Northeast only 41 percent of the southern born were white and 59 percent were nonwhite. The Old Northwest and Northeast each recorded about one million southern-born blacks, yet the heartland states were home to almost 1.6 million southern-born whites as compared with fewer than 700,000 southern-born whites in the Northeast. Thus southern newcomers to midwestern cities were predominantly white, whereas southern migrants to the Northeast were predominantly black. The result was a new cultural and ethnic mix that further distinguished Detroit from New York and Cincinnati from Boston.

The impact of southern whites was especially notable in those industrial centers most affected by the automobile boom. Even before World War I the Akron tire companies were drawing whites from West Virginia, and this stream of people northward continued in succeeding decades. During the 1930s Ohio author Ruth McKenney claimed that "nearly sixty-five percent of Akron's population was imported from the southern mountains;" rubber was "milled and steamed and hammered into tires by big drawling mountaineers from West Virginia and Tennessee and Alabama."[108] Flint also attracted far more southern whites than blacks, with a 1934 survey recording a southern white population of 10,597 compared with 2,737 southern blacks.[109] Because of the supposed prevalence of southern whites in Flint's Fenton Lawn subdivision, it was nicknamed "Little Missouri" or "Little Arkansas."[110] Detroit itself became the home of an army of white Southerners, the influx during World War II being especially noteworthy. A visitor to the Willow Run dormitories in 1943 reported: "Mountain dialects run heavy to the acre."[111] In a joke told often in wartime Detroit, one man asked another, "How many states are there in the Union?" "Forty-six," he answered. "Tennessee and Kentucky are now in Michigan."[112]

Like many African Americans, the white Southerners came north in search of higher pay and better jobs. "Rumors tell of inexhaustible opportunities in the city," reported a 1937 study of Cincinnati's many white Southerners, "and with the custom already established, it requires little initiative . . . to leave the mountains . . . for work in the city."[113] A survey of Detroit's World War II newcomers likewise found the lure of economic opportunity to be a powerful motive for the northward migration. When asked his reason for leaving the South, one migrant replied typically: "There's no work in Kentucky"; another said: "Wanted to get away from mining in West Virginia for a long time."[114] Patriotic sentiments and a willingness to do their part for the war effort also might have drawn Southerners to heartland defense plants. But in this case patriotism paid off. A study of one hundred families in a Detroit housing project revealed that their average weekly income rose more than 50 percent during the war.[115]

Despite such improved economic fortunes, white newcomers from Kentucky, Tennessee, and Arkansas remained among the poorest of the heartland urbanites. Like the blacks, white migrants were generally relegated to the most poorly paid, unskilled jobs. In 1934, 68 percent of the employed southern whites in Flint held unskilled jobs as compared with 54 percent of the total work force and 83 percent of Flint's black migrants from the South. Flint's southern whites were even less likely to be professionals than their black counterparts; only 1.7 percent of the white Southerners fell into the professional class, whereas 2.2 percent of the African Americans did so.[116] A Michigan factory executive said of the southern whites: "These people could do the unskilled jobs all right and were glad to get whatever wages were given to them."[117] With little hope for prosperity in Dixie, the newcomers to Michigan, Ohio, Indiana, and Illinois were willing to accept menial jobs and found even the lowest midwestern wages an improvement over their past economic condition.

Clustered along the lower rungs of the economic ladder, southern whites suffered from poor living conditions and inadequate housing. During the 1930s the housing of Flint's southern whites was, if anything, even worse than that of the city's black migrants. According to a Flint housing survey, 14 percent of southern white families resided in dwellings without running water, whereas 7.6 percent of the families of black newcomers and 6.1 percent of the population as a whole lived in such inadequate structures.[118] Migrants to Detroit during World War II could expect nothing better than grim rows of jerrybuilt defense housing. In *The Dollmaker,* a novel about a Kentucky family in wartime Detroit, author Harriette Arnow described their housing project as "rows of little shed-like buildings, their low roofs covered with snow, the walls of some gray-green stuff that seemed neither brick, wood, nor stone." The Kentucky family's cramped apartment was cut up into miniature rooms so "the place seemed all halls and walls and doors and windows," with the halls "scarce wider than [the mother's] shoulders."[119]

Though their worldly goods were not great, southern whites were able to find some spiritual solace in the midwestern cities. In every heartland center of southern migration, evangelists became a common phenomenon, presenting emotional revival meetings reminiscent of those back home in Dixie. In the mid-1920s evangelist Bob Lewis received a warm welcome from former Tennessee and Kentucky residents when he conducted a Christian crusade at Gary's Central Baptist Church. Gary's leading newspaper described Lewis as an "acrobatic loudspeaker" who wore "sheikish multi-colored, rubber-soled slippers, the mingled colors being banana yellow and coffee tan," but thousands thronged to hear the rakish preacher attack booze, vice, flappers, evolution, and the general immorality of the steel city.[120] During World War II migrants from the South's Bible Belt found a wide assortment of evangelists in Detroit. "Detroit is teeming with . . . tabernacles and evangelists," reported a national magazine in 1944, "complete with lighting effects, brass bands, robed choirs, stage properties and press agents." In a typical performance the evangelist was "leaping over the pulpit, vaulting piled chairs, clawing the air and sliding home, telling the folks what God [was] like."[121] Smaller storefront churches attracted many of the wartime migrants, offering a fundamentalist message in an informal, emotional setting. But both the storefront church and the big-time revival were cultural indicators of the changing population of heartland cities.

Such change, however, also brought cultural conflict. In the 1930s a study of Cincinnati's Southerners concluded that the typical migrant found "himself in a community swayed by a long-established German-Catholic culture in most respects out of sympathy with his own."[122] In Cincinnati and elsewhere, descendants of German immigrants claimed that the white Southerners deviated from midwestern norms; the newcomers spoke differently, worshipped differently, and lived differently. And the native heartlanders did not like the differences. No matter whether they came from the flatlands of western Kentucky and Tennessee or the mountains in the eastern section of these states, white Southerners were all derisively labeled as "hillbillies," a term that implied ignorance and laziness. According to the Office of War Information, most Detroiters during World War II regarded the Southerner as "clannish, dirty, careless, . . . illiterate and yokelish."[123]

Moreover, many Detroiters claimed that white migrants were largely responsible for the city's racial tensions. For example, a commentator in the *Detroit News* argued that the racial "fracas" of 1943 was owing in good measure to southern whites who had migrated to the Motor City "in vast numbers, bringing with them their Jim Crow notions of the Negro."[124] A social worker likewise said of the white newcomers: "They are ignorant and hold traditional southern attitudes toward the Negroes. . . . They constitute a thoroughly dislocated element in the population."[125] Responding to this tendency to blame white Southerners, a mountaineer in *The Dollmaker* contended: "They're allus talken about Klan-loven, nigger-haten Southerners, but I'm tellen th truth, they're more nigger-haters an Klan lovers up here than ever I did know about back home."[126] Yet few native Detroiters would have agreed with this irate Kentuckian. In the minds of long-time residents, Detroit was a happier, better city before either blacks or whites from the South descended upon it.

Many southern whites were equally displeased with their new midwestern neighbors. "We found Detroit a cold city, a city without a heart or a soul," wrote one Tennesseean in 1942. "So we are going back to Tennessee . . . where men and women are neighborly, and where even the stranger is welcome."[127] Since they did not face the prospect of racial oppression, white Southerners were, in fact, more likely to return to Dixie than their black counterparts. This was especially true when the economic cycle turned downward and jobs disappeared. For example, between 1930 and 1934 the southern white population of Flint dropped 35.1 percent, whereas the number of southern blacks fell 18.9 percent.[128] Yet most white migrants remained in the North, creating a new ethnic bloc in the Midwest's heterogeneous urban social structure.

Black and white Southerners where the principal newcomers to midwestern cities during the period from 1917 to 1945. Yet one other group also migrated northward to fill factory jobs left empty by the decline in European immigration. This group was the Mexicans, who were most heavily concentrated in Chicago and the Calumet region of northwestern Indiana. By 1930 they constituted 10 percent of the population of East Chicago, Indiana, and 3.5 percent of the residents of Gary.[129] Though in 1930 there were more than three times as many Mexicans in Chicago as in East Chicago, as yet they represented less than 1 percent of the Windy City's population. Even less significant was Detroit's Mexican community of sixty-five hundred persons, which accounted for only 0.4 percent of the Motor City's residents. In the Chicago and Gary region these newcomers already occupied approximately 14 percent of the jobs at the Inland Steel and United States Steel mills, and hundreds of Mexican migrants were also to be found in the meat packing plants.[130] Yet at the close of the 1920s they remained a minor element in the Midwest's industrial labor force.

During the economic depression of the 1930s many Mexican immigrants returned to their homeland, the number of Chicanos in Chicago dropping from twenty thousand to sixteen thousand. Labor shortages during World War II again drew migrants northward, so that the 1950 census recorded twenty-four thousand Mexicans in the Windy City.[131] At the end of World War II the Chicago Chicano community, however, was insignificant compared with the city's large Polish bloc or its growing black population, and in such heartland cities as Saint Louis, Cincinnati, and Indianapolis Mexicans remained a rarity. But already during the interwar period, a population pattern had developed that would become a permanent fact of midwestern life. Chicago and the Calumet region had established itself as the hub of Mexican-American settlement in the heartland, a distinction it would retain for decades to come.

Mexicans, southern whites, and southern blacks, all were additional elements to the population compound of the urban Midwest. Chicago, Cleveland, and Detroit had long been polyglot cities with residents from every European nation, but the great northward migration of the period 1917 to 1945 produced an even broader mix of people in the heartland metropolises. It was not, however, a happy combination. In the minds of many Midwesterners, blacks remained "niggers," white Southerners were "hillbillies," and Mexicans were "greasers." In the 1920s an East Chicago black said of Mexicans: "You can't understand them very well, and if you get into an argument with them you don't know what minute you will have them after you with knives."[132] A Mexican complained of European immigrants: "We get all the hard work and the Europeans get the easy work. They are mean and swear at us all the time."[133] In one city after another ethnic fissures were evident, and the influx of new migrants produced new tensions. It remained for future generations of Midwesterners to somehow patch together the ethnic pieces into a harmonious whole.

Facing Political Realities

During the early twentieth century, midwestern cities had been in the forefront of municipal reform. Reformers in Cleveland, Toledo, Detroit, and Dayton had offered different diagnoses and cures, but each of the sundry uplifters was dedicated to a belief in better urban rule, and each optimistically believed such rule could be realized. Pingree, Jones, and Johnson endeavored to create democratic cities, Leland thought morality could reign in the urban Midwest, and Patterson laid the groundwork for efficient, businesslike municipal government. All of these leaders were willing to crusade and experiment to create model metropolises that would lead the way for other urban centers in the nation. All sought to fashion cities on a hill, beacon lights for benighted American urbanites. From the 1890s to World War I, the flat heartland had more cities on a hill than it had hills.

By the 1920s and 1930s, however, the age of heady dreams and untarnished ideals was over. Rather than realizing a municipal paradise, the midwestern cities seemed to move a few steps closer to hell. Tales of corruption abounded, as did stories of gangster influence in politics. Much touted schemes for good government fell short of perfection, and in some cities "reform" administrations appeared no better than the unreformed regimes which had preceded them. In 1930 or 1940 Cleveland, Toledo, Detroit, Chicago, and even Dayton were no longer vaunted models of a brave new municipal future. Instead, newspapers and magazines throughout the nation presented Chicago as a shameful disgrace and Detroit as little better. By the 1930s the beacon light of midwestern municipal idealism had dimmed, and in some cities it apparently had been extinguished.

No midwestern city seemed more at odds with the reform ideals of an earlier age than Chicago. During the 1920s Chicago's dominant political figure was the loud-talking, sombrero-wearing, publicity-seeking Mayor William Hale Thompson. Known as "Big Bill," Thompson served as mayor from 1915 to 1923 and from 1927 to 1931, and in the course of his career he made Chicago politics a bad joke that elicited guffaws from people throughout the country. A long-time foe of the mayor, the *Chicago Tribune* editorialized: "Thompson is a buffoon in a tommyrot foundry, but when his crowd gets loose in the City Hall, Chicago has more need of Marines than any Nicaraguan town."[134] Writing in a national magazine, another critic blasted Thompson as a "political blunderbuss . . . indolent, ignorant of public issues, inefficient as an administrator, incapable of making a respectable argument, reckless in his campaign methods and electioneering oratory, . . . and congenitally demagogical."[135]

Faced with scandals in the public school system involving his closest henchmen, Thompson chose not to run for reelection in 1923. But to ensure that he remained in the public eye, Big Bill organized a much-publicized expedition to the South Seas in search of a mythical tree-climbing fish that the ex-mayor claimed could "live on land, . . . jump three feet to catch a grasshopper and . . . actually climb trees."[136] With much ado the bogus expedition set sail from Chicago, but Thompson quickly returned to the Windy City, having achieved his goal of keeping his name on the front pages.

By 1927 Big Bill was ready once again to capture the mayor's seat, then occupied by a reform Democrat William Dever who had aroused the ire of thirsty Chicagoans by attempting to enforce the national law prohibiting the manufacture and sale of alcohol. Responding to the public mood, Thompson ran on a platform that promised lax enforcement of the prohibition statute. "At this very hour," he told voters at a campaign rally, "there are police snooping about Chicago breaking down doors of homes to snoop around mattresses for a hip flask, or in the pantry for a little home brew, or in the basement or attic for a still. When I am mayor, I'll fire any cop who interferes with a citizen's personal liberty!" "Hooray for Big Bill! Hooray for beer!" cried the enthusiastic Chicago audience.[137] This was the type of campaign rhetoric Al Capone liked to hear. The Windy City's leading bootlegger and all-around gangster lined up wholeheartedly behind the ex-mayor, donating an estimated $100,000 to $250,000 to Big Bill's campaign fund and hanging a photograph of Thompson together with portraits of Washington and Lincoln on his office's bullet-proof walls.[138]

The second major plank of Thompson's platform was to rid the city of British influence and specifically to oust the public school superintendent who had permitted the use of history textbooks which supposedly offered a pro-British version of the American Revolution. In a display of pure demagoguery Thompson relentlessly attacked King George V of Great Britain and bellowed the slogan "America First!" "I wanta make the king of England keep his snoot out of America!" Thompson shouted to his followers. "That's what I want. I don't want the League of Nations! I don't want the World Court! America first, and last, and always! That's the issue of this campaign."[139] There was no evidence that King George was conspiring to take over Chicago, and the making of foreign policy regarding the League of Nations and World Court did not fall within the powers of the mayor of Chicago. Yet Thompson's hyper-patriotic, though irrelevant, message thrilled thousands of Chicagoans.

Meanwhile, the University of Chicago's Charles Merriam and the world-famous Jane Addams of Hull House, together with other local reformers, rallied behind the incumbent Mayor Dever. Their campaign slogan was "Dever and Decency," and their candidate contended quite reasonably that the job of mayor of Chicago had "to do with managing the business affairs of a big business city" and had "nothing to do with regulating international affairs."[140] On election day, however, Thompson won the mayor's office as Chicagoans opted for booze and balderdash rather than decency and reason.

Many outsiders viewed the election returns as clear proof that Chicago housed more political ignoramuses than any other city on earth. "They was trying to beat Bill with the better element vote," joked humorist Will Rogers. "The trouble with Chicago is that there ain't much better element."[141] The *Indianapolis Star* lambasted the Thompson victory as "a striking example of the potency of demagoguery and appeals to prejudice in American elections," and the *Saint Louis Star* proclaimed: "Chicago is still a good deal of a Wild West town, where a soapbox showman extracting white rabbits from a gentleman's plug hat still gets a better hearing than a man in a sober suit talking business."[142]

For the next four years under Big Bill's rule, Chicago earned an unenviable reputation as the nation's gangland capital. In the public's mind, the Windy City was no longer the urban laboratory of Jane Addams, a mecca of social reformers in search of solutions to city problems. It was now the city of Al Capone and Big Bill Thompson, a metropolis that had turned its back on morality and reform. When Capone's mobsters gunned down seven men in the Saint Valentine's Day Massacre of 1929, it only reinforced the public's belief that the Midwest's largest metropolis was outlaw territory and beyond the pale of decency.

Moreover, the Democratic political organization that ousted Thompson from power in the election of 1931 did not usher in an era of highminded rule by the likes of Merriam and Addams. Instead, during the 1930s and early 1940s Mayor Ed Kelly and Democratic County Chairman Pat Nash headed a classic partisan machine, doling out patronage to ward leaders in exchange for unquestioning loyalty to the party chieftains. One Democrat said of the autocratic Kelly: "Why, he could even give a lesson in bossism to Hitler and Stalin." Kelly himself explained: "To be a real mayor you've got to have control of the party. . . . You've gotta be a boss!"[143] Chicago's Democratic organization kept the water running, the traffic flowing, the parks mowed, and the schools open. Yet the idealism of Samuel "Golden Rule" Jones, Tom Johnson, and Edward Dunne was absent from Chicago's city hall.

Chicago was not the only heartland city whose reputation suffered from rumored links between politics and gangsterism. For example, by the close of the 1920s Detroit was a far different city from what Henry Leland hoped it would be. The Purple Gang and Licavoli Gang profited from gambling, prostitution, and running illicit liquor, and the Detroit Citizens League continued to battle futilely for more effective law enforcement. In 1930 Charles Bowles took office as mayor after an election campaign in which he pledged to clean up the city. Bowles, however, soon stirred the wrath of reformers when he fired his police commissioner for having ordered raids on houses of prostitution and gambling establishments. In retaliation, devotees of law and order with the support of the Citizens League took action to remove Bowles from office and a recall election was scheduled for July 22, 1930. The Citizens League's William Lovett viewed Bowles as "inadequate, inexperienced, and blundering," a man in which there appeared to be "no admixture of brains or municipal experience."[144] A League investigation also revealed that Bowles had accepted about $100,000 in campaign contributions from gamblers. Such a man had to be ousted from power.[145]

During the campaign to recall Bowles from office, gangster violence reached a new peak in the Motor City. In the first two weeks of July, mobsters slayed ten men, earning the month the label "Bloody July." Endorsing tougher law enforcement, on July 22 Detroiters voted to recall Bowles. Yet on the night of the election another gangland murder cast a pall on the city's already darkened reputation. Popular radio commentator Jerry Buckley was sitting in the lobby of a downtown hotel when three men walked up and fired eleven revolver shots into him. In his radio broadcasts Buckley had bitterly lambasted Bowles, but no one discovered any evidence that the slaying was in retaliation for the commentator's attacks on the defeated mayor. The sensational murder did, however, confirm in many minds that Detroit like Chicago was a city without law and order. Commenting on Buckley's death, the *Detroit Free Press* argued: "The government of the city of Detroit failed to maintain a decent check on banditry and gunmen, but allowed them to think that the town is wide open and 'easy.'"[146] "Is this city and this State to be ruled by the assassin or by the forces of organized government?" editorialized the *Detroit Times*.[147]

Across the nation headlines told of the gangland slayings of Chicago and Detroit; the blundering of Bowles and the buffoonery of Thompson received as much publicity as the democratic crusades of Pingree and Dunne had garnered a generation earlier. The two largest midwestern metropolises were not models of municipal success but instead good copy for scandal sheets. As in the case of Chicago, in Detroit the municipal authorities continued to provide the necessary services, and decent, competent men as well as inept misfits held the mayor's office. Yet neither city radiated the hope for better municipal rule as it once had.

Even John Patterson's city manager plan no longer seemed as promising a solution for heartland urban ills. Many midwestern cities adopted this scheme of government in the 1920s and 1930s, but in some of the largest heartland centers voters tired of it quickly. The plan was intended to achieve efficiency while preserving democracy. Yet many urbanites viewed the creation of an unelected municipal manager as a dangerous and unAmerican violation of the principles of democracy, and they perceived no compensating improvement in municipal administration. Mounting evidence indicated that manager rule did not necessarily eliminate partisan shenanigans nor schemes to cheat the taxpayer. Thus many midwestern voters remained unconvinced that city manager government was actually better government.

This was evident in Akron. In January 1920 city manager rule went into effect in the rubber capital, and from the very beginning problems arose. Rather than rising above politics, Akron's city manager immediately became the crux of political controversy, for a Republican-dominated city council chose the Republican elected to the largely ceremonial post of mayor as the first manager. In other words, the manager was not to be a nonpartisan, impartial administrator aloof from the political brawl, but instead he was the Republican mayor with a new title. In the past, however, the executive had been elected by the voters, whereas now this mayor garbed in the mantle of city manager was selected by politicians on the city council.[148]

The machinations of the Republican council brought howls from the Democrats who had backed adoption of the manager plan and laments from reformers who had optimistically anticipated a new regime of nonpartisan efficiency. The Democrat *Akron Evening Times* spoke for those "outraged by the prostitution of the new city charter to partisan ring politics upon its very first application." It especially lambasted those council members who did the dirty work in raping the new city charter," demanding their recall from office. Decrying the "swindle" and "conspiracy," the Democrats could only conclude that Akron was "placed in the grip of an unscrupulous political ring at the very outset of the new charter's life."[149]

Such partisan rhetoric did not bode well for the future of city manager government in Akron, and after three years of experience with the plan, Republicans, Democrats, and the electorate in general were ready for a change. The idea of shifting the initiative for policy-making to the city council seemed especially undesirable considering the long and dubious history of corrupt deals and partisan tricks among American municipal legislators. Yet the notion of allowing the appointed city manager a strong voice in determining policy struck the citizenry as undemocratic and unAmerican. The *Akron Beacon Journal* complained that the city manager was responsible only to the municipal council members, whom the press regarded as having "about the same principles as a reformed highwayman and just brains enough to keep out of an imbecile asylum." Moreover, the newspaper claimed that undemocratic manager rule strengthened that "small group of special interests" which found it "easier to control one man who ha[d] not been elected" than several who had.[150] Incompetent but powerful council members and an irresponsible executive capable of clandestine dealings, these seemed the hallmarks of Akron's manager plan. Such a combination won little favor, and even the Akron Chamber of Commerce which had originally sponsored manager rule took a neutral stance when a proposal repealing the plan appeared on the ballot in 1923.[151] A Citizens Committee did attempt to preserve the tarnished experiment, but the manager scheme suffered defeat and Akron returned to a strong mayor plan.[152]

In nearby Cleveland, city manager government met with the same fate. Ohio's largest city operated under a manager charter from 1924 to 1931, but as in Akron partisan politics and misgivings about an unelected executive proved the plan's undoing. From the very beginning, it was apparent that the scheme would not produce high-minded, nonpartisan rule. Attempting to ensure a continuation of politics as usual, the leaders of the local Republican and Democratic party organizations selected the first city manager and agreed on a division of patronage, with 60 percent of city jobs allocated to the majority GOP and 40 percent for the Democrats. The two party bosses pondered over who should occupy the manager's office, and in November 1923, six weeks before the new charter was to take effect, the Democratic leader Burr Gongwer telephoned the GOP chief Maurice Maschke and suggested the local Republican businessman William Hopkins. Maschke replied, "He would be great," and the decision was made. Moreover, according to Maschke, "Mr. Gongwer and I met frequently with Hopkins at his rooms in the Cleveland Athletic Club during December [and] discussed his cabinet and other major appointments." Hopkins did not automatically accept the suggestions of the party chieftains, but no two men had a greater say in the composition of Cleveland's first manager government than Maschke and Gongwer. Hopkins was just as amenable to their advice as any newly elected mayor.[153]

During his years in office, Hopkins proved a powerful manager who craved the limelight, stood at the center of local political controversy, and clearly determined municipal policy. Yet he was unelected, chosen by party leaders rather than voters, and this annoyed Clevelanders just as it troubled the citizenry of Akron. "I do feel humiliated and ashamed," said former mayor Newton Baker, "when I think of this city of a million people whose manager is picked up by an unseen hand from an invisible place, put in power and kept there, subject to the will of an influence over which the people have no control."[154] The Cleveland Federation of Labor expressed the same thought more bluntly when it contended: "The City Manager Plan is un-American, undemocratic and autocratic and should not be tolerated by anyone who desires to conserve the liberties of the people."[155] Many spokespersons for the ethnic minorities composing Cleveland's polyglot population agreed with this assessment. The city's most widely read Czech language newspaper warned: "Great banking interests have joined forces in support of the city manager system . . . providing for a lifelong dictator and making it impossible for you to perform your inalienable civic rights."[156] And a prominent black clergyman claimed that the city manager plan had deprived "the people of Cleveland of the privilege of choosing their ruler just as effectively as though they were excluded by the Constitution."[157]

In 1927, 1928, and 1929 proposals to repeal the manager plan appeared on the ballot, but by narrow margins they failed to win approval. Finally in 1931 the accumulated grievances toward the scheme resulted in its defeat at the polls and a return to more traditional mayoral rule.[158] Most Clevelanders agreed that the manager plan had not proved a panacea for the problems of urban government. It had eliminated neither partisan string-pulling nor patronage; moreover, under the plan city council members remained at best mediocre and at worst corrupt. Most damning of all, city manager rule seemed to deprive the voters of some of their voice in government. The electorate of Cleveland and Akron would not tolerate this.

Dayton did retain Patterson's scheme for efficient, businesslike administration, but during the interwar years manager government in that city gradually settled into a dull routine that aroused little attention. At the close of the 1930s a student of Dayton's manager regime wrote of the "indifferent complacency, toward which there was a decided tendency in the community at large." Rather than daring to attempt new solutions as it once had, Dayton's government was timid and reluctant to face the social and economic dilemmas that a decade of depression had produced. This observer contended: "It is to be regretted that Dayton, which started out so confidently in 1914 to point the way for other cities to follow, could not in 1938 show more of that same local resourcefulness."[159] Manager rule worked in Dayton, and government scandals did not rock the community. Yet the Ohio city was no longer in the vanguard; it was no longer pointing the way for the nation.

In one midwestern city, however, the spark of municipal idealism did flare during the interwar years. Long known for its benighted politics, Cincinnati adopted manager rule in 1924 and local reformers fought for good government during the following decade with an enthusiasm more typical of an earlier age. To ensure that manager government would not fall into the hands of party bosses as it had in Cleveland, in the first election under the new charter Cincinnati's reformers ran their own independent slate for the city council. Their platform was straightforward: "Business methods in government—freedom from political bosses."[160] It was an effective message, for on election day reform supporters of the new charter won six of the nine council seats and thus secured the privilege of naming the first city manager. In succeeding elections, reformers under the Charterite label continued to offer slates of council candidates and continued to win. After eight years under city manager government, Charterite Charles Taft could still write: "There is in this movement in Cincinnati the type of religious conviction which is not fanatical; which is not even ecstatic; which is hard-headed, and yet idealistic; a conviction, a faith that local good government is a possibility."[161]

Elsewhere in the Midwest, however, few people were writing such words. Cincinnati was the exception not the rule. The matronly Queen City had not been a trendsetter since its years of relative decline in the second half of the nineteenth century. Now in the 1930s its government won plaudits but did not stir municipal revolution across the country.

In fact, the age of municipal visionaries had passed. Midwesterners were still attempting to upgrade the quality of urban government and still ousting mayors like Bowles and challenging party chieftains like Maschke. But there was no Samuel Jones dreaming of a Christian cooperative commonwealth in Toledo nor a Tom Johnson transforming Cleveland into the world capital of the battle against Privilege. In 1932 while visiting the French Riviera Cleveland's Newton Baker met with Toledo's Brand Whitlock for the last time. The heir to Jones's reform mantle was "ill and old and tired," and Baker was a waning elder statesman. According to the former Cleveland mayor, their conversation was "that of two men who had seen the vast tragedies of life and, though disappointed that many of [their] hopes had not materialized were yet not disillusioned or willing to despair."[162] This same attitude seemed to sum up the spirit of urban government in the Midwest. Dashed hopes had tempered youthful enthusiasm, and the reform tradition had grown old like Baker and Whitlock. Yet many heartlanders continued to seek redemption from waste and corruption. Political passions had quieted and the maturing midwestern hubs had grown less militant in the cause of reform. Skepticism had won converts though cynicism had not yet triumphed.

The Suburban Trend

During the years between World War I and the end of World War II an increasing number of Midwesterners removed themselves from the arena of central-city politics by moving to the suburbs. Migration to outlying municipalities was evident in the late nineteenth century, but the centrifugal flow

TABLE 7

Percentage of Metropolitan Residents in Largest Midwestern Centers
Living outside the Central-City Limits

City	1920	1930	1940
Chicago	17.4	22.6	24.5
Detroit	20.5	25.5	29.3
Cleveland	13.9	24.6	27.7
Saint Louis	27.9	36.5	40.3
Milwaukee	16.8	22.2	25.7
Cincinnati	36.4	40.6	42.3

Sources: Bureau of the Census, Censuses of 1930 and 1940 (Washington: Government Printing Office, 1932, 1942).

accelerated in the 1920s and 1930s. The advent of the automobile enabled many middle-class heartlanders to wander farther from the urban core in search of an ideal home, and thousands of them did so. New subdivisions burgeoned along the metropolitan fringes and a bevy of "Heights," "Woods," and "Lawns" offered single-family dwellings ringed with grass and beyond the pall of big-city smoke.

In each of the Midwest's urban areas, the proportion of metropolitan residents living outside the central-city limits rose steadily during the 1920s and 1930s. As seen in Table 7, the percentage of those in the Cleveland metropolitan area who resided in the suburbs almost doubled between 1920 and 1940, and by the outbreak of World War II approximately a quarter of all residents in the metropolitan areas of Chicago, Detroit, and Milwaukee as well as Cleveland lived beyond the central-city limits. Because the metropolitan areas of Saint Louis and Cincinnati straddled state lines, an especially large portion of the population in these districts lived outside the central cities. A legal creation of the state of Missouri, the city of Saint Louis could not annex territory in Illinois nor could Cincinnati absorb parts of adjacent Kentucky. Consequently, independent satellite municipalities clustered along the east bank of the Mississippi River and the south shore of the Ohio River.

The growth in the proportion of suburbanites during the interwar period was in part owing to the migration of upper-middle-class Midwesterners to new elite communities. One of the most notable of these was Cleveland's Shaker Heights. During the first decade of the twentieth century Cleveland real estate developers Oris and Mantis Van Sweringen began purchasing land east of the city for the development of a model suburban town. But not until 1920, when the two brothers completed the Shaker Rapid Transit Line linking their suburban tract with downtown Cleveland, did Shaker Heights become a popular destination for upwardly mobile home buyers. From 1920 to 1930 the municipality's population soared from 1,600 to almost 17,800 with an average of three hundred new houses rising each year.

To ensure that their community remained attractive and appealed to the "best people," the Van Sweringen brothers imposed a comprehensive set of restrictions on the builders of these homes. The developers specified the ratio of house width to lot frontage, placing both a maximum and minimum limit on the breadth of proposed structures. Entrances had to be at the front of the house rather than the side, and asphalt shingle roofs and the use of artificial stone were forbidden. "No buff-colored brick shall be used in any event," the Van Sweringens announced in the booklet *Shaker Heights Standards,* "and no light-colored brick such as gray or white brick, or vertical-cut brick shall be used without the written consent of the Van Sweringen Company."[163] Arguing that "without the guidance of a competent architect, imagination [might] easily run to the freakish in residences," the brothers required that all prospective home builders hire "a graduate architect," or one of comparable credentials whose blueprints expressed "a thorough, technical knowledge of the highest and best in architecture, together with the ability to combine materials and prescribe color schemes."[164] Moreover, the Van Sweringen Company had to approve all home plans, and some styles of housing were expressly prohibited. "We do not believe that bungalows or houses of any similar type can have a proper setting in a built-up section, such as Shaker Heights is destined to be," the Van Sweringens explained, "so we have thought it necessary to exclude all buildings of that character from our property."[165] The Van Sweringens intended Shaker Heights to be an enclave of good taste where Cleveland's well-to-do could escape the ugliness and uncertainty of the big city. Their restrictions and specifications would supposedly guarantee the realization of this goal by preventing the construction of any tawdry or bizarre structures which might depress neighborhood property values and offend elite sensibilities.

The provisions mandating expensive building materials and high-priced architects also ensured that only the well-to-do could afford to build in the elite suburb. At the same time, deed restrictions limited sale of lots to Caucasians only. Thus Shaker Heights, like many other comparable communities throughout the Midwest, was designed to be tasteful, wealthy, and white. It was to provide a domestic refuge for the families of harried but affluent professionals and business leaders. The Van Sweringens envisioned it as a protected residential zone where the upper middle class could raise its children in an atmosphere superior to that of polyglot, proletarian Cleveland. "All that conserves home-spirit is cultivated," explained the brothers; "that which is inimical to it is barred."[166]

During the interwar period, Shaker Heights generally lived up to its developers' expectations. It remained a residential community with few business establishments. In the 1930s only about one-tenth of its employed residents worked in the suburb; most of the male breadwinners commuted to jobs in downtown Cleveland.[167] Shaker Heights women also transacted much of their business in the big city rather than in the sylvan suburb. They purchased groceries in Shaker Heights but bought most other items in Cleveland, and more than half of the suburb's shoppers visited downtown department stores at least once a week.[168] Though parents ventured into the urban core, children remained safely ensconced in Shaker Heights, where the schools won praise as the finest in the Cleveland area.

Shaker Heights could afford good schools, for in the 1930s as in the 1920s it remained the most elite of Cleveland's major suburbs. Eighty-two percent of Shaker Heights homes had seven or more rooms, and Cleveland newspapers carried real estate advertisements for Shaker Heights manses offering "6 bedrooms and four baths on second floor," "10 rooms and 3 baths with recreation room," and "12 rooms, 4 baths, including a library, sun room, and recreation room." By comparison only 34 percent of Cleveland's single-family dwellings had seven or more rooms.[169] Shaker Heights homes of the 1930s had the latest mechanical conveniences as well. Seventy-eight percent had refrigerators as compared with only 12 percent of Cleveland's residences.[170] Moreover, 31 percent of Shaker Heights families owned two or more automobiles, whereas only 2 percent of Cleveland's families did so.[171] Given their prosperity and the tastefulness of their surroundings, it was perhaps natural that residents of the model suburb were highly satisfied. In 1933 a survey revealed that 88 percent of Shaker Heights residents preferred their suburb to any other community in the Cleveland metropolitan area, and only 6.5 percent wanted to move out of their elite haven.[172] Apparently in Shaker Heights affluent heartlanders had found happiness.

Milwaukee's version of Shaker Heights was the village of Shorewood. Located along the shore of Lake Michigan north of the city, the village was originally named East Milwaukee and until the outbreak of World War I was best known as the site of an amusement park. By 1917 the shooting galleries and roller coasters had closed, but that year leaders of the community prepared their village for a more distinguished future by changing its name to Shorewood.[173] During the following decade, the honky-tonk hamlet with the new name became an exclusive residential suburb and a symbol of material success for Milwaukeeans. The population soared from 2,650 in 1920 to 13,479 in 1930 as mansions rose along the lakefront and less pretentious upper-middle-class homes filled the inland lots. As in the case of Shaker Heights, development was not haphazard but carefully controlled, and one boosterish description of the community proudly announced that "every foot of land was restricted, either by deed stipulation or village ordinance."[174]

By the 1930s Shorewood was proclaiming itself the "Model Twentieth Century Village."[175] According to an account published by the village government, it gave "an impression of shade and affluence" with "well-to-do business and professional people" making up the bulk of the population.[176] Like Shaker Heights, its school system was "one of the most elaborate in the country for a village of Shorewood's size," though many school employees could not afford to live in the village. "Of the six charwomen," the village publication explained, "four had to be recruited from outside because there were too few local candidates for the work."[177] The community was an elite residential refuge, and it intended to remain just that. This account insisted: "The village has no factories and wants none, limits its business area to a small shopping district, and self-consciously devotes its civic energies to making itself a pleasant place in which residents may live and spend their leisure."[178] This was the suburban ideal of heartlanders in the 1920s and 1930s. The most desirable suburbs were not for business; instead, they were designed to make residents forget their business.

Elsewhere similar communities were attracting affluent Midwesterners. In Columbus, King Thompson founded Upper Arlington in the second decade of the twentieth century, and between 1920 and 1930 the population rose fivefold from 620 to 3,059. "In this day of civic awakening it does not suffice merely that we live in a good, comfortable home on a good lot," the King Thompson Company told prospective customers. "It is still more important that we live in a community of good homes and amid people of aspirations similar to our own." Upper Arlington supposedly provided this as well as the opportunity to get "entirely away from the City's dust and smoke" and enjoy "numerous parks and winding streets" admitting of "varied and artistic settings and corresponding vistas."[179] Elite suburbs also appeared along the fringes of smaller cities. For example, in the words of its founder, Canton's Hills and Dales was "a community dedicated to the fine art of enjoyable living, to maintaining the highest ideals of home environment—where natural scenic beauty enhance[d] residences of dignity and worth."[180] Laid out in the 1920s, Hills and Dales became the showplace of Canton, a scenic retreat of large lots and winding drives where the city's elite clustered.

In one metropolitan area after another, well-to-do Midwesterners were moving to model communities tailor-made for their needs. Shaker Heights and Shorewood offered property restrictions that supposedly guaranteed the heavily mortgaged upper middle class would not suffer a decline in real estate values. These suburbs also supported schools that catered to the college bound and thus provided an education suitable to the class interests of the elite. Moreover, these communities conformed to elite standards of good taste and beauty as well as affording an escape from the environmental pollution spewing forth from big-city smokestacks. And the suburban villages satisfied the elite desire to separate business from home life by offering retreats removed from commerce and industry. Besides all this, the new suburbs pinned a badge of social status on their residents; an address in Hills and Dales or Shorewood was proof that one had arrived. At the same time, by moving to a posh suburb, the well-to-do could isolate themselves from people of lower rank. The very names of the communities emphasized that they were only for those who rose above the common herd. Thompson's village was not simply Arlington but Upper Arlington, and the Van Sweringens created Shaker Heights not a community with the less-elevated name of Shaker.

Yet the affluent were not the only ones seeking a suburban home. Many heartlanders of more modest means were also moving to communities beyond the central-city limits. For example, in 1927 Mills and Sons Company opened its Westwood project in Elmwood Park, a municipality adjoining Chicago's northwest side. Advertised as "The World's Largest Bungalow Development," Westwood offered small brick bungalows for those who could not afford a home in the elite North Shore suburbs.[181] West of Detroit, the Folker Company was developing the community of Garden City for auto workers in search of suburban homes. This developer advertised "farmlets" 147 feet wide and 135 feet deep where workers could grow fruits and vegetables in their spare time. "It offers the means of a great saving in your grocery bill," promised the Folker Company, "or the opportunity to live much better for less cash outlay." Garden City was touted as the "Sun Parlor of Detroit," but it was hardly an elegant parlor. In some subdivisions the so-called streets were simply graded, ditched, and then strewn with cinders; curbs, sewers, and asphalt were notably absent. There were no restrictions forcing lot owners to invest in expensive dwellings. Many Garden City residents constructed frame cottages on wooden posts protruding from the ground, and some built their garages first and lived in them until they could afford to erect a more substantial dwelling.[182]

In Cincinnati, the wealthy entrepreneur Mary Emery sought to build something better for the working class, creating in the 1920s the suburban community of Mariemont. According to the town planner Emery hired, "She became convinced that workers need primarily to live in comfortable and attractive homes amid a favorable environment if they are to develop a high working efficiency."[183] Thus Mariemont was to be a self-contained community with shops, schools, and recreation as well as tasteful houses and apartments. Unfortunately, the town proved so tasteful and consequently so expensive that it was largely beyond the means of the working class. The completed village became yet another middle-class suburb of Cincinnati.

But Mary Emery was not the only one who believed that properly planned suburban villages offered the best living environment for the working class. During the 1930s the federal government's Greenbelt program operated on this same assumption, creating three model suburban communities for persons of moderate means. Two of these New Deal towns were in the Midwest: Greenhills outside of Cincinnati and Greendale in the Milwaukee metropolitan area. Supporters of the Greenbelt communities could wax rhapsodic when speaking of the advantages of suburban life. One enthusiastic official of the program who moved to Greendale commented: "We are living close to nature and shall adjust ourselves to her for our benefit; we are able to recover our lost affinity to the soil." When Greendale opened in spring 1938, the *Milwaukee Sentinel* likewise predicted that its lucky residents would raise "radishes and roses and children" in an environment filled with "fresh air, grass and black dirt."[184]

New Deal officials, Mary Emery, Garden City auto workers, King Thompson, and the Van Sweringens all seemed to agree that the best hope for the good life rested with the suburban community. In an earlier age reformers dreamed that Cleveland and Toledo would become model communities, and sociologists optimistically sought the answers to urban problems in the laboratory of Chicago. By the 1930s, however, many Midwesterners appeared to be turning their backs on the maturing hubs and investing their hopes and fortunes in the suburban fringe. Depression-era idealists endeavored to remove the working class from Milwaukee and Cincinnati to Greendale and Greenhills. In these outlying towns America's laborers would supposedly find paradise. At the same time wealthy heartlanders opted to migrate beyond the central-city limits, spending their money to escape from urban ills rather than to cure them. In the competition for affluent residents, Cleveland was losing miserably to Shaker Heights and Milwaukee was far behind Shorewood. The heyday of the central cities was clearly passing. Throughout the Midwest suburbia was gaining ground, and no signs indicated any change in this trend.

7.

The Making of the Rust Belt

During the decades following World War II urban Midwesterners faced the ugly symptoms of aging. In the nineteenth century, heartland cities had been youthful marvels, growing at a breakneck pace and brimming with vitality. At the turn of the century, they were at the height of their powers, their achievements in manufacturing, government, architecture, and literature turning the heads of observers throughout the world. And in the 1920s and 1930s the heartland hubs appeared to move on to a duller but still distinguished middle-aged existence. By the 1950s, 1960s, and 1970s, however, Cleveland, Detroit, Chicago, and Milwaukee had turned gray, and at the beginning of the 1980s their feebleness was winning nationwide attention. They were the capitals of the rust belt, a decaying industrial swath that was no longer the nation's pride but instead had become a national problem.

During the second half of the twentieth century, then, debility and decay became the focus of attention in the urban Midwest. Revitalization was the watchword of all policymakers, and renewal plans proliferated. Everyone was seeking to lift the sagging face of the Midwest's cities; everyone was searching for a tonic to quicken the fainting urban heartbeat. Youth had passed, but hopes for a prosperous maturity survived.

The dangers of aging were first evident in the heartland's central cities. Migration to the suburbs and the failure of central cities to annex new territory meant that many of these hubs faced a seemingly perpetual spiral of population decline. As seen in Table 8, eight of the region's twelve largest cities lost population between 1950 and 1980. Moreover, during the 1970s eleven of these cities did so, with only Columbus recording population gains during every decade of the period. For some cities the decline was especially precipitous. Saint Louis's population dropped almost fifty percent during these thirty years, whereas Cleveland and Detroit lost more than a third of their inhabitants. The poor were most likely to remain in the central cities, and the wealthy were most likely to depart. Consequently, Saint Louis, Cleveland, Detroit, and the other declining cities increasingly became reservations for the impoverished, with expanding slums and a diminishing middle class.

During the 1950s and 1960s the urban cores rotted, but along the metropolitan fringe population increases and economic growth more than compensated for central-city decay. By the 1970s, however, the pattern changed and signs of decline once confined to the central cities spread throughout the

TABLE 8

The Largest Midwestern Cities, 1950 and 1980

City	1950 Population	Rank	1980 Population	Rank	Percentage of Change
Chicago	3,620,962	1	3,005,072	1	− 17.0
Detroit	1,849,568	2	1,203,339	2	− 34.9
Cleveland	914,808	3	573,822	5	− 37.3
Saint Louis	856,796	4	453,085	7	− 47.1
Milwaukee	637,392	5	636,212	4	− 0.2
Cincinnati	503,998	6	385,457	8	− 23.5
Indianapolis	427,173	7	700,807	3	+ 64.1
Columbus	375,901	8	564,871	6	+ 50.3
Toledo	303,616	9	354,635	9	+ 16.8
Akron	274,605	10	237,177	10	− 13.6
Dayton	243,872	11	203,371	11	− 16.6
Grand Rapids	176,515	12	181,843	12	+ 3.0

Sources: Bureau of the Census, Censuses of 1950 and 1980 (Washington: Government Printing Office, 1952 and 1983).

region. As seen in Table 9, in six of the twelve most populous midwestern metropolitan areas, the population dropped during the 1970s, and in three others the rate of growth was less than two percent. In the 1950s and 1960s local boosters claimed that the dismal population figures for the central cities of Saint Louis and Cleveland were simply a consequence of artificial and unchanging municipal boundaries. The metropolitan areas that constituted the "real" Saint Louis or the "true" Cleveland were still growing. But in the 1970s even this prop for local egos collapsed, forcing Midwesterners to recognize the economic weaknesses of their region. Residents of Indianapolis and Columbus might smile at the plus signs in their census columns, yet by nationwide standards even these metropolises were sluggish. The national average for population growth in metropolitan areas was 10.2 percent; not one of the major midwestern metropolises approached this figure, let alone the 55 percent posted by metropolitan Phoenix or the 54 percent for Orlando and environs.

By the early 1980s one did not have to consult census data to realize that the heartland was in the doldrums. From Youngstown to Rockford factories were closing, thousands were out of work, Cleveland was the butt of comedians' jokes, and the economic empire of Japan had flattened once-mighty Detroit. Americans were flocking to the Sunbelt, leaving behind the gray skies and shabby mills of the aging heartland. Revitalization schemes still aroused enthusiasm among never-say-die boosters, and in the late 1980s an economic upturn seemed to indicate that the worst had passed. Yet few people expected the Midwest to regain the economic preeminence it had

TABLE 9

The Midwest's Most Populous Metropolitan Areas, 1970 and 1980

Metropolitan Area	1970 Population	1980 Population	Percentage of Change
Chicago	6,974,755	7,103,624	+1.8
Detroit	4,435,051	4,353,413	−1.8
Saint Louis	2,410,884	2,356,460	−2.3
Cleveland	2,063,729	1,898,825	−8.0
Milwaukee	1,403,884	1,397,143	−0.5
Cincinnati	1,387,207	1,401,491	+1.0
Indianapolis	1,111,352	1,166,575	+5.0
Columbus	1,017,847	1,093,316	+7.4
Dayton	852,531	830,070	−2.6
Toledo	762,658	791,599	+3.8
Akron	679,239	660,328	−2.8
Gary-Hammond-East Chicago	633,367	642,781	+1.5

Sources: Bureau of the Census, Censuses of 1970 and 1980 (Washington: Government Printing Office, 1973 and 1983).

enjoyed in the early twentieth century, nor was anyone preparing for a mass migration from Florida and Arizona to Cleveland, Detroit, or Toledo. No matter the protestations of loyal heartlanders, a good deal of rust remained in the aging Midwest, and the problems of growing old would not soon disappear.

The Rusting of the Urban Heartland

Even before America's entry into World War II, many commentators were identifying and deploring the symptoms of urban decline. In 1939 a national magazine published an article titled "St. Louis: A City in Decay" which commented on "the desolation and desertion characterizing scores of blocks in the business district."[1] Early in 1941 a report of the Civic Committee on Conservation and Rehabilitation stated "the paramount question" before the Missouri metropolis: "Is the City of St. Louis progressing as a large metropolitan city should, or is it on the decline at a speed that eventually will mean destruction, abandonment, bankruptcy and a ghost city?" The organization answered this by noting that "the general trend of the city" was "on the decline."[2] Some observers were equally gloomy about Cleveland. In 1938 an article titled "Cleveland: A City Collapses" said of that city's population: "The number is being decreased at this minute by the steady outflux of citizens who have seen the fatal handwriting on the wall."[3] At the beginning of 1941 a study of downtown Cincinnati was only slightly more optimistic when it wrote of the need "to arrest decline" and contended that the Queen City stood "at the crossroads . . . between becoming a static or retrogressive community, or . . . becoming the great focal point for a large surrounding territory."[4] A report on downtown Milwaukee summarized prevailing opinion when it noted: "We now face the reality of cities that are old . . . but speedily declining." According to this 1941 commentary, "Every urban center confronts the task of safeguarding the substantial areas which have thus far held off the encroachments of spreading blight [and] rebuilding and rehabilitating those areas which have succumbed to decay."[5]

Responding to these cries, during the 1940s midwestern states enacted urban redevelopment legislation aimed at encouraging private investment in the distressed urban core. In 1941 both Illinois and Michigan adopted such measures, and within the next five years Missouri, Indiana, and Wisconsin followed suit, though Ohio did not act until 1949.[6] These laws either gave private corporations the power to condemn property for redevelopment or authorized municipalities to do so on behalf of private developers. Either way, recalcitrant slum owners would not be able to block the clearing of blighted properties for redevelopment. Some statutes also offered tax relief to anyone willing to risk money in the rebuilding of the city. Under Missouri law, during the first ten years after purchase of slum property, redevelopers would pay property taxes on only the assessed valuation of the raw land, exclusive of improvements and buildings. Any new structures erected during that first decade would be tax-exempt.

In Title I of the Housing Act of 1949 the federal government offered vital support for these urban redevelopment initiatives. Title I authorized Washington to fund two-thirds of the net cost of buying and clearing slum property, with local governments paying the remaining third. Together the federal government and the locality would provide developers with cleared sites on which these entrepreneurs were expected to erect handsome new structures. Apartments for decent, taxpaying residents and businesses generating jobs as well as tax revenues would supposedly sprout where worthless slums had formerly earned the city nothing but a bad reputation.

Taking advantage of Title I, many midwestern cities began to implement redevelopment schemes during the 1950s and early 1960s. Detroit's renewal authorities cleared slum land for a middle- and upper-income apartment complex known as Lafayette Park. The project's twenty-story Pavilion Apartments designed by famed architect Ludwig Mies van der Rohe opened to well-heeled tenants in 1959. Meanwhile, Saint Louis was constructing a middle-class housing scheme known as Plaza Square Apartments in the central business district and embarking on the Mill Creek Valley project, which was intended to include both housing and industry. Milwaukee's first urban renewal effort was the Lower Third Redevelopment Project, encompassing 31.5 acres which the local redevelopment authority intended to "be used primarily for the construction of commercial and light industrial facilities."[7] Similarly Cincinnati's Kenyon-Barr project was a 400-acre tract adjacent to the central business district, which the city cleared of twenty-five thousand impoverished black residents and set aside primarily for light industrial plants.

During the 1950s Cleveland had constructed some moderate-income housing under the federal urban renewal program, but by the beginning of the 1960s local authorities sought to create something more ambitious that might add luster to the aging city's tarnished reputation. The result was Erieview, a 163-acre downtown complex designed to include luxury apartments, hotels, stores, and offices. Originally described as "undoubtedly the most ambitious project so far undertaken under the Federal Urban Redevelopment Program," Erieview was representative of the grandiose dreams of urban heartlanders eager to take advantage of federal money and boost the sagging fortunes of their hometowns.[8] According to the master plan drafted by the distinguished architectural firm of I. M. Pei and Associates, Erieview would be an exciting, futuristic ensemble of slick, soaring high-rises and sleek, horizontal low-rises, all flanking tastefully landscaped parks and malls. Pei's drawings of flashing steel and glass structures offered a vision of modern splendor that would surely reestablish Cleveland as one of the brightest stars in the constellation of American cities.

Not all heartland renewal schemes entailed the leveling of superannuated structures to make way for gleaming modern complexes. On Chicago's south side the middle-class citizenry of Hyde Park-Kenwood were pursuing a different approach. Faced with an increasing number of illegal conversions of single-family houses into apartments and with the danger of racial conflict as blacks moved into the predominantly white district, in 1949 residents organized the Hyde Park-Kenwood Community Conference to foster improved property maintenance, to police zoning and housing code violations, and to nurture racial harmony. By 1952 the district's dominant institution, the University of Chicago, joined in the effort, for according to one resident, university officials were finally "forced to admit that if they didn't engage in community action, they might end up with a $200,000,000 investment in a slum, without anybody to do research or any students to educate."[9] The university-sponsored South East Chicago Commission threw its weight behind the program to halt illegal conversions, and it also drew up a renewal plan which provided for conservation and rehabilitation of existing buildings as well as spot clearance of structures deemed beyond salvation. In other words, bulldozers would not obliterate all buildings; instead, most would remain. The goal was an interracial but solidly middle-class neighborhood, and only buildings that threatened to lower the social status of the district had to be destroyed. In 1956 the federal government awarded $26 million in capital grant funds for the Hyde Park-Kenwood scheme, and during the next few years those structures which supposedly bred social decay fell before the wrecking ball, many of them replaced by handsome middle-class apartments designed by reputable modern architects.

Though Chicago, Cincinnati, Detroit, and Saint Louis garnered the largest

share of the Midwest's urban renewal funds, smaller heartland cities were
also endeavoring to combat blight with money from Washington. In Toledo
the redevelopment authority sought to combine clearance and rehabilitation
in an effort to upgrade the Chase Park residential neighborhood, and by the
early 1960s I. M. Pei and Associates was presenting a plan for renewal of
the downtown waterfront. With a thirty-story office tower flanked by low-
rise office blocks, two high-rise luxury apartment buildings, and "a plaza
where busy office workers" could "pause in their hurried day to rest and
enjoy a shady oasis," Pei's proposal was a junior-sized version of his plan
for Cleveland's Erieview.[10] Meanwhile, architects were drafting plans for a
64-acre tract on the western edge of downtown Dayton. An architecture
journal claimed that the planners had taken "particular care . . . to avoid
creating a 'Martian' or 'futuristic dream' type of presentation in favor of a
more realistic, economical outlook." But the Dayton scheme included an
ultra-modern arena-convention center with an adjacent hotel and a parking
garage whose roof "could most easily be used as a heliport," a new government center with a sixteen-story City-County Office Building, and three
luxury apartment towers offering a Park-Avenue lifestyle in the Buckeye
State's sixth largest city.[11] Akron's redevelopment authority cleared twenty-
three acres for the expansion of the University of Akron, initiated work on
a light industrial park, and launched a central business district project as a
response to "the deterioration of the downtown area over many years."[12]
Farther west in Madison, Wisconsin, city officials embarked on the Triangle
project intended to replace 52.5 acres of blighted houses and businesses
with tasteful high-rise and garden apartments of the type found on urban
drawing boards throughout the Midwest.[13]

In fact, the schemes for renewal in one city bore a striking resemblance
to those in every other community. The chief implement in the heartland's
proposed rebuilding seemed to be a cookie cutter designed to make Cleveland, Detroit, Akron, and Dayton look like every other renewed city in the
nation. Mies van der Rohe was building urban renewal structures not only
in Detroit but also in Baltimore, and I. M. Pei was not only planning the
future of Cleveland and Toledo but Boston as well. And their proposals for
each city embodied the same stylistic elements. Working in the fashionable
"International Style" of modern architecture, they and like-minded colleagues had little interest in regional or local diversity. Slick towers with
glass skins, high-rise apartments with balconies better suited to the Mediter-
ranean than the climatic extremes of the Midwest, and clean, landscaped
light industrial plants all were standard components of the renewed city, no
matter its location or its region. Except during the brief heyday of the Prairie
School, Midwesterners had traditionally aped the building styles and tastes
of Europe and the Atlantic seaboard. But the homogenized utopias of urban
renewal planners carried the heartland's look-alike propensities to the ex-
treme.

Plans for rebuilding midwestern cities, however, affected only a small portion of each metropolitan area. Outside their aged cores, the heartland metropolises remained strong and healthy during the 1950s and early 1960s with no need for revitalization. Climbing auto sales kept factories across the region humming, and high wage levels ensured that those employed on the assembly lines enjoyed a higher standard of living than workers anywhere else in the world. Detroit, Chicago, Cleveland, and Milwaukee still spelled jobs and money in the minds of many Americans. No one had yet coined the phrase rust belt; instead, the Midwest remained the land of chrome and steel, a symbol of America's prosperity and manufacturing might.

Yet incipient signs of economic trouble already were apparent to perceptive observers. After years of prosperity the auto industry faltered badly during the recession of the late 1950s. Making matters worse was a sudden upsurge in the sale of imported autos, a phenomenon Detroit had not faced before. In 1955 only 58,000 imported automobiles were sold in the United States, two years later the number climbed to 207,000 or 3.5 percent of total American sales, and in 1959 imports accounted for 10.2 percent of the market with 615,000 foreign autos sold that year.[14] During the early 1960s American manufacturers momentarily met the import challenge by introducing smaller compact models to compete with Volkswagen and other European producers. But by 1968 the foreign share of the American market was again over 10 percent, and the threat from imports had clearly become a permanent reality for heartland automakers and their suppliers. As yet Japanese models were of minor importance, with American sales for Toyota and Datsun each totalling only 3,000 cars in October 1967 as compared with the 42,000 automobiles marketed by Volkswagen. But that same year an automobile industry journal warned that the Japanese were "growing fast in the U.S. market," a fact that was "grim enough" for European producers and "perhaps grimmer in Detroit."[15]

During the 1950s and 1960s heartlanders also confronted a gradual decentralization of American vehicle production, meaning jobs for the South and West but no boost for midwestern fortunes. Michigan, Ohio, and Indiana remained the undisputed hub of auto and truck manufacturing, yet the Midwest's share of the industry was eroding. In 1947 the five states of the Old Northwest accounted for 78.3 percent of all employees in the American motor vehicle industry; by 1967 this figure was down to 68.3 percent, and five years later it had slipped to 65.8 percent.

More dramatic was the dispersion of tire manufacturing. Whereas in 1947 Ohio was the home of 43.0 percent of all tire industry employees, twenty years later the Buckeye State's share had dropped to 33.5 percent, and in 1972 it was only 25.0 percent. The combined work force at the Akron plants of the Goodyear, Firestone, Goodrich, and General Tire companies fell from fifty-one thousand in 1950 to thirty-seven thousand in 1970.[16] Meanwhile, the South proved the chief beneficiary of Akron's gradual decline, with Dixie's share of the nation's tire manufacturing work force rising from 13.7 percent in 1947 to 33.4 percent in 1972. Representative of this change was Goodyear's $73-million investment in a new tire factory in Union City, Tennessee. Announced in 1967, at that time it was the largest single construction project in the company's history.[17] At the beginning of the century Southerners had flocked northward to make tires in Akron. Now, however, the Rubber City's know-how and capital was migrating southward to build plants employing Southerners in their homeland.

Not only did heartland cities experience industrial decentralization, some also suffered the closing of major factories. For example, on December 9, 1963, Studebaker announced that it was moving its automobile manufacturing operations out of South Bend after more than a century as a leading employer in the community. Unable to compete with the auto industry's Big Three, Studebaker had stumbled along for more than a decade, and now in a last-ditch move it decided to transfer its remaining automobile production to its Canadian plant. Gradual cutbacks over the years meant that South Bend was no longer so dependent on the automaker. Yet the closing left jobless an estimated eight thousand workers, approximately 9 percent of the area's labor force.[18] "It's going to be a very serious blow to the economy of our area," admitted a chamber of commerce official, though with characteristic local pride he added that the city's other industries were "doing well." Indiana's governor also assured residents: "Every effort will be made by the state to ease this blow to the economy of South Bend and Indiana."[19] As yet most heartland hubs were maintaining their manufacturing might. But in coming years more and more midwestern governors and chamber of commerce leaders would be making similar statements as the heartland's industrial base gradually crumbled.

In fact, by the late 1960s and early 1970s heartland optimism was waning, and the urban horizon seemed to be darkening. One problem was a growing realization that urban renewal could not work miracles. Throughout the Midwest one project after another fell short of expectations. Saint Louis's Plaza Square Apartments failed to attract sufficient tenants, and in 1965 a national business magazine reported that the complex had been "in technical default" to the federal government "since the first payment was due."[20] Seven years later the luxury apartment blocks of the same city's Mansion House renewal project likewise went into default. "In Mansion House's nine years," reported the *St. Louis Post-Dispatch* in 1975, "there have been no payments on the principal to either the Government (which now holds the mortgage) [or] the previous note holders."[21] Meanwhile, redevelopment of Saint Louis's Mill Creek Valley had proceeded so slowly during the 1960s that its empty expanses of cleared land acquired the nickname "Hiroshima Flats."[22]

Elsewhere delays and bankruptcies also deflated hopes of urban revitalization. New buildings did not instantly sprout from the wastelands of Cleveland's Erieview, and much of the tract remained parking lots well into the 1970s. Those structures that did rise during the 1960s and 1970s were not always successful. According to one member of the city's Fine Arts Advisory Committee, the project's initial building, forty-story 100 Erieview Plaza, was a "piece of tin" whereas a second member of the committee labeled it a "block of nothing." A third member argued that New York-designed Erieview Plaza perhaps reflected the condescending, parochial outlook of New Yorkers toward Cleveland. In the minds of lofty Gothamites, a pedestrian glass and steel box was appropriate for Ohio.[23] At least Erieview Plaza readily attracted tenants, which was more than could be said of Erieview's Park Centre apartment and retail complex. Opened in 1973, the twin towers soon went bankrupt largely because of an inability to lease the retail space.[24] Meanwhile, renewal efforts in Toledo floundered. In 1968 one student of Toledo politics concluded that urban renewal in that city had progressed at a snail's pace because of: "disagreement over objectives; uncertainty in policy and administrative decisions; resistance from property owners; questions and objections from federal officials; demolition difficulties; and an undercurrent of political acrimony."[25]

Even in the smaller city of Madison, Wisconsin, renewal faced major obstacles and aroused noisy debate. The 52.5-acre Triangle project took two decades to complete; private builders could develop suburban tracts of that size in a single year. In the course of the Triangle project's history, opponents distributed "pink sheets" associating urban renewal with communism, former residents of the cleared tract held a picnic at which they hung the Madison Redevelopment Authority in effigy, and the authority's executive director resigned when he was arrested for operating a motor vehicle after losing his license for drunken driving. In 1974 a medical office building opened on the Triangle site, but it stood mostly vacant for a year before the mortgagee finally foreclosed on it.[26] As early as 1966 the local League of Women Voters reassured Madison residents that "neither Rome nor any urban renewal project was completed in a day."[27] Yet by the mid-1970s such bromides offered little consolation to an exasperated public.

Not all the news from the aging central cities was grim. New office buildings appeared in every city, changing the skylines and giving fresh hope to chamber of commerce boosters. In 1973 Chicago's Sears Tower was completed, securing for the birthplace of the skyscraper the honor of having the world's tallest office building. That same year Milwaukee's loftiest structure, the 601-foot First Wisconsin Center, likewise opened its doors to tenants, and the early 1970s witnessed the completion of four new towers of twenty or more stories in downtown Cleveland. After years of planning and preparation, the 630-foot Gateway Arch finally adorned the riverfront of Saint Louis, drawing much-needed tourist dollars to the beleaguered city. Both the Missouri metropolis and Cincinnati boasted of new downtown stadiums that attracted thousands of sports fans to the urban core.

One city after another pointed to glass and steel landmarks or concrete monuments which supposedly demonstrated the continuing vitality of the central business district. But going-out-of-business sales at downtown stores, rising crime rates, closing downtown movie palaces, and the deadly silence of the central business district after the office workers departed at

5:00 all seemed to point in a different direction. The aging urban core was surviving as a place of office employment but as little else. By the mid-1970s the optimism of earlier evangelists of urban revitalization appeared naive, and the expectations for central-city renaissance were waning.

Within a few years, however, Midwesterners faced not only the closing of downtown stores and theaters but also the seeming collapse of their entire economy. For heartland cities the late 1970s and early 1980s were the most dismal years of the post–World War II era. Plant closings accelerated, municipal governments teetered on the brink of bankruptcy, and the Midwest led the nation in unemployment. As the once-mighty industrial Midwest showed definite signs of debility, if not senility, commentators invented the term *rust belt* and applied it to the staggering heartland. In the 1950s Detroit was the city of chrome; by 1980 it was the hub of corrosion. "Cleveland is dead," announced the chairman of Cleveland's Democratic Party, though following passage of a needed tax increase he offered the slightly more optimistic diagnosis, "Cleveland is dying."[28] Few midwestern leaders were so blunt, but privately many were thinking as gloomily about their hometowns.

Youngstown won the dubious distinction of rust belt community par excellence. The economy of the aging steel center collapsed in the late 1970s and early 1980s when one mill after another shut down and transferred its workers to the unemployment lines. First, in September 1977 the Youngstown Sheet and Tube facility closed, putting forty-two hundred employees out of work. Responding to the announced closing, one veteran steelworker said, "It was like Pearl Harbor," and the local newspaper called it "the worst single blow ever suffered by the economy of the Mahoning Valley."[29] Then in January 1980 United States Steel shut its local works, idling thirty-five hundred workers, and Jones and Laughlin Steel did likewise, adding fourteen hundred men and women to the jobless rolls. By June 1980, the Youngstown area had 38 percent fewer manufacturing jobs than it had ten years earlier, the industrial work force having dropped from forty thousand to twenty-five thousand in a single decade.[30]

The shutdown generated many words but no adequate remedies. Seeking to pressure President Jimmy Carter into taking action to revive the local economy, one Youngstown group placed a full-page ad in the *Washington Post*. "Mr. President," it read, "Youngstown's job crisis is a moral issue. We need your help to keep self-help alive there and in the rest of Ohio."[31] Despite the plea, Youngstown failed to secure a Marshall Plan to rebuild its ruined economy. Some unemployed Youngstown residents blamed foreign competition for their woes, with one angry worker complaining: "The God-damn dirty Japs . . . killed my father in World War II, and now are taking food from my kids' table."[32] As Midwesterners were to discover, however, neither petitions to Washington nor brickbats aimed at Tokyo were to solve the problem. The heartland appeared to be in an irreversible decline, and Youngstown's steelworkers were among the casualties.

Youngstown residents found little consolation in the fact that they were not alone in their battle against economic decline. In nearby Akron, production of tires for passenger cars ceased in 1977, and five years later the volume manufacture of truck tires also came to a halt. By 1982 local rubber plants employed fewer than ten thousand workers compared with fifty-five thousand in the mid-1950s.[33] The leading rubber companies kept their headquarters and research facilities in the city, thereby cushioning the loss of manufacturing jobs and ensuring that Akron did not suffer as much as Youngstown. But no longer could anyone honestly refer to the rubber capital as the "City of Opportunity." Meanwhile, the headquarters of John Patterson's National Cash Register remained in Dayton, though the company moved out production facilities and thus eliminated fifteen thousand local jobs. In the 1970s the Dayton area lost 30 percent of its manufacturing positions, and in 1981 the city manager admitted: "This is a no-growth region. We're just kind of fighting the times."[34]

Farther west, Peoria was also feeling the impact of manufacturing decline. Beginning in 1979 the Hiram Walker distillery phased out its Peoria facility, eliminating nineteen hundred jobs in what was once the nation's great distilling center.[35] More seriously, Caterpillar Tractor fell on hard times, halving its work force in the Peoria area from thirty-seven thousand in 1979 to eighteen thousand in 1986. Throughout the post–World War II era, the giant manufacturer of earth-moving machinery had been the economic mainstay of the Illinois community, and its contraction affected every aspect of the local economy. Between 1977 and 1985 the value of building permits dropped by $32.6 million to $5.0 million, and the residential vacancy rate doubled in Peoria County during the first half of the 1980s.[36] To the north in Rockford, one-fourth of the labor force was unemployed during the dire winter of 1982 to 1983. "Like other factory cities across the Middle West," the *New York Times* later reported, "Rockford was bleeding away its jobs and its people."[37]

Moreover, the economic decline was apparent not only in second-level cities like Rockford and Peoria but in the heartland's largest metropolitan areas as well. When the nation's thirty-two largest metropolitan areas were ranked according to net employment growth from 1980 to 1982, all six of the major heartland metropolises were near the bottom of the list. Milwaukee was in twenty-first place, Detroit held twenty-sixth position, Saint Louis twenty-seventh, Chicago twenty-eighth, Cincinnati twenty-ninth, and Cleveland was dead last, ranking thirty-second. In fact, all the midwestern hubs except Milwaukee recorded job losses during this period, and the Wisconsin metropolis was barely in the positive column with a 0.6 percent gain in total employment. Cleveland suffered a loss of 4.6 percent of all its jobs during this three-year period, whereas Cincinnati experienced a drop of 1.9 percent and total employment in Chicago slipped 1.5 percent. The top eight metropolitan areas in terms of employment gains were all in the Sunbelt, with Houston and San Diego ranking first and second. Both recorded increases of better than 10 percent.[38]

No one familiar with the heartland had to rely on employment statistics and rankings to know that times were hard. The signs of decline were everywhere. On a cold morning in January 1983 over ten thousand job-hungry people gathered outdoors at a Milwaukee park to apply for a mere 175 openings announced by a local factory.[39] That same month employees at the downtown J. L. Hudson's store in Detroit also were looking for work, because that long-time retailing landmark was closing its doors. One customer of forty years admitted: "For me, Hudson's *was* Detroit and when it is gone, there will be nothing left.[40] Others who also felt there was nothing left in the Motor City packed their belongings and moved out. Reversing the migration pattern prevailing throughout most of the twentieth century, some Detroiters headed southward in search of jobs, turning especially to booming Texas. In 1981 the *Houston Chronicle* claimed a Sunday circulation of forty-two hundred newspapers in Michigan where prospective migrants perused the Texas want ads.[41]

Underlying the woes in Michigan was the weakness of the automobile industry. In 1981 General Motors recorded a corporate loss for the first time in six decades, and Ford skipped a quarterly dividend, the first such omission since the company's stock went public in the mid-1950s.[42] Meanwhile, Chrysler almost went out of business, and the frail giant did close its Dodge Main plant after more than sixty years of service. In 1978 American automakers sold 9.3 million cars, but by 1982 they were able to market only 5.8 million. Meanwhile, foreign producers, especially the Japanese, grabbed a larger share of the sales, accounting for 18 percent of the American market in 1978 and 27 percent in 1980.[43] This translated into particularly hard times for the auto-dependent heartland. General Motors company towns like Flint, Michigan, and Anderson, Indiana, regularly recorded the highest unemployment rates in the nation. Many observers believed that American automakers had run out of gas, leaving heartland cities in the middle of nowhere.

Cities with black majorities experienced special hardship. Having been abandoned by whites and some middle-class blacks, in the minds of most heartlanders these communities became off-limits for shopping, investment, commerce, or recreation. Business was poor everywhere in the Midwest, but in these racial reservations the economy seemed to be scraping bottom.

For example, everyone viewed East Saint Louis as a disaster area. During the 1970s the city's population dropped 21 percent, and by 1980, 95 percent of its fifty-five thousand inhabitants were black. For the most part, they were also poor, with almost 40 percent unemployed and at least half receiving some form of public aid. The total assessed valuation of property in East Saint Louis plummeted from $192 million in 1957 to only $32 million in 1980, and by 1981 over twelve hundred of the city's homes stood vacant and abandoned.[44] The few factories remaining in town were closing down. In 1979 Obear-Nester Glass Company ceased production, putting seven hundred people out of work, and the next year Hunter Packing Company followed suit, leaving another seven hundred jobless.[45] "Among its superlatives," observed one survey of

East Saint Louis, "it holds claim as the nation's most glaring example of urban decay."[46] The mayor contended that it also had the highest murder rate in the country.

A sad example of what an older city could become, East Saint Louis seemed headed for oblivion. "Many side streets are steeped in dilapidation," wrote one visiting journalist in 1981, "the abandonment distorted and magnified by open lots where houses have been demolished or are burnt-out shells. There, the tall grasses grow, weeds, bush, undergrowth, like mini-jungles."[47] Moreover, there was no dearth of government studies or sociological hand-wringing over the plight of East Saint Louis. As early as 1969 an East Saint Louis newspaper complained that the community was possibly "the most studied in the country[,] . . . a guinea pig for rich white school boys and the professoriate." "The city has been studied enough, dissected enough," the newspaper editorialized. "It is time ACTION is taken to arrest the downslide of the community."[48] Yet the studies and surveys continued, never achieving much other than publicizing East Saint Louis as a textbook example of urban debacle. In the early 1980s as in 1969, East Saint Louis was in desperate need of a miracle.

Another predominantly black city that was winning an equally bad reputation was Gary, Indiana. Despite annexation of a white residential area, between 1970 and 1980 Gary's population fell 13.4 percent and the black share rose from 53 percent to 71 percent. In 1974 one prominent black leader observed: "If things keep going as they are, Gary could be an all-black dead city."[49] Ten years later the city had not deviated from this supposedly fatal course. By 1985 the *Chicago Tribune* was reporting that one in every ten homes in Gary was vacant, but visitors to the boarded-up city generally thought that estimate was low.[50] Between 1972 and 1982 more than a third of the city's retailing establishments disappeared, as did 45 percent of the retail jobs. In 1981 the last downtown department store closed its doors, and four years later four of the five former department stores in the central business district were boarded up, with the Lake County Department of Public Welfare occupying the fifth.[51] The Gary National Bank likewise abandoned its downtown headquarters, moving its executive and administrative offices to the white suburban municipality of Merrillville. As if to further disassociate itself from the dying city of ill-repute, the bank changed its name to Gainer Bank.[52] In 1983 a local newspaper columnist wrote bitterly: "Gary has succumbed to a commercial cancer. Downtown is a shoppers' wasteland, the nearby neighborhoods blight areas."[53]

In one way Gary fared better than its fellow steel center of Youngstown. United States Steel did not close its mills in the Indiana city and thereby destroy the local economic base. Instead, the corporation invested in new equipment, making the Gary plant its flagship operation. Yet this spending resulted in more highly automated steel production that required less labor. From 1979 to 1982, employment in the local mills plummeted from thirty thousand to ten thousand, and despite an upturn in steel production in the mid-1980s, it continued to fall after 1982.[54] Gary was still making steel, but this was little consolation to the thousands of residents who lost their jobs and had no hope of regaining them.

Gary and East Saint Louis offered little encouragement to the region's boosters, but communities throughout the industrial Midwest had weathered hard times before. In the auto towns of Michigan, layoffs and economic woe were almost as predictable and expected as the change of the seasons. The early 1980s was, then, grim but not fatal; the downturn did not spell an end of hope for midwestern cities. Some urban heartlanders packed their belongings and moved southward, but most remained.

By the mid-1980s, however, heartland commentators were becoming notably more optimistic about the fate of many of the region's cities. The economy bottomed out during the tough winter of 1982 to 1983 and then headed upward. Midwestern cities generally were not in the vanguard of recovery, continuing to trail behind Sunbelt frontrunners. But there were signs of better times, and many observers were claiming that the heartland's older central cities were not as troubled as previously thought. In addition, rising unemployment and a wave of foreclosures in the oil towns of Texas made the Midwest seem not so shabby by comparison. Talk of renaissance revived, and chamber of commerce boosters pointed to every new building and each additional job as evidence that the heartland hubs were coming back.

Especially encouraging was a central business district building boom that actually began during the late 1970s and early 1980s but accelerated in the mid-1980s and produced scores of new skyscrapers. "Chicago's downtown building boom," reported the *Tribune,* "will hit record levels in 1986, after an eight-year investment binge that has produced a 'Super Loop' of new offices, hotels and apartment buildings."[55] In 1987 a magazine article titled "BOOM!" announced: "More construction has taken place in central Chicago during the last eight years than at any time since the Great Fire."[56] The *Cincinnati Enquirer* described the 1980s as "the most successful decade of office growth in Cincinnati's history" and "a feast for developers of downtown office space."[57] In the early 1970s the inventory of office space in the Queen City's central business district grew at an annual average of 175,000 square feet; in the 1980s the rate of growth was about 450,000 square feet a year.[58] To the north in Cleveland, downtown office space increased 35 percent from 1979 to 1986, with three new buildings opening in 1983 and two in 1985.[59] The most notable addition was the forty-five-story Sohio Building, but by the close of the 1980s construction of the fifty-two-story Society Center had begun. Moreover, the director of downtown development of the city's Growth Association was definitely bullish on Cleveland's future. "We should be America's dynamic downtown of the 90s," he observed in a 1989 publication.[60] Meanwhile, in 1985 a thirty-story office tower was completed in Milwaukee, followed later in the decade by a twenty-eight-story office building and a looming thirty-seven-story structure. Lauding Milwaukee as "a city on the move," a 1989 magazine article said of this latter high-rise:

"The golden brilliance of its towering peak reflects not only the morning sun, but also this city's newfound exuberance."[61]

Contributing to the supposed exuberance in some cities was the development of new downtown retail malls. For example, in August 1982 the $70-million Grand Avenue mall opened in Milwaukee. This three-level arcade stretched four blocks, linking the city's two major department stores. According to one study of the mall, tenants for its 150 shops "were carefully chosen to create a 'festival' atmosphere, while at the same time offering a variety of general merchandise, home furnishings, apparel, and specialty goods."[62] It was, then, to be both fun and practical, a place where one could do necessary shopping and enjoy it. This combination proved successful, and many claimed Grand Avenue was the midwife of downtown Milwaukee's rebirth. Late in 1983, a midwestern architecture journal observed: "Downtown Milwaukee is full of activity and, to a large degree, the mall is the reason the people are there."[63] That same year another study claimed "the Grand Avenue's most significant contribution to Milwaukee" was "the improved image it . . . established for downtown."[64] Two years later an executive of the Milwaukee Redevelopment Corporation seconded this, arguing that "the success of the Grand Avenue meant a complete 180-degree turn in the sentiment about investing in Downtown Milwaukee." "It used to be okay to work Downtown," he observed. "Now it's a place people want to go to see and be seen."[65]

In the mid-1980s Saint Louis boosters sought similar results in their hometown by applying a double dose of retailing stimulant to their superannuated central business district. In August 1985 Saint Louis residents celebrated the opening of both St. Louis Centre and Union Station, the former with two hundred shops anchored by the city's two leading department stores and the latter with eighty shops, twenty-two restaurants, and a 550-room hotel. Expressing the euphoria of the moment, a sales clerk at St. Louis Centre commented: "For years we've been hearing about what a dead city this is, and now, suddenly, it's had new life breathed back into it."[66] Others also proclaimed the rebirth of the Missouri metropolis. An architecture magazine dubbed Saint Louis "the turn-around city of the 1980s," but with unusual modesty the boosterish mayor claimed it was only "the turning-around city of the '80s."[67]

Elsewhere mayors were attempting to enliven their aging cities by promoting entertainment facilities. In Cleveland a combination of public and private money funded the restoration of three movie houses on Playhouse Square as a multi-theater complex for the performing arts. Along the Cuyahoga River, a warehouse-industrial district known as the Flats was also becoming a fashionable nightclub district, attracting the dollars of young professionals in the Cleveland area. But when Cleveland was chosen as the site for the Rock and Roll Hall of Fame, many local observers believed their city had truly arrived. Writing of the upcoming dedication of the Rock and Roll Hall of Fame, a publication sponsored by the Greater Cleveland Growth

Association predicted: "In the early 1990s the focus of the music world, from London to Manhattan to Hollywood, will be riveted on Cleveland for what surely will be one of the most spectacular openings in American entertainment history."[68] The city nicknamed "the mistake on the lake" in the late 1970s was now supposedly to become a show business star.

In Cleveland, Saint Louis, Milwaukee, and throughout the Midwest, "renaissance" was a popular refrain. Even smaller cities whose original birth and history of growth had been none too spectacular were claiming to be reborn. According to a regional magazine, Superior, Wisconsin, a city that had been depressed almost from the date of its founding, was "quietly transforming itself into one of the glittering jewels of the Lake Superior region." "Superior has enjoyed a renaissance in the past five years," this 1990 account proclaimed, "that is the talk of Wisconsin and the envy of many downstate communities."[69] One downstate city that was not envious was Racine, for it too was supposedly reborn. "If the renaissance of Racine is part miracle," wrote one enthusiastic commentator in 1989, "it is no myth."[70] That same year a regional magazine in Northern Indiana published an article on Elkhart with the subtitle "The Rebirth Continues."[71] In small cities as well as their larger brethren the theme was the same: the heartland communities were coming back.

One midwestern city trumpeted its success so loudly that some observers claimed it was immune from the corroding ills of the rust belt. That was Indianapolis, the self-proclaimed star of heartland revival. Under the leadership of super-booster Mayor William Hudnut, Indianapolis tried to shed its traditional image as "Naptown" and "India-no-place." In 1982 Hudnut broke ground for the sixty-thousand-seat Hoosier Dome stadium, and two years later he found a tenant for the mammoth structure when he lured the Colts professional football team from Baltimore. That year Hudnut proudly proclaimed: "We are becoming major league, growing, I hope, to greatness."[72] When the Colts arrived, *Time* magazine seconded this assessment, declaring, "India-no-place is no more."[73] Hudnut and like-minded citizens of the Hoosier metropolis meanwhile were campaigning to secure for their city the title of amateur sports capital of America. Culminating this effort, in 1987 Indianapolis hosted the Pan American Games, the first city in the United States to do so since 1959. Meanwhile, in 1986 the city's historic Union Station reopened after a $65-million renovation which transformed the railway depot into a "festival marketplace" with more than one hundred shops and restaurants as well as a 276-room Holiday Inn. During the first year after its reopening, Union Station became Indianapolis's chief attraction, drawing more than 13 million visitors. Brimming with bumptious vitality, irrepressible Indianapolis won endless accolades. The *Wall Street Journal* dubbed it the "Star of the Snow Belt," for *Newsweek* it was the "Cinderella of the rust belt," the *Chicago Sun-Times* named it "a Corn Belt city with Sun Belt sizzle," and *Smithsonian* magazine extolled the once-ignored community as "a born-again Hoosier diamond in the rust."[74]

The rosy rhetoric of revival, however, only masked the continuing problems plaguing midwestern cities. In fact, the purported renaissance of heartland hubs was not as real or as dramatic as publicists claimed. During the 1980s as in the 1970s, the population of most of the major central cities continued to fall. The rate of decline was slower than in the 1970s, but Cleveland, Saint Louis, Detroit, and Chicago were still shrinking. The populations of the leading metropolitan areas also either continued to slip or inched upward at a modest pace, and nowhere did the census bureau discover Sunbelt sizzle in the Corn Belt. "Fizzle" better described some heartland metropolises, and even such hardy performers as Columbus and Indianapolis looked like laggards next to sunny San Jose, San Diego, Phoenix, or Orlando. The Sunbelt's star was still rising and clearly eclipsing midwestern advances.

Moreover, the positive publicity of the late 1980s largely focused on increases in service and office employment, ignoring the persistent erosion of the Midwest's industrial base. Throughout the country, experts wrote of America entering a postindustrial era, an age when manufacturing was becoming less significant and white collars were supplanting blue. Such a change was especially threatening to the Old Northwest. No region had traditionally been so dependent on manufacturing; since the late nineteenth century the bedrock of the heartland's greatness had been its factories. Now in a supposedly postfactory era, the winds of change did not seem to be blowing in the Midwest's direction.

After 1982 manufacturing fortunes did improve in the heartland, but the modest industrial comeback failed to foster a dynamic growth in jobs. Just as U.S. Steel automated its Gary mills to save on labor costs, so other manufacturers sought to boost production without increasing employment. "Because of a growing reliance on automation and new technologies," the *New York Times* reported in a 1990 article on the industrial Midwest, "some factories look as if they have been hit by a kind of economic neutron bomb, which left assembly lines running at full speed but eliminated most of the people who worked on them."[75] Employment figures supported this conclusion. During the 1980s the Chicago area, for example, lost 188,000 jobs in heavy industry, a drop of 33 percent.[76] Heartland auto manufacturers survived the 1980s, though their performance offered little support to claims of renaissance. By the close of the 1980s, General Motors and its company town of Flint had become a sad joke. In his popular film *Roger & Me*, Michael Moore depicted the devastating impact of huge General Motors layoffs on the Michigan city, ridiculing the unfeeling incompetence of the giant automaker and in the process further blackening Flint's already dismal image. Japanese automakers did invest in the heartland during the 1980s, thus offering new jobs to midwestern auto workers. Yet they studiously avoided locating their plants in major urban areas. Instead, they chose to build their factories in corn fields outside of Marysville, Ohio, Lafayette, Indiana, and Bloomington, Illinois. The Japanese clearly preferred areas where labor unions were weak, where the population was rock-rib Republican, and where the workers would be overwhelmingly white. This they found in the rural Midwest rather than in unionized, Democratic, heterogeneous Detroit, Cleveland, or Chicago.

Moreover, in the 1980s as in the 1970s some heartland cities remained notorious for their symptoms of decline and decay. For example, no amount of cosmetic rhetoric about renaissance could hide Detroit's blemishes. In the late 1980s Detroit's inventory of abandoned buildings grew at the rate of twenty-four hundred a year, and in the last six months of 1989 the city's busy wrecking crews leveled three thousand abandoned structures. Few new buildings were taking the place of these derelict dwellings and businesses. Though Detroit had once been renowned for its high rate of home ownership, in 1987 the city issued only two building permits for construction of single-family houses and none for two-family units.[77] Demolition thus resulted in vacant lots rather than new housing. In 1989 some Detroiters sighted tumbleweed rolling down the city's deserted streets. Others spotted a ring-necked pheasant strolling around downtown, the city's many vacant lots with their high weeds providing good cover for these game birds. A local magazine said of such occurrences: "They feed a feeling that Detroit is not all that far from returning to the wilds from which it came."[78] One consolation for other midwestern cities was that they were not as bad off as Detroit. In 1990 an editorial in none-too-dynamic Toledo commented on "the erosion of Detroit." "It is difficult," the newspaper argued, "to reverse a course on which a city is slipping down to Third World status."[79]

Cities that were attempting to reverse their course continued to face problems with implementing revitalization schemes. In the late 1980s as in the 1960s and 1970s many renewal projects seemed to progress at a snail's pace, resulting in despair rather than boosted morale. In 1985 Cincinnati's Elder-Beerman department store closed, and on its site city planners projected an office showpiece known as Fountain Square West. Yet the project stalled, and the store stood vacant for the remainder of the decade, an empty hulk literally and figuratively casting a shadow over the heart of Cincinnati's central business district. Meanwhile, in 1988 the nearby Ayres department store went out of business, and its building was slated to be renovated as Tower Place, a center for specialty shops. But that project also proceeded at a discouraging rate so that by 1990 the *Cincinnati Enquirer* was commenting on both "the debilitating delays on Fountain Square West, [and] the slow development of Tower Place."[80] Though both schemes could eventually prove boons to the Queen City's central business district, the momentary lack of progress was fatal for some downtown retailers. "People in city hall tell us the future is bright once Tower Place opens," complained one shop owner. "But that is the future. We need help today." "I've been downtown for nine years," commented another retailer in 1990, "and this is the slowest it's ever been. Several stores have pulled out, and the promised building has not taken place."[81]

At the same time, Indianapolis's slow-moving efforts at retail revitalization also stirred criticism. Throughout the 1980s city officials were absorbed in planning and negotiating the construction of a mammoth downtown mall known as Circle Centre. By 1989 wrecking balls were leveling buildings on the site of the proposed mall, but it still was not clear what tenants could be lured to the complex and when it would be completed. "They're tearing everything down, and there's no mall," complained one downtown jeweler in 1990. "Awaiting Circle Centre mall for more than a decade," a local magazine observed, "Indianapolis now has a miniature Grand Canyon in its midsection, a huge debt and still no Downtown shopping center." According to this publication, the project had "hit more snags than cheap polyester."[82]

Delays deflated hopes of renaissance, but even more damaging were completed projects that misfired. In the 1980s as in earlier decades, some renewal schemes failed miserably, further depressing local spirits. The classic example was Toledo's Portside. Opened in May 1984 as part of an eleven-acre riverfront renewal project, Portside was a festival marketplace developed by the renowned James Rouse who had earlier created such famed and festive retailing malls as Boston's Quincy Market and Baltimore's Harborplace. Regarded nationally as the Michelangelo of urban renaissance, Rouse was supposedly to act as the long-awaited savior of Toledo's faltering downtown. Yet six years after Portside's gala dedication, the number of shops and restaurants in the waterfront mall had dropped from seventy to seventeen, and the project was struggling to survive. In May 1990 a Cleveland developer tried to put together a deal to renovate Portside and reopen it as a complex of nightclubs and restaurants.[83] By September of that year, however, hopes for renovation had waned. A visiting journalist wrote of the white elephant marketplace: "The minimum maintenance is noticeable from the main entrance, an octagonal vestibule that reeks of urine." "One set of escalators isn't working," he reported, "plants have wilted and the decorative water fountains are dry and filled with trash."[84] That same month the leading restaurant in the complex finally moved out, forcing the closing of Portside.[85] Backers of the scheme had predicted that it would attract five million visitors each year, but by the beginning of the 1990s it was one more example of Toledo's decline. Expressing the city's humiliation, one reporter commented: "The two-level shopping center, once trumpeted as a life raft for Toledo's floundering downtown, is sinking itself."[86]

But Toledo was not the only loser among the heartland cities. Some urban centers were improving their image, yet the term rust belt persisted and was still applied to the industrial Midwest. At the close of the decade, a Chicago business journal concluded that "Chicago merely survived the 1980s." Together with its fellow heartland metropolises it had overcome difficulties but had not flourished. This same journal claimed, "In the 1990s, we may well do much more."[87] Other observers, however, felt differently. "The decline of the Midwest is inevitable," the chairman of the University of Chicago's economics department argued in 1990. According to this pedant, "For many young people, the Midwest is a less attractive region to live and work."[88] Though "bullish" on his home state, an Ohio historian came to much the same conclusion. "If you were to walk down the street in any city in any state in the union," he observed, "and stop people at random to ask them where they think the action is today, not one in a thousand would say in Ohio."[89] Thus the doubts remained, and fears of Sunbelt superiority persisted. The economic pulse of the manufacturing heartland was not steady enough to silence detractors nor faint enough to quiet boosters.

The Continuing Migration

During the two decades following 1945, as in the years before, the migration of Southerners to the Midwest continued. Heartland auto plants, rubber factories, steel mills, and machine tool works flourished, fueling the demand for a fresh army of laborers from the South. And so long as the Midwest offered greater economic opportunities than Dixie, the flow northward remained unabated. Only in the late 1960s and the 1970s when the heartland economy lost its relative advantage over the South did the movement cease and in some areas reverse itself. Yet on the whole, the postwar era was a period in which the Midwest became increasingly southern in its population.

Moreover, as in the decades before 1945, the southern migration remained predominantly white. By 1970, 2,503,797 southern-born whites lived in the five states of the Old Northwest as compared with only 1,267,266 southern-born nonwhites. Of the region's southern natives, 66.4 percent were white but only 33.6 percent were black, and in each of the five states white Southerners outnumbered African-American natives of Dixie. As in earlier years, this migration pattern contrasted markedly with that of the Northeast, where 47.2 percent of the southern born were white and 52.8 percent were nonwhite. In 1970 as in 1950 the number of black Southerners in the Northeast and Old Northwest was approximately the same, but the heartland had two and a half times as many white Southerners as the Northeast. Both before and after World War II, the Great Southern Migration was predominantly white in the Midwest but predominantly black in the Northeast.

The influx of white Southerners was especially impressive in Ohio and Indiana. By 1970 white southern natives constituted almost 10 percent of the Buckeye State's population and over 9 percent of the inhabitants of the Hoosier State. In contrast, they accounted for 5 percent of Michigan's population and 4 percent of the residents of Illinois. Yet even these states had a larger proportion of white Southerners than the major eastern industrial states. For example, white southern natives made up 2.8 percent of Pennsylvania's population and a mere 1.5 percent of New York's inhabitants. Among the midwestern states only Wisconsin had such a small proportion of white Southerners among its residents.

Many of these white Southerners settled in the older central cities of the

Old Northwest. Despite the concentration of blacks in the aging urban hubs, in 1970 southern-born whites outnumbered southern-born blacks in six of the region's eleven largest cities. In Akron, Columbus, and Indianapolis, they were approximately twice as numerous as black natives of Dixie, whereas in Cincinnati they outnumbered black Southerners by 50 percent, in Dayton by almost 40 percent, and in Toledo by about 30 percent. White southern natives made up more than 10 percent of the population of each of these cities, excepting Toledo; and in Dayton, the most heavily white southern city, their share was almost 13 percent. White Southerners were even more prevalent in some of the Midwest's working-class suburbs. Huber Heights was a community of small look-alike brick homes north of Dayton, and by 1970, 21 percent of its nineteen thousand inhabitants were southern born. In nearby unincorporated Northridge, southern natives made up 30 percent of the population, and in Dayton's south-side industrial suburb of Moraine, 40 percent of the residents had been born below the Mason-Dixon Line. Similarly, in the Cincinnati working-class suburb of Norwood 34 percent of the thirty thousand residents were southern natives.

One did not have to look at the census returns, however, to realize that white Southerners had become a major element of the population in many midwestern communities. Fundamentalist and pentecostal churches catering to the newcomers became increasingly common, and between 1953 and 1963 the fastest-growing denomination in Ohio was the Southern Baptist church. Southern Baptist membership soared almost fivefold, and the number of churches affiliated with that denomination rose from 55 to 254.[90] Meanwhile, in 1952 the Arkansas-born evangelist Rex Humbard established his head-quarters in Akron where he found the rubber capital's southern population ripe for down-home gospel preaching. Beginning his Akron crusade in a rented theater, over the next quarter century Humbard built an evangelical empire that included the majestic Cathedral of Tomorrow in suburban Cuyahoga Falls and a nearby broadcast production center beaming his ministry to 700 radio and 656 television stations. His style remained pure Dixie, but that proved popular enough in southern-tinged Akron to fill the Cathedral of Tomorrow each Sunday morning.[91]

Astute politicians also recognized the changes wrought by the newcomers. These changes were apparent in the late 1960s and early 1970s when segregationist presidential candidate George Wallace stunned many political pundits and frightened liberals by garnering an unexpectedly large number of votes in the industrial Midwest. Part of the Alabaman's heartland support came from voters whose roots were in the South. Running as an independent candidate in the presidential election of 1968, he outpolled both Richard Nixon and Hubert Humphrey in Moraine and won an impressive one-fourth of the ballots in Norwood.[92] For many heartland newcomers Wallace was not an invader from an alien region; he was a good old boy from back home.

A good number of longtime midwestern residents did not welcome these Baptist Dixiecrats with their different practices, ideas, and customs. The newcomers generally were poor and had little schooling. Moreover, some of them did not conform to what native-born Midwesterners regarded as standards of civilized behavior. "Those people are creating a terrible problem in our city," complained one Indianapolis woman in 1956. "For some reason or other, they absolutely refuse to accommodate themselves to any kind of decent, civilized life."[93] Detroiters agreed with this assessment. A 1951 survey conducted by Wayne University asked a sample of Detroit residents to identify "undesirable people" who were "not good to have in the city." The most common reply was criminals or gangsters, the choice of 26 percent of those surveyed. But the second most frequent response was poor southern whites or hillbillies, the answer of 21 percent of the respondents. In contrast, only 13 percent named blacks and 6 percent foreigners.[94] For Motor City residents the hated hillbilly was a pariah second only to rapists, murderers, and thieves.

During the postwar era, native Midwesterners leveled numerous charges against the newcomers. Many regarded them as filthy, unsanitary, and ignorant about health and hygiene. A Chicago real estate broker claimed, "They'd just as soon use the floor for a toilet as go to the bathroom. We'd rather rent to a Negro, a Mexican, or a Filipino than to a white person from the South."[95] Offering a less heated assessment, a Cincinnati doctor observed: "They have no conception of what we consider adequate medical standards."[96] The supposed violence and criminality of the migrants also aroused antagonism. "Frankly," a Cincinnati police officer commented, "they're responsible for a disproportionate amount of the lawbreaking in the city."[97] A Chicago bartender complained: "These hillbillies fight a lot, and they use knives when they do. Chicago fellows don't fight that way."[98] Moreover, heartland natives contended that the sexual mores of the newcomers differed from those of the Midwest. A Cincinnati police officer claimed that the Southerners had no idea of statutory rape. "'If they're big enough, they're old enough' is likely to be their attitude toward girls," he observed. According to this officer, "Incest is another matter which a lot of mountaineers see differently than we do. . . . They can't see why it's any business of the police what they do with their sex life."[99]

Employers shared these negative attitudes toward the southern migrants. They would employ them if they needed help, but some firms preferred not to do so. In the late 1940s a Chicago employer remarked: "I told the guard at the plant gate to tell the hillbillies that there were no openings. It was easy enough, you know. The guard could tell which ones were from the South by their speech."[100] The manager of a Cincinnati firm explained his misgivings about southern workers: "They seem to do everything wrong because of lack of training and poor physical stamina. They're not used to tough competition."[101] Given such preconceptions among midwestern employers, southern newcomers were handicapped in their efforts to get ahead. Consequently, economic necessity forced many to live in central-city "hillbilly ghettoes." Even the "successful" southern migrants were employed chiefly in blue-collar jobs, which could lead at best to a house in Huber Heights.

In the minds of many native Midwesterners the Southerners were, then, lazy, immoral, violent, and dirty. The newcomers were from a different culture, which the longtime residents either did not understand or did not like. A 1964 article on "Chicago's Hillbilly Ghetto" described the white Southern migrants as "undernourished, uneducated, unwanted, and unable to cope with a society that does not understand them or their ways."[102] Though perhaps unduly grim, this generalization expressed the difficulties facing thousands of heartland newcomers.

Less numerous but more highly publicized were the black migrants moving northward. Most clustered in the older central cities, and during the course of the postwar era their share of the central-city population increased markedly. As seen in Table 10, at midcentury in none of the Midwest's twelve largest cities did blacks constitute as much as 20 percent of the population. By 1980 in ten of the twelve cities the black share was better than 20 percent, and in six of these cities African Americans represented more than one-third of the populace. In 1950 only one-sixth of all Detroit residents were black; thirty years later African Americans made up more than three-fifths of the Motor City's population. Likewise, in Chicago the black share went from 14 percent to 40 percent and in Saint Louis from 18 percent to 46 percent. During the postwar era Indianapolis annexed virtually all of the county in which it was located. Despite this massive addition of white suburban territory, the black proportion of the Hoosier capital's population climbed to 22 percent.

Though inner-city ghettoes won the lion's share of media attention, by the 1960s and 1970s an increasing number of blacks were moving to the suburbs. This was especially evident in Cleveland's eastern suburbs. During the first two decades after World War II, blacks expanded throughout the city's east side, and by the mid 1960s they were moving across the city limits into the independent municipalities of East Cleveland and Shaker Heights. As late as 1960 more than 98 percent of all blacks in the Cleveland metropolitan area lived in the central city, and more than one-third of the 6,455 blacks residing in suburbia were live-in servants or residents of institutions situated in outlying communities. Yet by 1965 approximately 25,000 African Americans lived in suburban Cleveland, and during the second half of the decade the number rose at a pace of 7,000 a year.[103]

Many suburbs feared that a rapid influx of blacks combined with white flight would produce an all-black suburban ghetto of depressed property values. Between 1960 and 1967 the black share of East Cleveland's population went from 2.4 percent to an estimated 44.6 percent, and according to one study, "from 1963 to 1967, block after block underwent rapid transition."[104] During the 1960s a consultant for the city of East Cleveland claimed that the community was "the first real test of the proposition that a viable racially integrated community [could] be created in America."[105] In the fol-

TABLE 10

Percentage of Blacks in Total Population in Largest Midwestern Cities,
1950 and 1980

City	1950	1980
Chicago	13.6	39.8
Detroit	16.2	63.1
Indianapolis	15.0	21.8
Milwaukee	3.4	23.1
Cleveland	16.2	43.8
Columbus	12.4	22.1
Saint Louis	17.9	45.6
Cincinnati	15.5	33.8
Toledo	8.2	17.4
Akron	8.7	22.2
Dayton	14.0	36.9
Grand Rapids	3.9	15.7

Sources: Bureau of the Census, Censuses of 1950 and 1980 (Washington: Government Printing Office, 1952 and 1983).

lowing decade, however, the suburb clearly flunked this test. "East Cleveland is now a thumbnail portrait of modern urban America," reported the *Cleveland Plain Dealer* in 1984. "Its 37,000 residents, overwhelmingly black, are mostly working-class people; nearly a quarter of them live in poverty." Once the home of John D. Rockefeller, the East Cleveland of the 1980s was "worlds away from the wealthy enclave it was at the turn of the century."[106] By 1980, 86 percent of its population was black, and most whites had definitely chosen to abandon the suburb rather than to stay and mix with blacks.

More successful at achieving integration was Shaker Heights, where racial transition proceeded at a slower pace. As early as the late 1950s blacks began moving into the upper-middle-class suburb, arousing fears among Shaker Heights residents that white homeowners would panic and sell out. Responding to this threat of white flight, in 1957 residents of the Ludlow area near the western edge of Shaker Heights founded a community association. According to its first president, this group endeavored to maintain a "happy, peaceful, and prosperous" neighborhood as integration proceeded.[107] Through block clubs, parties, and small meetings, the association calmed the fears of whites then living in the neighborhood. But by the early 1960s it faced the problem of attracting white home buyers to a neighborhood which real estate brokers and home lenders had identified as turning black and thus inappropriate for whites. To combat the problem, residents established the Ludlow Company, which helped whites finance the purchase of homes in the community. Moreover, the community association urged real estate brokers to stop using "blockbusting" tactics aimed at speeding white flight and accelerating racial turnover. All this proved successful, and during the late 1960s and 1970s the black share of Ludlow's population remained relatively stable at 55 percent.[108]

With equal success Shaker Heights's Lomond neighborhood association fought to ensure an integrated community. It too loaned money to whites for down payments on homes in "heavily integrated blocks." Moreover, it lobbied to secure a city ordinance outlawing "for sale" signs, which many regarded as psychological instigators of panic selling by whites.[109] In the 1970s Chicago's western suburb of Oak Park employed some of the same techniques to ensure integration rather than a rapid transition from all white to all black. According to one student of the suburb, by 1977 Oak Park "was being touted in the local and national press as a case of successful neighborhood racial integration."[110]

Shaker Heights and Oak Park, however, were the exceptions rather than the rule. In fact, during the second half of the twentieth century the Midwest was the most residentially segregated region of the nation. According to a study of racial segregation by residence in thirty-eight of the nation's largest metropolitan areas, in 1980 the four most segregated metropolises were Cleveland, Detroit, Chicago, and Milwaukee with Saint Louis ranking sixth and Indianapolis in eighth place. Moreover, this was not a new phenomenon. An examination of census data from 1960 showed Chicago, Milwaukee, and Cleveland to be the three most segregated metropolises, and according to an analysis of 1970 data the industrial Midwest held four of the top five places.[111] One of the distinctive characteristics of the midwestern city was, then, the unusual degree of racial segregation in residence. Throughout the nation blacks tended to live in black neighborhoods and whites in white neighborhoods. But nowhere were there fewer mixed residential districts than in the industrial Midwest. In 1960, 1970, and 1980 the heartland was a region of racially pure neighborhoods.

Attempts to integrate white areas of midwestern cities stirred considerable racial animosity during the 1960s and 1970s. For example, in 1966 the Reverend Martin Luther King, Jr., came to Chicago and launched the Open City campaign. Seeking to open neighborhoods previously closed to blacks, the campaign's organizers argued: "Every man is entitled to full access of buying or renting housing that is sound, attractive, and reasonably priced." To achieve this end, 450 Open City demonstrators marched on the all-white, working-class neighborhood of Gage Park, carrying signs which read "end slums" and "a prejudiced child is a crippled child." In Gage Park they met a mob of four thousand white counter-demonstrators and faced a barrage of rocks, bricks, and bottles. Expressing the frustration of Gage Parkers who had previously retreated before black residential advances, one white resident complained: "Now they want to come in and drive us out again. Well, we have to protect our neighborhood. This is a matter of self-preservation."[112]

Even more provocative was a 1966 march on Chicago's all-white working-class suburb of Cicero. At this demonstration two thousand National Guardsmen backed up by a small army of Illinois State Police and Cook County sheriff's deputies attempted to protect 250 marchers from a militant mob of three thousand whites. A tough town, which had formerly housed the headquarters of Al Capone, Cicero was hardly a bastion of calm, nonviolent discourse. "Marching in Cicero comes awfully close to a suicidal act," the Cook County sheriff warned.[113] The demonstrators survived, though in the case of both Cicero and Gage Park they achieved little. In 1980 Cicero remained virtually all white, a continuing symbol of the residential segregation endemic to the Midwest, and blacks accounted for less than 1 percent of the population of Gage Park.

Residential segregation, however, offered one significant advantage to midwestern blacks. With their numbers concentrated in the central cities or in certain all-black suburbs, they were better able to secure public office and wield political power. In heavily black municipalities, African Americans could use their ballots to oust white officialdom and take control. Had blacks been scattered evenly throughout the metropolitan area, they would have remained a minority in every political unit. Their voice would have been as weak in Chicago as in Cicero. Segregation ensured that they enjoyed local power bases, and by the 1960s the heartland's black politicians were ready to build on these bases.

Electoral victories in Cleveland and Gary testified to the success of their efforts. These were the first major municipalities in the nation to elect black mayors, and in each city the large African-American community mobilized to put one of its own number in power. Moreover, in both cities voting split along race lines, with an overwhelming percentage of whites casting their ballots for the white candidate and virtually all blacks opting for the black contestant.

In 1965 black state legislator Carl Stokes had come within twenty-one hundred votes of defeating Cleveland's incumbent white mayor Ralph Locher, and two years later he was eager to try again for the Ohio city's top job. He defeated Locher in the Democratic primary but in the general election faced the GOP's Seth Taft, a white patrician who had graduated from Yale and was the grandson of President William Howard Taft. Stokes's strategy was to emphasize race loyalty in black neighborhoods and deplore voting along racial lines in white areas. According to Taft, "It was a double campaign because over in the Negro part of the city the ministers and the newspaper editors and everybody were saying, 'Vote color,' and over in the white community Stokes was saying, 'No, don't vote color—consider a person on his qualifications, not on account of his color.'"[114] The latter message convinced relatively few whites, for on election day Stokes squeezed by to victory, winning approximately 95 percent of the black ballots but only 19 percent of the white vote.[115] In a normal year, the overwhelming majority of working-class Cleveland whites cast Democratic ballots; but in this election, race outweighed party loyalty, and they lined up behind a high-toned Republican Ivy Leaguer.

This was to become a familiar story in the older central cities of the Midwest. In a mayoral contest between a black and a white, party, class, and policy counted for little. Race determined the voter's choice. For example, at the same time Stokes was vying with Taft, a young black attorney in Gary, Richard Hatcher, was attempting to end white rule in the Hoosier steel center. Challenging the candidate of the white Democratic organization in the party primary, Hatcher proclaimed himself the liberator of the African-American masses. "No longer shall we be stampeded to the polls like a bunch of cattle by a cynical, corrupt, bigoted, political machine," he told his black followers. "Plantation politics is dead."[116] After winning the primary, Hatcher faced a Republican challenger in the general election. In the overwhelmingly Democratic city, the Republican contender usually had no chance of victory, but the white Democratic party chairman was openly hostile to Hatcher. Questioning the black candidate's heavy reliance on racial appeals, the party chairman claimed: "Hatcher is making a career out of being a Negro."[117] Gary's white Democrats felt likewise, and on election day Hatcher won with 96 percent of the black vote but only 14 percent of the white ballots.[118]

In 1973 Detroit was to join the list of heartland cities with African-American mayors. That year the black contender Coleman Young defeated his white opponent. Though neither candidate sought to stir racial antagonism, the results resembled those of Gary and Cleveland. Young carried 92 percent of the black ballots; his foe won the endorsement of 91 percent of white voters.[119]

During the 1980s racial rifts dominated Chicago politics with election returns reflecting the black-white polarization evident in other midwestern hubs. In 1983 black Congressman Harold Washington won the Democratic primary for mayor and faced white Republican Bernard Epton in the general election. Like Stokes, Hatcher, and Young, Washington mobilized African-American voters by appealing to racial pride. "It's our turn," he told a black audience. "Every group, when it reaches a certain population percentage, automatically takes over. They don't apologize . . . they just move in and take over."[120] Though Epton disavowed racism, many felt his campaign slogan "Epton for Mayor—Before It's Too Late" had definite racial implications, and a nationally syndicated columnist called it "a lightly coated message to whites to resist the election of the city's first black mayor."[121] Chicago's black newspaper editorialized: "In this city where segregation is a baptismal font in which nearly all whites dip their fingers, a mayoral contest in which a Black candidate is opposed by a white candidate—there is no way to keep race out of the contest."[122]

The election returns supported this judgment, for in Chicago as in Detroit, Gary, and Cleveland, voters cast their ballots according to race. Virtually all blacks sided with Washington and 82 percent of non-Hispanic whites were in the Epton column. Party affiliation swayed few voters; a remarkable 79 percent of all white Democrats marked ballots for the Republican candidate.[123] Two days before the election a local newspaper commiserated that "it was black for black and white for white," leaving Chicago "a city divided against itself."[124] Yet the data on residential segregation indicated that the city had long been divided against itself. The election returns in 1983 were just the political expression of a long-standing phenomenon.

In Chicago, Detroit, Gary, Cleveland, and elsewhere in the heartland, race continued to polarize urban life and politics throughout the first four decades following World War II. By the 1970s and 1980s the Midwest was no longer a magnet drawing black newcomers from the South; the great migration of the twentieth century had ceased. But the division between blacks and whites persisted, and nowhere was this more evident than in midwestern residential patterns and politics.

In the Chicago mayoral elections of the 1980s another group of newcomers began demonstrating their political clout. Support from Chicago's Hispanics gave Harold Washington his winning margin in 1983, and Latino votes spelled victory for white Mayor Richard M. Daley in 1989. Migrants from Mexico had become a significant factor in Chicago life, and in a city divided between black and white they held the deciding ballots. By 1980, 14 percent of Chicago's residents were Hispanic, and the number was growing. This was the emerging third force in the volatile ethnic arena of the Windy City.

Yet beyond Chicago and the Calumet region of northwestern Indiana, Hispanics remained a minor, if not insignificant, element of the heartland population. In California, Texas, Florida, and New York the influx of Mexicans, Cubans, and Puerto Ricans was perhaps the most significant demographic fact of life of the post–World War II era. With the arrival of thousands of Spanish-speaking newcomers, bilingualism became a major issue in these areas, as did illegal immigration. Yet most of the heartland remained remote from these concerns. By 1980 Latinos constituted less than 1 percent of the population in Indianapolis, Columbus, Cincinnati, Akron, and Dayton, and only slightly above 1 percent in Saint Louis. Of the major midwestern cities, Milwaukee was second to Chicago in percentage of the population that was Hispanic. But Hispanics accounted for only 4 percent of the residents of the Wisconsin city. Of the twenty-two cities in the United States with over 500,000 population, Columbus tied for dead last in percentage of Latinos, whereas Indianapolis ranked twentieth, Detroit seventeenth, and Cleveland fifteenth. When the 170 American cities with over 100,000 residents were ranked according to the percentage of Hispanics in the population, Evansville ended up in last place and Akron in second to last position. Outside of the local Taco Bell, Evansville and Akron residents had little chance to savor the Hispanic flavor affecting so much of the United States.

In fact, by 1980 the Midwest was no longer a region of newcomers. During the nineteenth century it had drawn migrants from the Atlantic seaboard,

Germany, Poland, and Bohemia. In the twentieth century the Poles and Czechs continued to arrive, but by the close of World War I a new migration from the South was redrawing the Midwest's demographic map. The late twentieth-century heartland was, by comparison, a region of stability experiencing a slow outward flow of people but relatively undisturbed by the arrival of migrants from other lands or sections. In 1980, 75 percent of the residents of the Old Northwest were natives of the states in which they resided; in contrast only 68 percent of all Americans were born in their state of residence. In every one of the eight midwestern metropolitan areas of one million or more population, more than 70 percent of the persons were born in the same state where they then resided. These figures were far higher than those for the boom cities of the Sunbelt. Only 22 percent of the residents of the Fort Lauderdale-Hollywood metropolitan area were born in Florida, and only 31 percent of the inhabitants of metropolitan Phoenix were natives of Arizona. Moreover, the heartland was no longer one of the chief destinations for foreign immigrants. The Indianapolis and Cincinnati metropolitan areas had the smallest share of foreign-born residents of any of the nation's metropolitan areas, having one million or more inhabitants. With 10.5 percent of its population of foreign birth, metropolitan Chicago had the largest foreign-born contingent in the Midwest. Yet the Windy City seemed all-American compared with the Miami metropolitan area, where over a third of the residents hailed from abroad, and greater Los Angeles, where 22 percent of the people were natives of another nation.

All of these figures added up to the conclusion that midwestern cities no longer were magnets attracting people in search of opportunity and advancement. In the late twentieth century, the once polyglot cities of the heartland were not beacons of hope for foreigners. Except for the Chicago region, heartland metropolitan areas attracted relatively few newcomers from south of the Rio Grande or from anywhere else for that matter. The Midwest of the last quarter of the century was not a land of migrants. It was a region of those who had stood fast and held firm despite the economic buffeting of the 1970s and 1980s. The continuing rift between blacks and whites meant that it was not an ethnically homogeneous or harmonious region. But the great social and ethnic divide in the Midwest was no longer between oldtimers and newcomers. By the close of the century, both blacks and whites, both descendants of "hillbillies" and scions of Teutonic families, had deep roots in the Midwest.

The Suburban Heartland

In the mid-twentieth century as in the late nineteenth century, the Midwest remained a region of owner-occupied homes. According to the 1950 census, Michigan led the nation in percentage of dwellings that were owner-occupied, Indiana was in fourth place, and all of the states of the Old Northwest, except Illinois, were well above the national average for owner occupancy. Moreover, the twelve metropolitan areas with the highest rates of owner occupancy were all in either Michigan, Indiana, or Ohio. Almost three-fourths of the residents of the Flint and South Bend metropolitan areas owned their own homes, and better than two-thirds of the families in the Akron, Fort Wayne, Grand Rapids, and Youngstown areas likewise paid no tribute to a landlord. By comparison, fewer than half the dwellings in the Northeast were owner occupied. Apartment living and rent paying remained less common in heartland cities than in the metropolises of the Atlantic coast or California, and working-class Midwesterners were less likely than their southern counterparts to lease their modest dwellings. Single-family homes surrounded by neat yards continued to characterize the metropolitan landscape of the Midwest, and home ownership remained a commonly sought goal of most urban heartlanders.

Thanks in part to low-cost mortgages insured by the federal government, the heartland dream of home ownership was becoming a reality for even more Midwesterners in the years following World War II. Throughout the nation, suburban housing projects were arising along the metropolitan fringes, with row after row of Cape Cod cottages and prefabricated ranch houses displacing corn fields, pastures, orange groves, and tracts of cotton. With its tradition of home ownership, the Midwest seemed an especially fertile field for such single-family subdivisions. Suburban sprawl thus became a phenomenon common to Cleveland, Detroit, Chicago, Saint Louis, and other heartland metropolises. The centrifugal flow of population accelerated during the postwar era with thousands of new recruits joining the army of suburban Midwesterners.

Typical of postwar suburban boomtowns was the new community of Rolling Meadows, twenty-five miles northwest of Chicago's central business district. Laid out in the early 1950s by developer Kimball Hill, Rolling Meadows offered two- or three-bedroom ranch homes to thousands of white working-class Chicagoans who previously had been unable to afford the advantages of suburbia. A survey from 1954 showed that the typical Rolling Meadows home buyer was a young, blue-collar Roman Catholic who had fought in World War II. Though more established and affluent residents in nearby suburbs derisively labeled the community "Meadow Ghetto," "Rolling Mudholes" or "Plywood City," many working-class newcomers to suburbia regarded the development of look-alike, prefabricated houses as a dream come true. Recalling her early days in Rolling Meadows, one refugee from the concrete of Chicago said: "I can remember sitting out waiting to see the first touch of green that would be our front lawn; and until you've done that—you just haven't lived!"[125]

About fifteen miles west of Rolling Meadows, building contractor Leonard Besinger was laying out the equally ambitious subdivision of Meadowdale. Like Kimball Hill, Besinger sought primarily to cater to blue-collar home buyers, and consequently the homes were inexpensive and prefabricated. Dedicated to cutting costs, Besinger dispensed with basements and substituted carports for garages. Moreover, as in the case of Rolling Meadows the project proved highly profitable for the builder. To handle the thousands of prospective buyers who descended on Meadowdale each weekend during the mid-1950s, Besigner introduced what he referred to as a "'supermarket' type of selling." From the sprawling parking lot, customers were channeled to six model homes and from there to a movie theater with "a large cinemascope screen" where they saw a film with "stereophonic sound" depicting the advantages of life in Meadowdale. Finally buyers proceeded to the sales office where they were given a number. When their number was called, they stepped up to the counter to select a lot and house style.[126]

Besinger found that customers were willing to wait two or three hours for their number to be called, for Meadowdale like Rolling Meadows represented the realization of a lifetime ambition. "Out here we have a six-room house with a big yard," exulted a meat cutter with four children. Prior to moving to Meadowdale he had "a four-room apartment on the second floor of a building on the Northwest Side, with only a gangway for a backyard for the kids." A milkman said of his new suburban home: "You have all the city conveniences—shopping, with parking, and schools—in a community like this. Everybody makes you welcome and you become a part of the community."[127] During the 1950s highbrow critics and affluent detractors scoffed at Meadowdale and its ilk. In their eyes such subdivisions, with street after street of identical houses and seemingly identical families, bred a stultifying homogeneity and a dismal uniformity. But the milkman and the meat cutter found suburbia a refreshing change from the cold impersonality and debilitating congestion of the big city.

All across the Midwest, suburbs were filling with new families eager for a yard, a house, and membership in the PTA. Between 1950 and 1960 the population of the Detroit suburb of Livonia soared from 17,534 to 66,702, and in the mid 1950s the local chamber of commerce advertised the Livonia area as "The Hottest Spot in America."[128] Meanwhile, the northern Detroit suburb of Warren seemed even hotter, skyrocketing in population from a mere 727 in 1950 to 89,246 in 1960. South of Cleveland the satellite city of Parma tripled in population during the 1950s, and on the northwestern outskirts of Saint Louis the community of Florissant rose tenfold in number of residents.

Retailers read these figures and soon turned their attention toward suburbia as well. Before World War II most residents of suburban municipalities continued to shop regularly at central-city department stores and downtown specialty shops. In their outlying communities they bought groceries and drugs but little else. After World War II, however, the center of American retailing moved from the urban core to the outskirts, as suburban shopping malls with branches of the big department stores offered merchandise formerly found only downtown. Northland Shopping Center in the Detroit suburb of Southfield became a model for others throughout the nation. At the time of its opening in 1954, Northland boasted of eighty stores with fifteen more projected, 160 acres of parking, and an elaborate landscaping scheme that included nineteen hundred evergreens and eighteen thousand ground-cover plants.[129]

During the following two decades every heartland city was to acquire its own version of Detroit's Northland, but the greatest of the huge retailing centers was Woodfield Mall in the Chicago suburb of Schaumburg. Opened in 1971, with 220 stores on three levels, it claimed to be the "world's largest shopping center under one roof."[130] By 1976 the *Chicago Tribune* was label-ing it "the Super Bowl of retailing." Each Saturday 250,000 shoppers de-scended on the mall, giving it a temporary population almost equal to that of Rockford and Peoria combined. Moreover, chartered buses came from as far away as Ohio loaded with shoppers eager to experience the retailing excitement of the nation's number-one mall.[131] While the big stores along State Street in downtown Chicago were closing their doors, Schaumburg was establishing itself as the shopping mecca of the Midwest.

In fact, by the 1960s and 1970s an increasing number of traditionally tran-quil residential suburbs were becoming commercial hubs, with research cen-ters and office parks as well as shopping malls. One of the first to establish itself as a center of office employment was the Saint Louis suburb of Clayton. As early as 1948 the Famous-Barr Department Store built a branch in Clay-ton, and four years later Brown Shoe Company completed a sprawling, low-rise office building in the community. In 1959 the city council repealed its five-story limit on building height, and this reform ushered in a heyday of commercial construction. In 1962 two office towers, one thirteen stories and the other sixteen stories, were erected, and within a few years a structure of twenty-six stories joined them. By 1966 the *St. Louis Post-Dispatch* com-mented that the skyline of Clayton "no longer blended into the county's amorphous urban sprawl, but now appeared more like a little Tulsa or per-haps an Omaha, than just another incorporated outskirt of St. Louis."[132] Moreover, the building boom continued, transforming Clayton into an office center rivaling that of downtown Saint Louis.

By 1980 an increasing number of businesses were clustering along the heartland's suburban expressways, and these giant thoroughfares were be-coming the new main streets of the Midwest. One of the best examples of this phenomenon was the Chicago area's East-West Tollway between Oak Brook and Naperville. By the mid-1980s, seventy-seven thousand workers earned their living in the 12 million square feet of office space along this eighteen-mile stretch of superhighway. Others profited from the corridor's construction boom that resulted in the inventory of office space more than doubling between 1980 and 1985.[133] Among the largest enterprises located near the highway were the Bell Laboratories and the Amoco Research Cen-ter, both of which contributed to Naperville's growing reputation as a center of high technology. Moreover, business was expanding westward along the tollway, bringing growth and prosperity to Aurora. "Today the land may be fields flecked with dandelions," reflected an architectural journal in 1989, "but tomorrow it's the site of the slick and shiny corporate homes of Toyota, Hyundai, Farmers Insurance, and a number of other companies that are finding Aurora . . . the place to be."[134] Many predicted that Aurora would be Illinois's second largest city by 2010, and so long as the East-West Toll-way kept channeling business into the community the prediction seemed more than justified.

In the late twentieth century, then, midwestern suburbia was no longer a residential refuge with few stores and fewer offices. Many heartlanders spent virtually their entire lives in suburbia, rarely crossing the line into the central city. They slept in their suburban homes, worked in suburban offices or plants, and shopped in suburban malls. Moreover, the proportion of twenty-four-hour suburbanites was growing. Whereas in 1960 only 36 percent of all employed persons in the Detroit metropolitan area both lived and worked in the suburbs, by 1980, 62 percent did so.[135] In 1989 a Wisconsin traffic study revealed that about as many commuters traveled westward from Milwaukee County to suburban Waukesha County during the morning rush hour as commuted eastward toward the central city. Such a finding was not surprising, for between 1979 and 1987 Waukesha County garnered more than 80 percent of all the new jobs created in the Milwaukee metropolitan area.[136] In both the Milwaukee and Detroit areas, the central city was no longer as central to the economy of the metropolis as it had once been. For many metropolitan residents, it was just a deteriorating hulk that they rarely visited and had little desire to frequent.

Midwestern metropolises were not as unfocused and centerless as some Sunbelt areas. Homes, condominiums, stores, and offices stretched along Florida's east coast, held together only by a common expressway; and in California's Silicon Valley, San Jose, Santa Clara, Mountain View, and Sunnyvale sprawled into one another, forming a seemingly endless stream of settlement with all the personality of a plastic cup. In contrast, Chicagoland still radiated from the Loop and the Sears Tower remained an unmistakeable landmark announcing to all travelers that here was the center of the metropolis. Yet the East-West Tollway seemed the wave of the future. Linear corridors of business were replacing old-fashioned downtowns, and Naperville and Waukesha County were the hottest locations in the relatively chilly economic climate of the Midwest.

The Continuing Tradition of Cultural Colonialism

Though the economy, ethnic composition, and settlement patterns of midwestern cities changed through the course of their history, one constant was the continuing sense of cultural inferiority. In 1980 as in 1880 or in 1830, there remained a nagging belief that heartland urbanites were removed from the centers of thought and intellectual creation in the nation and the world. Except during Chicago's brief golden age of the early twentieth century, heartlanders and outsiders alike perceived the region as a consumer of culture rather than a creator. It exported grain and automobiles, but imported ideas and entertainment. It was a cultural imitator rather than an innovator. Heartland cities supported huge art museums and superb symphony orchestras, thereby attempting to prove their worth. Yet during the late twentieth century residents of the Atlantic and the Pacific coasts did not envy the midwestern metropolises for their cultural attainments nor did they view heartland cities as trendsetters. To a Californian or a New Yorker, Cleveland, Detroit, Indianapolis, and Saint Louis were down-at-the-heel, doughty matrons, sporting last year's cultural fashions.

Many Midwesterners remained proud of their self-proclaimed solid American values and embraced a persisting belief that their region was the keeper of the national flame, the guardian of American virtue. Heartlanders were firmly convinced that they were not as rude as New Yorkers, not as shallow or rootless as Californians, and not as narrow or ignorant as Southerners. The midwestern way of life supposedly represented America at its best. But the late twentieth century was an age of diminishing nationalism, and consequently the Midwest's image as a bastion of Americanism was less appealing than it once had been. By the 1980s and 1990s the heartland's traditional merits simply counted for less, and the region seemed of declining significance in the evolution of the nation's culture. In any case, the Midwest's ideological purity did not ensure it primacy as a generator of ideas and entertainment. The East and West coasts enjoyed a lead in determining what Americans thought, what they viewed, what they laughed at, and what they sang.

The rise of television as the nation's chief medium of entertainment and information reinforced the image of the Midwest as a cultural colony. New York City and Los Angeles were to dominate television broadcasting, and producers and executives on the East and West coasts would determine what millions of heartlanders would watch every evening. Similarly, the national news broadcasts came from New York and Washington, D.C., and news directors on the Atlantic seaboard decided for the midwestern audiences what was indeed "news" and what deserved maximum coverage. New Yorkers and Californians packaged the entertainment and information heartlanders received, and increasingly the Midwesterner's vision of the world was seen through the lenses of the Atlantic and Pacific coasts.

For a short time in the late 1940s and early 1950s it appeared that Chicago might develop into a television hub. The nationwide popularity of such locally produced programs as "Kukla, Fran, and Ollie" and "Garroway at Large," starring Dave Garroway, seemed to promise a leading role for the Windy City in the television era. In fact, during Chicago's shortlived television heyday, radio star Fred Allen came to the city and announced: "They ought to tear down [New York's] Radio City and rebuild it in Chicago and call it Television Town."[137] Yet by 1953 Garroway had moved to New York, and Chicago's early hopes for broadcasting glory had waned.

In the competition for supremacy in television broadcasting, New York and Los Angeles had advantages that Chicago could not match. For example, New York City's preeminence in the advertising industry meant that it was a preferred site for broadcasting. In 1951 *Time* magazine explained: "Most of the advertising agencies who pay TV's biggest bills have headquarters in New York; with large sums at stake, they prefer to have their programs produced and staged close at hand where they can keep a firm finger in the pie."[138] Once filmed programming supplanted live broadcasts, Los Angeles took the upper hand. It had the movie studios and sound stages necessary for filming television programs, and Hollywood thus became the capital both of broadcasting and motion pictures. Moreover, the Broadway theaters of New York and movie studios of Los Angeles ensured a concentration of talent in both cities. By comparison the show business population of Chicago was miniscule. A Chicago television producer would have to import talent; in Los Angeles every waiter or waitress was a latent star looking for his or her big break.

Not only did Midwesterners spend much of their time viewing the products of other regions, the popular music they enjoyed was also largely imported. New York remained the center of the musical theater, and Nashville was the capital of the growing country and western music industry. Los Angeles was another great recording center and perhaps the dominant city in fashioning the popular tastes of America. Chicago did develop its own style of blues music which attracted many black listeners in the late 1940s and early 1950s. The 1960s witnessed the decline of blues and the rise of Chicago soul, this latter style spawning dozens of recording companies and distributors along "Record Row" on the city's near south side. During the 1970s, however, Chicago lost its grip on the black music market. Speaking of Chicago's role in the development of blues and soul, in 1974 one veteran performer concluded: "It was great history, but unfortunately for the last ten years, that's mostly what it has been—history."[139]

Attracting a wider audience among white listeners than Chicago blues or soul, the Motown sound of Detroit was the heartland's chief contribution to popular music, and it earned the beleaguered Motor City a brief stint in the show business limelight. Eager to lift its sagging reputation, Cleveland claimed to be the birthplace of rock and roll and won designation as the site of the Rock and Roll Hall of Fame. Cleveland's claim, however, rested on the fact that a local disc jockey had been an early promoter of rock music. No one ever heard of the Cleveland sound nor could the Ohio city boast of any native of the stature of Elvis. Saint Louis had been the childhood home of such music stars as Chuck Berry and Tina Turner, but that city garnered only the Bowling Hall of Fame. In the minds of many observers, this designation seemed appropriate. The Midwest was deemed a region of pot-bellied bowlers and not the glitzy hub of show business.

Throughout the post–World War II era, then, the urban Midwest did not set national or international trends in popular thought or entertainment.

Instead, heartland cities remained cultural colonies of the East and West coasts. Californians and New Yorkers did not look to Cleveland or Saint Louis to discover the latest fashions. Los Angeles residents did not sit before their television sets to view the newest entertainment offering from Chicago. And New Yorkers did not tune in to Detroit for the latest in national news. In the late twentieth century, America's perimeter was clearly in charge of the nation's mind. The heartland remained a follower.

During the post–World War II era midwestern cities likewise achieved only limited success as centers of higher learning. State legislatures authorized funds to found urban universities or strengthen existing institutions. Thus Illinois created a new campus of the state university on the near west side of Chicago, Indiana founded a branch of Purdue and Indiana universities in Indianapolis, and in 1955 Wisconsin merged the two-year Milwaukee extension with a state teachers college to form the University of Wisconsin-Milwaukee. Meanwhile, Michigan assumed control of Detroit's municipally supported Wayne University, and Ohio similarly strengthened former municipal universities in Toledo, Akron, and Cincinnati by making them state institutions. In Cleveland and Youngstown colleges founded by the YMCA also became state universities, further enhancing higher education in urban Ohio. Yet none of these institutions had a reputation rivaling those of the finest universities of the East nor even the leading universities in their own states. The urban campuses suffered the stigma of being perceived as branches; in the minds of most people the "real" University of Wisconsin remained in Madison, Champaign-Urbana was the true home of the University of Illinois, and Indiana University was in Bloomington not Indianapolis. In the popular imagination, the newer urban universities remained colonies of the long-established institutions in the region's smaller cities.[140]

By the 1970s and 1980s universities were deemed growth industries generating high-tech industrial development as well as providing stable employment for thousands. Yet during this boom age for higher education, the Midwest's chief cities generally were not among the most distinguished hubs of scholarship. In the 1980s as in the 1920s and 1930s, the University of Chicago was the only university in a large midwestern city to rank among the nation's most prestigious institutions, and Northwestern in nearby Evanston was the only elite suburban university in the heartland. By comparison Baltimore could boast of Johns Hopkins, Philadelphia of the University of Pennsylvania, New York City took pride in Columbia, and the Boston metropolis was home to both Harvard and Massachusetts Institute of Technology. Midwestern state legislatures had appropriated large sums to ensure that higher education was available to urban dwellers, and the city universities admirably taught and trained thousands of students. Moreover, they made notable strides as centers of research. Yet at the end of the twentieth century, a lack of prestigious institutions still distinguished most of the largest midwestern cities from their eastern counterparts. In higher education circles no one ever equated Detroit with Boston.

One area in which the urban Midwest previously showed distinction was architecture. Chicago gave birth to the skyscraper, and many of the greatest architects in America practiced there. No American achieved greater immortality in the field than Frank Lloyd Wright, and the Midwest's Prairie School was one of the liberating forces unleashing the modern aesthetic throughout the world.

After World War II Chicago retained a distinguished position in architecture, but the Windy City and the Midwest in general failed to recapture the visionary audacity of the Prairie School years. The great German architect Ludwig Mies van der Rohe did settle in Chicago where he established himself as a living icon for worshippers of modern architecture. Yet his architecture was not a declaration of cultural independence for the heartland. Labeled the "International Style," Mies's abstract aesthetic was purposely devoid of any geographic or regional association. The Prairie architects were Midwesterners whose regional outlook underlay their architectural style and their rebellion against convention. Mies was a German architect whose aesthetic was fully developed prior to arriving in America and who pointedly ignored local traditions. He built the same in Barcelona as in Chicago, the same in Baltimore as in Detroit. In other words, he was an architect who happened to end up in the Midwest; he was not a midwestern architect.

Chicago's most successful postwar architectural firm, Skidmore, Owings, and Merrill(SOM), was loyal to the internationalism of Mies rather than the regionalism of Wright. Founded in the 1930s by two Indiana natives, SOM established branch offices on the East and West coasts and practiced an architecture so devoid of regional style that many casual observers did not realize that its head office was actually in Chicago and not New York.[141] Appropriately, the most acclaimed buildings of both Mies and SOM were along New York's Park Avenue where they set the style for future Gotham office towers. By contrast, in the late 1950s that superannuated *enfant terrible* Frank Lloyd Wright built New York's bizarre Guggenheim Museum, a structure about as appropriate to its Fifth Avenue location as a circus tent. It was the prairie iconoclast's final nose-thumbing gesture at the capital of the eastern establishment.

So long as Mies remained headquartered in Chicago, he lent his prestige to the Windy City, and admirers from throughout the world looked to the Midwest's largest metropolis for inspiration. With his death in 1969, however, Chicago's position in the world of architecture fell, and according to one observer, in the 1970s "Chicago architecture seemed suddenly to have been left behind in a provincial backwater."[142] In 1976 a group of Windy City architects who called themselves the "Chicago Seven" did take up the standard of rebellion in the spirit of their Prairie School predecessors. Yet in 1981 one architecture critic commented: "Chicago is architecturally exactly what it is in other ways, a provincial capital with one eye on New York and Europe and the other on its own jingoistic pride." Because of this outlook, it too often wanted "to ape more 'legitimate' and recognized styles" as fast as possible, resulting in what this critic referred to as "a constantly shifting Chicago Bandwagon School."[143] The leader of the "Chicago Seven," Stanley Tigerman, also recognized the continuing sense of inferiority engrained in Chicagoans. "Isolated by geography," wrote Tigerman in 1987, "Chicago continuously yearns to be reassured by its continental counterparts that it is alright to be separated from the boundaries of this great nation."[144]

Reassurances, however, were not always forthcoming. Instead, in the late twentieth century, as in previous decades, condescending comments by architects and critics heightened the regional sense of inadequacy. In the late 1980s a prominent avant-garde architect told the editor of a midwestern architecture journal that the heartland was "just the sort of quiet place where the seeds of experiment [could] be sown and allowed to grow without interference," and he compounded his condescension by suggesting that Ohio was "innocent enough to take risks."[145] In a letter to the editor, a Chicago architect took exception to "this view of the Midwest as a sort of intellectual void," but most heartlanders were used to such mindlessly parochial attitudes regarding their region.[146] According to Stanley Tigerman, "Chicago is perceived by Easterners as similar to that great, unapproachable rock centering Australia—it is compelling for a great distance but, ultimately, not really inhabitable."[147] After more than 150 years of heartland urban settlement, Tigerman and others still faced the assumption that midwestern cities were barely civilized habitations, deadly quiet outposts in the remote interior.

During the 1980s some Chicagoans continued to garner laurels within the architectural profession, but local practitioners were discouraged by the willingness of Windy City developers to hire out-of-town talent for a number of major projects. A Japanese architect was responsible for the American Medical Association building, a Spaniard designed a Wacker Drive skyscraper, and the New York firm of Kohn Pedersen Fox received five major commissions in downtown Chicago.[148] In the field of architecture Chicago remained a producer and not just a consumer. Yet some Chicagoans looked upon these outside creations in the same way a Detroiter viewed Toyotas and Mazdas. They were a visible threat to one of the city's chief claims to fame. Moreover, no reincarnation of Frank Lloyd Wright walked the streets of the Illinois metropolis shaking the nation's architectural establishment. In the area of building design, unlike in the world of popular entertainment, Chicago was still a contender, though the confidence and daring of earlier years was perhaps lacking.

Certainly heartland architects fared much better than the region's painters or sculptors. During the post–World War II era, New York City was the recognized capital of the art world, and to win a place in the art history books any aspiring artist had to head for Manhattan. Given the presumed preeminence of New York City, one could no more become an internationally acclaimed artist in Detroit or Chicago than one could become a movie star in Cleveland or Saint Louis. Moreover, to be taken seriously by critics in the 1950s and 1960s, anyone who dared remain west of the Appalachians had to produce works in the New York style. To employ a style contrary to the standards dictated by New York was to ensure opprobrium as a reactionary or as an unsophisticated dabbler.

The leading art museums reinforced this sense of cultural colonialism. Ever since their founding in the late nineteenth and early twentieth centuries, these museums had viewed their role as that of missionaries of culture. They brought the great creations of Europe before the eyes of Midwesterners, thereby seeking to enhance heartlanders' appreciation of art. Their primary mission was to import art rather than to nurture or create it. The renaissance palaces of painting and sculpture arising in Chicago and Detroit and their neoclassical counterparts in Cleveland and Saint Louis endeavored to uplift the Midwest by making it more like Europe and the eastern seaboard. These museums never sought to challenge artistic dogma or to incite rebellion against the cultural capitals of the world. Most were associated with local schools of art which offered training in painting, drawing, and sculpture. But this training conformed to accepted Atlantic seaboard standards, and again the goal was to teach the styles of Europe and the East so that Midwesterners could keep up with artistic fashion. In any case, in America the mark of a great art institution was its collection and not its students.

In keeping with this tradition, heartland museums of the post–World War II decades often tendered little support or encouragement to local artists. When the Chicago Art Institute made contemporary acquisitions during the 1950s and 1960s, it generally bought works by New York or European painters and sculptors. In fact, the Art Institute was known for its unsympathetic attitude toward Chicago artists of the postwar era.[149] The opening of Chicago's Museum of Contemporary Art in 1967 seemed to promise better times for the local art community. But the museum's first director made clear that "it would be pointless to coddle Chicago artists for the sake of pleasing narrow interests."[150] Unfortunately for local artists, no one could accuse the Museum of Contemporary Art of coddling. When it celebrated its tenth anniversary with a major retrospective exhibition, only four of the eighty-five artists represented in the show were from Chicago.[151]

Detroit's Institute of Art also proved apathetic, if not hostile, toward local creators. During the 1940s and 1950s the institute maintained a separate gallery within the museum which exhibited the work of Michigan artists, but in 1963 this showcase for local talent was dismantled because the space was needed for other exhibits.[152] Moreover, since 1911 the institute had held the annual "Exhibition for Michigan Artists." Yet during the 1960s and 1970s the insensitivity and indifference of museum officials largely destroyed this tradition. In 1973 the art critic for the *Detroit News* lambasted the institute's "increasing neglect of the local art community." According to this critic, "This neglect shows up in the condescending . . . Michigan exhibitions; in a refusal to search out and encourage really creative artists who work here;

in a disregard for informing the public about local art and in a generally negative attitude toward the best galleries which often provide the only consistent platform for contemporary art."[153]

The Detroit Institute of Art, Chicago Art Institute, Museum of Contemporary Art, and many other midwestern museums faced the same indictment. They remained focused on the world beyond the heartland and could see little merit in the works created virtually within the shadow of their institutions. Midwestern museum directors and curators, like most of the art establishment, viewed America's interior as the provinces, and no institution seriously aspiring to greatness could allow itself to succumb to provincial tastes or talents. Those governing the leading museums believed that Chicago and Detroit deserved only the best in art and the best supposedly came from New York, not from Illinois or Michigan.

As a result of this attitude, the Midwest's largest museums reflected little of their own locality. The Detroit Institute of Art was a good place to visit if one wanted to forget that one was in Detroit. One could wander through the galleries decked with baroque and rococco treasures and escape from the reality of the Motor City. Moreover, that was the idea behind the midwestern art museum. In 1980 as in 1900 it was supposed to be an outpost of culture charged with civilizing, but not succumbing to, the material world of automakers and grain handlers.

During the 1970s New York City's grip on the art world did loosen slightly, and a group of Chicago artists labeled the Imagists won international recognition. In the early 1980s one critic perceiving an Imagist influence on Gotham actually went so far as to refer to "the Chicagoization of New York."[154] Likewise, a body of Detroit artists known as the "Cass Corridor School" attracted national attention to a degree previously unknown in the Motor City. Yet New York remained the art capital of the world, and a sense of provincialism continued to hang like a pall over heartland creators. In 1987 an assistant at a Chicago gallery complained: "It's a no-win situation. If we concentrate on Chicagoans, we don't get the best collectors. But we don't get them anyway because they buy in New York."[155] Expressing a widely held view, one Windy City gallery owner explained: "The problem with being in Chicago is that we are removed." And another knowledgeable commentator concluded, "It's very hard to have a big New York career if you live in Chicago."[156]

By the 1980s some Midwesterners were turning to the West rather than to the East for artistic inspiration. For example, in 1988 a Chicago artist and columnist in a midwestern art journal departed for Los Angeles, which he believed had "the rapidly coalescing energy of cultural production" that might transform it "into the equal of New York as a center of the artworld of the 21st century." "I have seen an enormous amount of growth and change in the Chicago art scene over the past decade," he wrote in his last column for midwestern readers. "But the exodus of ambitious artistic talents continues, and it has not been offset by an influx of emigres from New York or the West Coast."[157] In other words, the United States was developing two magnets for artistic achievement, one in the East and one in the West, and the Midwest's greatest metropolis could not match the pull of either.

Outside Chicago the sense of cultural inferiority reached even greater proportions. In 1987 a Saint Louis art critic wrote: "Many times I've heard St. Louis people refer to Chicago, let alone New York, as a big deal, and in the silence of subtext I understand an implicit competition in which St. Louis, for the speaker, is the loser."[158] That same year the former director of a contemporary art gallery in Indianapolis said much the same thing more simply when she referred to the Hoosier capital's "incredible inferiority complex."[159] The attitude of some locals did not offer any boost to heartland spirits. In 1988 a staff member of the Cleveland Museum of Art admitted that the institution's annual show of local creations "was barely tolerated" by the museum personnel, "knowledgeable as they [were] about trends in New York and everything."[160] Another publication claimed the staff regarded this showcase of local talent "as a thankless, if necessary onus."[161] Even more devastating to the heartland ego was the judgment of the "Michigan editor" of a midwestern art journal. In 1987 he publicly proclaimed: "Detroit is a hick town [and] anything that is not facile will find meager rewards waiting in Detroit."[162]

New York not only dominated the art world of the postwar era, it also retained its position as the nation's literary capital. As the home of the leading publishers and the principal agents, it dominated the book trade and literary fashion, and no midwestern city could rival it. With universities becoming the chief patrons of creative writing, poets and novelists increasingly dispersed throughout the nation to every sylvan campus where a steady paycheck was forthcoming. Consequently, by the 1980s Gotham was not the residence of a majority of the nation's prominent literary practitioners, and unlike painters, writers did not feel compelled to flock to Manhattan or face oblivion.[163] But New York continued to possess an unequaled allure for those who made a living working with words and ideas. Books and articles appeared about an elite known as the "New York intellectuals;" by comparison no one heard of any coterie of Detroit or Cleveland intellectuals.

James Farrell and Nelson Algren did carry on the Chicago literary tradition in the 1930s, 1940s, and 1950s, and in the 1970s University of Chicago professor Saul Bellow won the Nobel Prize for literature. Yet Chicago was not the literary mecca it had been in the early twentieth century. Nor did literary insurgents in the Windy City win the admiration of audiences worldwide. In the second half of the twentieth century Chicago was just one more city with its share of talent.

Moreover, Chicago was no longer the compelling literary symbol it had once been. At the turn of the century, in one novel after another, Chicago had been a major character looming over the human protagonists. It had symbolized competitive materialism and the terrible, yet awe-inspiring, forces of urbanization and industrialization. By the second half of the twentieth century, such themes were passé; the city and the machine failed to stir the mind of the novelist or the poet. Consequently, the symbol of Chicago no longer maintained its grip on the literary imagination nor appeared so frequently in the pages of fiction or verse.

In fact, by the 1980s Chicago remained in pretty much the same cultural relationship to New York as it had a century earlier. It was still subordinate, still walking two steps behind Gotham, and still fretful about catching up. "There is a gnawing sense of inadequacy," wrote one observer of Chicago in the early 1980s, "it sees itself as the second city—second, that is, to New York, though it may well nowadays be third or fourth or fifth."[164] Moreover, that characterization could apply not only to Chicago but to the urban Midwest as a whole. Culturally, the heartland's cities remained colonies of the Atlantic and Pacific coasts and they knew it. The centers of entertainment, information, art, and literature were beyond the boundaries of Ohio, Illinois, or Michigan. Nor were Midwesterners as eager as they once were to shed their colonial status. The fires of cultural insurgency that once warmed the Prairie School and the Robin's Egg Renaissance now burned less brilliantly. Instead, residents of the aging hubs tuned in to the news from Washington, then watched a Hollywood sitcom, and possibly perused the *New York Times* best-seller list to see what was worth reading.

After Two Centuries

The year 1987 marked the two hundredth anniversary of the creation of the Northwest Territory and the 150th birthday of the city of Chicago. In 1988 Cincinnatians joined in the celebrations with a series of events commemorating their city's bicentennial. No matter whether midwestern metropolises were marking their bicentennial or sesquicentennial, the message was the same. The heartland hubs had indeed grown old. By the 1990s the urban heartland was beginning its third century, and the cities of the industrial Midwest could look back on a wealth of experiences. Over the course of two hundred years, they had accumulated a heritage studded with success but troubled by occasional failure.

Among their most notable achievements was their rise to economic greatness during the nineteenth and early twentieth centuries. The region successfully overcame the physical isolation that plagued it during its earliest years of settlement. Railroads supplemented, and in some cases supplanted, the rivers, lakes, and canals as much-needed arteries of access to the outside world. Consequently, Chicago, Saint Louis, Detroit, Cleveland, and Milwaukee were able to develop into centers of commerce and industry rather than remaining simple trading outposts. They became central to the nation's economy, fashioning its machinery and processing its foodstuffs.

Moreover, the Midwest and its cities were to assume a central position in the nation's perception of itself. By the beginning of the twentieth century, Ohio, Indiana, Illinois, Michigan, and Wisconsin were not only at the heart of America's economy, they also seemed to embody the American spirit as no other area did. According to popular opinion, the Midwest was the most American region of the nation and the most democratic. People from the heartland were deemed typically American, and the region's greatest hero, Abraham Lincoln, became the physical embodiment of the nation's conception of democracy and the chief icon of its political faith. In the popular imagination Boston was too Brahmin to be truly American, New York too foreign, New Orleans too Creole, and Los Angeles and San Francisco too crazy. Chicago, though, was deemed the all-American metropolis, and such lesser hubs as Indianapolis, Columbus, Fort Wayne, and Peoria also seemed examples of pure Americana. In fact, according to common parlance, if something "played in Peoria," it appealed to the great American masses. Peoria and similar heartland centers were regarded as the litmus test for American taste and mentality.

Yet this emerging sense of centrality did not assuage all heartland doubts. Feelings of cultural inferiority continued to nag at residents of midwestern cities. Imitation of Europe and the East Coast persisted, and only a few

figures like Frank Lloyd Wright were confident enough to snub the traditional centers of arts and learning and seek to create what they regarded as
an American and democratic culture in the Midwest. Despite a sense of
being better than the East in terms of ideology and Americanism, Midwesterners continued to look to New York, London, and Paris for ideas, art, and
entertainment.

Residents of heartland cities thus conceived of themselves at the center
of the nation but at the same time one step removed from the heart of
civilization. The very name "Middle West" implied the dual sense of centrality and isolation characterizing the region. Chicago and Detroit were at
the middle of America's economy and the national self-perception. But with
regard to higher culture, they remained the West, a fringe area beyond the
vital core.

Meanwhile, millions of migrants to the region testified to the lure of its
economic triumphs while at the same time drawing into question its image
as 100 percent American. Germans flooded heartland cities in the nineteenth
century, though the number of Slavic newcomers had increased markedly
by 1900. Moreover, the Irish, Scandinavians, Italians and virtually every
other nationality could claim settlements of lesser size in the polyglot midwestern cities. The next layer of new residents came from the American
South, with both blacks and whites finding homes north of the Ohio River.
Especially numerous were the white migrants from Dixie who added a new
southern tinge to the cities of Ohio, Indiana, and Michigan.

The newcomers continued to arrive by bus, train, and automobile in Chicago, Detroit, and Cleveland so long as the heartland remained a region of
economic opportunity. By the 1970s and 1980s, however, it was no longer a
leading magnet for money or people. It had grown old, and its image had
changed from industrial dynamo to tired has-been. Aging took its heaviest
toll in the central cities, but in both city and suburb times were tough. The
economic heart of America was moving to the South and West, leaving the
Midwest's pulse fainter. Moreover, economists claimed that America had
entered a postindustrial age, and thus by definition the industrial Midwest
was out of date and out of step. Postindustrial Atlanta, Dallas, and San
Diego had assumed the advantage.

Though the region's cities had passed from youth to maturity to old age,
this did not necessarily mean that death was imminent. Chicago, Milwaukee,
Detroit, Saint Louis, and Cleveland would survive in future decades even
though they counted for less in the affairs of the nation and the world. By
the close of the twentieth century, however, it did seem as if the concept of
the city was becoming less meaningful in the Midwest and the nation as a
whole. Distinctions between rural and urban had blurred, especially in such
densely populated areas as the industrial Midwest. Most Ohioans or Hoosiers living in areas designated by the census bureau as rural were not farmers or isolated rubes. The chief differences between them and their brothers
and sisters in metropolitan areas were that they had larger yards and com-

muted farther to work. Moreover, an increasing number of so-called suburbs did not fit the suburban image. Naperville, Illinois, was not a bedroom community but a center of business as well as a place of residence. Similarly, Troy, Southfield, and other municipalities of Oakland County were the principal generators of what economic vitality remained in southeastern Michigan; the Motor City's engine had died. And the future of southeastern Wisconsin seemed to rest with Waukesha County and not Milwaukee. The term *suburb* implied a position of subordination and dependence on the dominant central city. That type of relationship was becoming less common.

Thus after two centuries, the patterns of settlement in the industrial Midwest continued to change. Perhaps by the 1990s the notion of "cities" of the heartland was a conceptual anachronism. Population sprawled across the region and amorphous megapolises were supplanting clearly focused urban centers. Who could accurately define where the Dayton metropolitan area gave way to Greater Cincinnati or where the Milwaukee metropolis began and Chicagoland ended? Certainly the so-called cities did not conform to the notion of "urban" prevailing in 1850 or 1900. Over the course of two centuries the Midwestern metropolises had changed from trading outposts, pinpoints of habitation in the overwhelming wilderness, to industrial giants with billows of smoke testifying to their manufacturing might, and finally to vast conurbations defying definition.

Notes

The Urban Heartland

1. See Timothy R. Mahoney, *River Towns in the Great West: The Structure of Provincial Urbanization in the American Midwest, 1820–1870* (Cambridge, U.K.: Cambridge University Press, 1990); Timothy R. Mahoney, "Urban History in a Regional Context: River Towns on the Upper Mississippi, 1840–1860," *Journal of American History* 72 (September 1985): 318–39; David R. Goldfield, "The New Regionalism," *Journal of Urban History* 10 (February 1984): 171–86.

1. Creating the Urban Network

1. J. W. Scott, "Our Cities—Atlantic and Interior," *The Merchants' Magazine* 19 (October 1848): 386.

2. Charles Cist, *Cincinnati in 1841: Its Annals and Future Prospects* (Cincinnati: Charles Cist, 1841), p. 275.

3. Charles N. Glaab, "Jesup W. Scott and a West of Cities," *Ohio History* 73 (Winter 1964): 6.

4. Ibid.

5. J. W. Scott, *The Future Great City of the World* (Toledo: Blade Steam Book and Job Print, 1868); Glaab, "Scott," pp. 3–12. See also J. W. Scott, "Our American Lake Cities," *Hunt's Merchants' Magazine* 31 (October 1854): 403–13; J. W. Scott, "Westward Movement of the Center of Population, and of Industrial Power of North America," *Hunt's Merchants' Magazine* 36 (February 1857): 198–202; J. W. Scott, "The Great City of the Interior: On Lake or River?" *Hunt's Merchants' Magazine* 37 (July 1857): 47–49; J. W. Scott, "Our Cities in 1862 and 1962," *The Merchants' Magazine and Commercial Review* 47 (November 1862): 401–409.

6. James Hall, *The West: Commerce and Navigation* (Cincinnati: H. W. Derby and Company, 1848), pp. 227–28.

7. Cist, *Cincinnati in 1841,* p. 275.

8. Mrs. Steele, *A Summer Journey in the West* (New York: John S. Taylor and Company, 1841), pp. 239–40.

9. Henry D. Shapiro and Zane L. Miller, eds., *Physician to the West: Selected Writings of Daniel Drake on Science and Society* (Lexington, Ky.: University Press of Kentucky, 1970), p. 91.

10. A. N. Marquis, ed., *The Industries of Cincinnati* (Cincinnati: A. N. Marquis and Company, 1883), pp. 17–18; James Flint, *Letters from America* (Edinburgh, U.K.: W. and C. Tait, 1822), p. 125.

11. Flint, *Letters from America,* p. 211; Richard C. Wade, *The Urban Frontier: Pioneer Life in Early Pittsburgh, Cincinnati, Lexington, Louisville, and St. Louis* (Chicago: University of Chicago Press, 1959), p. 171.

12. Charles Frederic Goss, *Cincinnati, the Queen City, 1788–1912* (Chicago: S. J. Clarke Publishing Company, 1912), 1: 140.

13. A Septuagenarian, "A Review Commercial and Literary," *Genius of the West* 4 (February 1855): 34.

14. B. Drake and E. D. Mansfield, *Cincinnati in 1826* (Cincinnati: Morgan, Lodge, and Fisher, 1827), p. 75; Walter Stix Glazer, "Cincinnati in 1840: A Community Profile," Ph.D. diss., University of Michigan, 1968, p. 45.

15. James Taylor Dunn, ed., "'Cincinnati Is a Delightful Place': Letters of a Law Clerk, 1831–34," *Bulletin of the Historical and Philosophical Society of Ohio* 10 (October 1952): 263.

16. Richard T. Farrell, "Cincinnati in the Early Jackson Era, 1816–1834: An Economic and Political Study," Ph.D. diss., Indiana University, 1967, p. 31; Drake and Mansfield, *Cincinnati in 1826,* p. 77; Richard Smith, *A Review of the Trade and Commerce of Cincinnati* (Cincinnati: Cincinnati Gazette, 1853), p. 7. For statistics on 1846–47, see Hall, *The West,* pp. 323–28.

17. "The Commercial Growth and Greatness of the West: As Illustrating the Dignity and Usefulness of Commerce," *The Merchants' Magazine* 17 (November 1847): 503; Hall, *The West,* p. 313; Maria L. Varney, "Letters from the Queen City," *The Herald of Truth* 2 (July 1847): 84.

18. Margaret Walsh, *The Rise of the Midwestern Meat Packing Industry* (Lexington, Ky.: University Press of Kentucky, 1982), p. 94.

19. Charles Fenno Hoffman, *A Winter in the West* (New York: Harper and Brothers, 1835), 2: 136, 138; Cincinnati Federal Writers' Project, *They Built a City* (Cincinnati: Cincinnati Post, 1938), pp. 80–81. See also Harriet Martineau, *Retrospect of Western Travel* (London: Saunders and Otley, 1838), 2: 233.

20. Varney, "Letters from the Queen City," p. 84.

21. *Cincinnati, Columbus, Cleveland and Erie Railroad Guide* (Columbus: Ohio State Journal Company, 1854), p. 6.

22. Drake and Mansfield, *Cincinnati in 1826,* pp. 64–66.

23. William Smith, *Annual Statement of the Trade and Commerce of Cincinnati* (Cincinnati: Gazette Company Print, 1855), p. 8.

24. Charles Cist, *Sketches and Statistics of Cincinnati in 1851* (Cincinnati: William H. Moore and Company, 1851), p. 257.

25. Ibid., p. 169.

26. Smith, *Trade and Commerce of Cincinnati,* p. 9.

27. Varney, "Letters from the Queen City," pp. 83–84.

28. *Cincinnati . . . Railroad Guide,* p. 10.

29. Timothy Flint, *Recollections of the Last Ten Years* (Boston: Cummings, Hilliard, and Company, 1826), pp. 40–41.

30. Jed Dannenbaum, *Drink and Disorder: Temperance Reform in Cincinnati from the Washingtonian Revival to the WCTU* (Urbana: University of Illinois Press, 1984), p. 75.

31. Ibid., p. 76.

32. Howard C. McClary, *150 Years of Community Service: The Story of the Cincinnati Union Bethel 1830–1980* (Cincinnati: Cincinnati Union Bethel, 1980), p. 8; Dannenbaum, *Drink and Disorder,* pp. 75–76.

33. Drake and Mansfield, *Cincinnati in 1826,* p. 38.

34. Ibid.; Cist, *Cincinnati in 1841,* p. 101.

35. Cist, *Cincinnati in 1841,* pp. 99–102.

36. McClary, *150 Years,* p. 3. See also George E. Stevens, *The City of Cincinnati, A Summary of Its Attractions, Advantages, Institutions and Internal Improvements, with a Statement of Its Public Charities* (Cincinnati: George S. Blanchard and Company, 1869), pp. 122–23.

37. Shapiro and Miller, *Physician to the West,* p. 102.

38. Richard C. Wade, "The Negro in Cincinnati, 1800–1830," *Journal of Negro History* 39 (January 1954): 55. See also Henry L. Taylor, "On Slavery's Fringe: City Building and Black Community Development in Cincinnati, 1800–1850," *Ohio History* 95 (Winter–Spring 1986): 28.

39. Henry Howe, *Historical Collections of Ohio* (Cincinnati: Henry Howe, 1851), pp. 226–28. See also C. G. Woodson, "The Negroes of Cincinnati Prior to the Civil War," *Journal of Negro History* 1 (January 1916): 14–15.

40. The three eastern cities in which Germans outnumbered other nationalities were Allegheny, Pennsylvania (today part of Pittsburgh), Buffalo, New York, and Reading, Pennsylvania. The two southern cities with a German concentration were Baltimore and Louisville. Three of these five exceptions, Allegheny, Buffalo, and Louisville, bordered on the Midwest region.

41. Carl Wittke, "The Germans of Cincinnati," *Bulletin of the Historical and Philosophical Society of Ohio* 20 (January 1962): 3–14; William A. Baughin, "The Development of Nativism in Cincinnati," *Bulletin of the Cincinnati Historical Society* 22 (October 1964): 240–55; Robert G. Vitz, *The Queen and the Arts: Cultural Life in Nineteenth-Century Cincinnati* (Kent, Ohio: Kent State University Press, 1989), p. 41.

42. Cist, *Cincinnati in 1841,* p. 33.

43. Larry Gara, ed., "A Correspondent's View of Cincinnati in 1839," *Bulletin of the Historical and Philosophical Society of Ohio* 9 (April 1951): 139.

44. Dunn, "'Cincinnati Is a Delightful Place,'" p. 269.

45. Robert W. Lovett, "Augustus Roundy's Cincinnati Sojourn, 1838–1845," *Historical and Philosophical Society of Ohio Bulletin* 19 (October 1961): 260.

46. Frances Trollope, *Domestic Manners of the Americans* (New York: Alfred A. Knopf, 1949), pp. 43, 45.

47. Cist, *Cincinnati in 1851,* p. 326.

48. Ibid., p. 164.

49. Glazer, "Cincinnati in 1840,"pp. 250–51.

50. Cist, *Sketches . . . Cincinnati in 1851,* p. 108.

51. "The Cincinnati Observatory," *Cincinnati Miscellany* (May 1845), p. 254.

52. Cist, *Sketches . . . Cincinnati in 1851,* pp. 104, 106.

53. Ibid., p. 106.

54. Kathleen J. Kiefer, "Flying Sparks and Hooves: Prologue," *Cincinnati Historical Society Bulletin* 28 (Summer 1970): 102. See also John H. White, Jr., "The Steam Fire Engine: A Reappraisal of a Cincinnati 'First,'" *Cincinnati Historical Society Bulletin* 28 (Winter 1970): 317–35.

55. Timothy Flint, "Editor's Address," *The Western Monthly Review* 1 (May 1827): 10.

56. *The Genius of the West* 3 (August 1854): frontispiece advertisement.

57. Septuagenarian, "Review Commercial and Literary," p. 36.

58. "Editor's Budget," *The Western Monthly Magazine and Literary Journal* 1 (June 1837): 363.

59. Vitz, *The Queen and the Arts,* p. 21.

60. William D. Gallagher, "Periodical Literature," *Western Literary Journal and Monthly Review* 1 (November 1844): 6.

61. A Septuagenarian, "Reminiscences of Men and Events in the West," *The Genius of the West* 4 (April 1855): 106.

62. Walter Sutton, *The Western Book Trade: Cincinnati as a Nineteenth-Century Publishing and Book-Trade Center* (Columbus: Ohio State University Press, 1961), p. 67; Vitz, *The Queen and the Arts,* p. 56.

63. Vitz, *The Queen and the Arts,* p. 23.

64. T. W. Whitley, "The Western Art Union," *The Herald of Truth* 4 (July 1848): 75; Cist, *Sketches . . . Cincinnati in 1851,* p. 128.

65. Vitz, *The Queen and the Arts,* p. 33.

66. Ibid., p. 48.

67. Whitley, "Western Art Union," p. 75.

68. *The Indiana Gazetteer* (Indianapolis: Douglass and Maguire, 1833), p. 111.

69. Walsh, *Midwestern Meat Packing,* p. 94. See also John T. Windle and Robert M. Taylor, Jr., *The Early Architecture of Madison, Indiana* (Madison, Ind.: Historic Madison, 1986), p. 12.

70. Betty Lou Amster, *New Albany on the Ohio: Historical Review 1813–1963* (New Albany, Ind.: New Albany Sesquicentennial, 1963), p. 23; Victor M. Bogle, "New Albany within the Shadow of Louisville," *Indiana Magazine of History* 51 (December 1955): 303, 310.

71. "New Albany, Indiana," *Hunt's Merchants' Magazine* 41 (August 1859): 182; Amster, *New Albany*, p. 36. See also Victor M. Bogle, "New Albany: Mid-Nineteenth Century Economic Expansion," *Indiana Magazine of History* 53 (June 1957): 127–46.

72. Timothy Flint, *The History and Geography of the Mississippi Valley* (Cincinnati: E. H. Flint, 1833), 1: 310.

73. Alex. Mackay, *The Western World; or, Travels in the United States in 1846–47* (London: Richard Bentley, 1849), 3: 53.

74. "Trade and Commerce of St. Louis," *The Merchants' Magazine* 15 (August 1846): 168.

75. Hall, *The West*, pp. 250–51.

76. John Hogan, *Thoughts about the City of St. Louis, Her Commerce and Manufactures* (Saint Louis: Republican Steam Press Print, 1854), p. 6; Wyatt Winton Belcher, *The Economic Rivalry between St. Louis and Chicago 1850–1880* (New York: Columbia University Press, 1947), p. 41.

77. Frances D. Gage, "Aunt Fanny's Removal to the West—First Impressions of St. Louis," *Ohio Cultivator* 9 (15 January 1853): 30.

78. Hogan, *Thoughts about . . . St. Louis*, pp. 13, 17.

79. Gage, "Aunt Fanny's Removal," p. 31.

80. Elbert Jay Benton, *Cultural Story of an American City, Cleveland* (Cleveland: Western Reserve Historical Society, 1944), 2: 7–8.

81. Edmund H. Chapman, *Cleveland: Village to Metropolis*, 2d ed. (Cleveland: Western Reserve Historical Society, 1981), p. 46.

82. "Cleveland, Ohio—Western Reserve, etc.," *The National Magazine and Industrial Record* 7 (December 1845): 614–15; John G. Clark, *The Grain Trade in the Old Northwest* (Urbana: University of Illinois Press, 1966), p. 59.

83. "Cleveland, Ohio," p. 615.

84. Homer Hoyt, *One Hundred Years of Land Values in Chicago* (Chicago: University of Chicago Press, 1933), p. 26.

85. Bessie L. Pierce, *A History of Chicago* (New York: Alfred A. Knopf, 1937), 1: 62.

86. Excerpt from Harriet Martineau, *Society in America* reprinted in *Reminiscences of Early Chicago* (Chicago: R. R. Donnelley and Sons, 1912), pp. 27–28.

87. Hoyt, *Land Values in Chicago*, p. 19; excerpts from Charles Fenno Hoffman, *A Winter in the West* reprinted in *Reminiscences of Early Chicago*, p. 15.

88. "City of Chicago, Illinois," *The Merchants' Magazine* 18 (February 1848): 166.

89. Pierce, *History of Chicago*, 1: 69; Hoyt, *Land Values in Chicago*, p. 42.

90. A. T. Andreas, *History of Chicago* (Chicago: A. T. Andreas, 1884), 1: 135.

91. J. W. Norris, *General Directory and Business Advertiser of the City of Chicago for the Year 1844* (Chicago: Ellis and Fergus, 1844), p. 15. For further information on the boom and bust associated with canal construction, see James William Putnam, *The Illinois and Michigan Canal: A Study in Economic History* (Chicago: University of Chicago Press, 1918).

92. Milo Milton Quaife, ed., *The Development of Chicago 1674–1914* (Chicago: Caxton Club, 1916), p. 214.

93. George Newman Fuller, *Economic and Social Beginnings of Michigan* (Lansing: Wynkoop Hallenbeck Crawford Company, 1916), pp. 135, 148).

94. Ibid., p. 136. See also Clarence M. Burton, *When Detroit Was Young* (Detroit: Burton Abstract and Title Company, 1951), p. 42.

95. Almon Ernest Parkins, *The Historical Geography of Detroit* (Lansing: Michigan Historical Commission, 1918), p. 186.

96. Ezra C. Seaman, "Detroit, Michigan," *The Merchants' Magazine* 20 (March 1849): 285.

97. Samuel Freeman, *The Emigrant's Hand Book, and Guide to Wisconsin* (Milwaukee: Sentinel and Gazette Power Press Print, 1851), p. 53.

98. Kathleen Neils Conzen, *Immigrant Milwaukee 1836–1860* (Cambridge, Mass.: Harvard University Press, 1976), p. 12; Bayrd Still, *Milwaukee: The History of a City* (Madison: State Historical Society of Wisconsin, 1948), p. 25.

99. Still, *Milwaukee,* p. 127.

100. Roger D. Simon, "Foundations for Industrialization, 1835–1880," *Milwaukee History* 1 (Spring and Summer 1978): 48; Conzen, *Immigrant Milwaukee,* p. 14; Still, *Milwaukee,* p. 72.

101. W. D. Root, *Sandusky in 1855—City Guide and Business Directory* (Sandusky, Ohio: Bill, Cooke and Company, 1855), pp. 17–18.

102. Ibid., pp. 18, 20. See also "Sandusky City," *The Merchants' Magazine* 19 (September 1848): 287–90.

103. Randolph C. Downes, *Canal Days* (Toledo: Historical Society of Northwestern Ohio, 1949), p. 89.

104. Ibid., p. 91. See also John H. Doyle, *A Story of Early Toledo* (Bowling Green, Ohio: C. S. Van Tassel, 1919), pp. 32–50; Tana Mosier Porter, *Toledo Profile: A Sesquicentennial History* (Toledo: Toledo Sesquicentennial Commission, 1987), pp. 31–43.

105. Rebecca S. Shoemaker, "Michigan City, Indiana: The Failure of a Dream," *Indiana Magazine of History* 84 (December 1988): 327.

106. Ibid., p. 335.

107. Ibid., p. 333.

108. Lee D. Dahl, "The Origins of Conflict between Southport and Racine," in Nicholas C. Burckel, ed., *Kenosha: Historical Sketches* (Kenosha, Wis.: Kenosha Community History Committee, 1986), p. 54.

109. Ibid., p. 55. See also John D. Haeger, "Capital Mobilization and the Urban Center: The Wisconsin Lakeports," *Mid-America* 60 (April–July 1978): 75–93; Irving Cutler, *The Chicago-Milwaukee Corridor: A Geographic Study of Intermetropolitan Coalescence* (Evanston, Ill.: Northwestern University, 1965), pp. 19–26; "City of Racine, Wisconsin," *Hunt's Merchants' Magazine* (May 1857): 552–57.

110. Oscar Eugene Olin, *Akron and Environs* (Chicago: Lewis Publishing Company, 1917), p. 57.

111. Warren Jenkins, *The Ohio Gazetteer and Traveller's Guide* (Columbus: Isaac N. Whiting, 1841), p. 55.

112. William Henry Perrin, ed., *History of Summit County* (Chicago: Baskin and Battey, 1881), p. 338; James A. Braden, ed., *A Centennial History of Akron 1825–1925* (Akron: Summit County Historical Society, 1925), p. 69.

113. *The Indiana Gazetteer, or Topographical Dictionary of the State of Indiana* (Indianapolis: E. Chamberlain, 1850), p. 388. See also Timothy Edward Howard, *A History of St. Joseph County Indiana* (Chicago: Lewis Publishing Company, 1907), 1: 357; Dean R. Esslinger, *Immigrants and the City: Ethnicity and Mobility in a Nineteenth-Century Midwestern Community* (Port Washington, N.Y.: Kennikat Press, 1975), p. 21; *South Bend and the Men Who Have Made It* (South Bend: Tribune Printing Company, 1901), p. 22.

114. *History and Directory of Kent County, Michigan* (Grand Rapids: Dillenback and Leavitt, 1870), p. 121. See also Z. Z. Lydens, ed., *The Story of Grand Rapids* (Grand Rapids: Kregel Publications, 1966), pp. 5–24; Charles F. Clark, comp., *Michigan State Gazetteer and Business Directory for 1863–4* (Detroit: Charles F. Clark, 1863), pp. 323–26.

115. *The History of Winnebago County, Ill., Its Past and Present* (Chicago: H. F. Kett and Company, 1877), pp. 401, 406.

116. Ibid., p. 116.

117. James Harrison Kennedy, *A History of the City of Cleveland* (Cleveland: Imperial Press, 1896), p. 299.

118. Ibid., pp. 295–300; W. Scott Robison, ed., *History of the City of Cleveland, Its Settlement, Rise and Progress* (Cleveland: Robison and Cockett, 1887), pp. 42–43; Benton, *Cultural Story of Cleveland,* 2: 22–24.

119. Edward D. Holton, "Commercial History of Milwaukee," *Report and Collections of the State Historical Society of Wisconsin for the Years 1857 and 1858* 4 (1859): 272.

120. Ibid., p. 274. See also Frank A. Flower, *History of Milwaukee, Wisconsin* (Chicago: Western Historical Company, 1881), pp. 496–508; Still, *Milwaukee,* pp. 39–41.

121. Braden, *Centennial History of Akron,* p. 48; Olin, *Akron and Environs,* p. 63.

122. Charles A. Church, *History of Rockford and Winnebago County, Illinois* (Rockford, Ill.: New England Society of Rockford, 1900), pp. 157–59; Charles A. Church, *Past and Present of the City of Rockford and Winnebago County, Illinois* (Chicago: S. J. Clarke Publishing Company, 1905), p. 36; *Winnebago County,* pp. 400–401, 403–404; C. Hal Nelson, *Sinnissippi Saga: A History of Rockford and Winnebago County, Illinois* (Rockford, Ill.: Winnebago County Illinois Sesquicentennial Committee, 1968), p. 74.

123. Opha Moore, *History of Franklin County, Ohio* (Topeka, Kan.: Historical Publishing Company, 1930), 1: 123–24.

124. Ibid., p. 124; William T. Martin, *History of Franklin County* (Columbus: Follett, Foster and Company, 1858), p. 264.

125. *The Columbus Business Directory for 1843–4* (Columbus: J. R. Armstrong, 1843), pp. 3–8; Martin, *History of Franklin County,* pp. 264–71; Moore, *History of Franklin County,* 1: 125–26; Jacob H. Studer, *Columbus, Ohio: Its History, Resources, and Progress* (Columbus: Jacob H. Studer, 1873), pp. 14–15.

126. *Columbus Directory for 1843–4,* p. 60.

127. Ibid., pp. 54–55. See also Martin, *History of Franklin County,* pp. 314–15.

128. *A. C. Howard's Directory, for the City of Indianapolis* (Indianapolis: A. C. Howard, 1857), pp. 3–7; Ignatius Brown, *Logan's History of Indianapolis from 1818* (Indianapolis: Logan and Company, 1868), pp. 2–4; Donald F. Carmony, "Genesis and Early History of the Indianapolis Fund, 1816–1826," *Indiana Magazine of History* 38 (March 1942): 17–30; John W. Reps, *The Making of Urban America: A History of City Planning in the United States* (Princeton, N.J.: Princeton University Press, 1965), pp. 272, 274–75.

129. Paul M. Angle, *"Here I Have Lived:" A History of Lincoln's Springfield 1821–1865* (New Brunswick, N.J.: Rutgers University Press, 1935), p. 56; William E. Baringer, *Lincoln's Vandalia: A Pioneer Portrait* (New Brunswick, N.J.: Rutgers University Press, 1949), pp. 73–74.

130. Baringer, *Lincoln's Vandalia,* pp. 104–109; Angle, *Lincoln's Springfield,* pp. 56–57, 75.

131. Edward J. Russo, *Prairie of Promise: Springfield and Sangamon County* (Woodland Hills, Calif.: Windsor Publications, 1983), p. 15.

132. Baringer, *Lincoln's Vandalia,* p. 109.

133. Angle, *Lincoln's Springfield,* pp. 57–58.

134. William W. Upton, "Locating the Capital of the State of Michigan," *Michigan History Magazine* 23 (Summer 1939): 283.

135. Daniel S. Durrie, *A History of Madison* (Madison: No publisher, 1874), pp. 45–47; Lyman C. Draper and others, "Naming of Madison and Dane County and the Location of the Capitol," *Collections of the State Historical Society of Wisconsin*

6 (1872): 388–96; Reuben Gold Thwaites, *The Story of Madison 1836–1900,* 3d ed. (Madison: Roger Hunt, 1986), pp. 4–5; David V. Mollenhoff, *Madison: A History of the Formative Years* (Dubuque, Iowa: Kendall Hunt Publishing Company, 1982), p. 22.

136. Justin L. Kestenbaum, *Out of a Wilderness: An Illustrated History of Greater Lansing* (Woodland Hills, Calif.: Windsor Publications, 1981), p. 30. See also Upton, "Locating the Capital," pp. 282–83.

137. Frank E. Robson, "How Lansing Became the Capital," *Historical Collections, Michigan Pioneer and Historical Society* 11 (1887): 241.

138. Ibid., p. 240.

139. Thwaites, *Madison,* p. 5.

140. Rosamond Reed Wulsin, ed., "A New Englander's Impressions of Cincinnati in 1820—Letters by William Greene," *Bulletin of the Historical and Philosophical Society of Ohio* 7 (April 1949): 119.

141. Dunn, "'Cincinnati Is a Delightful Place,'" pp. 273–75.

142. *Columbus Directory for 1843–4,* p. 39.

143. Brown, *Logan's History of Indianapolis,* pp. 19, 34; W. R. Holloway, *Indianapolis: A Historical and Statistical Sketch of the Railroad City* (Indianapolis: Indianapolis Journal Print, 1870), p. 83.

144. Angle, *Lincoln's Springfield,* p. 92.

145. J. G. Knapp, "Early Reminiscences of Madison," *Collections of the State Historical Society of Wisconsin* 6 (1872): 386.

146. "Shall the State Fair Be Fixed Permanently at Columbus?" *Ohio Cultivator* 7 (1 December 1851): 361; "Hotels and Hospitality of Columbus," *Ohio Cultivator* 7 (15 October 1851): 312.

147. "Ohio State Board of Agriculture," *Ohio Cultivator* 8 (15 December 1852): 376–77. For information on other state institutions in Columbus, see Studer, *Columbus,* pp. 347–63, 368–81.

148. Jacob Piatt Dunn, *Greater Indianapolis* (Chicago: Lewis Publishing Company, 1910), 1: 110.

149. *Documents of the General Assembly of the State of Indiana at the Twenty-Ninth Session, Commencing December 1, 1845* (Indianapolis: J. P. Chapman, 1846), 2: 92.

150. *Journal of the Assembly of the State of Wisconsin, 1852* (Madison: Charles T. Wakeley, 1852), pp. 228–31, 250–52.

151. *Documents Accompanying the Journal of the Senate of the State of Michigan, at the Annual Session of 1850* (Lansing: R. W. Ingals, 1850), Senate Document no. 5, p. 1; Edwin O. Wood, *History of Genesee County, Michigan* (Indianapolis: Federal Publishing Company, 1916), 1: 592; Samuel W. Durant, *History of Kalamazoo County, Michigan* (Philadelphia: Everts and Abbott, 1880), pp. 161–62.

152. Charles V. DeLand, *DeLand's History of Jackson County, Michigan* (No place: B. F. Bowen, 1903), p. 111; *Documents Accompanying the Journal of the House of Representatives of the State of Michigan, at the Annual Session in 1838* (Detroit: John S. Bagg, 1838); pp. 330–33.

153. Carl E. Black, "Origin of Our State Charitable Institutions," *Journal of the Illinois State Historical Society* 18 (April 1925): 175–94; Minnie Wait Cleary, "History of the Illinois School for the Deaf," *Journal of the Illinois State Historical Society* 35 (December 1942): 368–71; Don Harrison Doyle, *The Social Order of a Frontier Community: Jacksonville, Illinois 1825–70* (Urbana: University of Illinois Press, 1978), pp. 68–73.

154. Sherry O. Hessler, "'The Great Disturbing Cause' and the Decline of the Queen City," *Bulletin of the Historical and Philosophical Society of Ohio* 20 (July 1962): 177.

155. Ibid.

156. William Prescott Smith, *The Book of the Great Railway Celebrations of 1857* (New York: D. Appleton and Company, 1858), p. 94.

157. Ibid., pp. 93–106; Carl Abbott, *Boosters and Businessmen: Popular Economic Thought and Urban Growth in the Antebellum Middle West* (Westport, Conn.: Greenwood Press, 1981), p. 165; Hessler, "'The Great Disturbing Cause,'" p. 175; John F. Stover, *Iron Road to the West: American Railroads in the 1850s* (New York: Columbia University Press, 1978), p. 137.

158. Smith, *Great Railway Celebrations*, p. 94.

159. Walsh, *Midwestern Meat Packing*, p. 59.

160. Hogan, *Thoughts about . . . St. Louis*, p. 7.

161. J. Thomas Scharf, *History of Saint Louis City and County* (Philadelphia: Louis H. Everts and Company, 1883), 2: 1148; James Neal Primm, *Lion of the Valley: St. Louis, Missouri* (Boulder, Colo.: Pruett Publishing Company, 1981), p. 215.

162. Scharf, *History of Saint Louis*, 2: 1142–62; Belcher, *Economic Rivalry*, pp. 73–74, 78–81; Primm, *Lion of the Valley*, pp. 214–21.

163. Primm, *Lion of the Valley*, pp. 287–88; Scharf, *History of Saint Louis*, 2: 1012–13.

164. *Annual Review of the Business of Chicago, for the Year 1852* (Chicago: No publisher, 1853), p. 15.

165. Belcher, *Economic Rivalry*, pp. 69–71.

166. Abbott, *Boosters and Businessmen*, p. 138.

167. John S. Wright, *Chicago: Past, Present, Future* (Chicago: John S. Wright, 1868), p. x.

168. *A Guide to the City of Chicago* (Chicago: T. Ellwood Zell and Company, 1868), p. 31.

169. Ibid.

170. *Howard's Directory . . . Indianapolis*, p. 43.

171. O. H. Smith, *Early Indiana Trials and Sketches* (Cincinnati: Moore, Wilstach, Keys and Company, 1858), p. 286; George W. Hawes, *Indiana State Gazetteer and Business Directory for 1860 and 1861* (Indianapolis: George W. Hawes, 1860), p. 175; *Howard's Directory . . . Indianapolis*, p. 52.

172. Smith, *Early Indiana Trials*, p. 114.

2. The Emerging Center of Urban America

1. "Chicago Heard of Abroad," *The Lakeside Monthly* 11 (February 1874): 179; Frank Carpenter, "The East and the West," *The Lakeside Monthly* 11 (February 1874): 175, 177.

2. Census Office, *Manufactures of the United States in 1860* (Washington: Government Printing Office, 1865); Census Office, *Compendium of the Eleventh Census: 1890* (Washington: Government Printing Office, 1894), pp. 706–11.

3. Census Office, *Manufactures in 1860;* Census Office, *Compendium of Eleventh Census*, pp. 706–709.

4. *Industrial History of Milwaukee* (Milwaukee: E. E. Barton, 1886), pp. 54–56.

5. *The Industries of Detroit* (Detroit: J. M. Elstner, 1887), p. 51.

6. A. N. Marquis, ed., *The Industries of Cincinnati* (Cincinnati: A. N. Marquis and Company, 1883), p. 43.

7. *Ninth Annual and Tenth Statistical Report of the Board of Trade of Cincinnati, for the Commercial Year Ending January 1, 1878* (Cincinnati: James Barclay, 1878), p. 81.

8. *Half-Century's Progress of the City of Chicago* (Chicago: International Publishing Company, 1887), p. 32. For an account of the relationship between Chicago's development and the natural resources in its expanding hinterland, see William Cronon, *Nature's Metropolis: Chicago and the Great West* (New York: W. W. Norton and Company, 1991).

9. I. J. Isaacs, comp., *The Industrial Advance of Indianapolis* (Indianapolis: A. R. Baker, 1887), p. 27.

10. *Columbus, Ohio and Its Resources* (Columbus: Ohio State Journal, 1890), p. 3; Columbus Board of Trade, *The City of Columbus—The Capital of Ohio and the Great Railway Center of the State* (Columbus: G. L. Manchester, 1885).

11. David C. Klingaman, "The Nature of Midwest Manufacturing in 1890," in David C. Klingaman and Richard K. Vedder, eds., *Essays on the Economy of the Old Northwest* (Athens, Ohio: Ohio University Press, 1987), pp. 281–84.

12. J. D. Pickands, *Annual Statement of the Trade, Commerce and Manufactures of the City of Cleveland, for the Year 1867* (Cleveland: Fairbanks, Benedict and Company, 1868), p. 22.

13. X. X. Crum, *Annual Report of the Cleveland Board of Trade* (Cleveland: Leader Printing Company, 1885), p. 191; Henry Howe, *Historical Collections of Ohio* (Columbus: Henry Howe and Son, 1889), 1: 501.

14. Almon Ernest Parkins, *The Historical Geography of Detroit* (Lansing: Michigan Historical Commission, 1918), pp. 299–300; Bernhard C. Korn, *The Story of Bay View* (Milwaukee: Milwaukee County Historical Society, 1980), pp. 49–56; "Milwaukee and Her Iron Industry," *The Milwaukee Monthly Magazine* 5 (January 1873): 23–25; "Milwaukee," *The Milwaukee Monthly Magazine* 9 (January 1875): 7–9.

15. "Milwaukee and Her Iron Industry," pp. 23–24.

16. *Industries of Detroit,* pp. 52–53.

17. Silas Farmer, *History of Detroit and Wayne County and Early Michigan,* 3d ed. (Detroit: Silas Farmer and Company, 1890), p. 804.

18. "Milwaukee and Her Iron Industry," p. 25.

19. "Milwaukee," *The Milwaukee Monthly Magazine* 8 (December 1874): 476; Walter F. Peterson, *An Industrial Heritage: Allis-Chalmers Corporation* (Milwaukee: Milwaukee County Historical Society, 1978), p. 14.

20. Bessie Louise Pierce, *A History of Chicago* (New York: Alfred A. Knopf, 1957), 3: 155, 163; *Chicago Commerce, Manufactures, Banking, and Transportation Facilities 1884* (Chicago: S. Ferd. Howe and Company, 1884), pp. 118–21; Elmer A. Riley, *The Development of Chicago and Vicinity as a Manufacturing Center Prior to 1880* (Chicago: University of Chicago, 1911), pp. 112–15.

21. *Youngstown, Past and Present* (Cleveland: Wiggins and McKillop, 1875), pp. 68–69.

22. James Stanford Bradshaw, "Grand Rapids, 1870–1880: Furniture City Emerges," *Michigan History* 55 (Winter 1971): 334; Ellen Arlinsky and Marg Ed Kwapil, *In Celebration of Grand Rapids* (Woodland Hills, Calif.: Windsor Publications, 1987), p. 131.

23. Z. Z. Lydens, ed., *The Story of Grand Rapids* (Grand Rapids: Kregel Publications, 1966), p. 303. See also William Widdicomb, "The Early History of the Furniture Industry in Grand Rapids," *Publications of the Historical Society of Grand Rapids* 1 (1909): 63–76; Arthur S. White, "Grand Rapids Furniture Centennial," *Michigan History Magazine* 12 (April 1928): 267–79.

24. C. Hal Nelson, ed., *Sinnissippi Saga: A History of Rockford and Winnebago County, Illinois* (Rockford: Winnebago County Illinois Sesquicentennial Committee, 1968), p. 144.

25. Sharon Darling, *Chicago Furniture: Art, Craft, and Industry 1833–1983* (New York: W. W. Norton and Company, 1984), p. 45.

26. Ibid.

27. Ibid., p. 46.

28. Edward P. Duggan, "Machines, Markets, and Labor: The Carriage and Wagon Industry in Late-Nineteenth Century Cincinnati," *Business History Review* 51 (Autumn 1977): 310–12; *History of Cincinnati and Hamilton County, Ohio* (Cincinnati: S. B. Nelson and Company, 1894), p. 323.

29. Henry L. Hunker, *Industrial Evolution of Columbus, Ohio* (Columbus: Ohio State University, 1958), p. 49; *Columbus and Its Resources,* p. 34. See also Alfred E. Lee, *History of the City of Columbus, Capital of Ohio* (New York: Munsell and Company, 1892), 2: 326–27; Levi T. Strader, *Facts and Figures of Franklin County, Ohio* (Columbus: No publisher, 1899), pp. 95–96.

30. Timothy Edward Howard, *A History of St. Joseph County, Indiana* (Chicago: Lewis Publishing Company, 1907), 1: 394–99; Carl Crow, *The City of Flint Grows Up* (New York: Harper and Brothers, 1945), pp. 24–37.

31. *Seven Days in Chicago* (Chicago: J. M. Wing and Company, 1877), p. 46.

32. Bessie Louise Pierce, ed., *As Others See Chicago: Impressions of Visitors, 1673–1933* (Chicago: University of Chicago Press, 1933), p. 257.

33. L. Schick, *Chicago and Its Environs: A Handbook for the Traveler* (Chicago: L. Schick, 1891), p. 120; Pierce, *As Others See Chicago,* p. 224.

34. *Seven Days in Chicago,* p. 46; *Half-Century's Progress of Chicago,* p. 51. See also *Chicago Commerce 1884,* pp. 78–93.

35. Robert E. Tyson, *History of East St. Louis* (East Saint Louis: John Haps and Company, 1875), pp. 122–25; L. U. Reavis, *Saint Louis, The Future Great City of the World,* 4th ed. (Saint Louis: E. F. Hobart and Company, 1873), pp. 240–42; Cincinnati Federal Writers' Project, *They Built a City: 150 Years of Industrial Cincinnati* (Cincinnati: Cincinnati Post, 1938), p. 95; Margaret Walsh, *The Rise of the Midwestern Meat Packing Industry* (Lexington, Ky.: University Press of Kentucky, 1982), pp. 74–75; Isaacs, *Industrial Advance of Indianapolis,* pp. 33–34.

36. *Fifty-Fourth Annual Report of the Cincinnati Chamber of Commerce and Merchants' Exchange for the Year Ending December 31, 1902* (Cincinnati: Ohio Valley Company, 1903), p. 182.

37. Alfred Lief, *"It Floats": The Story of Procter and Gamble* (New York: Rinehart and Company, 1958), pp. 54, 56; Cincinnati Writers' Project, *They Built a City,* pp. 102–13. See also *History of Cincinnati and Hamilton County,* pp. 322–23.

38. *Industrial History of Milwaukee,* pp. 58–59.

39. Thomas C. Cochran, *The Pabst Brewing Company: The History of an American Business* (New York: New York University Press, 1948), p. 74.

40. Roger D. Simon, "Foundations for Industrialization, 1835–1880," *Milwaukee History* 1 (Spring and Summer 1978): 44; Riley, *Development of Chicago as a Manufacturing Center,* p. 122.

41. William J. Langson, comp., *Fifteenth Annual Report of the Trade and Commerce of Milwaukee, for the Year Ending December 31, 1872* (Milwaukee: Daily Sentinel Book and Job Printing House, 1873), p. 24.

42. C. M. Woodward, "The City of St. Louis," *The New England Magazine* 5 (January 1892): 616. See also James Neal Primm, *Lion of the Valley—St. Louis, Missouri* (Boulder, Colo.: Pruett Publishing Company, 1981), pp. 347–49.

43. Jerry Klein, *Peoria!* (Peoria: Visual Communications, 1985), pp. 73, 76.

44. Sharon Mallman, "The Store That Gimbel Built," *Historical Messenger of the Milwaukee County Historical Society* 31 (Autumn 1975): 76–80.

45. Cecil C. Hoge, Sr., *The First Hundred Years Are the Toughest* (Berkeley: Ten Speed Press, 1988), pp. 12–22; Perry Duis, *Chicago—Creating New Traditions* (Chicago: Chicago Historical Society, 1976), p. 106.

46. James C. Worthy, *Shaping an American Institution: Robert E. Wood and Sears, Roebuck* (Urbana: University of Illinois Press, 1984), pp. 19–26; Hoge, *First Hundred Years,* pp. 18–22; Duis, *Chicago,* pp. 106–107.

47. John B. Jentz, "Artisan Culture and the Organization of Chicago's German Workers in the Gilded Age, 1860 to 1890," in Hartmut Keil, ed., *German Workers' Culture in the United States 1850 to 1920* (Washington: Smithsonian Institution Press, 1988), p. 60.

48. George J. Lankevich, ed., *Milwaukee: A Chronological and Documentary History* (Dobbs Ferry, N.Y.: Oceana Publications, 1977), p. 111.

49. Robert P. Porter, Henry Gannett, and William C. Hunt, *Progress of the Nation 1790 to 1890—U.S. Census of 1890* (Washington: Government Printing Office, 1894), p. xcii.

50. Census Office, *Compendium of Eleventh Census,* pp. 604–605.

51. Jentz, "Artisan Culture," pp. 60–61.

52. Guido Andre Dobbert, *The Disintegration of an Immigrant Community: The Cincinnati Germans, 1870–1920* (New York: Arno Press, 1980), p. 32.

53. Hartmut Keil, "Immigrant Neighborhoods and American Society: German Immigrants on Chicago's Northwest Side in the Late Nineteenth Century," in Keil, ed., *German Workers' Culture,* p. 29.

54. Dobbert, *Disintegration of an Immigrant Community,* pp. 32–33.

55. Randolph C. Downes, *Lake Port, Lucas County Historical Series* (Toledo: Historical Society of Northwestern Ohio, 1951), p. 347; Robert E. Samuelson and Judith L. Kitchen, *Architecture: Columbus* (Columbus: Foundation of the Columbus Chapter of the American Institute of Architects, 1976), p. 36; Melvin G. Holli and Peter d'A. Jones, eds., *Biographical Dictionary of American Mayors, 1820–1980* (Westport, Conn.: Greenwood Press, 1981), pp. 180–81, 277, 380–81.

56. Holli and Jones, *Biographical Dictionary,* pp. 180–81.

57. Census Office, *Compendium of Eleventh Census,* pp. 604–605.

58. Michael F. Funchion, "Irish Chicago: Church, Homeland, Politics, and Class—The Shaping of an Ethnic Group, 1870–1900," in Peter d'A. Jones and Melvin G. Holli, eds., *Ethnic Chicago* (Grand Rapids: William B. Eerdmans Publishing Company, 1981), p. 24.

59. Ibid., p. 22.

60. Hans Norman, "Swedes in North America," in Harald Runblom and Hans Norman, eds., *From Sweden to America: A History of the Migration* (Minneapolis: University of Minnesota Press, 1976), p. 252.

61. Odd S. Lovoll, *A Century of Urban Life: The Norwegians in Chicago before 1930* (Northfield, Minn.: Norwegian-American Historical Association, 1988), p. 163.

62. Ibid., p. 157.

63. Ibid., pp. 155–56. See also Philip S. Friedman, "The Americanization of Chicago's Danish Community, 1850–1920," *Chicago History* 9 (Spring 1980): 36, 38.

64. Lovoll, *Century of Urban Life,* pp. 159, 161, 332.

65. C. Hal Nelson, ed., *We, the People of Winnebago County* (Rockford, Ill.: Winnebago County Bicentennial Commission, 1975), p. 66. For population figures, see Census Office, *Compendium of Eleventh Census,* pp. 623–24.

66. Census Office, *Compendium of Eleventh Census,* p. 606.

67. Frank Serafino, *West of Warsaw* (Hamtramck, Mich.: Avenue Publishing Company, 1983), p. 9.

68. Henry B. Leonard, "Ethnic Cleavage and Industrial Conflict in Late Nineteenth Century America: The Cleveland Rolling Mill Company Strikes of 1882 and 1885," *Labor History* 20 (Fall 1979): 524–48.

69. Gerd Korman, *Industrialization, Immigrants and Americanizers: The View from Milwaukee, 1866–1921* (Madison: State Historical Society of Wisconsin, 1967), p. 66.

70. *Seventh Biennial Report of the Bureau of Labor Statistics of Illinois, 1892* (Springfield, Ill.: H. W. Rokker, 1893), pp. 368, 380–81.

71. Kenneth L. Kusmer, *A Ghetto Takes Shape: Black Cleveland, 1870–1930* (Urbana: University of Illinois Press, 1976), p. 10; David M. Katzman, *Before the Ghetto: Black Detroit in the Nineteenth Century* (Urbana: University of Illinois Press, 1973), p. 62; Allan H. Spear, *Black Chicago: The Making of a Negro Ghetto, 1890–1920* (Chicago: University of Chicago Press, 1967), p. 12; Iola Hessler Silb-

erstein, *Cincinnati Then and Now* (Cincinnati: League of Women Voters of the Cincinnati Area, 1982), p. 306.

72. Darrel E. Bigham, *We Ask Only a Fair Trial: A History of the Black Community of Evansville, Indiana* (Bloomington: Indiana University Press, 1987), p. 22.

73. Bureau of the Census, *Statistics of Women at Work* (Washington: Government Printing Office, 1907), p. 131.

74. *Thirteenth Annual Report of the Bureau of Statistics of Labor . . . for the Year 1889* (Columbus, Ohio: Westbote Company, 1890), p. 20.

75. *Sixth Annual Report of the Bureau of Labor and Industrial Statistics* (Lansing, Mich.: Robert Smith and Company, 1892), p. ix.

76. *Fifth Biennial Report of the Department of Statistics, for 1893–94* (Indianapolis: William B. Burford, 1894), pp. 3, 58.

77. Census Office, *Report of Population of the United States at the Eleventh Census: 1890—Part II* (Washington: Government Printing Office, 1897), p. clxx. For information on the increasing number of female office workers in the Midwest's largest city, see Lisa M. Fine, *The Souls of the Skyscraper: Female Clerical Workers in Chicago, 1870–1930* (Philadelphia: Temple University Press, 1990).

78. *Sixteenth Annual Report of the Bureau of Labor Statistics . . . for the Year 1892* (Norwalk, Ohio: Lansing Printing Company, 1893), p. 356.

79. Ibid., p. 355.

80. *Thirteenth Report of Bureau of Statistics of Labor*, p. 33.

81. Klingaman, "Midwest Manuacturing," p. 286.

82. *Sixteenth Annual Report of the Commissioner of Labor, 1901* (Washington: Government Printing Office, 1901), p. 29.

83. *Fourth Biennial Report of the Department of Statistics for 1891–92* (Indianapolis: William B. Burford, 1892), pp. 28–29.

84. *Ninth Annual Report of the Bureau of Labor Statistics . . . for the Year 1885* (Columbus, Ohio: Westbote Company, 1886), p. 146.

85. *Fourth Report of Department of Statistics*, p. 39.

86. *Thirteenth Report of Bureau of Statistics of Labor*, p. 57.

87. James M. Morris, "William Haller, 'The Disturbing Element,'" *The Cincinnati Historical Society Bulletin* 28 (Winter 1970): 279.

88. "Salutatory," *The Labor Review* 1 (March 1880): 1.

89. Richard Oestreicher, "Socialism and the Knights of Labor in Detroit, 1877–1886," *Labor History* 22 (Winter 1981): 17. See also Richard Oestreicher, *Solidarity and Fragmentation: Working People and Class Consciousness in Detroit, 1875–1900* (Urbana: University of Illinois Press, 1986).

90. David T. Burbank, *Reign of the Rabble: The St. Louis General Strike of 1877* (New York: Augustus M. Kelley, 1966), p. 53; Primm, *Lion of the Valley*, p. 328.

91. Burbank, *Reign of the Rabble*, p. 78; Primm, *Lion of the Valley*, p. 329.

92. Burbank, *Reign of the Rabble*, p. 61.

93. Ibid., p. 178.

94. Pierce, *Chicago*, 3: 250.

95. Richard Schneirov, "Chicago's Great Upheaval of 1877," *Chicago History* 9 (Spring 1980): 8, 14.

96. B. J. Griswold, *The Pictorial History of Fort Wayne, Indiana* (Chicago: Robert O. Law Company, 1917), p. 498. For an account of the strike of 1877 in another Indiana city, see Nick Salvatore, "Railroad Workers and the Great Strike of 1877: The View from a Small Midwest City," *Labor History* 21 (Fall 1980): 522–45.

97. Philip Van Patten, "Socialistic Labor Party—Summary of Proceedings of the Nat. Ex. Committee," *The Labor Review* 1 (March 1880): 14; Oestreicher, "Socialism in Detroit," p. 22.

98. Pierce, *Chicago*, 3: 256.

99. Paul Avrich, *The Haymarket Tragedy* (Princeton, N.J.: Princeton University Press, 1984), p. 85.

100. Ibid., p. 84.

101. *Fourth Biennial Report of the Bureau of Labor Statistics of Illinois, 1886* (Springfield, Ill.: H. W. Rokker, 1886), pp. 479–80.

102. Pierce, *Chicago* 3: 277; Eugen Seeger, *Chicago, the Wonder City* (Chicago: George Gregory Printing Company, 1893), p. 255.

103. Pierce, *Chicago,* 3: 278.

104. Seeger, *Chicago,* p. 270.

105. *Second Biennial Report of the Bureau of Labor and Industrial Statistics, 1885–1886* (Madison: Democrat Printing Company, 1886), pp. 321, 337; Korn, *Bay View,* pp. 84–90; Milwaukee Writers' Project, *History of Milwaukee County* (Milwaukee: Milwaukee Public Library, 1947), pp. 239–40.

106. *Second Report of Bureau of Labor Statistics, 1885–1886,* pp. 321, 371.

107. *Fourth Report of Bureau of Labor Statistics of Illinois,* pp. 493, 495.

108. Seeger, *Chicago,* p. 270.

109. Ray Ginger, *The Bending Cross: A Biography of Eugene Victor Debs* (New Brunswick, N.J.: Rutgers University Press, 1949), p. 142.

110. Stanley Buder, *Pullman: An Experiment in Industrial Order and Community Planning, 1880–1930* (New York: Oxford University Press, 1967), p. 182.

3. Skyscrapers, Symphonies, and Ballparks

1. *Chicago Tribune,* 10 December 1889, p. 2.

2. Bessie Louise Pierce, *A History of Chicago* (New York: Alfred A. Knopf, 1940), 2: 326; Edmund H. Chapman, *Cleveland: Village to Metropolis,* 2d ed. (Cleveland: Western Reserve Historical Society, 1981), p. 113; George J. Lankevich, ed., *Milwaukee: A Chronological and Documentary History* (Dobbs Ferry, N.Y.: Oceana Publications, 1977), p. 26; James Neal Primm, *Lion of the Valley—St. Louis, Missouri* (Boulder, Colo.: Pruett Publishing Company, 1981), pp. 200–201; Harold M. Mayer and Richard C. Wade, *Chicago: Growth of a Metropolis* (Chicago: University of Chicago Press, 1969), p. 138; Carol Poh Miller and Robert Wheeler, *Cleveland: A Concise History, 1796–1990* (Bloomington: Indiana University Press, 1990), p. 94; Clay McShane, *Technology and Reform: Street Railways and the Growth of Milwaukee, 1887–1900* (Madison: State Historical Society of Wisconsin, 1974).

3. Thomas S. Hines, *Burnham of Chicago: Architect and Planner* (New York: Oxford University Press, 1974), p. 47; Carl W. Condit, *The Chicago School of Architecture* (Chicago: University of Chicago Press, 1964), p. 26.

4. Homer Hoyt, *One Hundred Years of Land Values in Chicago* (Chicago: University of Chicago Press, 1933), p. 153; Condit, *Chicago School,* p. 12; Joseph and Caroline Kirkland, *The Story of Chicago* (Chicago: Dibble Publishing Company, 1894), 2: 348.

5. Hines, *Burnham,* p. 67; *Chicago Tribune,* 7 November 1890, p. 1. For a contemporary account of John W. Root's life and work, see *The Inland Architect and News Record* 16 (January 1891): 85–92.

6. Hugh Morrison, *Louis Sullivan: Prophet of Modern Architecture* (New York: W. W. Norton and Company, 1935), pp. 156–62; Condit, *Chicago School,* p. 128.

7. Kirkland, *Chicago,* 2: 349.

8. Perry Duis, *Chicago—Creating New Traditions* (Chicago: Chicago Historical Society, 1976), p. 29.

9. *Industrial Chicago* (Chicago: Goodspeed Publishing Company, 1891), 1: 168; Condit, *Chicago School,* p. 27.

10. *American Architect* 48 (10 August 1895): 62–63; Robert V. Prestiano, "'The Inland Architect': A Study of the Contents, Influence, and Significance of Chicago's

Major, Late Nineteenth Century Architectural Periodical," Ph.D. diss., Northwestern University, 1973, pp. 95–96.

11. Kirkland, *Chicago,* 2: 347.

12. Karl Baedeker, ed., *The United States with an Excursion into Mexico: A Handbook for Travellers—1893,* reprint ed. (New York: DaCapo Press, 1971), p. 282.

13. George McGue and Frank Peters, *A Guide to the Architecture of St. Louis* (Columbia, Mo.; University of Missouri Press, 1989), pp. 42, 45.

14. Eric Johannesen, *From Town to Tower* (Cleveland: Western Reserve Historical Society, 1983), p. 21.

15. W. Hawkins Ferry, *The Buildings of Detroit: A History,* rev. ed. (Detroit: Wayne State University Press, 1980), p. 137.

16. Robert P. Porter, Henry Gannett, and William C. Hunt, *Progress of the Nation 1790 to 1890—U.S. Census of 1890* (Washington: Government Printing Office, 1894), pp. 932–47; *Report on Farms and Homes: Proprietorship and Indebtedness in the United States at the Eleventh Census: 1890* (Washington: Government Printing Office, 1896), pp. 32, 366–71.

17. *Report on Farms and Homes: 1890,* pp. 32, 366–71.

18. Silas Farmer, *History of Detroit and Wayne County and Early Michigan,* 3d ed. (Detroit: Silas Farmer and Company, 1890), p. 804.

19. John W. Root, "The City House in the West," *Scribner's Magazine* 8 (October 1890): 425.

20. Robert B. Fairbanks, *Making Better Citizens: Housing Reform and the Community Development Strategy in Cincinnati, 1890–1960* (Urbana: University of Illinois Press, 1988), pp. 14–15.

21. *Fourth Annual Report of the Commissioner of Labor, 1888* (Washington: Government Printing Office, 1889), p. 17.

22. Porter, Gannett, and Hunt, *Progress of the Nation—Census of 1890,* p. cxcv; *Fourth Report of Commissioner of Labor,* p. 18.

23. Landscape Research, *Built in Milwaukee: An Architectural View of the City* (Milwaukee: City of Milwaukee, 1980), p. 44.

24. Ibid., pp. 68–69.

25. Hartmut Keil, "Immigrant Neighborhoods and American Society: German Immigrants on Chicago's Northwest Side in the Late Nineteenth Century," in Hartmut Keil, ed., *German Workers' Culture in the United States 1850 to 1920* (Washington: Smithsonian Institution Press, 1988), pp. 31–33.

26. Barbara M. Posadas, "A Home in the Country: Suburbanization in Jefferson Township, 1870–1889," *Chicago History* 7 (Fall 1978): 143.

27. "Humboldt Park," *The Real-Estate and Building Journal* 26 (22 March 1884): 136.

28. Tana Mosier Porter, *Toledo Profile: A Sesquicentennial History* (Toledo: Toledo Sesquicentennial Commission, 1987), p. 58.

29. "South Chicago," *The Real-Estate and Building Journal* 26 (23 February 1884): 88–89.

30. William Payne, *Cleveland Illustrated: A Pictorial Hand-Book of the Forest City* (Cleveland: Fairbanks, Benedict and Company, 1876), p. 187.

31. Charles C. Savage, *Architecture of the Private Streets of St. Louis: The Architects and the Houses They Designed* (Columbia, Mo.: University of Missouri Press, 1987); David T. Beito, "Owning the 'Commanding Heights': Historical Perspectives on Private Streets," in *Public-Private Partnerships: Privatization in Historical Perspective* (Chicago: Public Works Historical Society, 1989), pp. 1–47.

32. R. D. McKenzie, *The Metropolitan Community* (New York: McGraw-Hill Book Company, 1933), p. 337.

33. Henry B. Teetor, *The Past and Present of Mill Creek Valley* (Cincinnati: Cohen and Company, 1882), p. 203.

34. Geoffrey J. Giglierano and Deborah A. Overmyer, *The Bicentennial Guide to Greater Cincinnati: A Portrait of Two Hundred Years* (Cincinnati: Cincinnati Historical Society, 1988), p. 587.

35. Everett Chamberlin, *Chicago and Its Suburbs* (Chicago: T. A. Hungerford and Company, 1874), p. 397; Michael H. Ebner, *Creating Chicago's North Shore: A Suburban History* (Chicago: University of Chicago Press, 1988), p. 68.

36. Ebner, *Creating Chicago's North Shore,* p. 65.

37. Powell A. Moore, *The Calumet Region: Indiana's Last Frontier* (Indianapolis: Indiana Historical Bureau, 1959), pp. 141–77.

38. Ibid., pp. 216–56.

39. Helen Corbin Monchow, *Seventy Years of Real Estate Subdividing in the Region of Chicago* (Evanston, Ill.: Northwestern University, 1939), pp. 103–104.

40. *50 Years of Inland Steel 1893–1943* (Chicago: Inland Steel Company, 1943), pp. 5, 9.

41. Moore, *Calumet Region,* pp. 165–66.

42. George B. Anderson, *One Hundred Booming Years: A History of Bucyrus-Erie Company 1880–1980* (South Milwaukee: Bucyrus-Erie Company, 1980), p. 20.

43. Helen Lefkowitz Horowitz, *Culture and the City: Cultural Philanthropy in Chicago from the 1880s to 1917* (Chicago: University of Chicago Press, 1989), p. 76; Helen Lefkowitz Horowitz, "The Art Institute of Chicago: The First Forty Years," *Chicago History* 8 (Spring 1979): 2.

44. Horowitz, *Culture and the City,* p. 75; Horowitz, "Art Institute of Chicago," p. 2.

45. Horowitz, *Culture and the City,* p. 53; Horowitz, "Art Institute of Chicago," p. 4.

46. "Chicago's Higher Evolution," *Dial* 13 (1 October 1892): 205–206; Horowitz, *Culture and the City,* p. 84.

47. Stefan Germer, "Picture at an Exhibition," *Chicago History* 16 (Spring 1987): 12; Montague Marks, "My Note Book," *The Art Amateur* 13 (November 1885): 110; John D. Kysela, "Sara Hallowell Brings 'Modern Art' to the Midwest," *The Art Quarterly* 27 (1964): 154–55.

48. "Cincinnati," *Atlantic Monthly* 20 (August 1867): 246.

49. Kenneth R. Trapp, "Art Palace of the West: Its Beginnings," in *Art Palace of the West: A Centennial Tribute 1881–1981* (Cincinnati: Cincinnati Art Museum, 1981), pp. 26–27.

50. Elizabeth Williams Perry, *A Sketch of the Women's Art Museum Association of Cincinnati 1877–1886* (Cincinnati: Robert Clarke and Company, 1886), pp. 59–60; Trapp, "Art Palace of the West," p. 21.

51. For a history of the funding and building of the museum, see *Cincinnati Museum Association—Fifth Annual Report* (Cincinnati: Robert Clarke and Company, 1886), pp. 9–14.

52. *The Detroit Museum of Art—Historical Report* (Detroit: John F. Eby and Company, 1891), pp. 3–36; Wallace E. Clayton, *The Growth of a Great Museum: An Informal History of the Detroit Institute of Arts* (Detroit: Founders Society Detroit Institute of Arts, 1966), pp. 11–29.

53. "Milwaukee Art Gallery," *Milwaukee Literary Messenger,* 5 (November 1873): 345.

54. Lillian B. Miller, "The Milwaukee Art Museum's Founding Father: Frederick Layton (1827–1919) and His Collection," in *1888—Frederick Layton and His World* (Milwaukee: Milwaukee Art Museum, 1988), pp. 21–29.

55. Horowitz, *Culture and the City,* p. 80.

56. Robert C. Vitz, *The Queen and the Arts: Cultural Life in Nineteenth-Century Cincinnati* (Kent, Ohio: Kent State University Press, 1989), p. 86.

57. George P. Upton, "The Cincinnati Musical Festival," *The Lakeside Monthly*

9 (June 1873); 475; Vitz, *The Queen and the Arts,* p. 88; "The Cincinnati Musical Festival," *Milwaukee Literary Review* 5 (May 1873): 125.

58. Upton,"Cincinnati Musical Festival," p. 473; Vitz, *The Queen and the Arts,* p. 86.

59. "Cincinnati Musical Festival," *Milwaukee Literary Review,* p. 125.

60. Vitz, *The Queen and the Arts,* p. 89; "Cincinnati Musical Festival," *Milwaukee Literary Review,* p. 127.

61. Vitz, *The Queen and the Arts,* pp. 89–90.

62. *Sixth Biennial Musical Festival, at Cincinnati . . . 1884* (Cincinnati: Festival Association, 1884), p. 15.

63. Vitz, *The Queen and the Arts,* p. 91.

64. Ibid., p. 109.

65. Ibid.

66. Ibid.

67. Ibid., p. 110.

68. Ibid., p. 115.

69. Ibid.

70. Horowitz, *Culture and the City,* p. 39; Duis, *Chicago,* p. 89.

71. Horowitz, *Culture and the City,* p. 41; Duis, *Chicago,* p. 89.

72. Oskar Burckhardt, *Der Musikverein von Milwaukee 1850–1900, Eine Chronik* (Milwaukee: Musikverein, 1900), p. 10.

73. Ibid., p. 124.

74. Ibid., pp. 93–95.

75. Ann Bakamjian Reagan, "Eugen Luening and the Milwaukee Musical Society," *Milwaukee History* 6 (Autumn 1983): 96.

76. Ibid., p. 97.

77. Randolph C. Downes, *Lake Port, Lucas County Historical Series* (Toledo: Historical Society of Northwestern Ohio, 1951), p. 354.

78. La Vern J. Rippley, *The Columbus Germans* (Columbus: Columbus Männerchor, 1968), p. 10.

79. Jacob H. Studer, *Columbus, Ohio: Its History, Resources, and Progress* (Columbus, Ohio: Jacob H. Studer, 1873), p. 443.

80. George Theodore Probst, *The Germans in Indianapolis 1840–1918* (Indianapolis: German-American Center and Indiana German Heritage Society, 1989), p. 95.

81. F. Karl Grossman, *A History of Music in Cleveland* (Cleveland: Case Western Reserve University, 1972), pp. 76–78.

82. *Cincinnati Gazette,* 18 November 1881, p. 5; Bruce Weber, "Frank Duveneck and the Art Life of Cincinnati, 1865–1900," in *The Golden Age: Cincinnati Painters of the Nineteenth Century Represented in the Cincinnati Art Museum* (Cincinnati: Cincinnati Art Museum, 1979), p. 26.

83. Lonnie Wheeler and John Baskin, *The Cincinnati Game* (Wilmington, Ohio: Orange Frazer Press, 1988), pp. 26, 30.

84. Joseph S. Sterns, Jr., "The Team That Couldn't Be Beat: The Red Stockings of 1869," *Queen City Heritage* 46 (Summer 1988): 51.

85. Wheeler and Baskin, *Cincinnati Game,* p. 27.

86. Peter Levine, *A. G. Spalding and the Rise of Baseball: The Promise of American Sport* (New York: Oxford University Press, 1985), p. 13.

87. Gunther Barth, *City People: The Rise of Modern City Culture in Nineteenth-Century America* (New York: Oxford University Press, 1980), p. 171.

88. Levine, *Spalding,* p. 22.

89. Audrey Olson, "The Nature of an Immigrant Community: St. Louis Germans, 1850–1920," *Missouri Historical Review* 66 (April 1972): 352.

90. Klaus Ensslen, "German-American Working-Class Saloons in Chicago," in

Keil, *German Workers' Culture*, p. 162; Probst, *Germans in Indianapolis*, pp. 82, 89–90.

91. Norton Mezvinsky, "The White-Ribbon Reform 1874–1920," Ph.D. diss., University of Wisconsin, 1959, pp. 52–53.

92. Ibid., p. 54.

93. *Cleveland World*, comp., *"The World's" History of Cleveland* (Cleveland: Cleveland World, 1896), pp. 123–24.

94. Helen E. Tyler, *Where Prayer and Purpose Meet* (Evanston, Ill.: Signal Press, 1949), pp. 19–34.

95. Ibid., p. 127.

4. Automobiles and Reform

1. Allan Nevins, *Ford: The Times, the Man, the Company* (New York: Charles Scribner's Sons, 1954), 1: 156–57.

2. Bureau of the Census, *Manufactures 1909* (Washington: Government Printing Office, 1913), p. 809; Bureau of the Census, *Manufactures 1919* (Washington: Government Printing Office, 1923), p. 868.

3. Bureau of the Census, *Manufactures 1909*, p. 809; Bureau of the Census, *Manufactures 1919*, p. 868.

4. Carl Crow, *The City of Flint Grows Up* (New York: Harper and Brothers, 1945), pp. 37–54, 71–77; Edwin O. Wood, *History of Genesee County Michigan* (Indianapolis: Federal Publishing Company, 1916), 1: 774–75; Timothy E. Howard, *A History of St. Joseph County Indiana* (Chicago: Lewis Publishing Company, 1907), 1: 399; Albert George Ballert, *The Primary Functions of Toledo, Ohio* (Chicago: University of Chicago, 1947), pp. 27, 180–82.

5. Justin L. Kestenbaum, *Out of a Wilderness: An Illustrated History of Greater Lansing* (Woodland Hills, Calif.: Windsor Publications, 1981), pp. 71–73; Frank B. Woodford and Arthur M. Woodford, *All Our Yesterdays: A Brief History of Detroit* (Detroit: Wayne State University Press, 1969), pp. 256–57; William Stocking, "Fifty Years of Industrial Progress in Detroit," *Michigan History Magazine* 10 (October 1926): 617; Ottilie M. Leland with Minnie Dubbs Millbrook, *Master of Precision: Henry M. Leland* (Detroit: Wayne State University Press, 1966), p. 61.

6. Leland and Millbrook, *Master of Precision*, pp. 65–78.

7. Woodford and Woodford, *All Our Yesterdays*, p. 263; Stocking, "Fifty Years," p. 617; Leland and Millbrook, *Master of Precision*, p. 70; Melvin G. Holli, "The Impact of Automobile Manufacturing upon Detroit," *Detroit in Perspective* 2 (Spring 1976): 179; Melvin G. Holli, ed., *Detroit* (New York: New Viewpoints, 1976), p. 119.

8. Stocking, "Fifty Years," pp. 617–18; Holli, "Impact of Automobile," p. 180; Holli, *Detroit*, p. 119.

9. Nevins, *Ford*, 1: 452.

10. Holli, *Detroit*, pp. 134–35.

11. Nevins, *Ford*, 1: 475.

12. Charles K. Hyde, "'Dodge Main' and the Detroit Automobile Industry, 1910–1980," *Detroit in Perspective* 6 (Spring 1982): 6, 10.

13. Nevins, *Ford*, 1: 533, 535.

14. Holli, *Detroit*, pp. 134–35.

15. Frank Serafino, *West of Warsaw* (Hamtramck, Mich.: Avenue Publishing Company, 1983), pp. 38–40; Bureau of the Census, *Population 1920* (Washington: Government Printing Office, 1922), 3: 495.

16. Kestenbaum, *Out of a Wilderness*, p. 74.

17. Wood, *Genesee County*, 1: 777.

18. John Ihlder, "Flint: When Men Build Automobiles Who Builds Their City?" *Survey* 36 (2 September 1916): 549; Richard W. Judd, *Socialist Cities: Municipal*

Politics and the Grass Roots of American Socialism (Albany: State University of New York Press, 1989), p. 96.

19. Wood, *Genesee County,* 1: 777.

20. Ibid., p. 775.

21. Ballert, *Primary Functions of Toledo,* p. 182.

22. Richard H. Keehn, "Industry and Business," in John A. Neuenschwander, ed., *Kenosha County in the Twentieth Century: A Topical History* (Kenosha, Wis.: Kenosha County Bicentennial Commission, 1976), pp. 180, 184–85.

23. "Akron Produces 41.4 Per Cent. of American Rubber Goods," *Akron, Ohio* 7 (April 1920): 1; "Continued Expansion Expected for Akron's Rubber Industry," *Akron, Ohio* 7 (February 1920): 3.

24. Maurice O'Reilly, *The Goodyear Story* (Elmsford, N.Y.: Benjamin Company, 1983), p. 46; Karl H. Grismer, *Akron and Summit County* (Akron, Ohio: Summit County Historical Society, 1952), p. 378; Hugh Allen, *Rubber's Home Town: The Real-Life Story of Akron* (New York: Stratford House, 1949), p. 172.

25. "Interesting Figures Tell Story of Akron's Rapid Growth," *Akron, Ohio* 7 (January 1920): 2.

26. P. W. Litchfield, "Houses and Water Are Akron's Greatest Need," *Akron, Ohio* 4 (January 1917): 1.

27. O'Reilly, *Goodyear Story,* p. 46. For the development of the Ohio rubber industry, see also William D. Overman, "The Rubber Industry in Ohio," *Ohio Historical Quarterly* 66 (July 1957): 278–89.

28. Grimser, *Akron,* p. 379; O'Reilly, *Goodyear Story,* p. 43.

29. Allen, *Rubber's Home Town,* p. 171.

30. Grismer, *Akron,* p. 378.

31. Edward Thornton Heald, *The Stark County Story* (Canton: Stark County: Historical Society, 1952), 3: 14, 21, 23.

32. Stuart W. Leslie, *Boss Kettering* (New York: Columbia University Press, 1983), pp. 38–57; Clarence K. Wildasinn, "Development of Industry in Dayton, Ohio," unpublished paper, Ohio State University, 1928, pp. 31–32.

33. Logan Esarey, *History of Indiana* (Dayton, Ohio: Dayton Historical Publishing Company, 1924), 3: 261.

34. Herbert W. Rice, "Charles Jeremiah Smith and His Sons," *Historical Messenger* 3 (March 1956): 6–8.

35. Workers of the Writer's Program, Illinois, *Rockford* (Rockford, Ill.: Graphic Arts Corporation, 1941), pp. 83–86; Nevins, *Ford,* 1: 456.

36. Raymond A. Mohl and Neil Betten, "The Failure of Industrial City Planning: Gary, Indiana, 1906–1910," *Journal of the American Institute of Planners* 38 (July 1972): 205.

37. Elliott Flower, "Gary, The Magic City," *Putnam's Magazine* 5 (March 1909): 644.

38. Mohl and Betten, "Failure of Industrial City Planning," p. 206.

39. Ibid.

40. Ibid., p. 205.

41. Ibid., p. 211; Flower, "Gary," p. 647.

42. Mohl and Betten, "Failure of Industrial City Planning," p. 212.

43. James B. Lane, *"City of the Century": A History of Gary, Indiana* (Bloomington: Indiana University Press, 1978), p. 105.

44. George W. Hilton and John F. Due, *The Electric Interurban Railways in America* (Stanford, Calif.: Stanford University Press, 1960), pp. 255, 275; William D. Middleton, *The Interurban Era* (Milwaukee: Kalmbach Publication, 1961), p. 140; Glen A. Blackburn, "Interurban Railroads of Indiana," *Indiana Magazine of History* 20 (December 1924): 400–36; Esarey, *Indiana,* 3: 251.

45. Hilton and Due, *Interurban Railways,* p. 91.

46. Edward A. Leary, *Indianapolis: The Story of a City* (Indianapolis: Bobbs-Merrill Company, 1971), p. 173.

47. Kestenbaum, *Out of a Wilderness,* pp. 68–69.

48. "Continued Expansion . . . for Akron's Rubber Industry," p. 3.

49. Hazen S. Pingree, "Detroit: A Municipal Study," *The Outlook* 55 (6 February 1897): 441; Holli, *Detroit,* p. 115.

50. Melvin G. Holli, *Reform in Detroit: Hazen S. Pingree and Urban Politics* (New York: Oxford University Press, 1969), p. 79.

51. Samuel M. Jones, *The New Right* (New York: Eastern Book Concern, 1899), pp. 87, 91.

52. James H. Rodabaugh, "Samuel M. Jones—Evangel of Equality," *Quarterly Bulletin of Historical Society of Northwestern Ohio* 15 (January 1943): 41.

53. Holli, *Reform in Detroit,* p. 103.

54. Thomas F. Campbell, "Municipal Ownership" in David D. Van Tassel and John J. Grabowski, *The Encyclopedia of Cleveland History* (Bloomington: Indiana University Press, 1987), p. 699; C. H. Cramer, *Newton D. Baker* (Cleveland: World Publishing Company, 1961), p. 46.

55. Tom L. Johnson, *My Story* (New York: B. W. Huebsch, 1913), p. xxxv; Carol Poh Miller and Robert Wheeler, *Cleveland: A Concise History, 1796–1990* (Bloomington: Indiana University Press, 1990), p. 106.

56. Holli, *Reform in Detroit,* p. 72.

57. Jones, *New Right,* pp. 105, 375.

58. Rodabaugh, "Samuel M. Jones," p. 29.

59. Miller and Wheeler, *Cleveland,* p. 107.

60. Frederic C. Howe, *The Confessions of a Reformer* (New York: Charles Scribner's Sons, 1925), p. 109.

61. Ibid.

62. Donald E. Pitzer, "Revivalism and Politics in Toledo: 1899," *Northwest Ohio Quarterly* 41 (Winter 1968–69): 15; Morgan J. Barclay, "Reform in Toledo: The Political Career of Samuel M. Jones," *Northwest Ohio Quarterly* 50 (Summer 1978): 84.

63. Thomas F. Campbell, "Mounting Crisis and Reform: Cleveland's Political Development," in Thomas F. Campbell and Edward M. Miggins, eds., *The Birth of Modern Cleveland, 1865–1930* (Cleveland: Western Reserve Historical Society, 1988), p. 307.

64. Lincoln Steffens, "A Tale of Two Cities," *McClure's Magazine* 25 (July 1905): 301; Hoyt Landon Warner, *Progressivism in Ohio 1897–1917* (Columbus: Ohio State University Press, 1964), p. 38; Rodabaugh, "Samuel M. Jones," p. 38.

65. Warner, *Progressivism in Ohio,* p. 36.

66. Holli, *Reform in Detroit,* p. 71.

67. Steffens, "Tale of Two Cities," p. 302.

68. Howe, *Confessions of a Reformer,* p. 113.

69. Steffens, "Tale of Two Cities," p. 305.

70. Howe, *Confessions of a Reformer,* p. 113.

71. Jones, *New Right,* p. 87.

72. Jack Tager, *The Intellectual as Urban Reformer: Brand Whitlock and the Progressive Movement* (Cleveland: Press of Case Western Reserve University, 1968), p. 79. See also Brand Whitlock, "The City and Civilization," *Scribner's Magazine* 52 (November 1912): 633.

73. Tager, *Intellectual as Urban Reformer,* p. 85.

74. Ibid., p. 97.

75. Jean L. Stinchcombe, *Reform and Reaction: City Politics in Toledo* (Belmont, Calif.: Wadsworth Publishing Company, 1968), p. 34.

76. Cramer, *Baker,* p. 47.

77. Ibid., pp. 55, 58.

78. Lloyd Wendt and Herman Kogan, *Bosses in Lusty Chicago: The Story of Bathhouse John and Hinky Dink* (Bloomington: Indiana University Press, 1971), p. 40.

79. Wendt and Kogan, *Bosses in Lusty Chicago*, p. 41.

80. John D. Buenker, "Edward F. Dunne: The Limits of Municipal Reform," in Paul M. Green and Melvin G. Holli, eds., *The Mayors: The Chicago Political Tradition* (Carbondale, Ill.: Southern Illinois University Press, 1987), pp. 33, 42.

81. Ibid., p. 43.

82. Ibid., p. 33.

83. David V. Mollenhoff, *Madison: A History of the Formative Years* (Dubuque, Iowa: Kendall Hunt Publishing Company, 1982), p. 308.

84. Ibid., p. 311.

85. Leland and Millbrook, *Master of Precision,* p. 167; Jack D. Elenbaas, "The Boss of the Better Class: Henry Leland and the Detroit Citizens League, 1912–1924," *Michigan History* 58 (Summer 1974): 140.

86. Elenbaas, "Boss of the Better Class," p. 136.

87. William P. Lovett, *Detroit Rules Itself* (Boston: Richard G. Badger, 1930), p. 77; Elenbaas, "Boss of the Better Class," pp. 143–44.

88. Elenbaas, "Boss of the Better Class," pp. 149–50.

89. Lovett, *Detroit Rules Itself,* p. 27.

90. William P. Lovett, "Pingree of Detroit—Demagogue or Statesman?" *National Municipal Review* 8 (November 1919): 595–97.

91. Raymond R. Fragnoli, *The Transformation of Reform: Progressivism in Detroit—and after, 1912–1933* (New York: Garland Publishing, 1982), p. 95.

92. Lovett, *Detroit Rules Itself,* pp. 24, 26.

93. Fragnoli, *Transformation of Reform,* p. 128.

94. Ibid., p. 149.

95. Ibid., p. 137.

96. Ibid., p. 143.

97. Ibid., p. 166. For slightly different figures, see Lent D. Upson, "Detroit Adopts a New Charter," *National Municipal Review* 7 (September 1918): 530.

98. Upson, "Detroit Adopts a New Charter," p. 530.

99. Chester E. Rightor, *City Manager in Dayton* (New York: Macmillan Company, 1919), p. 2; Judith Sealander, *Grand Plans: Business Progressivism and Social Change in Ohio's Miami Valley, 1890–1929* (Lexington, Ky.: University Press of Kentucky, 1988), pp. 86–87, 94; Landrum Bolling, *City Manager Government in Dayton* (Chicago: Public Administration Service, 1940), pp. 8–9.

100. Sealander, *Grand Plans,* pp. 89–91.

101. Ibid., p. 100.

102. Bolling, *City Manager Government in Dayton,* p. 11.

103. For a list of city manager cities, see "City Manager Movement," *National Municipal Review* 9 (April 1920): 245–47.

104. Judd, *Socialist Cities,* p. 23.

105. Robert F. Hoxie, "'The Rising Tide of Socialism': A Study," *The Journal of Political Economy* 19 (October 1911): 611, 616.

106. Robert F. Hoxie, "The Socialist Party in the November Elections," *The Journal of Political Economy* 20 (March 1912): 212.

107. Hoxie, "Rising Tide," p. 613.

108. Marvin Wachman, *History of the Social-Democratic Party of Milwaukee 1897–1910* (Urbana: University of Illinois Press, 1945), p. 15.

109. Walter Thomas Mills, "Wisconsin Socialists," *The Vanguard* 5 (April 1907): 171.

110. Ibid.

111. Wachman, *Social-Democratic Party,* pp. 64, 81.

112. Victor L. Berger, "What Is the Matter with Milwaukee?" *The Independent* 68 (21 April 1910): 840.

113. Wachman, *Social-Democratic Party,* pp. 78–81.

114. Berger, "What Is the Matter?" p. 841.

115. Hoxie, "Rising Tide," p. 630.

116. Edward S. Kerstein, *Milwaukee's All-American Mayor: Portrait of Daniel Webster Hoan* (Englewood Cliffs, N.J.: Prentice-Hall, 1966), p. 79.

117. Robert C. Reinders, "Daniel W. Hoan and Municipal Reform in Milwaukee, 1910–1920," *Historical Messenger of the Milwaukee County Historical Society* 21 (June 1965): 44.

118. Daniel W. Hoan, *City Government: The Record of the Milwaukee Experiment* (New York: Harcourt, Brace and Company, 1936), p. 71. For more information on Milwaukee Socialism, see Frederick I. Olson, "Milwaukee's Socialist Mayors: End of an Era and Its Beginning," *Historical Messenger of the Milwaukee County Historical Society* 16 (March 1960): 3–8; Sally M. Miller, "Casting a Wide Net: The Milwaukee Movement to 1920," in Donald T. Critchlow, ed., *Socialism in the Heartland: The Midwestern Experience, 1900–1925* (Notre Dame, Ind.: University of Notre Dame Press, 1986), pp. 18–45.

119. Judd, *Socialist Cities,* pp. 73, 89.

120. Paul H. Douglas, "The Socialist Vote in the Municipal Elections of 1917," *National Municipal Review* 7 (March 1918): 136–38; James R. Simmons, "The Socialist Party in Indiana, 1900–1925," in Critchlow, *Socialism in the Heartland,* p. 55.

121. Judd, *Socialist Cities,* p. 100.

122. Ibid., p. 95.

123. Ibid., pp. 103–105.

124. Ibid., p. 106.

125. Clarence H. Young and William A. Quinn, *Foundation for Living: The Story of Charles Stewart Mott and Flint* (New York: McGraw-Hill Book Company, 1963), p. 46.

126. Ibid., p. 47.

127. Ibid., p. 51.

128. Judd, *Socialist Cities,* p. 76.

129. Ibid., p. 143.

130. John T. Walker, "The Dayton Socialists and World War I: Surviving the White Terror," in Critchlow, ed., *Socialism in the Heartland,* p. 131.

131. Ibid., p. 121. See also Judd, *Socialist Cities,* p. 149; Bolling, *City Manager Government in Dayton,* p. 24; Sealander, *Grand Plans,* pp. 107–108,

132. Sealander, *Grand Plans,* pp. 108–109; Walker, "Dayton Socialists," p. 127; Judd, *Socialist Cities,* p. 149.

133. Hoxie, "Socialist Party in November Elections," p. 216.

134. Frank P. Zeidler, "Dan Hoan, Successful Mayor," *Historical Messenger of the Milwaukee County Historical Society* 17 (March 1961): 24.

135. Will C. Conrad, "Carl Sandburg's Milwaukee Days," *Historical Messenger of the Milwaukee County Historical Society* 9 (June 1953): 10.

136. Jane Addams, *Twenty Years at Hull House* (New York: New American Library, 1961), p. 114. For a summary of activities at Hull House, see Robert A. Woods and Albert J. Kennedy, eds., *Handbook of Settlements* (New York: Charities Publication Committee, 1911), pp. 54–59.

137. Addams, *Twenty Years,* p. 76.

138. Ibid., p. 81.

139. Ibid., p. 224.

140. Ibid., p. 152.

141. Ibid., pp. 41–42.

142. Ibid., p. 42.

143. Ibid.

144. Albion W. Small, "Scholarship and Social Agitation," *American Journal of Sociology* 1 (March 1896): 564; Steven J. Diner, *A City and Its Universities: Public Policy in Chicago, 1892–1919* (Chapel Hill: University of North Carolina Press, 1980), p. 29.

145. Diner, *A City and Its Universities,* p. 32; Steven J. Diner, "Department and Discipline: The Department of Sociology at the University of Chicago, 1892–1920," *Minerva* 13 (Winter 1975): 524.

146. Ellen Fitzpatrick, *Endless Crusade: Women Social Scientists and Progressive Reform* (New York: Oxford University Press, 1990), p. 41.

147. Howard E. Wilson, "Social Welfare in Chicago," in Iona M. R. Logie, *Careers in the Making* (New York: Harper and Brothers, 1931), p. 45.

148. Woods and Kennedy, *Handbook of Settlements,* p. 69.

149. Wilson, "Social Welfare," p. 41.

150. Ibid., p. 44.

151. Barry D. Karl, *Charles E. Merriam and the Study of Politics* (Chicago: University of Chicago Press, 1974), p. 53.

152. Fitzpatrick, *Endless Crusade,* p. 81.

153. Woods and Kennedy, *Handbook of Settlements,* p. 301.

154. John J. Grabowski, "Social Reform and Philanthropic Order in Cleveland, 1896–1920," in Harry F. Lupold and Gladys Haddad, eds., *Ohio's Western Reserve: A Regional Reader* (Kent, Ohio: Kent State University Press, 1988), p. 231.

155. Ibid., p. 236.

156. Woods and Kennedy, *Handbook of Settlements,* p. 83.

5. In the Cultural Vanguard

1. David F. Burg, *Chicago's White City of 1893* (Lexington, Ky.: University Press of Kentucky, 1976), p. 115.

2. Ibid., p. 148; Charles M. Kurtz, *Illustrations from the Art Gallery of the World's Columbian Exposition* (Philadelphia: George Barrie, 1893), pp. 9–10, 14.

3. Burg, *Chicago's White City,* pp. 235, 238.

4. Ibid., p. 178.

5. Ibid., p. 301.

6. Ibid., p. 176.

7. Ibid., p. 300.

8. Charles Zueblin, "'The White City' and After," *The Chautauquan* 38 (December 1903): 374.

9. William H. Wilson, *The City Beautiful Movement* (Baltimore: Johns Hopkins University Press, 1989), pp. 53–74.

10. Thomas S. Hines, *Burnham of Chicago: Architect and Planner* (New York: Oxford University Press, 1974), p. 160; Thomas S. Hines, "The Paradox of 'Progressive' Architecture: Urban Planning and Public Building in Tom Johnson's Cleveland," *American Quarterly* 25 (October 1973): 428; Holly M. Rarick, *Progressive Vision: The Planning of Downtown Cleveland 1903–1930* (Cleveland: Cleveland Museum of Art, 1986), p. 14.

11. Rarick, *Progressive Vision,* p. 15; Hines, *Burnham,* p. 160; Hines, "Paradox of 'Progressive' Architecture," p. 429.

12. Rarick, *Progressive Vision,* p. 24.

13. Ibid.; Hines, *Burnham,* p. 168; Hines, "Paradox of 'Progressive' Architecture," p. 441.

14. Edward A. Roberts, "Civic Art in Cleveland, Ohio," *The Craftsman* 9 (October 1905): 48.

15. Rarick, *Progressive Vision,* p. 27.

16. Roberts, "Civic Art," pp. 45–56.

17. Eric Johannesen, "Cleveland's Group Plan," *Inland Architect* 31 (November–December 1987), p. 32.

18. Frederic C. Howe, *The Confessions of a Reformer* (New York: Charles Scribner's Sons, 1925), p. 113; Hines, *Burnham,* p. 158.

19. Charles Moore, *Daniel H. Burnham: Architect Planner of Cities* (Boston: Houghton Mifflin Company, 1921), 2: 102; Hines, *Burnham,* p. 316.

20. Hamlin Garland, "The New Chicago," *The Craftsman* 24 (September 1913): 555; Hines, *Burnham,* p. 312.

21. Moore, *Burnham,* 2: 147; David Van Zanten, "Daniel Hudson Burnham 1846–1912," *Inland Architect* 31 (November–December 1987): 26.

22. Hines, *Burnham,* p. 334. See also Carl W. Condit, *Chicago 1910–29: Building, Planning, and Urban Technology* (Chicago: University of Chicago Press, 1973), pp. 69–72.

23. Moore, *Burnham,* 2: 101; Hines, *Burnham,* p. 315.

24. Hines, *Burnham,* p. 326.

25. Ibid., p. 333.

26. Graham Romeyn Taylor, "The New Chicago," *Charities and The Commons* 19 (1 February 1908): 1551.

27. Hines, *Burnham,* pp. 343–44.

28. Thomas J. Schlereth, *Cultural History and Material Culture: Everyday Life, Landscapes, Museums* (Ann Arbor, Mich.: UMI Research Press, 1990), p. 240.

29. Ibid., p. 241. See also Dana F. White, *The Urbanists, 1865–1915* (New York: Greenwood Press, 1989), p. 257.

30. Schlereth, *Cultural History,* pp. 253–55.

31. Giorgio Ciucci, Francesco Dal Co, Mario Manieri-Elia, and Manfredo Tafuri, *The American City: From the Civil War to the New Deal* (Cambridge, Mass.: MIT Press, 1983), p. 100.

32. Mel Scott, *American City Planning since 1890* (Berkeley: University of California Press, 1971), p. 108.

33. L. M. McCauley, "Municipal Art in Chicago: A Civic Renaissance Planned for the Western Metropolis," *The Craftsman* 9 (December 1905): 321.

34. Garland, "New Chicago," pp. 558, 565.

35. Timothy J. Garvey, *Public Sculptor: Lorado Taft and the Beautification of Chicago* (Urbana: University of Illinois Press, 1988), p. 8. See also McCauley, "Municipal Art," pp. 338–39.

36. M. J. Lowenstein, comp., *Official Guide to the Louisiana Purchase Exposition* (Saint Louis: Official Guide Company, 1904), pp. 46, 48.

37. Mark Bennitt and Frank Parker Stockbridge, comps., *History of the Louisiana Purchase Exposition* (Saint Louis: Universal Exposition Publishing Company, 1905), p. 554.

38. *A City Plan for Saint Louis* (Saint Louis: Civic League of Saint Louis, 1907), p. 14.

39. Ibid., p. 8.

40. Ibid., pp. 37, 53; Scott, *American City Planning,* p. 73.

41. Dwight F. Davis, "The Neighborhood Center—A Moral and Educational Factor," *Charities and the Commons* 19 (1 February 1908): 1505.

42. Ibid., p. 1506.

43. David M. Bluestone, "Detroit's City Beautiful and the Problem of Commerce," *Journal of the Society of Architectural Historians* 47 (September 1988): 258.

44. Ibid.

45. Shirley Leckie, "Brand Whitlock and the City Beautiful Movement in Toledo, Ohio," *Ohio History* 91 (1982): 5, 14, 16; Brand Whitlock, "The City and Civilization," *Scribners* 52 (November 1912): 623.

46. Landscape Research, *Built in Milwaukee: An Architectural View of the City* (Milwaukee: City of Milwaukee, 1980), pp. 127–29.

47. Plan Commission, *The Plan of the City of Columbus* (Columbus, Ohio: City of Columbus, 1908), pp. 7, 47–56.

48. Michael Maloney and Kenneth J. Remenschneider, *Indianapolis Landscape Architecture* (Washington: Landscape Architecture Foundation, 1983), pp. 36–39.

49. John Nolen, *Madison: A Model City* (Boston: John Nolen, 1911), pp. 137, 150; David V. Mollenhoff, *Madison: A History of the Formative Years* (Dubuque, Iowa: Kendall Hunt Publishing Company, 1982), p. 345.

50. Nolen, *Madison*, p. 45; Mollenhoff, *Madison*, pp. 346–47.

51. George W. Maher, "The City Plan Movement and Improvement for Springfield, Illinois," in Christian K. Laine, *Landmark Springfield: Architecture and Urbanism in the Capital City of Illinois* (Chicago: Metropolitan Press Publications, 1985), p. 17.

52. H. Allen Brooks, *The Prairie School* (New York: W. W. Norton and Company, 1976), p. 7; Frank Lloyd Wright, "Louis Henry Sullivan, Beloved Master," in H. Allen Brooks, ed., *Prairie School Architecture—Studies from 'The Western Architect'* (New York: Van Nostrand Reinhold Company, 1983), pp. 301–303.

53. Frank Lloyd Wright, *In the Cause of Architecture* (New York: Architectural Record Books, 1975), p. 55.

54. Richard Guy Wilson, "Chicago and the International Arts and Crafts Movements: Progressive and Conservative Tendencies," in John Zukowsky, *Chicago Architecture 1872–1922: Birth of a Metropolis* (Munich: Prestel-Verlag, 1987), p. 217.

55. George W. Maher, "The Western Spirit," *The Western Architect* 9 (November 1906): 113–14.

56. William Drummond, "The Work of Guenzel and Drummond," in Brooks, *Prairie School Architecture*, pp. 220, 223.

57. George W. Maher, "Northwestern University Campus—An American Ideal," *The Inland Architect and News Record* 51 (March 1908): 15.

58. John S. Van Bergen, "A Plea for Americanism in Our Architecture," in Brooks, *Prairie School Architecture*, p. 247.

59. "The Work of Tallmadge & Watson, Architects," in Brooks, *Prairie School Architecture*, p. 268.

60. Wright, *In the Case of Architecture*, p. 56.

61. "George W. Maher, A Democrat in Architecture," in Brooks, *Prairie School Architecture*, p. 162.

62. George W. Maher, "The Western Spirit," *The Western Architect* 9 (December 1906): 126.

63. Wilson, "Chicago and the International Arts and Crafts Movement," p. 217; Brooks; *Prairie School*, pp. 4–5.

64. "Trier Center Neighborhood, Winnetka, Ill.," in Brooks, *Prairie School Architecture*, p. 8. For more on Griffin, see Christopher Vernon, "Walter Burley Griffin, Landscape Architect," in John S. Garner, ed., *The Midwest in American Architecture* (Urbana: University of Illinois Press, 1991), pp. 217–29.

65. Frank Lloyd Wright, "The Art and Craft of the Machine," in *Catalogue of the Fourteenth Annual Exhibition of the Chicago Architectural Club* (Chicago: Chicago Architectural Club, 1901), no page numbers.

66. Robert C. Twombly, *Frank Lloyd Wright: His Life and Architecture* (New York: John Wiley and Sons, 1979), pp. 220–23.

67. Sharon Darling, *Chicago Furniture: Art, Craft, and Industry 1833–1983* (New York: W. W. Norton and Company, 1984), p. 250.

68. Ibid., p. 258.

69. Ibid., p. 261.

70. Wright, *In the Cause of Architecture,* p. 56; Joseph Connors, *The Robie House of Frank Lloyd Wright* (Chicago: University of Chicago Press, 1984), p. 6.

71. Darling, *Chicago Furniture,* p. 268.

72. Abram Garfield, "The Architecture of Cleveland," *Art and Archaeology* 16 (October–November 1923): 154.

73. Wilhelm Miller, "How the Middle West Can Come into Its Own," *Country Life in America* 22 (15 September 1912): 12, 14; Mara Gelbloom, "Ossian Simonds: Prairie Spirit in Landscape Gardening," *The Prairie School Review* 12 (Second Quarter 1975): 6.

74. Gelbloom, "Ossian Simonds," pp. 9–10. See also Robert E. Grese, "Ossian Cole Simonds," in William H. Tischler, ed., *American Landscape Architecture: Designers and Places* (Washington: Preservation Press, 1989), pp. 74–77.

75. Leonard K. Eaton, "Jens Jensen and the Chicago School," *Progressive Architecture* 41 (December 1960): 145.

76. Leonard K. Eaton, *Landscape Artist in America: The Life and Work of Jens Jensen* (Chicago: University of Chicago Press, 1964), p. 16.

77. Ibid., p. 40.

78. Ibid., p. 47. For more on the influence of the Prairie School of landscape architecture on Chicago's parks, see *Prairie in the City: Naturalism in Chicago's Parks, 1870–1940* (Chicago: Chicago Historical Society, 1991).

79. Wilhelm Miller, "The Prairie Style of Landscape Architecture," *Architectural Record* 40 (December 1916): 591.

80. Eaton, *Landscape Artist,* p. 75; Laine, *Landmark Springfield,* p. 106.

81. Eaton, *Landscape Artist,* p. 58.

82. Ibid., p. 38.

83. Charles E. White, Jr., "Insurgent Architecture in the Middle West," *Country Life in America* 22 (15 September 1912): 16.

84. Miller, "Prairie Style of Landscape Architecture," p. 591.

85. *Chicago Tribune,* 28 October 1917, Part 8, p. 5; Kenny J. Williams, *A Storyteller and a City: Sherwood Anderson's Chicago* (DeKalb, Ill.: Northern Illinois University Press, 1988), p. 41; Anthony Grosch, "H. L. Mencken and Literary Chicago," *Chicago History* 14 (Summer 1985): 4.

86. Williams, *Storyteller and a City,* p. 42.

87. Alson J. Smith, *Chicago's Left Bank* (Chicago: Henry Regnery Company, 1953), pp. 3, 21.

88. Williams, *Storyteller and a City,* p. 42.

89. Hamlin Garland, *Crumbling Idols* (Cambridge, Mass.: Harvard University Press, 1960), pp. 114, 117–19, 121, 134.

90. Jean Holloway, *Hamlin Garland: A Biography* (Austin: University of Texas Press, 1960), p. 102.

91. *The Chap-Book* 9 (15 July 1898), no page numbers.

92. Herbert E. Fleming, "The Literary Interests of Chicago—V," *American Journal of Sociology* 11 (May 1906): 800.

93. *The Chap-Book* 9 (15 July 1898), no page numbers.

94. Hamlin Garland, *A Daughter of the Middle Border* (New York: Sagamore Press, 1957), p. 23; Henry Regnery, "Stone, Kimball, and the Chap-Book," *Chicago History* 4 (Summer 1975): 90.

95. Rolf Achilles, "The Chap-Book and Posters of Stone & Kimball at the Newberry Library," *Journal of Decorative and Propaganda Arts* (Fall 1989): 67.

96. Henry B. Fuller, *The Cliff-Dwellers* (New York: Harper and Brothers, 1893), pp. 38, 43–44; Bernard R. Bowron, Jr., *Henry B. Fuller of Chicago: The Ordeal of a Genteel Realist in Ungenteel America* (Westport, Conn.: Greenwood Press, 1974), pp. 129, 131; Williams, *Storyteller and a City,* p. 33.

97. Fuller, *Cliff-Dwellers,* p. 134; Helen Lefkowitz Horowitz, *Culture and the*

City: Cultural Philanthropy in Chicago from the 1880s to 1917 (Chicago: University of Chicago Press, 1989), p. 177.

98. Henry B. Fuller, *With the Procession* (Chicago: University of Chicago Press, 1965), p. 203; Williams, *Storyteller and a City,* p. 34.

99. Williams, *Storyteller and a City,* p. 36.

100. Ibid., p. 38.

101. Robert Bray, "Hamlin Garland's Rose of Dutcher's Coolly," in James Nagel, ed., *Critical Essays on Hamlin Garland* (Boston: G. K. Hall and Company, 1982), p. 344.

102. Theodore Dreiser, *Sister Carrie* (New York: Doubleday, Page and Company, 1900), pp. 9, 17, 28.

103. Ibid., pp. 16, 18.

104. Theodore Dreiser, *The Titan* (New York: John Lane Company, 1914), pp. 4, 6.

105. Garland, *Daughter of the Middle Border,* pp. 222, 229.

106. Theodore Dreiser, *A History of Myself; Newspaper Days* (New York: Horace Liveright, 1931), p. 1.

107. Floyd Dell, *Homecoming* (New York: Farrar and Rinehart, 1933), pp. 232, 237–38; James Albert Gazell, "The High Noon of Chicago's Bohemias," *Journal of the Illinois State Historical Society* 65 (Spring 1972): 54–59; Donald F. Tingley, "The 'Robin's Egg Renaissance': Chicago and the Arts, 1910–1920," *Journal of the Illinois State Historical Society* 63 (Spring 1970): 40–41.

108. Tingley, "'Robin's Egg Renaissance,'" p. 42.

109. Sherwood Anderson, *Sherwood Anderson's Memoirs* (New York: Harcourt Brace and Company, 1942), p. 241; Williams, *Storyteller and a City,* p. 144.

110. Sherwood Anderson, *Windy McPherson's Son* (New York: B. W. Huebsch, 1922), pp. 121, 138; Williams, *Storyteller and a City,* pp. 46, 53.

111. Sherwood Anderson, *Marching Men* (New York: B. W. Huebsch, 1921), pp. 155–56; Williams, *Storyteller and a City,* p. 98.

112. Anderson, *Memoirs,* p. 294; Tingley, "'Robin's Egg Renaissance,'" p. 48.

113. Floyd Dell, *The Briary Bush* (New York: Alfred A. Knopf, 1921), p. 55; Bernard Duffey, *The Chicago Renaissance in American Letters: A Critical History* (East Lansing, Mich.: Michigan State College Press, 1954), p. 181.

114. See, for example, reviews of *Rose of Dutcher's Coolly,* one of which refers to Garland's depiction of life in the Midwest as "grossly indecent in spirit and rudely animal in substance." Nagel, *Critical Essays on Garland,* p. 65.

115. Daniel J. Cahill, *Harriet Monroe* (New York: Twayne Publishers, 1973), p. 24.

116. Connors, *Robie House,* pp. 67–69.

117. Cahill, *Monroe,* p. 42.

118. Horowitz, *Culture and the City,* p. 203.

119. Cahill, *Monroe,* p. 51.

120. Smith, *Chicago's Left Bank,* p. 37.

121. Ibid.

122. Duffey, *Chicago Renaissance,* pp. 185–86.

123. Smith, *Chicago's Left Bank,* p. 33.

124. Duffey, *Chicago Renaissance,* p. 175.

125. Tingley, "'Robin's Egg Renaissance,'" p. 50.

126. Duffey, *Chicago Renaissance,* p. 191; Smith, *Chicago's Left Bank,* p. 27. For other studies of Chicago literature, see Robert C. Bray, *Rediscoveries: Literature and Place in Illinois* (Urbana: University of Illinois Press, 1982); and Carl S. Smith, *Chicago and the American Literary Imagination 1880–1920* (Chicago: University of Chicago Press, 1984).

127. *Chicago Tribune,* 28 October 1917, Part 8, p. 5; Grosch, "Mencken and Chicago," p. 19.

128. Smith, *Chicago's Left Bank,* pp. 17–18.

129. Grosch, "Mencken and Chicago," pp. 19–20.

130. Smith, *Chicago's Left Bank,* p. 243. See Fred Millet, *Contemporary American Authors* (New York: Harcourt, Brace, 1940).

131. Anderson, *Memoirs,* p. 199; Thomas J. Schlereth, "A Robin's Egg Renaissance: Chicago Culture, 1893–1933," *Chicago History* 8 (Fall 1979): 144.

6. After the Heyday

1. Arthur Pound, *Detroit, Dynamic City* (New York: D. Appleton-Century Company, 1940), pp. 333–34.

2. Sidney Fine, *Sit-Down: The General Motors Strike of 1936–1937* (Ann Arbor: University of Michigan Press, 1969), p. 107.

3. Ellen Arlinsky and Marg Ed Kwapil, *In Celebration of Grand Rapids* (Northridge, Calif.: Windsor Publications, 1987), p. 59.

4. Tana Mosier Porter, *Toledo Profile: A Sesquicentennial History* (Toledo: Toledo Sesquicentennial Commission, 1987), p. 78.

5. E. D. Kennedy, *The Automobile Industry* (New York: Reynal and Hitchcock, 1941), p. 67; Albert George Ballert, *The Primary Functions of Toledo, Ohio* (Chicago: University of Chicago, 1947), p. 182.

6. Helen M. Strong, "Cleveland: A City of Contacts," *Economic Geography* 1 (July 1925): 201.

7. Cincinnati Federal Writers' Project, *They Built a City: 150 Years of Industrial Cincinnati* (Cincinnati: Cincinnati Post, 1938), p. 185.

8. Ruth McKenney, *Industrial Valley* (New York: Harcourt, Brace and Company, 1939), no page number.

9. Hugh Allen, *The House of Goodyear* (Cleveland: Corday and Gross, 1943), pp. 226–46.

10. Michael Edgerton and Kenan Heise, *Chicago: Center for Enterprise* (Woodland Hills, Calif.: Windsor Publications, 1982), 2: 347.

11. Sharon Darling, *Chicago Furniture: Art, Craft, and Industry 1833–1983* (New York: W. W. Norton and Company, 1984), pp. 293–94.

12. Edgerton and Heise, *Chicago,* p. 348.

13. Rosemary Feurer, "Shoe City, Factory Towns: St. Louis Shoe Companies and the Turbulent Drive for Cheap Rural Labor, 1900–1940," *Gateway Heritage* 9 (Fall 1988): 2.

14. Ibid., p. 5.

15. Bayrd Still, *Milwaukee: The History of a City* (Madison: State Historical Society of Wisconsin, 1948), p. 486.

16. Kennedy, *Automobile Industry,* pp. 115–37.

17. Allen, *House of Goodyear,* p. 213. See also Maurice O'Reilly, *The Goodyear Story* (Elmsford, N.Y.: Benjamin Company, 1983), pp. 47–49.

18. Kennedy, *Automobile Industry,* p. 120.

19. Spurgeon Bell and Ralph J. Watkins, *Industrial and Commercial Ohio* (Columbus: Ohio State University, 1928), 2: 765.

20. Ibid., 2: 689.

21. *Akron Chamber of Commerce Official Bulletin* 8 (January 1921): 1.

22. "'Work and Save' Did Spell Akron Future," *Akron Chamber of Commerce Official Bulletin* 8 (July–August 1921): 4.

23. Bell and Watkins, *Industrial and Commercial Ohio,* 2: 766.

24. Ibid., 2: 765.

25. Bureau of the Census, *Manufactures: 1929* (Washington: Government Printing Office, 1933), 2: 265, 1227.

26. S. M. Dubrul, "Significance of the Findings," in *The Dynamics of Automobile Demand* (New York: General Motors Corporation, 1939), p. 139; Pound, *Detroit,* p. 337.

27. Kennedy, *Automobile Industry,* pp. 226, 242; Karl H. Grismer, *Akron and Summit County* (Akron, Ohio: Summit County Historical Society, 1952), p. 476.

28. Charles W. Boas, "Locational Patterns of the Michigan Passenger Automobile Industry: 1900–1957," *Papers of the Michigan Academy of Science, Arts, and Letters* 44 (1959): 310; Justin L. Kestenbaum, *Out of a Wilderness: An Illustrated History of Greater Lansing* (Woodland Hills, Calif.: Windsor Publications, 1981), p. 100.

29. Porter, *Toledo Profile,* p. 90; Kennedy, *Automobile Industry,* pp. 244–46.

30. Richard H. Keehn, "Industry and Business," in John A. Neuenschwander, ed., *Kenosha County in the Twentieth Century: A Topical History* (Kenosha, Wis.: Kenosha County Bicentennial Commission, 1976), pp. 187–88; Charles K. Hyde, "'Dodge Main' and the Detroit Automobile Industry, 1910–1980," *Detroit in Perspective* 6 (Spring 1982): 15.

31. Kennedy, *Automobile Industry,* p. 241.

32. Census Bureau, *Manufactures: 1929,* 2: 1227.

33. Fine, *Sit-Down,* p. 104.

34. Still, *Milwaukee,* pp. 479, 485.

35. Federal Writers' Project, *They Built a City,* pp. 14–15.

36. Iwan Morgan, "Fort Wayne and the Great Depression: The Early Years, 1929–1933," *Indiana Magazine of History* 80 (June 1984): 143.

37. Still, *Milwaukee,* pp. 479, 481.

38. Melvin G. Holli, ed., *Detroit* (New York: New Viewpoints, 1976), p. 172.

39. Ibid.

40. Daniel W. Hoan, *Inaugural Address of Daniel W. Hoan* (Milwaukee: City of Milwaukee, 1932), p. 3.

41. Bureau of the Census, *Manufactures 1939* (Washington: Government Printing Office, 1942), 1: 50.

42. Still, *Milwaukee,* p. 498.

43. Porter, *Toledo Profile,* p. 89.

44. Grismer, *Akron,* p. 482.

45. Fine, *Sit-Down,* pp. 4–5.

46. Holli, ed., *Detroit,* p. 180.

47. Automobile Manufacturers Association, *Sit-Down* (No place: No publisher, 1939), p. 6.

48. Fine, *Sit-Down,* p. 331.

49. Ibid., "Everybody's Doing It," *Time* 29 (29 March 1937): 12.

50. Automobile Manufacturers Association, *Sit-Down,* p. 6.

51. Ibid., pp. 30, 32; Kestenbaum, *Out of a Wilderness,* pp. 102, 104.

52. Pound, *Detroit,* p. 330.

53. Ibid., p. 339.

54. Grismer, *Akron,* pp. 486–87.

55. Robert M. Taylor, Jr., Errol Wayne Stevens, Mary Ann Ponder, and Paul Brockman, *Indiana: A New Historical Guide* (Indianapolis: Indiana Historical Society, 1989), p. 193.

56. Ibid., p. 386.

57. Jon W. Lundin, *Rockford: An Illustrated History* (Chatsworth, Calif.: Windsor Publications, 1989), p. 121.

58. David D. Van Tassel and John J. Grabowski, eds., *The Encyclopedia of Cleveland History* (Bloomington: Indiana University Press, 1987), p. 1073.

59. Alan Clive, *State of War; Michigan in World War II* (Ann Arbor: University of Michigan Press, 1979), p. 34.

60. Sallie M. Manassah, David A. Thomas, and James F. Wallington, *Lansing: Capital, Campus, and Cars* (East Lansing, Mich.: Contemporary Image Advertising, 1986), p. 63.

61. Ibid.

62. Clive, *State of War,* pp. 34, 36.

63. Ibid., p. 95.

64. Ibid., p. 30.

65. Ibid., pp. 31, 111.

66. Melvin G. Holli, "The Great War Sinks Chicago's German *Kultur,*" in Melvin G. Holli and Peter d'A. Jones, eds., *Ethnic Chicago,* rev. ed. (Grand Rapids: William B. Eerdmans Publishing Company, 1984), p. 467.

67. Ibid.

68. George Theodore Probst, *The Germans in Indianapolis 1840–1918* (Indianapolis: German-American Center and Indiana German Heritage Society, 1989), pp. 152–53.

69. Van Tassel and Grabowski, *Encyclopedia of Cleveland History,* p. 1072.

70. Holli, "Great War Sinks German *Kultur,*" p. 508; Rudolf A. Hofmeister, *The Germans of Chicago* (Champaign, Ill.: Stipes Publishing Company, 1976), pp. 71–72, 76.

71. Holli, "Great War Sinks German *Kultur,*" p. 485; Writers' Program of the Works Projects Administration, *Cincinnati: A Guide to the Queen City and Its Neighbors* (Cincinnati: Wiesen-Hart Press, 1943), p. 94.

72. Hofmeister, *Germans of Chicago,* p. 77.

73. Ibid., pp. 73–74; Holli, "Great War Sinks German *Kultur,*" p. 502; Van Tassel and Grabowski, *Encyclopedia of Cleveland History,* p. 1072.

74. Probst, *Germans in Indianapolis,* p. 153.

75. Hofmeister, *Germans of Chicago,* p. 79.

76. Audrey L. Olson, *St. Louis Germans, 1850–1920* (New York: Arno Press, 1980), p. 233.

77. Holli, "Great War Sinks German *Kultur,*" p. 511.

78. Darrel E. Bigham, *We Ask Only a Fair Trial: A History of the Black Community of Evansville, Indiana* (Bloomington: Indiana University Press, 1987), p. 108.

79. Lee Williams, "Newcomers to the City: A Study of Black Population Growth in Toledo, Ohio, 1910–1930," *Ohio History* 89 (Winter 1980): 6, 11.

80. John Hope Franklin, *From Slavery to Freedom: A History of American Negroes,* 2d ed. (New York: Alfred A. Knopf, 1956), p. 464.

81. James R. Grossman, *Land of Hope: Chicago, Black Southerners, and the Great Migration* (Chicago: University of Chicago Press, 1989), p. 259.

82. Ibid., p. 167.

83. Ibid.

84. Paul S. Taylor, "Mexican Labor in the United States: Chicago and the Calumet Region," *University of California Publications in Economics* 7 (1932): 42.

85. Grossman, *Land of Hope,* p. 184.

86. Taylor, "Mexican Labor," p. 40.

87. Grossman, *Land of Hope,* p. 183.

88. Kenneth L. Kusmer, *A Ghetto Takes Shape: Black Cleveland, 1870–1930* (Urbana: University of Illinois Press, 1976), p. 191.

89. Taylor, "Mexican Labor," p. 157.

90. Thomas J. Schlereth, "A Robin's Egg Renaissance: Chicago Culture, 1893–1933," *Chicago History* 8 (Fall 1979): 151.

91. Chadwick Hansen, "Social Influences on Jazz Style: Chicago, 1920–30," *American Quarterly* 12 (Winter 1960): 498.

92. Allan H. Spear, *Black Chicago: The Making of a Negro Ghetto 1890–1920* (Chicago: University of Chicago Press, 1967), pp. 202, 211.

93. Ibid., p. 211.

94. David Allan Levine, *Internal Combustion: The Races in Detroit 1915–1926* (Westport, Conn.: Greenwood Press, 1976), p. 137.

95. Ibid.

96. Taylor, "Mexican Labor," p. 115.

97. Kusmer, *Ghetto Takes Shape,* p. 187.

98. Elliott M. Rudwick, *Race Riot at East St. Louis July 2, 1917* (Carbondale, Ill.: Southern Illinois University Press, 1964), pp. 49–50.

99. Ibid., pp. 67–68, 165.

100. Ibid., p. 69.

101. Grossman, *Land of Hope,* p. 179; Spear, *Black Chicago,* p. 216.

102. Clive, *State of War,* p. 133.

103. Ibid.

104. Ibid., pp. 141–42.

105. Ibid., pp. 157–60; Dominic J. Capeci, Jr., and Martha Wilkerson, "The Detroit Rioters of 1943: A Reinterpretation," *Michigan Historical Review* 16 (Spring 1990): 49–72.

106. Richard Polenberg, *America at War: The Home Front, 1941–1945* (Englewood Cliffs, N.J.: Prentice-Hall, 1968), p. 112.

107. Alfred McClung Lee and Norman D. Humphrey, *Race Riot (Detroit, 1943)* (New York: Octagon Books, 1968), p. 90.

108. McKenney, *Industrial Valley,* no page number.

109. Erdmann Doane Beynon, "The Southern White Laborer Migrates to Michigan," *American Sociological Review* 3 (June 1938): 337.

110. Ibid., p. 340.

111. Clive, *State of War,* p. 174.

112. Ibid., p. 179.

113. Grace G. Leybourne, "Urban Adjustments of Migrants from the Southern Appalachian Plateaus," *Social Forces* 16 (December 1937): 241.

114. Clive, *State of War,* p. 172.

115. Ibid., p. 175.

116. Beynon, "Southern White Laborer," p. 338.

117. Ibid., p. 339.

118. Ibid., p. 340.

119. Harriette Arnow, *The Dollmaker* (New York: Avon Books, 1972), pp. 169, 171–72.

120. James B. Lane, *"City of the Century": A History of Gary, Indiana* (Bloomington: Indiana University Press, 1978), p. 110.

121. Brewster Campbell and James Pooler, "Hallelujah in Boom Town," *Colliers* 113 (1 April 1944): 18–19.

122. Leybourne, "Urban Adjustments of Migrants," p. 242.

123. Clive, *State of War,* pp. 179–80.

124. Lee and Humphrey, *Race Riot,* p. 91.

125. Ibid., p. 92.

126. Arnow, *Dollmaker,* p. 540; Clive, *State of War,* p. 180.

127. Clive, *State of War,* p. 182.

128. Beynon, "Southern White Laborer," p. 337.

129. Julian Samora and Richard A. Lamanna, *Mexican-Americans in a Midwest Metropolis: A Study of East Chicago* (Los Angeles: University of California, Los Angeles, 1967), p. 5.

130. Taylor, "Mexican Labor," p. 46.

131. Louise Año Nuevo Kerr, "Mexican Chicago: Chicano Assimilation Aborted, 1939–1954," in Holli and Jones, *Ethnic Chicago,* pp. 270, 282. For Mexican-Ameri-

cans in Detroit, see Norman D. Humphrey, "The Migration and Settlement of Detroit Mexicans," *Economic Geography* 19 (October 1943): 358–61.

132. Taylor, "Mexican Labor," p. 230.

133. Ibid., p. 114.

134. Lloyd Wendt and Herman Kogan, *Big Bill of Chicago* (Indianapolis: Bobbs-Merrill Company, 1953), p. 251.

135. Ibid., p. 275.

136. Ibid., p. 216.

137. Ibid., p. 263.

138. Ibid., pp. 250, 268.

139. Ibid., p. 248.

140. Ibid., p. 253; John R. Schmidt, *"The Mayor Who Cleaned Up Chicago": A Political Biography of William E. Dever* (DeKalb, Ill.: Northern Illinois University Press, 1989), pp. 157–58.

141. Schmidt, *"Mayor Who Cleaned Up Chicago,"* p. 167; Wendt and Kogan, *Big Bill,* p. 274.

142. Wendt and Kogan, *Big Bill,* p. 275; Schmidt, *"Mayor Who Cleaned Up Chicago,"* p. 167.

143. Roger Biles, *Big City Boss in Depression and War: Mayor Edward J. Kelly of Chicago* (DeKalb, Ill.: Northern Illinois University Press, 1984), pp. 47, 49.

144. Raymond R. Fragnoli, *The Transformation of Reform: Progressivism in Detroit—And After, 1912–1933* (New York: Garland Publishing, 1982), p. 343.

145. Ibid., p. 344.

146. "Detroit's Murderous Election Climax," *Literary Digest* 106 (9 August 1930): 10.

147. Ibid. See also Frank B. Woodford and Arthur M. Woodford, *All Our Yesterdays: A Brief History of Detroit* (Detroit: Wayne State University Press, 1969), pp. 307–309; Robert Conot, *American Odyssey* (New York: William Morrow and Company, 1974), pp. 266–67.

148. *Akron Evening Times,* 23 December 1919, p. 1; 5 January 1920, p. 1; *Akron Beacon Journal,* 23 December 1919, p. 1; 5 January 1920, p. 1; 6 January 1920, p. 4; 8 January 1920, p. 1.

149. *Akron Evening Times,* 23 December 1919, p. 1; 2 January 1920, p. 6. See also *Akron Evening Times,* 26 December 1919, p. 6; 7 January 1920, p. 6.

150. *Akron Beacon Journal,* 11 August 1923, p. 1; 13 August 1923, p. 1. See also *Akron Beacon Journal,* 9 August 1923, pp. 1, 14.

151. For a comparison of the chamber of commerce stance in 1918 and 1923, see "New Charter Proposed for Akron," *Akron, Ohio: Official Publication Akron Chamber of Commerce* 5 (September 1918): 1; "Charter Amendments Will Eliminate City Manager," *Akron Chamber of Commerce* 10 (July–August 1923): 1.

152. P. M. Burke, "The Akron Primary Vote," *City Manager Magazine* 5 (September 1923): 26–28; Earl Willis Crecraft, "Akron Drops City Manager," *National Municipal Review* 12 (November 1923): 639–40.

153. Robert C. Ray, "A History of the First City Manager Government in Cleveland," Master's thesis, Ohio State University, 1936, pp. 36–37, 43; *Cleveland News,* 24 October 1931, p. 4; Louis Browdy, "Cleveland's City Manager Survives," *The Nation* 129 (4 September 1929): 246; William G. Shepherd, "This City Upset the Mayor's Chair," *Collier's* 75 (14 February 1925): 9, 44. Maurice Maschke revealed the details of his joint effort with Gongwer in his "Memoirs" published in the *Cleveland Plain Dealer* in August 1934. He also spoke at length of his role in the selection of Hopkins in a speech before the City Club in October 1931. See Maurice Maschke Papers, Ohio Historical Society, Columbus, Ohio.

154. *Cleveland Plain Dealer,* 1 November 1931, p. 1.

155. Randolph O. Huus, "The Attack on Cleveland's Council-Manager Charter,"

National Municipal Review 17 (February 1928): 70; Ray, "History of Manager Government in Cleveland," p. 63.

156. *Cleveland American,* 7 November 1927, p. 1.

157. *Cleveland Gazette,* 17 August 1929, p. 1.

158. *Cleveland Plain Dealer,* 4 November 1931, pp. 1, 4, 6, 14; "Some Facts and Comments on the Election," *Greater Cleveland* 7 (12 November 1931): 39–42.

159. Landrum R. Bolling, *City Manager Government in Dayton* (Chicago: Public Administration Service, 1940), p. 64.

160. Charles P. Taft, *City Management: The Cincinnati Experiment* (New York: Farrar and Rinehart, 1933), p. 76.

161. Ibid., p. 237.

162. C. H. Cramer, *Newton D. Baker: A Biography* (Cleveland: World Publishing Company, 1961), p. 63.

163. John R. Stilgoe, *Borderland: Origins of the American Suburb, 1820–1939* (New Haven: Yale University Press, 1988), p. 245; *Shaker Village Standards* (Cleveland: Van Sweringen Company, 1925), pp. 13–14.

164. Stilgoe, *Borderland,* p. 242.

165. Ibid., p. 241; *Shaker Village Standards,* p. 3.

166. Stilgoe, *Borderland,* p. 246; *Shaker Village Standards,* p. 14.

167. Mary Schauffler, *The Suburbs of Cleveland: A Field Study of the Metropolitan District Outside the Administrative Area of the City* (Chicago: University of Chicago, 1945), p. 114.

168. Ibid., pp. 381–82.

169. Ibid., pp. 179–80.

170. Ibid., p. 183.

171. Ibid.

172. Ibid., p. 434.

173. Federal Writers' Project, *Shorewood* (Shorewood, Wis.: Village of Shorewood, 1939), pp. 49–55.

174. Ibid., p. 60.

175. Ibid., p. 57.

176. Ibid., pp. 12, 57.

177. Ibid., pp. 58–59.

178. Ibid., p. 11.

179. King Thompson Company, *The Country Club District* (Columbus: King Thompson Company, no date), no page numbers. See also Marjorie Garvin Sayers, ed., *History of Upper Arlington, A Suburb of Columbus, Ohio* (Columbus, Ohio: Upper Arlington Historical Society, 1977), pp. 3–13.

180. Edward T. Heald, *The Stark County Story* (Canton, Ohio: Stark County Historical Society, 1955), 4: 782.

181. Daniel J. Prosser, "Chicago and the Bungalow Boom of the 1920s," *Chicago History* 10 (Summer 1981): 92.

182. Garden City Historical Commission, *Early Days in Garden City* (Garden City, Mich.: Garden City Historical Commission, 1962), pp. 47–53, unpaged illustration of Folker advertisement.

183. John Nolen, *New Towns for Old* (Boston: Marshall Jones Company, 1927), pp. 121, 123.

184. Arnold R. Alanen and Joseph A. Eden, *Main Street Ready-Made: The New Deal Community of Greendale, Wisconsin* (Madison: State Historical Society of Wisconsin, 1987), p. 55.

7. The Making of the Rust Belt

1. Charles Edmundson, "St. Louis: A City in Decay," *Forum* 102 (November 1939): 200–201.

2. *St. Louis Post-Dispatch,* 12 February 1941, p. 4A.

3. Walter Abbott, "Cleveland: A City Collapses," *Forum* 100 (September 1938): 99–100.

4. Walter S. Schmidt, *Proposals for Downtown Cincinnati* (Chicago: Urban Land Institute, 1941), p. 1.

5. K. Lee Hyder and Howard J. Tobin, *Proposals for Downtown Milwaukee* (Chicago: Urban Land Institute, 1941), p. 5.

6. Seward H. Mott and Max S. Wehrly, "State Legislation for Urban Redevelopment," *American Planning and Civic Annual* (1946), pp. 94–98; "Illinois Enacts Neighborhood Redevelopment Corporation Law," *American City* 56 (August 1941): 37; *Annual Report of the Chicago Plan Commission, 1941* (Chicago: Chicago Plan Commission, 1942), p. 15; *Twenty-third Annual Report, City Plan Commission, Detroit, 1941* (Detroit: City Plan Commission, 1942), pp. 10–11; *Urban Redevelopment Legislation in the United States: A Comparative Analysis* (Chicago: American Society of Planning Offices, n.d.); "The Status of Urban Redevelopment: A Symposium," *Urban Land* 7 (October 1948): 1; Jon C. Teaford, *The Rough Road to Renaissance: Urban Revitalization in America, 1940–1985* (Baltimore: Johns Hopkins University Press, 1990), pp. 34, 106.

7. *First Report 1959—Redevelopment Authority of the City of Milwaukee* (Milwaukee: Redevelopment Authority of Milwaukee, 1959), p. 5; Bertil Hanson, *A Report on the Politics of Milwaukee* (Cambridge, Mass.: Joint Center for Urban Studies, 1961), pp. VI-9–VI-10.

8. Eric Johannesen, *Cleveland Architecture, 1876–1976* (Cleveland: Western Reserve Historical Society, 1979), p. 223; Teaford, *Rough Road to Renaissance,* p. 148.

9. Muriel Beadle, *The Hyde Park-Kenwood Urban Renewal Years* (Chicago: Author, 1967), p. 13; Teaford, *Rough Road to Renaissance,* p. 118. For additional accounts of the Hyde Park-Kenwood efforts, see Julia Abrahamson, *A Neighborhood Finds Itself* (New York: Harper and Brothers, 1959); Peter H. Rossi and Robert A. Dentler, *The Politics of Urban Renewal: The Chicago Findings* (New York: Free Press of Glencoe, 1961); Harvey S. Perloff, *Urban Renewal in a Chicago Neighborhood: An Appraisal of Hyde Park-Kenwood Renewal Program* (Chicago: Hyde Park Herald, 1955); James V. Cunningham, *The Resurgent Neighborhood* (Notre Dame, Ind.: Fides Publishers, 1965), pp. 69–85; Arnold R. Hirsch, *Making the Second Ghetto: Race and Housing in Chicago, 1940–1960* (Cambridge, U.K.: Cambridge University Press, 1983), pp. 135–70.

10. "Riverview Project," *Ohio Architect* 21 (November 1963): 6; "Toledo Urban Renewal," *Ohio Architect* 20 (March 1962): 4–7; Jean L. Stinchcombe, *Reform and Reaction: City Politics in Toledo* (Belmont, Calif.: Wadsworth Publishing Company, 1968), pp. 135–43; Tana Mosier Porter, *Toledo Profile: A Sesquicentennial History* (Toledo: Toledo Sesquicentennial Commission, 1987), pp. 127–28.

11. "Focus on the Future," *Ohio Architect* 19 (March 1961): 5, 8, 10.

12. *Urban Renewal—Akron, Ohio—1957–1965* (Akron: Citizens for Progress, 1965), no page numbers.

13. Ronald Hammer, "Political History of Urban Renewal in Madison," honors thesis, University of Wisconsin, 1975; *Current Status of Urban Renewal in Madison* (Madison: League of Women Voters, 1966), p. 7.

14. "Imports Hit New Record Despite Domestic Sub-Compact Challenge," *Ward's 1971 Automotive Yearbook* (Detroit: Ward's Communications, 1971), p. 11; Lawrence J. White, *The Automobile Industry since 1945* (Cambridge, Mass.: Harvard University Press, 1971), pp. 15–16.

15. Clare Cotton, "Auto World," *Ward's Quarterly* 3 (Winter 1967): 11.

16. Maurice O'Reilly, *The Goodyear Story* (Elmsford, N.Y.: Benjamin Company, 1983), p. 213.

17. Ibid., p. 149.

18. Robert M. Taylor, Jr., Errol Wayne Stevens, Mary Ann Ponder, and Paul Brockman, *Indiana: A New Historical Guide* (Indianapolis: Indiana Historical Society, 1989), p. 527.

19. *Chicago Tribune,* 10 December 1963, Section 3, p. 5.

20. "Saint Louis Snaps Out of a Long, Costly Lull," *Business Week,* no. 1881 (18 September 1965): 202; Teaford, *Rough Road to Renaissance,* p. 158.

21. *St. Louis Post-Dispatch,* 3 August 1975, p. 3A; 24 August 1975, p. 1B; Teaford, *Rough Road to Renaissance,* p. 216.

22. Teaford, *Rough Road to Renaissance,* p. 157.

23. Jim Tolan and Dan Cook, *Cleveland's Changing Skyline* (Cleveland: Cleveland Landmarks Press, 1984), p. 19.

24. Ibid., p. 44.

25. Stinchcombe, *Reform and Reaction,* p. 143.

26. Hammer, "Urban Renewal in Madison," pp. 17–18, 22.

27. *Status of Urban Renewal in Madison,* p. 9.

28. William Hershey, *Ohio Cities in Trouble* (Akron, Ohio: Akron Beacon Journal, 1981), p. 7.

29. Thomas G. Fuechtmann, *Steeples and Stacks: Religion and Steel Crisis in Youngstown* (Cambridge, U.K.: Cambridge University Press, 1989), pp. 55–56, 66.

30. Hershey, *Ohio Cities in Trouble,* p. 17; Terry F. Buss and F. Stevens Redburn, *Shutdown at Youngstown: Public Policy for Mass Unemployment* (Albany: State University of New York Press, 1983), p. 23.

31. Buss and Reburn, *Shutdown at Youngstown,* p. 25.

32. Feuchtmann, *Steeples and Stacks,* p. 73.

33. "Whatever Happened to Akron?" *Forbes* 130 (22 November 1982): 170.

34. Hershey, *Ohio Cities in Trouble,* pp. 9–10.

35. Milton Derber, *Labor in Illinois: The Affluent Years, 1945–80* (Urbana: University of Illinois Press, 1989), p. 306.

36. *Overall Economic Development Plan, Peoria County, Illinois* (Peoria, Ill.: Peoria County Board and Peoria City Council, 1986), pp. 15–17, 19.

37. *New York Times,* 8 October 1990, p. 1.

38. Randall W. Eberts, "Business Openings and Closings: Ranking Cleveland," *REI Review: A Report on Regional Economic Issues* (December 1985), p. 35.

39. Jack Norman, "Congenial Milwaukee: A Segregated City," in Gregory D. Squires, ed., *Unequal Partnerships: The Political Economy of Urban Redevelopment in Postwar America* (New Brunswick, N.J.: Rutgers University Press, 1989), p. 193.

40. "The Death of a Landmark," *Newsweek* 100 (27 December 1982): 54; Teaford, *Rough Road to Renaissance,* p. 292. See also *Detroit Free Press,* 4 January 1983, p. 4C; 17 January 1983, pp. 1A, 11A; and 19 January 1983, pp. 1A, 5A, 8A.

41. Alfred J. Watkins, "Capital Punishment for Midwestern Cities," in Barry Checkoway and Carl V. Patton, eds., *The Metropolitan Midwest: Policy Problems and Prospects for Change* (Urbana: University of Illinois Press, 1985), p. 107.

42. John B. Rae, *The American Automobile Industry* (Boston: Twayne Publishers, 1984), p. 156.

43. Ibid., pp. 151, 153, 156.

44. Ben Dobbin, "East St. Louis: Treadmill to Oblivion," *Illinois Issues* 7 (November 1981): 6, 9.

45. Derber, *Labor in Illinois,* p. 326; Ben Dobbin, "East St. Louis: Down but Not Out," *Illinois Issues* 7 (December 1981): 7.

46. Dobbin, "East St. Louis: Treadmill to Oblivion," p. 6.

47. Ibid., p. 8.

48. Robert Mendelson, William Tudor, Sally Ferguson, and Sophie Junz, *East St. Louis—Studied and Re-studied* (Edwardsville, Ill.: Southern Illinois University, 1969), p. iv.

49. *Washington Post,* 2 December 1974, p. A2.

50. *Chicago Tribune,* 4 August 1985, Section 1, p. 16.

51. Ibid.

52. Ibid.; "Gary, Ind.: A City Federal Millions Haven't Helped," *U.S. News & World Report* 93 (22 November 1982): 80.

53. *Gary Post-Tribune,* 5 May 1983, p. A1.

54. Robert A. Catlin, "The Decline and Fall of Gary, Indiana," *Planning* 54 (June 1988): 14.

55. *Chicago Tribune,* 22 October 1986, p. 1; Teaford, *Rough Road to Renaissance,* p. 271.

56. Patrick Barry, "BOOM!" *Chicago Times* 1 (September–October 1987): 27; Teaford, *Rough Road to Renaissance,* p. 271.

57. *Cincinnati Enquirer,* 31 July 1990, pp. A-1, A-6.

58. Ibid., p. A-6.

59. Cleveland City Planning Commission, *Cleveland Civic Vision 2000 Downtown Plan* (Cleveland: Cleveland City Planning Commission, 1988), p. 11.

60. Ned Whelan, *Cleveland: Shaping the Vision* (Chatsworth, Calif.: Windsor Publications, 1989), p. 246.

61. Dave Jensen, "Milwaukee: A City On the Move," *North Shore* 12 (August 1989): 72–73.

62. J. Thomas Black, Libby Howland, and Stuart I. Rogel, *Downtown Retail Development: Conditions for Success and Project Profiles* (Washington: Urban Land Institute, 1983), p. 36.

63. David A. Greenspan, "The Grand Avenue," *Inland Architect* 27 (November–December 1983): 28.

64. Black, Howland, and Rogel, *Downtown Retail Development,* p. 38.

65. Helen Pauly, "Renaissance Men," *Milwaukee Magazine* 10 (August 1985): 46. See also Norman, "Congenial Milwaukee," pp. 193–94; Carla Crane, "Milwaukee—A Downtown on the Move," *Urban Land* 47 (February 1988): 8–9; *Developments: A Newsletter on Milwaukee's Planning and Development Activities—Special Issue: Downtown Retail Center* (August 1979).

66. *St. Louis Post-Dispatch,* 26 August 1985, p. 3A; Teaford, *Rough Road to Renaissance,* p. 273.

67. Vincent C. Schoemehl, Jr., "Economics, Politics and City Design," *Places: A Quarterly Journal of Environmental Design* 6 (Summer 1990): 16.

68. Whelan, *Cleveland,* p. 243.

69. Elizabeth and William Beck, "Superior, Wisconsin: Renaissance of a Superior Port City," *Lake Superior Magazine* 11 (January 1990): 33.

70. Tom Davis, "Racine Looks to the Lake," *Wisconsin Trails* 30 (August 1989): 28.

71. "Elkhart: The Rebirth Continues," *Heritage Country* 10 (Fall and Winter 1989): 57.

72. Rita J. Bamberger and David W. Parham, "Leveraging Amenity Infrastructure: Indianapolis's Economic Development Strategy," *Urban Land* 43 (November 1984): 13.

73. William H. Hudnut III with Judy Keene, *Minister/Mayor* (Philadelphia: Westminister Press, 1987), p. 15.

74. Donald Dale Jackson, "Indianapolis: A Born-Again Hoosier Diamond in the Rust," *Smithsonian* 18 (June 1987): 70, 73. See also Sam Stall, "State of the Union," *Indianapolis Monthly* 9 (April 1986): 60–76; and Cynthia Davidson-Powers, "Indianapolis: Parking Spaces, Bricks and Races," *Inland Architect* 31 (July–August 1987): 34–41.

75. *New York Times,* 8 October 1990, p. C10.

76. *Crain's Chicago Business* 12 (18–31 December 1989): 14.

77. *Columbus Dispatch,* 4 January 1990, p. 7A.

78. Ric Bohy, "Ain't Nobody Gonna Run Me Out!" *Detroit Monthly* 12 (October 1989): 50.

79. *Toledo Blade,* 16 September 1990, Section F, p. 4.

80. *Cincinnati Enquirer,* 30 July 1990, p. A-4.

81. Ibid.

82. Julia Spalding, "The Once and Future Mall," *Indianapolis Monthly* 13 (August 1990): 73, 75. See also Kevin Callahan, "How Shopping Shapes the City: The Advent of Circle Centre," *Inland Architect* 31 (July–August 1987): 42–48.

83. *Toledo Blade,* 24 May 1990, pp. 1, 10.

84. *Columbus Dispatch,* 2 September 1990, p. 2B.

85. *Toledo Blade,* 5 September 1990, pp. 1, 7.

86. *Columbus Dispatch,* 2 September 1990, p. 2B. See also Cynthia Davidson-Powers, "Proud Maumee," *Inland Architect* 30 (September–October 1986): 22–25; Donna Owens, "Toledo's Redevelopment Program," in *Advancing Cleveland* (Cleveland: Cleveland State University, 1986), pp. 67–80; and Stephen Phillips, "Toledo: After the Fall," *Ohio Magazine* 13 (March 1991): 12–15.

87. *Crain's Chicago Business,* 18–31 December 1989, p. 14.

88. *New York Times,* 8 October 1990, p. C10.

89. John Fleischman, "The Return of Buckeye Nationalism," *Ohio Magazine* 13 (January 1991): 23.

90. *Ohio Almanac 1970* (Lorain, Ohio: Lorain Journal Company, 1969), p. 270.

91. *Cleveland Plain Dealer,* 1 September 1979, p. 6-C; 20 January 1983, p. 3B; 22 January 1983, p. 8-C.

92. *Ohio Almanac 1970,* p. 435.

93. James A. Maxwell, "Down from the Hills and into the Slums," *The Reporter* 15 (13 December 1956): 27.

94. Lewis M. Killian, *White Southerners,* rev. ed. (Amherst, Mass.: University of Massachusetts Press, 1985), p. 98.

95. Ibid., p. 107.

96. Maxwell, "Down from the Hills," p. 28.

97. Ibid.

98. Killian, *White Southerners,* p. 108.

99. Maxwell, "Down from the Hills," p. 28.

100. Killian, *White Southerners,* p. 97.

101. Maxwell, "Down from the Hills," p. 28.

102. Hal Bruno, "Chicago's Hillbilly Ghetto," *The Reporter* 30 (4 June 1964): 28; Killian, *White Southerners,* p. 91.

103. Arthur D. Little, Inc., *East Cleveland: Response to Urban Change* (East Cleveland: City of East Cleveland, 1969), p. 7.

104. Ibid., pp. 3, 27.

105. Ibid., p. vi.

106. *Cleveland Plain Dealer,* 9 December 1984, p. 25A.

107. David D. Van Tassel and John J. Grabowski, eds., *The Encyclopedia of Cleveland History* (Bloomington: Indiana University Press, 1987), p. 644.

108. Ibid.

109. Ibid., p. 640.

110. Carole Goodwin, *The Oak Park Strategy: Community Control of Racial Change* (Chicago: University of Chicago Press, 1979), pp. 1–2.

111. Lawrence J. R. Herson, *The Urban Web: Politics, Policy, and Theory* (Chicago: Nelson-Hall Publishers, 1990), p. 413.

112. Alan B. Anderson and George W. Pickering, *Confronting the Color Line: The Broken Promise of the Civil Rights Movement in Chicago* (Athens, Ga.: University of Georgia Press, 1986), pp. 201, 223–24, 226.

113. Ibid., pp. 259, 277.

114. Estelle Zannes, *Checkmate in Cleveland: The Rhetoric of Confrontation during the Stokes Years* (Cleveland: Press of Case Western Reserve University, 1972), p. 49.

115. Jon C. Teaford, *The Twentieth-Century American City: Problem, Promise, and Reality* (Baltimore: Johns Hopkins University Press, 1986), p. 148.

116. William E. Nelson, Jr., and Philip J. Meranto, *Electing Black Mayors: Political Action in the Black Community* (Columbus: Ohio State University Press, 1977), p. 245.

117. Ibid., p. 285; James B. Lane, *"City of the Century:" A History of Gary, Indiana* (Bloomington: Indiana University Press, 1978), p. 288.

118. For analyses of the general election returns, see Nelson and Meranto, *Electing Black Mayors*, pp. 317–318; Alex Poinsett, *Black Power Gary Style: The Making of Mayor Richard Gordon Hatcher* (Chicago: Johnson Publishing Company, 1970), p. 94.

119. Teaford, *Twentieth-Century American City*, p. 148. See also Wilbur C. Rich, *Coleman Young and Detroit Politics: From Social Activist to Power Broker* (Detroit: Wayne State University Press, 1989).

120. Doris Graber, "Media Magic: Fashioning Characters for the 1983 Mayoral Race," in Melvin G. Holli and Paul M. Green, eds., *The Making of the Mayor: Chicago 1983* (Grand Rapids: William B. Eerdmans Publishing Company, 1984), p. 72.

121. Paul Kleppner, *Chicago Divided: The Making of a Black Mayor* (DeKalb, Ill.: Northern Illinois University Press, 1985), pp. 210–11.

122. Graber, "Media Magic," p. 74.

123. Don Rose, "How the 1983 Mayoral Election Was Won: Reform, Racism, and Rebellion," in Holli and Green, *The Making of the Mayor*, p. 122; Kleppner, *Chicago Divided*, p. 221.

124. Kleppner, *Chicago Divided*, p. 239.

125. Esther Perica, *They Took the Challenge: The Story of Rolling Meadows* (Rolling Meadows, Ill.: Rolling Meadows Library, 1979), pp. 47, 50.

126. Carolyn J. Bullinger, ed., *Dundee Township 1835–1935* (Carpentersville, Ill.: Crossroads Communications, 1985), pp. 155–56.

127. Ibid., p. 157.

128. Dominic P. Paris, *Footpaths to Freeways: The Story of Livonia* (No place: No publisher, 1975), p. 223.

129. Arthur A. Hagman, ed., *Oakland County Book of History* (Pontiac, Mich.: Sesqui-Centennial Executive Committee, 1970), pp. 273, 279; Edward Thornton Heald, *The Stark County Story* (Canton, Ohio: Stark County Historical Society, 1955), 4: 402–403.

130. *Chicagoland's Community Guide—Thirteenth Annual Edition* (Chicago: Law Bulletin Publishing Company, 1976), p. 163.

131. *Chicago Tribune*, 16 December 1976, Section 7, p. 1.

132. Dickson Terry, *Clayton: A History* (Clayton, Mo.: City of Clayton, 1976), p. 275.

133. Robert T. Dunphy, "Suburban Mobility: Reducing Reliance on the Auto in DuPage County, Illinois," *Urban Land* 46 (December 1987): 7; Robert Cervero, *America's Suburban Centers: The Land Use-Transportation Link* (Boston: Unwin Hyman, 1989), p. 177.

134. Cynthia Davidson-Powers, "The New Main Street?" *Inland Architect* 33 (July–August 1989): 34. See also Sidney K. Robinson, "Aurora on the Edge," *Inland Architect* 33 (July–August 1989): 30–36.

135. William G. Johnston, Jane Newitt, and David Reed, *Michigan Beyond 2000* (Lanham, Md.: University Press of America, 1987), p. 111.

136. *Milwaukee Journal,* 2 November 1989, pp. 1A, 10A. For more on the postsuburban metropolises of the late twentieth century, see Joel Garreau, *Edge City: Life on the New Frontier* (New York: Doubleday, 1991).

137. Joel Sternberg, "Television Town," *Chicago History* 4 (Summer 1975): 108.

138. Ibid., p. 117.

139. Robert Pruter, *Chicago Soul* (Urbana: University of Illinois Press, 1991), p. 349. See also Mike Rowe, *Chicago Blues: The City and the Music* (New York: Da Capo Press, 1975).

140. See Leslie L. Hanawalt, *A Place of Light: A History of Wayne State University* (Detroit: Wayne State University Press, 1968), pp. 406–17; Frank R. Hickerson, *The Tower Builders: The Centennial Story of the University of Toledo* (Toledo: University of Toledo, 1972), pp. 297–343; and Alvin W. Skardon, *Steel Valley University: The Origin of Youngstown State* (Youngstown, Ohio: Youngstown State University, 1983), pp. 244–62.

141. Nathaniel Alexander Owings, *The Spaces in Between: An Architect's Journey* (Boston: Houghton Mifflin Company, 1973); Christopher Woodward, *Skidmore, Owings & Merrill* (New York: Simon and Schuster, 1970).

142. Heinrich Klotz, "The Chicago 'Renaissance,'" in Maurizio Casari and Vincenzo Pavan, eds., *Beyond the International Style: New Chicago Architecture* (New York: Rizzoli International Publications, 1981), p. 33.

143. Nory Miller, "Chicago Revisited," in Casari and Pavan, *New Chicago Architecture,* p. 45.

144. Stanley Tigerman, "Daniel Burnham: Paradigm or Pariah?" *Inland Architect* 31 (November–December 1987): 62.

145. Cynthia Chapin Davidson, "In Search of the Avant-Garde," *Inland Architect* 34 (May–June 1990): 33; Cynthia Chapin Davidson, "Taking Risks: Eisenman in Ohio," *Inland Architect* 34 (May–June 1990): 44.

146. John Clark, "Craft vs. Theory," *Inland Architect* 34 (September–October 1990): 2.

147. Tigerman, "Daniel Burnham," pp. 62–63.

148. *Chicago Tribune,* 9 April 1989, Section 13, pp. 4–5, 22; Mary Alice Molloy, *Chicago since the Sears Tower: A Guide to New Downtown Buildings,* rev. ed. (Chicago: Inland Architect Press, 1990); Kelley L. Blevins, "School's Out," *Town and Country* 144 (September 1990): 284; Joseph Crump, "Less Is Skidmore," *Chicago* 40 (February 1991): 79–80.

149. Charles A. Lewis and Cynthia Yao, eds., *Chicago: The City and Its Artists 1945–1978* (Ann Arbor: University of Michigan Museum of Art, 1978), pp. 5, 19.

150. Ibid., p. 5.

151. Ibid., p. 6.

152. Dennis Barrie et al., *Artists in Michigan, 1900–1976: A Biographical Dictionary* (Detroit: Wayne State University Press, 1989), p. 33.

153. Ibid.

154. For a discussion of this, see Peter Schjeldahl, "'Chicagoization': Some Second Thoughts on the Second City," *New Art Examiner* 12 (May 1985): 28.

155. Eleanor Heartney, "Second to What? Chicago 1987," *New Art Examiner* 14 (May 1987): 24.

156. Ibid., pp. 24, 26.

157. Buzz Spector, "Remembering the Midwest," *Dialogue: An Art Journal* 11 (September–October 1988): 7.

158. Joanna Frueh, "Under the Arch: Art in St. Louis," *New Art Examiner* 15 October 1987): 30.

159. Stephen Sylvester, "Landscape, Regionalism, and Moving On," *Dialogue: An Art Journal* 10 (March–April 1987): 17.

160. Amy Sparks, "Rooted in the Past, Wary of the Present, the Cleveland Museum Resists Contemporary Art," *New Art Examiner* 15 (May 1988): 36.

161. Douglas Utter, "Ohio's Juried Exhibitions Come of Age," *Dialogue: Arts in the Midwest* 13 (November–December 1990): 19.

162. Vincent A. Carducci, "Detroit: Art and Transmission," *New Art Examiner* 14 (January 1987): 38.

163. Joseph Epstein, *Plausible Prejudices: Essays on American Writing* (New York: W. W. Norton and Company, 1985), pp. 25–30.

164. Miller, "Chicago Revisited," p. 45.

Index

Index

JON C. TEAFORD is Professor of History at Purdue University. He is the author of a number of previous books on American urban history, including *City and Suburb: The Political Fragmentation of Metropolitan America, 1850–1970* and *The Rough Road to Renaissance: Urban Revitalization in America, 1940–1985*.